MISS MILES

Miss Miles

or

A Tale of Yorkshire Life
60 Years Ago

MARY TAYLOR

With an Introduction by
Janet H. Murray

New York   Oxford
OXFORD UNIVERSITY PRESS
1990

Oxford University Press

Oxford   New York   Toronto
Delhi   Bombay   Calcutta   Madras   Karachi
Petaling Jaya   Singapore   Hong Kong   Tokyo
Nairobi   Dar es Salaam   Cape Town
Melbourne   Auckland

and associated companies in
Berlin   Ibadan

Library of Congress Cataloging-in-Publication Data
Taylor, Mary, 1817–1893.
Miss Miles, or, A tale of Yorkshire life 60 years ago / Mary
Taylor : with an introduction by Janet H. Murray.

p.   cm.
Originally published : London : Remington & Co., 1890.
ISBN 0-19-506492-5
1. Murray, Janet Horowitz, 1946–   II. Title.   III. Title: Miss
Miles.   IV. Title: Tale of Yorkshire life 60 years ago.
PR5549.T35M57   1990
823'.8—dc20   90-31290

2 4 6 8 10 9 7 5 3 1
Printed in the United States of America

Contents

CONTENTS.

Introduction to the Oxford Edition
of *Miss Miles*

Janet Horowitz Murray

> Mary alone has more energy and power in her nature
> than any ten men you can pick out. . . . It is vain to
> limit a character like hers within ordinary bound-
> aries—she will overstep them. I am morally certain
> Mary will establish her own landmarks. , . . (Ws
> no. 107, 3 January 1841)

So predicted Charlotte Brontë of her closest friend—a prediction that Mary Taylor fulfilled in her life and in her writings.
Her unconventional and feminist views, her outspoken nature,
her love of adventure and travel, her delight in self-reliance,
and her fierce loyalty to her friends yielded a rich and vigorously lived life and an intensely felt and profoundly feminist
novel. Mary Taylor worked on *Miss Miles* from her early womanhood until the end of her life. Although it is not autobio-
graphical, it reflects her lifelong advocacy of independence for
women and her lifelong experience of women's courage and
sustaining friendships.

Mary Taylor (1817–1893) was brought up by her Radical
Yorkshire wool trading family to value exertion and to question authority. Her independence of spirit was apparent from
her schoolgirl years, and distinguished her from the equally
intense but much more socially timid Charlotte Brontë. Their
schoolmate Ellen Nussey remembered their last days at Miss
Wooler's school:

> Then came a time that both Charlotte and Mary were so pro-
> ficient in schoolroom attainments there was no more for them

> to learn, and Miss Wooler set them Blair's *Belle Lettres* to
> commit to memory. We all laughed at their studies. Charlotte
> persevered, but Mary took her own line, flatly refused, and ac-
> cepted the penalty of disobedience going supperless to bed
> for about a month before she left school. When it was moon-
> light, we always found her engaged in drawing on the chest
> of drawers, which stood in the bay window, quite happy and
> cheerful. (Stevens 10)

The fifteen year old's rebellion displays character traits Mary
would affirm throughout her life—a surprisingly serene disre-
gard for authority, a scorn for the useless busywork that was
so often recommended for women, and a clearly felt need for
meaningful activity.

Charlotte Brontë has left us a portrait of Mary at this period
of her life in the character of Rose Yorke in *Shirley,* a portrait
Mary Taylor affectionately appreciated as presenting her as
"a little lump of perfection" (Stevens, Letter 21):

> Rose is a still, sometimes a stubborn girl now: her mother
> wants to make of her such a woman as she is herself—a woman
> of dark and dreary duties—and Rose has mind full-set, thick-
> sown with the germs of ideas her mother never knew. It is
> agony to her often to have these ideas trampled on and re-
> pressed. She has never rebelled yet; but if hard driven she will
> rebel one day, and then it will be once for all.

Mary's own mother, Ann Waring Taylor, was a cold, Cal-
vinistic chapel-goer who (unlike the Miles family and their
friends) emphasized the punitive aspects of her religion. In
later years Mary told a young friend that "my mother was
never a mother to me," and described how she and her younger
sister Martha would conspire to evade their mother's prudish
and inhibiting spirit (S. Taylor 13). Significantly, it was after
her father's death—when she would have been expected to
make her home with her mother—that Mary began to seek her
fortune on the Continent and eventually in New Zealand. In
fact, she did not return to England until after her mother's
death.

Taylor's Radical father, on the other hand, seems to have
doted on her and to have encouraged her to take an active

role in the boisterous political discussions that marked the Taylor family life. Brontë captures the tenderness in their relationship:

> Rose loves her father: her father does not rule her with a rod of iron; he is good to her. He sometimes fears she will not live, so bright are the sparks of intelligence, which, at moments, flash from her glance and gleam in her language. This idea makes him often sadly tender to her. (*Shirley*, Chapter 9)

Miss Wooler was similarly reported to exclaim that Mary was "too pretty to live" (Stevens 10). This anxiety was probably often expressed about much-loved children at a time when one out of five children did not live to adulthood. But with Mary Taylor these fears were particularly unfounded, since she had an exceptionally strong constitution. It was not her delicate health but her assertive, disruptive nature—the "sparks of intelligence" which "flash from her glance and gleam in her language"—that made Mary appear out of place and therefore at risk in a world in which middle class women were expected to look to men for their opinions and to meet their destinies with passive acceptance.

Young Mary's outspokenness and unconventional behavior extended to her romantic life. She seems to have had a crush on Branwell Brontë, with the disastrous consequences Charlotte details in this letter to Ellen Nussey:

> Did I not once tell you of an instance of a Relative of mine who cared for a young lady till he began to suspect that she cared more for him and then instantly conceived a sort of contempt for her—? You know to what I allude—never as you value your ears mention the circumstance—but I have two studies—*you* are my study for the success, the credit, and the respectability of a quiet, tranquil character. Mary is my study—for the contempt, the remorse—the misconstruction which follow the development of feelings in themselves noble, warm—generous—devoted and profound—but which being too freely revealed—too frankly bestowed—are not estimated at their real value. God bless her—I never hope to see in this world a character more truly noble—she would *die* willingly for one she loved—her intellect and her attainments are of the very highest standard. (Stevens 17; WS no. 106)

Charlotte and Mary destroyed almost all of their correspondence—presumably because it was much more frank and critical than Charlotte's letters to Ellen Nussey—so we do not have Mary's version of this flirtation. However, it is hard to imagine a less suitable match than the straightforward, ambitious, morally earnest Mary, and the maudlin, fearful, self-destructive Branwell. The rest of Charlotte's reflections on Mary's attachment were destroyed by Ellen Nussey, except for the reflection that Mary would probably never marry—a prediction that proved true.

Certainly much of Mary's romantic energies were focused on travel. Charlotte captures this quality in Rose Yorke:

> [I] long to travel . . . I mean to make a way to do so, if one is not made for me. I cannot live always in Briarfield. The whole world is not very large compared with creation: I must see the outside of our own round planet at least. . . . I am resolved that my life shall be a life . . . [not] a long slow death like yours in Briarfield Rectory. (*Shirley*, Chapter 23)

This scene between the vital Rose Yorke and the placid, immobilized Caroline Helstone is particularly poignant because it echoes Mary's last meeting with Charlotte before leaving for New Zealand. Here is Mary's account of that difficult parting:

> When I last saw Charlotte (Jan. 1845) she told me she had quite decided to stay at home. She owned she did not like it. Her health was weak. She said she would like any change at first, as she had liked Brussels at first, and she thought that there must be some possibility for some people of having a life of more variety and more communion with human kind, but she saw none for her. I told her very warmly that she ought not to stay at home; that to spend the next five years at home, in solitude and weak health, would ruin her; that she would never recover it. Such a dark shadow came over her face when I said "Think of what you'll be five years hence!" that I stopped, and said, "Don't cry, Charlotte!" She did not cry, but went on walking up and down the room, and said in a little while, "But I intend to stay, Polly." (Stevens 161; Gaskell, Chapter XIII)

Charlotte's acceptance of her isolation and poverty frightened and enraged her friend. Throughout her life Mary deplored passivity and isolation as leading to morbid religiosity and even insanity. In *Miss Miles,* Miss Everard presents the spectre of a woman long used to isolation who indulges herself with an imaginary companion—a fate she urges young Maria to shun in words that echo Mary's to Charlotte: "Think of what you'll be like after ten years of solitude!" (129).

Mary often encouraged her friends to move on both physically and emotionally, by setting an example and by writing passionate and encouraging letters. After her father died in 1841, Mary went off to Europe with her sister Martha, and wrote back descriptions of the art and architecture which inspired Charlotte with a "vehement impatience of restraint and steady work . . . a strong wish for wings . . . an urgent thirst to see, to know, to learn" (WS no. 119). When Martha died of cholera in Brussels in 1842, Mary sought relief from her grief in a wider range of activity and shocked her friends by taking a teaching post in an all boys' school in Germany. It was Mary who provided Charlotte and Emily with the motivation and the practical guidance to go to school in Brussels ("her own strong energetic language heartened me on," wrote Charlotte [WS no. 123]), and it was Mary whose letter of advice later broke the spell that had kept Charlotte in Brussels alone and miserable, pining for her married professor, M. Heger.

It was perhaps inevitable that Mary's love of activity and scorn for feminine paralysis would propel her to a frontier environment where she could use her energies to better purpose than in England. Charlotte had known for years that Mary wanted to move to New Zealand with one of her brothers and she understood the reasons why:

> Mary has made up her mind she can not and will not be a governess, a teacher, a milliner, a bonnetmaker nor housemaid. She sees no means of obtaining employment she would like in England, so she is leaving it. (WS no. 112, 2 April 1841)

Yet when the plans were finally made, Charlotte felt "as if a great planet fell out of the sky" (WS no. 183, 16 September 1844).

Like Maria and Dora in *Miss Miles*, Mary and Charlotte bridged their separation with eagerly written and received letters, letters in which Mary reported on her progress toward independence and often scolded Charlotte for being too passive and self-denying. For both of them the letters had the effect of affirming parts of their intellects and personalities which the surrounding world ignored or inhibited; they were psychological lifelines stretched out across the globe. Too few of these letters survive—only those impersonal enough to be shared with Ellen Nussey. And yet we can still sense the flavor of their friendship and hear the tone of moral examination and compassionate support that Mary captured again in Maria's and Dora's relationship.

In 1850 Mary shared her exhilaration at her success in becoming self-sufficient:

> I have set up shop! I am delighted with it as a whole—that is it is as pleasant or as little disagreeable as you can expect an employment to be that you earn your living by. The best of it is that your labour has some return and you are not forced to work on hopelessly without result. (Stevens, Letter 20)
>
> * * *
>
> I have wished for 15 years to begin to earn my own living. Last April I began to try. It is too soon yet to say with what success. I am woefully ignorant, terribly wanting in tact, and obstinately lazy, and almost too old to mend. Luckily there is no other chance for me; so I must work. (Stevens, Letter 21)

Taylor's insistence on her own laziness is characteristic of her down-to-earth idealism. She saw herself not as a great adventurer, but as a person whose dignity depended on becoming as self-sufficient as she could. She found all the details of keeping shop and dealing with the wider world of merchants unfamiliar and confusing at first. She had to overcome shyness and ignorance in herself and in Ellen, as well as opposition and even ridicule in the community. But she threw herself into the work, "as fierce as a dragon" in Ellen's words, and succeeded in establishing a thriving business (Stevens, Letter 21).

Perhaps the hardest obstacles for Mary to overcome were her tendencies toward reclusiveness and her preference for spending her time in more intellectual pursuits rather than in visiting warehouses and keeping account books. It was remembered of her that

> once a year, her brothers sent her out a lot of books and for 2 days after it arrived she would pace up and down her backyard or garden quite oblivious to everything, while customers who knew her ways just wandered in and out and took what they wanted, and always left the right amount in payment. (S. Taylor 7–8)

Of all the news she received she was, of course, most interested in Charlotte's literary success, and she eagerly read the novels when they finally reached her hemisphere. She did not hesitate to criticize her lionized friend ("You are a coward and a traitor," she announced when she saw excerpts from *Shirley* which argued too weakly for a woman's right to work) or to give her honest literary opinions (*Jane Eyre* "surprised me by being so perfect as a work of art," but "You are very different from me in having no doctrine to preach. . . . Has the world gone so well with you that you have no protest to make against its absurdities?") (Stevens, Letters 20 and 16). She frequently chided Charlotte for impractical selflessness and urged her to "Look out for [monetary] success in writing. You ought to care as much for that as you do for going to Heaven" (Stevens, Letter 19). For her own part, she looked forward to learning from Charlotte's mistakes in order to negotiate better terms with her future publishers. Her plan was to make her fortune in New Zealand, and then to return to England and publish a travel book that would prepare the way for her novel.

Mary's happiest time in Wellington began when she was joined in August 1849 by her cousin Ellen Taylor, who became her roommate and partner in the shop. She wrote to Ellen Nussey about the relief she felt at having her cousin's company:

we talk over things that I never could talk about before she came. Some of them had got to look so strange I used to think sometimes I had dreamt them. Charlotte's books were of this kind. Politics were another thing where I had all the interest to myself and a number of opinions of my own I had got so used to keep to myself that at last I thought one side of my head filled with crazy stuff. (Stevens, Letter 22)

As Mary describes it, Ellen's arrival rescued Mary from the danger she describes in *Miss Miles*—a mental imbalance brought on by severe emotional and intellectual isolation. But Ellen died in December 1851, leaving Mary on her own once more. Mary wrote to Charlotte of the death in "a long letter which wrung my heart so in its simple, strong, truthful emotion, I have only ventured to read it once." Charlotte continued:

She fears she shall now in her dreary solitude become "a stern, harsh, selfish woman"—this fear struck home—again and again I have felt it for myself—what is *my* position to Mary's?

I should break out in energetic wishes that she would return to England—if reason would permit me to believe that prosperity and happiness would there await her—but I see no such prospect. May God help her as only God can help. (Stevens 106–7)

But despite Charlotte's concern, Mary was probably the better-off of the two in dealing with loneliness and grief. As she had after the death of her sister, she threw herself into activity as the best cure she knew for the heartaches of life.

If I had more time I should get melancholy. No one can prize activity more than I do little interest [though] there is in it. I never long am without it but a gloom comes over me. The cloud seems to be always there behind me and never quite out of sight but when I keep on at a good rate. Fortunately the more I work the better I like it—I shall take to scrubbing the floor before it's dirty and polishing pans on the outside in my old age.—It is the only thing that gives me an appetite for dinner. (Stevens, Letter 24)

From this comment and others it is clear that Mary was not immune to the paralysis and morbid self-absorption so common among Victorian women, but that she had developed an effective way of countering it by marshaling her considerable physical energies toward active engagement with the world. The result was that far from becoming a "stern, harsh, selfish woman," she remained open to close friendships all her life. Even in her last thirty years as the oddly dressed, bookish village recluse back in her native Yorkshire, she was regularly visited by younger women who looked to her for guidance and understanding.

Two stories Mary liked to tell her friends make clear how she dealt with the terrors and losses of her adventurous life. Once, while hiking in Switzerland, she found herself alone on a glacier in an icy, barren landscape and separated from her lodge by a deep crevasse. She retreated in horror from the opening, hiding her face in her hands, and imagining that she would freeze before her friends could find her. Then she opened her eyes, mustered her strength, and returned to the gap, only to find that she could easily step over it after all (*Swiss Notes* 186–87). In the other story, Taylor described how shortly after Ellen Taylor's death she was awakened by ghostly footsteps on her verandah; she then heard the sound of the door opening and felt something press against her side with a long drawn breath. She put her hands over her eyes but then thought, "If I don't look and see what it is that will haunt me all my life." When she did look the ghost turned out to be Henry Taylor's dog (S. Taylor 18–19). Although both stories are comic, the terror they describe is very real. The point of each is clear: survival depends upon facing your fears with your eyes open. They are apt moral fables for the sturdy woman who boasted herself "freer from headaches and other ailments than any other person on board" during the long, dangerous journey to New Zealand (WS no. 199; Stevens 58).

Mary's faith in the active life made her singularly resistant to the cult of feminine self-sacrifice. While Charlotte and Ellen Nussey encouraged one another to ever higher standards of self-denial, Mary consisetntly denounced self-sacrifice as morally degrading. Her tone and sentiments have a startlingly modern ring to them, as witnessed by this letter to Ellen Nussey on the question of whether Charlotte should forego her marriage to Arthur Nichols to gratify her father's need for attention. It is hard to believe the letter was written in 1854.

> You talk wonderful nonsense about C. Brontë in your letter. What do you mean about "bearing her position so long, and enduring to the end"? and still better—"bearing our lot whatever it is". If it's Charlotte's lot to be married shouldn't she bear that too? or does your strange morality mean that she should refuse to ameliorate her lot when it lies in her power. How would she be inconsistent with herself in marrying? Because she considers her own pleasure? If this is so new for her to do, it is high time she began to make it more common. It is an outrageous exaction to expect her to give up her choice in a matter so important, and I think her to blame in having been hitherto so yielding that her friends can think of making such an impudent demand. (Stevens, Letter 26)

It is characteristic of Mary Taylor that she ends not by sympathizing with Charlotte in her suffering, but by blaming her for her passivity in not seeking her own pleasure. Similarly, she set up the test for her heroine Maria, who must defy the "customs of the country" to give herself the chance for happiness with Branksome. For Taylor, women had an absolute duty to act in their own interests and to defy convention if necessary to do so.

In 1855 Charlotte Brontë died, and Mary received a request from Elizabeth Gaskell to write her reminiscences of her friend. Mary confided in Ellen Nussey that "I can never think without gloomy anger of Charlotte's sacrifices to the selfish old man [her father]." Gaskell's *The Life of Charlotte Brontë* offered Mary the opportunity to "set the world right" concerning Charlotte's character, and her eloquent letters were widely excerpted in the biography. Although neither Taylor nor Gaskell could explicitly condemn the Reverend Brontë, Taylor's descriptions of Charlotte's life (including the recollection of the parting between the friends cited above) made clear the extent of Charlotte's unhappiness and self-sacrifice. Although she remained anonymous (only identifying herself as "Mary" in the *Brontë* biography, and—unlike Ellen Nussey—refusing to publicly discuss Charlotte afterwards), Taylor in effect made her public writing debut through her defense of her friend's reputation.

Meanwhile, *Miss Miles* remained unfinished.

In 1859 Mary returned to England, collected her inheritance of L3000, and built herself a house in Yorkshire. It was a time of intense feminist activity in England, including open agitation for the Married Women's Property Acts and for wider educational and professional opportunities. Taylor contributed to the movement by writing articles for the woman-run *Victoria Magazine* in which she urged women that their "first duty" was to be self-supporting. The articles were popular enough to be collected into a book in 1870, which was the first time her full name appeared in print. Taylor's feminism is strikingly devoid of bitterness toward men, whose selfishness she takes for granted. Instead she holds women responsible for listening to men's advice against their own interests. She uses a variety of personas from ingenue to elderly housewife, but most often she takes the stance of a fellow sinner and sufferer, addressing her readers like friends meeting over tea:

> No answer me: Are we right, one and all, in folding our hands, even though we bear both our wants and our idleness with patience, and though some of us feel no present evil and can shut our eyes to the future? It is customary; it is feminine, in the sense that women generally do it; and it is approved of by most men. But is it right? Is there any merit in bearing privation rather than exerting ourselves to remove it? (*First Duty* 18)

In effect she was extending the circle of her inspiring letters from her immediate friends to women at large. She continued to write for *Victoria Magazine* in the 1870s, even turning her hand to some short stories, which perhaps marked her return to writing fiction. In all of her journalistic pieces, Taylor articulated a strong sense not merely of women's wrongs, but of what women could be, psychologically and morally, in conditions of greater freedom.

Taylor indulged her love of travel with regular trips to Switzerland. In 1874 she took four younger women with her and they wrote a travel memoir together, *Swiss Notes by Five Ladies* (1875). Taylor is portrayed as the "Frau Mutter" who makes all the arrangements, worries over her charges, and insists on scaling every peak despite her age and her shortness of breath. The role of the motherly companion who encourages young girls to seek adventure was one she obviously enjoyed and continued to play with these young women and others. One of them later said that "under her rather hard, abrupt manners she [Mary] had the kindest heart of anyone she ever knew and that if anyone were worried or in trouble she [Mary] knew it instinctively" (S. Taylor 3–4). In her later life, then, Taylor seems to have been able to give to others the constructive motherly attention she missed so much in her own family.

Throughout her adventures, Taylor was intermittently working on *Miss Miles* and rereading it at intervals, always with pleasure and interest in the scenes she had described. In 1852 she reported to Charlotte that the novel

> does not get on fast though I have written about 1 volume and a half [i.e. about 300 pages]. It's full of music, poverty, disputing, politics, and original views of life. I can't for the life of me bring the lover into it nor tell what he's to do when he comes. Of the men generally I can never tell what they'll do next. The women I understand pretty well, and rare tracasserie there is among them,—they are perfectly *feminine* in that respect at least. (Stevens 24)

Her focus on women's tracasserie—their daily troubles—as she half-mockingly remarks, makes for an unusually shaped novel, one without a conventional love story and whose heroines may not appear "feminine" to her Victorian readers. Although with experience she gained more confidence in depicting men and their concerns, *Miss Miles* remained a woman-centered story. It also remained characteristically womanly in form: not the narration of exaggerated or violent events, but the meticulous detailing of the texture of community itself and of the quotidian exertion of individual force and courage. *Miss Miles* grows by accretion. Its hold on the reader is like the magnetism of a close friendship. Much of the novel's power is based upon the intimacy of the narrator's voice, distanced by time from the story she is telling (as the subtitle indicates), but involved very deeply in her heroines' struggles to make sense of their lives and to face the vicissitudes of their time with courage and moral strength.

Insofar as it does conform to mainstream nineteenth century fictional conventions, *Miss Miles* is a bildungsroman—a novel of the education of youth. As a woman's bildungsroman, however, it has a different form from the journey of, say, Pip or David Copperfield from ignorance to moral enlightenment. There are four protagonists rather than one, and each individual journey of discovery is traced within a web of motherliness and friendship among women. All four protagonists move from enclosure in a secure family to vulnerable isolation. All confront poverty, loneliness, and societal constraints that threaten to immobilize them and to force them into painfully inauthentic situations. The successful characters overcome their isolation by forming bonds with other women which enable them to move toward secure independence.

Sarah, the "Miss Miles" of the title, moves beyond her working-class family in her efforts to become a "lady." Her struggle to preserve the intense ties of childhood while gaining a wider field of action for herself allows Taylor to dissect the whole social network of Repton. Sarah's fresh eyes and outspoken tongue provide the satiric bite of the novel and flavor it with a down-to-earth, racy Yorkshire humor. Maria and Dora are thrown out into the world by the deaths of their parents. Their friendship is the emotional center of the novel, and they are clearly the characters with whom Taylor herself is most fully identified. Amelia, the most sheltered, privileged, and "lady-like" protagonist, sees her family collapse around her when her father is bankrupted, and becomes an outcast in her own home because of her principled nature. The lifelong bond between Dora and Maria is balanced by the tentative friendship between Sarah and Amelia. Just as Dora is sustained through poverty by Maria's encouragement, Amelia is offered the chance of escape from her demoralizing gentility through her friendship with the down-to-earth Sarah.

Much like Pip in *Great Expectations,* who must learn to be a moral, self-supporting man rather than a status-oriented "gentleman," the four protagonists of *Miss Miles* struggle with whether they want to be passive, respectable "ladies" or self-sufficient women. In contrast to the false standards of ladylike behavior, the virtues celebrated by the novel are courage in isolation, loyalty to friends, frugality, disdain for status and convention, and, above all, active self-help over passive suffering. The psychology underlying the characterization of all four heroines assumes that women are debilitated and degraded by dependency and passivity, and that they gain spirit and strength by comforting one another and—most of all—by acting in their own interests. It also assumes that the greatest protection for the vicissitudes of life that a young woman can have is a mother who has urged her to be strong and moral rather than passive and dependent on men.

Because this is a *feminist* bildungsroman, the theme of learning takes on special significance. The women are portrayed as powerless from ignorance. Old Miss Everard in particular epitomizes the misery that grows from not understanding one's own business interests. Maria and Dora are not able to supply one another with any information that might help them overcome their difficulties. Sarah seeks an education to learn how to prosper, but soon learns that Miss Bell is almost as much in the dark as she herself is on this crucial question. Little by little the women come to understand how the world works, to overcome their shyness and confusion, and to learn how to deal with landlords, singing teachers, business managers, and others beyond their domestic circle. Taylor charts the exhilaration that comes with each of these steps, culminating in Miss Everard's unexpected delight in their becoming businesslike and confident like men.

Although Taylor did succeed in "bringing the lover into" her story, she carefully subordinated romantic interest to the central theme of the women's growing independence. Sarah and Maria have lovers who must prove themselves superior to the corrupting environment of male denigration of women before they are accepted by their sweethearts. Sarah has the distinction of being perhaps the only romantic heroine in the nineteenth century to punch her lover in the face. Although the scene with Sammy is comic, the misunderstanding between them is the cause of believable misery, and Taylor means for us to take seriously Sarah's fear of humiliation in a world in which women are thought of as no more than kittens to be played with.

Amelia's story is the most melodramatic and narrowly political. Her death from enforced idleness parodies the convention of the ingenue dying from a broken heart. Yet there is real pathos in Amelia's wavering between keeping to her ideals and "groveling for companionship" in her family (290), and there is almost tragic force behind Amelia's declaration to her mother and sisters after the disaster at Mrs. Overton's ball that "I will never again do what you tell me, or believe a word you say" (390). Mrs. Turner, of course, like Mrs. Wells, represents the destructive mothering that Taylor sees as virtually fatal to their daughters because it enforces a dependence on men.

But whatever the limits of romance in the other heroines' lives, it is perhaps more interesting that the outspoken Dora has no suitor at all and shows no longing for one. (She does long for and get a business manager, however!) In fact the climax of the novel involves Dora's passionate cry not for love but for justice. In Chapter XXIII the relatively unsocialized Dora asks Maria to sponsor her in a public lecture in Repton. Dora's angry temperament and her deep bitterness over her personal wrongs pose a threat to Maria's tenuous footing in the existing social and economic order. If the unstable Dora offends the people of Repton, Maria will lose her pupils. The starvation conditions in Repton make Maria's choice quite serious. Her generous response to her friend's plea marks the high point in her moral development, the crowning moment of what Taylor clearly sees as a noble friendship:

Dora got up and seized her hand as if to prevent the coming refusal.

" 'Ria you are my friend, I call upon you as my friend. I am not insane, I know very well that I go a long way to ruin you if I fall, but, Maria, help me. 'Ria! I am sinking under water, and I want a hand."

"Dora, is it right? Are you sure?"

"I am sure."

"Then I will help you with my whole heart! Never mind what comes of it, tell me what to do." (327)

Maria's decision to help Dora sets up a crucial test for her own lover, Branksome, and indeed for the entire community of Repton, as she goes from rich to poor, church-goer to dissenter, looking for sponsors. Most importantly, Maria herself is energized by her commitment to her friend and is able to speak out more freely and to feel the relief that comes from action: her "spirits rose, necessity drove her forward, and the terrible ordeal, sitting motionless in presence of danger, was over" (330).

The Dora/Maria story is in its way a version of the stories told in *Jane Eyre* and *Wuthering Heights:* the conflict between the childish, unsocialized woman and the grown-up, socialized woman. Maria is a calm, controlled schoolteacher like Miss Temple in *Jane Eyre,* but drawn with interiority. Taylor makes it clear that Maria's placidity is the result of a more favorable family life than her bitter friend Dora's. And though it is the rebellious Dora who is in need of protection by her better-established friend—just as young Jane Eyre was in need of protection in the destructive microcosmic patriarchy of Lowood—Taylor emphasizes that, unlike Miss Temple, the respectable Maria is as much in need of her women friends (including even Sarah Miles, whose parents come to her rescue) as they are of her. Most interestingly, instead of soothing and suppressing the rebellious, raging, unsatisfied Dora (as Miss Temple does with Jane), Maria sanctions her and gives her a platform. The triumphant solidarity between Maria and Dora is as much a wishful rewriting of Charlotte's and Mary's lives as it is of *Jane Eyre*. In life, Mary was powerless to rescue Charlotte from Haworth and her long martyrdom to her selfish old father. Charlotte was powerless to help Mary establish independence and return to England. In the fictional world of *Miss Miles,* however, Maria's friendship liberates Dora from the isolation of an exploitative male household, and Dora's self-assertion energizes Maria to exercise her authority as a schoolteacher within the community. The socialized and unsocialized women gain strength from one another.

Taylor's faith in exertion differs from conventional Victorian cant about "self-help" because she knows quite well that, as Sarah and Maria both learn, "we may do our best and wisest and fail after all." Maria responds to this knowledge by continuing to "dress the doll" of daydreams for the future, even though there was something of "insanity" in living always on false hopefulness (312–16). Sarah also decides that "Hope is pretty well all we have in the world" (145). The last sentence of the novel reinforces this realistic view of the uncertainty of life, telling us that the main characters "had many changes, and many sorrows, so we had better leave them in sight of that paradise which never comes but at the end of a novel."

But if Taylor refuses to guarantee happiness ever after to her characters, she does guarantee them their integrity. The two marriages at the end of the novel are based on equality and mutual respect. The women's occupations bring them a good living and a satisfying connection to the public world. Sarah and Dora, the outspoken ones, literally find their public voices in finding their professions in singing and lecturing. Maria's and Miss Everard's schoolkeeping represents an ideal that Mary and Charlotte cherished from girlhood—not so much for themselves since they were too demanding to enjoy teaching—but as an emblem of self-possession and self-sufficiency. By opening their eyes to the dangers around them and facing them straight on, by standing up for themselves and for one another, and by caring more for autonomy than for status, Taylor's heroines are rewarded not so much with love and wealth, but with the chance to live their lives in that "atmosphere of truth" that Sarah cherishes so deeply in old Sykes' house (368).

Early in the novel, Sarah astonishes Maria by lamenting that "I am not wise enough for what I have to do and have to go through in life." Maria feels much the same about herself (149). In telling their stories so realistically, without offering large rewards or exaggerating the courage of the characters she admired, Taylor was trying to capture that wisdom for herself and her readers. Perhaps that is why she held onto *Miss Miles* all her life—to be sure it contained all she knew about the world before passing it on. The publication of *Miss Miles* when she was 73 years old was Mary Taylor's last great act of friendship toward women: the women she had known in her youth, whose struggles it indirectly records; the women she had mothered in later life, who were her immediate audience; and the women who have come after her and who are as haunted by the great riddles of work, courage, and integrity as the "upright and downright" Yorkshire lass of 160 years ago.

Bibliography

Elizabeth C. Gaskell. *The Life of Charlotte Brontë*. ed. Alan Shelston. Harmondsworth, England: Penguin, 1975.

Janet Horowitz Murray. *Strong-Minded Women*. New York: Pantheon, 1982; New York: Penguin, 1984.

Janet Horowitz Murray. "The First Duty of Women: Mary Taylor's Writings in *Victoria Magazine*." *Victorian Periodicals Review*. 23(4) Winter 1990.

Joan Stevens. *Mary Taylor, Friend of Charlotte Brontë: Letters from New Zealand and Elsewhere*. New York: Oxford University Press, 1972. Auckland, New Zealand: Auckland University Press, 1972.

Mary Taylor. *The First Duty of Women: A Series of Articles Reprinted from "The Victorian Magazine," 1865–1870*. London: Emily Faithfull, 1870.

[Mary Taylor, Grace Hirst, Fanny Middleton Richardson, Minnie Nielson, and Marion Ross.] *Swiss Notes by Five Ladies*. Leeds, England: Inchbold & Beck, 1875.

T. [Mary Taylor]. "Feminine Suffrage and the *Pall Mall Gazette*." *Victoria Magazine* 11: 211–21, 1868.

T. "Feminine Profitable Labour." *Victoria Magazine*. 15: 555–63, 1870.

M. Taylor. "The Revolt and the Revolters" (Lead Article, July). *Victoria Magazine*. 17: 193–204, 1870.

M. Taylor. "Plain Sewing" (Lead Article, September). *Victoria Magazine*. 19: 385–93, 1872.

M. Taylor. "The Shah on English Laws Relating to Women. A Dialogue That Might Have Been." *Victoria Magazine.* 21: 358–65, 1873.

M. T. [Mary Taylor]. "A Servant Girl's History." *Victoria Magazine.* 27: 503–12, 1876.

Susan M. Taylor [daughter of Edward Taylor, grandniece of Mary Taylor]. Untitled Manuscript Notebook, Recording Interview with Grace Hirst, Friend of Mary Taylor. Haworth Parsonage Library. Undated.

Thomas J. Wise and John Alexander Symington (eds.). *The Brontës: Their Lives, Friendships, and Correspondence.* 4 vols. [The Shakespeare Head Brontë, referred to here as WS.] Oxford: Oxford University Press, 1932.

List of Yorkshire Terms
and German Phrases

Yorkshire Dialect Words in *Miss Miles*

a'warters	on weekdays
addle	earn
agate	going, going on
agen	against
allus	always
bairn	child
brass	money
capped	astonished, puzzled
clam	go hungry
creel	frame for holding oatcakes
dree his own wierd	suffer his own fate
faal	ugly, ill-tempered
fettle, fettling	tidying, scouring
frame	get on, succeed
fratch	quarrel
gaumless	stupid
hallacked	loitered, idled
I'st	I must
i' t' gate	in the way
mell	speak, concern oneself about
mense	neaten, tidy up
lake	play, go idle
loin	lane

nobbud	nothing but
oud	old
pop-shop	pawn shop
roar	cry
siding	clearing away
summat	something
thoil	bear, endure
throddy	plump
threeped me down	shouted me down
tull	to
wer sens	ourselves

German Phrases in *Miss Miles*

p. 1 "Die Goldene zeit des Werdens": The Golden Time of Becoming.

p. 64 "Je gelehrte je verkehrter": The more educated, the more mixed-up.

p. 219 "Wir menschen werden wunderbar geprüft. Wir konnten's nicht ertragen hät' uns nicht, Dir schöne leichtsinn die natur verlichen": We humans get tested in the most wondrous ways. We would not be able to stand it, If Nature had not given us the ability to take things lightly.

p. 241 "Sicherlich es muss das beste / Irgendwo zu finden seyn": Surely the best must be able to be found somewhere.

p. 260 "auf Freiers fuss": going a-courting.

p. 373 "Eine anhang von sinnlichkeit die sich niemals concentrirt": An appendage of a sensuality that never gets focused.

MISS MILES

CHAPTER I.

DIE GOLDENE ZEIT DES WERDENS.

THAT sort of structure indefinitely called a mill has the power of gathering round it a kind of architecture more useful than ornamental. Trim gentility and retired leisure never seek its neighbourhood, and the picturesque cottages with diamond-paned windows, many-coloured thatch, and earthen floors, disappear under its influence. Their place is taken by weather-tight buildings with slated roofs, stone floors, and sash windows—repulsive to aestheticism, but cheering to the eyes of real philanthropists.

Such a change was passing over the village of Repton sixty years ago. It lay in a narrow valley in the West Riding of Yorkshire, with a stream and a lane running down the middle of it. On each side of these were green fields stretching upwards towards the heather that covered the high land for miles round. A road, still called the New Road, crossed the lane at right angles connecting the two nearest towns. On one side of the valley stood the great house of the landowner, Mr. Everard—whose necessities had made him let the ground for the mill—and the church and the vicarage were opposite on the other. Somewhat higher up the valley was the new chapel, and after this, perhaps, the most important building was the shop at the corner made by the lane and the road.

All this lay wrapped in December snow when our story opens. A thick fog had covered it all day, but at dusk a keen north wind had swept the valley, and the frost made the burr of the clogs and the shouts of the children sound loud and clear. As the lights began to appear in the windows, a small crowd collected round the door of the shop where John Miles and his wife were prepared to serve till midnight, for it was Saturday, and it was a good year, and it was near to Christmas, and for all these reasons everyone was determined to spend their money.

It had not been always so with this isolated village, nor with England generally for the fifty years before. The scanty population of the country lived thinly scattered on the barren land. They grew their own oatmeal and bacon, and, perhaps, milk, and wanted little else. Towards the end of the eighteenth century three bad harvests followed in succession. In January, 1800, a bullock was roasted whole on the ice of the Thames, and the hills of the West Riding were covered in June with deep snow. The poor were in famine; rents were not paid. Many a wealthy family came down in the world, and many of the class below them were brought face to face with poverty. There was discontent among the starving people that the rulers thought dangerous; no one could say why it came, and no one could find a remedy.

It was in this year that a strange man came to the great house wanting a strange thing. He would like to buy, or lease, a few fields near the Beck and build a mill there. He was no gentleman in appearance, and his speech would have been unintelligible to anyone not born in the neighbourhood. Even in his own dialect he was not fluent enough to make Mr. Everard understand how he hoped to be able to give five times the old rent for the fields and yet drive a profitable trade.

But for years Mr. Everard had gone downhill. Rents were lower, burdens heavier, and prospects darker. He consented to lease the fields—not to sell them. Oh, no! they should come back to his family some time, though he might be dead and gone. His successors might even pull down the mill and restore the land to its old condition, when the good times came back again.

So the mill rose and prospered, in ugly proximity to the great house, the church, and the vicarage. The "trim gentility" of the place somehow hated it more than it deserved, for they had not the eyes to see its compensating good qualities. The poor took to it, fully appreciating the higher wages, and not caring in the least about the ugliness, nor even the dirt and smoke.

There was another cause for the enmity that then existed between the upper classes and the lower through the country.

It has been written with authority that had it not been for Wesley and Whitfield the name of Christ would have been unknown in that part of Yorkshire. Before Wesley, the little earnest religion there was existed among some sort of conventiclers, who were fined for meeting, fined for not going to church, and otherwise thwarted and oppressed.

Perhaps partly by this means the lukewarm and time-serving members were winnowed out of the little flock that had kept their Puritan proclivities, and they remained united and earnest. With immense difficulty they succeeded in building a small chapel—an eyesore and a wickedness to the vicar of the parish—and, after the mill had brought comparative prosperity, this was succeeded by a much larger one. Chapel-going became the fashion, and if the religion was not so earnest or so fruitful in good works as it ought to have been, why, it is not the first time such a thing has been true of churches, established or otherwise. The population, as a whole, were in opposition—in religion, because the only sincerity known to them had been among the Dissenters; in politics, because the vicar was zealously loyal and Tory, which in those days was almost the same thing. They were triumphant when the mill was in full work, and not docile when they were in want. These times came alternately, but not many of them learnt to minimize the effect of the one by the other.

On this particular Saturday before Christmas, in the house or living-room behind the shop, Sarah Miles was "cleaning up." She had washed the floor, replaced the chairs, and dusted the furniture, and now prepared to end her labours by washing the door-step. As she opened the door, she took a look up the lane and down the lane, sure of seeing someone she knew, and probably someone to speak to. She soon made out a girl of her own age standing outside the crowd and peering into the shop. She called to her—

"Eh, Harriet, lass!"

To whom thus Harriet—

"Sarah, haven't ye done yet? Jim Sugden an' me's been teeming water down ever sin drinkin' time, and it's t' grandest slide ye ever seed i' yer life!"

"I'm comin'," Sarah shouted, as she swept the steps with her cloth and then dashed the water into the open drain, and gently deposited the pail within the door.

Then, drying her bare arms on her canvas pinafore, she joined the boys and girls at the corner. She and Harriet were the two tallest; nearly fourteen, and well-grown, fine lasses, in dark-blue print, rough pinafores, and fuzzy hair.

"Here's Sarah!" shouted someone, and was nearly pushed down in the snow by Sarah for his zeal.

"Cannot ye hod yer din?" she said. "Mother 'll hear ye!"

Then they all tramped up the hill, Sarah critically eyeing the slide as she went along. She led off on the way down, and it was no slight test of activity to do so. The hill was steep, the causeway often interrupted, and the ground rough. The only way to avoid being thrown down by such obstacles was to regain the perpendicular by a desperate leap forwards, or to take a run when they could not slide, and so running, leaping, flying, to make their way to the bottom. Again and again they tramped up the hill, and flew down, each time leaping into the snow-drift at the bottom till all were assembled. They were laying in a stock of courage, health, and energy that would benefit them for the whole of their natural lives. True, they were most of them forbidden to do it, but they were blessed with a healthy instinct that set authority at defiance.

Sarah's draught of energy was cut short by her own carelessness.

"Jim Sugden's fallen," someone cried.

"Jim, ye mun go last," Sarah observed, without the slightest expectation that her orders would be attended to. "I think nought o' folks as falls."

"Go last yer sen, Sarah," was the answer.

It did not seem a very desirable privilege to go first, for any-one who fell was not only severely hurt, but all the others fell on to him, and then abused him for spoiling the fun.

"I never fall," Sarah shouted again, and these loud words fell on her mother's ears as the door was accidentally opened by a customer. She went and called her daughter.

The door of the house opposite opened, sending a gleam of yellow light across the snow, which disappeared immediately. Then several voices answered at once—

"She is not here."

The mother was not deceived. She had seen her daughter enter the house opposite, and, satisfied with having put an end to her uncivilized proceedings, went no farther. The other children stood about looking lost. After a while they tried the slide again, but the charm was gone. They grew afraid in the darkness, and, standing still, began to shiver with cold, and slipped off quietly, each to his own home.

The house Sarah had entered was bright and clean, but the day's work was not done yet, for a bowl of dough stood on the hearth, and the house-mother was rolling out cakes at a table under the window. There was a staircase opposite the door, and a bed half hidden behind it with blue and white checked curtains. A man sat smoking by the fire, and a round table stood near him. Sarah walked familiarly up to the fire and sat down on the fender, leaning her shoulder against the oven and putting out her hands to the blaze.

After a while the woman asked her—

"Ye've done cleaning, Sarah?"

"Aye."

"And ye dunnot want to get to your knitting?" the old man asked, with a smile.

"No."

There was another silence, which was broken by the sound of clogs and the loud voices and laughter of a troop of girls.

"There's t' lasses," said the father, and, parting from their companions, three girls burst into the room and walked up to the fire.

"Eh, but it's cold! Mother, haven't ye done yet? Now, Sarah, lass, how goes it?"

They had all three bare arms, fuzzy heads, and canvas pinafores. Head, arms, and pinafores shone with oil.

"Mother, we've bought t' cap."

"Ha' ye, lasses? Let's look at it."

"I daren't tak it out o' t' paper. Sarah, ye do it."

Sarah unfolded the paper, which the girl had carefully held by the two corners ever since she came in, and produced for inspection a net cap with a wide border, plentifully stuck over with blue ribbon. The old woman came to examine it, rolling-pin in hand. The girls tried it on her head, and then on Sarah's. They described others they had seen, and would have liked to buy, and said—

"T' new folk"—the milliners—"were reight folk enough, and not a bit proud, but they couldn't talk reight," meaning that they had not the broad accent of the Repton people. "It's for ye, mother."

Then the conversation turned again on the caps and finery, and then, naturally, on the means of purchasing some of it. The mother demurred; she thought they should wait a bit, well knowing that time would bring other wants, and this one would be forgotten.

"Wait! What for, mother? Is there ought on at t' shop?"

The mother would not say. She asked how they thought they could pay for everything and have fine caps besides. Sarah told them there was nothing owing at the shop, she had heard her mother say so that morning.

A shout of laughter followed the announcement.

"Well, I declare I never heerd t' like on't! Not to heve

nought on at t' shop, and munnot get nought nauther! We'll heve it t' next wage day, will n't we, lasses?"

Amidst the merriment the old man leaned forward to light his pipe.

"It's fine times for ye bairns. All on ye plenty o' work an' nought bud yer sens to think on. What 'll ye do when ye've each on ye gotten a two or three childer an' maybe nought to put i' their mouths?"

"There's good years an' bad years," said the youngest, after a pause, which arose out of the difficulty of admitting that they would or would not have any children; "an' in a bad year no one never gets no comfort wi' thinking on a good year, so it's no use spoiling a good year wi' thinking on a bad un."

"If folk will have such lots o' bairns they mun tak t' consequences," said the eldest.

She had already starved in her lifetime, and knew the same thing might happen again.

"Ye'll see Peggy 'ull be an old maid," said her mother, pointing at her with the rolling-pin.

"If I am, I's heve less to clam!"

"Keep thee i' that mind, Peggy," said her father.

"What's thou gotten agen wedding?" asked his wife. "Thou'rt better off than if thou'd never been wed."

"Why, maybe I am, wife; but t' lass 'll go her own gate, so I may as well speak my own mind."

It grew late. The mother took the last bread out of the oven; the girls "cleaned themselves," and Sarah, hearing her father closing the shop windows, crossed the road, entered by the house door, and went straight upstairs to bed.

Her friend on the slide was also her companion at chapel next day. They joined hands on the way thither, sat together among the Sunday scholars, and employed most of the time in discussing their own affairs. Only when the singing began did they attend to the service. Sarah's out-door habits had strengthened her lungs. She was gifted with a good ear and an appreciation of musical effect, and when there were any "grand things" to be sung she lent her aid with all her heart. Especially on winter afternoons the two friends would congratulate each other on the early darkness, and enjoy the time with true artistic feeling when the congregation rose in the dusk after the long sermon, and the service closed with—nobody knows what. A hymn it was called, but the worshippers were not critical, and devotional feeling as expressed in music is not very definite. At Repton they used large license, and were merry, pugnacious, or amatory, without the slightest consciousness of the incongruity of their behaviour.

As Sarah cleared the table after tea, while her father, mother, and brother turned their chairs to the fire, she asked leave to go and see Aunt Jane.

"Sarah," said her mother, "where were you last night?"

"I was sliding down t' hill."

"I went an' called, an' ye never spoke."

" 'Cause I'd gone into Willanses."

"I've told you before I will n't have ye running out wi' all t' lads an' t' lasses i' t' town. What 'll come o' such ways, think ye? A great girl like you! Are ye allus going to run out whenever ye can find a lot o' bairns to go wi' ye? Can any good come on it, think ye?"

"Ye mud let me go to t' school."

Her brother and father laughed. School had been Sarah's favourite object for the last half year. She took up fancies of that kind, no one knew why, and held to them with great pertinacity.

"You've given up going to t' Sunday school," said her mother; "what more learning would you have?"

"They set me nought but chapters, an' kept me agate teaching other folk."

"It would be better if ye thought more o' t' chapters, Sarah. Go your ways to your Aunt Jane, an' don't be running about i' t' town gate."

Sarah slipped out, sprang across the road, passed the Willanses, and ran down the causeway about two hundred yards to a cottage door.

The room she entered was very like the one in which she had spent her last evening. There was no staircase. The round table was by the fire, and a sloping board stood beneath the window with a web of dark-coloured cloth stretched over it, half lying before and half behind it. A pair of burling irons—tweezers for picking light-coloured specks out of cloth—lay on the window-sill.

Aunt Jane was wiping the table after tea. When her niece came in she turned her head and said—

"Now, Sarah, lass, is that thee?"

Sarah sat down on the fender. Aunt Jane hung up the towel and took her chair. It was no part of Sarah's manners to speak when she had nothing to say. She put her chin on her hand and her elbow on her knee, and looked into the fire till the spirit moved her, and then—

"Aunt Jane, did ye ever see aught o' fine folk?"

"Why, I've been i' place. I seed something of 'em there."

"What were they like?"

"Why, they were much like other folk, nobbud they could do nought—couldn't hug (carry) a bairn, nor nought. An' some on 'em were t' biggest fools I ever seed."

"Is Mrs. Dodds a fool?"

"Nay, I've nought again her."

"Is Mrs. Turner, where our Jane is, a fool?"

"Aye, a reight 'un! An' isn't a lady nauther."

"Mrs. Turner isn't a reight lady, an' they reckon to be t' grandest folk i' Repton!"

"Happen they are, for that matter."

"An' Mrs. Overton, what's she?"

"I know nought about her. What do ye want wi' such folk?"

"I do want summat wi' 'em."

"Why, what for?"

" 'Cause I do."

Sarah inclined to be sulky. To have a reason which you cannot put into words is as bad as to have no reason at all, and people in that dilemma, it is well known, make up for the want by an extra allowance of temper.

"And you want to go to school?"

"Yes, I do."

"What for, I wonder?"

" 'Cause I do."

A silence.

"You told me to keep agate asking my mother to let me go, an' said she'd let me at last. And now ye're asking me what I want it for! What have ye agen it?"

"I've nought agen it, but if ye think o' taking after t' fine folk ye'll never come to no good. They plague their lives out wi' spending more nor they have; an' then they're shamed o' earning aught."

"But they addle (earn) more nor we do, else how can they spend so much? An' if I went t' school an' learnt what they do—"

"Sarah, ye talk like a fool! If ye'll find me a fine lady 'at's been t' boarding school 'at addles more nor I do mysen, I'll go servant to her again. Grander they are, an' less they do."

"Now, Aunt Jane, that's one o' your cross speaks! They spend lots o' brass; where do they get it?"

The door burst open, and Harriet Sykes came in.

"Sarah, are ye there? Come home to your mother's! There's our Sam, an' Reuben Halsy, and Sydney Wynde, an' they're going all about gathering for a new chapel—an' your John's with 'em—'cause Thomas an' Mr. Sanders won't let 'em have no singing as they want. I heard 'em say about t' power o' music, an' bringing souls to Christ."

She had run all the way, partly from excited curiosity, and partly because it was dark, then she knelt against the fender, unfolding the pinafore that was rolled round her arms, and repeating coaxingly—

"Now do, Sarah!"

"Go yoursen."

"I don't like; there's so many folk. What are ye agate on, 'at ye mun stop here?"

"Aye, go thy ways, Sarah. She's thinking o' nought but what t' fine folks does."

"Sarah, what mun ye be running after t' grand folks for? They never put a hand to nought, an' they know nought but what's o' no use."

"Thou knows nought about it! If they dunnot do your work, they maybe do summat better. They're like!"

"Go thy ways wi' thee," her aunt exclaimed, and Sarah rose from the fender, and the two left the house.

The room that Sarah had cleaned the day before was somewhat superior to those already described; the invariable round table was there on one side of the fire. The bed, turned up to look like a cupboard, was opposite, with a chair on each side of it. Three more chairs stood usually opposite the two windows, and these had crimson moreen curtains, and a window-seat in each. As Sarah entered she took her friend by the hand and led her round the assembled company to the window-seat behind her mother, where, half hidden by the curtain, she surveyed the company. Mr. and Mrs. Miles sat on each side of the fire, and their son John next to his father. Sammy Sykes, too, Harriet's brother, she knew well enough, as also his friend, Sydney Wynde. Sydney was not a Reptonian; he was a slight-limbed, small-mouthed youth, wearing a green coat with velvet collar, and an abundance of shirt wrist-band. Sarah's instinct did not approve of him. It was evident he could not fight his way in the world, and this being the thing he most wanted to do, what was he good for? He was young Sykes's model in dress and demeanour, though the pupil half despised his master while he copied him.

Near the round table, and resting his arm on it, sat Ruben Halsy, a long, thin man, stooping more from lymphatic temperament than hardship, with dull eyes, sunk cheeks, and a great development of jaw. Such a face rode about under Don Quixote's helmet, and worked to about as much purpose in the world.

When the girls had seated themselves with great appearance of gravity and respect, he went on, stroking the table with his finger-ends—

"And you see, Mrs. Miles, I would willingly be the humble

instrument in God's hands to bring anyone to worship Him, instead of spending their Sundays in wickedness. I don't say I can do it, but—" he looked at Mrs. Miles and stopped.

"Well, you can persuade them to come to chapel if you have a gift that way, you know. There's one open for 'em, and if they won't come to that I doubt they won't to another."

"Ye'll see they'll come to ours," said Sammy Sykes, "when we've got it, so ye may as well subscribe and get it built."

"Aye, aye," said the old shopkeeper, "there's to be some grand play-acting at your chapel 'at 'll fetch 'em all up."

Sammy laughed.

"Indeed, Mr. Miles, we wish everything to be done decently, and in order. Many people don't approve of the form of worship in Mr. Somers' chapel. I hope we are all free to think for ourselves, and I hope we all do think; at least I pray that those who don't may be brought to reflect and tremble, and to cry out with the gaoler."

"Those that wish to worship God can do it as it is well enough—" It was an understood thing that Rueben Halsy never finished a sentence, but always had to be interrupted. "Folks are as free as they like, and there's no religion in just getting up new chapels."

"Now come, mother," said Sammy, "we've made up our mind to have it, so what's t' use o' talking?"

"It caps me (astonishes me), when ye start o' laking wi' ought, 'at I should ha' to pay for it!" This from old Miles.

"There's no laking about it, old man. It's going to be as good a chapel as any on 'em. Ye've built a chapel your sen afore now, an' other folks has had to help you."

"Eh, lads, ye little know! These are different times thro' when t' our chapel wor built!"

"Aye, that are they!" the old woman responded.

"Did ye never ask nobody for nought i' those days?"

'Happen we did; but they were a different sort o' folk that built t' oud chapel. They're most on 'em dead an' gone now, but I believe there was hardly a man among them, or a woman either, that had not the root of the matter in them. They had a deal to bide too, and little to spend. Lads and lasses couldn't addle their living i' those days! T' oud chapel was thought of many a year before it was built; an' when we prayed in it t' first time we called it Ebenezer, for we never thought to have been helped so far."

"Aye," said Sam, "an' t' oud devil down t' loine 'cited folk to come thro' Baumforth t' week after, an' break every pane o' glass i' t' hoile for ye, cause he couldn't get no Repton folk to do it."

"T' oud devil" was the vicar of the parish.

"Ye say more nor ye know when ye say that, Sammy, an' if ye didn't make so free wi' foul names, maybe it would be better for ye."

"Why, there's nought so holy in oud Nick 'at a man mud stick at his name!"

"If he weren't so oft in your mouths maybe he'd be farther out o' your hearts."

"Then 'twor'n't just him 'at I wor speaking o'. No, bud somebody like him."

"There's one thing you young things knows well enough, and that is other folks' shortcomings. If ye did not give your mind so much to that maybe ye'd have more time for your own!"

"Now you know well enough he did all 'at ever he could to hinder that chapel being built."

"I don't say but he did. Nevertheless, I do say hitherto hath the Lord helped us, and I had rather keep in that frame of mind, that I shall have His help in time to come. And what have you to complain of? He has not hindered your chapel building!"

"No; but he would if he could."

"Keep your money in your pocket, Sam. Ye'll get no good by spending it that way."

"We're not looking for worldly advantages, Mrs. Miles," said old Reuben, who was expecting to be preacher in it.

"Look ye to yourself, Reuben, an' then ye'll be right, whatever other folks are."

"Indeed I am aware of my many shortcomings, I humbly own."

"Come on, Mr. Halsy," said Sam, standing up, "we must go somewhere else. Mr. Miles will give us something, I know, and so will Mrs. Miles—now I know you will"—turning round to her as he went out.

"Go your ways, Sammy, and tak' better care o' your brass."

"It was time to go," said Sam outside the door, where they waited till the old man had shaken hands with all the family. "He'd ha' stalled (tired) 'em to death."

"I reckon we'st ha' to give 'em something," said old Miles to his wife when the door was closed.

There was a schism among the frequenters of the chapel in Repton. Thirty years before a few earnest men, such as old Sykes and John Miles, had held together in their belief, and, aided by their sincerity and some persecution, had succeeded in building a small place, where they worshipped as they would. It had thriven and increased, until in the more recent times, when the mill had made a little more saving possible, the congregation had built the place that now stood up, large, bare, ugly, and defiant before the eyes of the vicar of the parish. But as wealth and popularity increased, zeal declined, and the present pastor, Mr. Somers, had no other morality than to repeat the principles of the most influential part of his congregation. He was not unfaithful; he was true to his principles, though he did not originate them, nor could he have done so, but he did his best. He worked diligently, though the fire that had warmed the old generation was no longer there, and the young people each had an opinion. To have an opinion was all they had learnt from their predecessors. They set up for themselves, and they got that unfortunate predilection for the form that marks those that do not quite understand the substance. They would have some singing, having found that it was attractive elsewhere, and found also that they liked it themselves. There was no reason why they should not have it, nor, as old Miles remarked, was there any reason why they should. But Mr. Somers had unfortunately put his foot down as to the old simple service, and he soon found his congregation leaving him. The old people looked on in silent grief. They knew themselves no longer the strongest. Some were dead, and some were fallen away. The best of them let things go with the hopelessness of age and the toleration of a wide experience. But they hoped nothing from it.

CHAPTER II.

HOLD FAST TO THE FAITH WITHOUT WAVERING.

"Mother, may I go down to the Sykes's when I've done?"

Sarah said this next day as she "sided up" after tea.

Her mother looked round, and answered slowly—

"Yes, when ta's done."

Sarah set the house in order and ran down the lane. As she expected, Sammy Sykes was at home, as well as his father and sister; there was also Sydney Wynde.

"Now, Sarah lass," said they all in turn, as she took her seat among them without further ceremony; she often did so. Yet those who knew her ways saw that she had come for an express purpose. No one was surprised when she began without preface—

"What do you mean about a new chapel, Sammy? What ails ye at t' oud 'un? Is Reuben Halsy better than Mr. Somers?"

Sammy knew that neither his father nor Mr. Miles thought much of their pastor, and answered boldly—

"We'll have things better wi' him. We'll have some better singing."

"Aye," said his father, "ye've gotten too much o' yer own way wi' Somers, an' ye think ye'll heve it all out wi' t'other chap."

"Why do you let him, then?" she said, turning sharply round to the old man.

"Eh, bairn, lads mun spend their brass."

At which Sarah's eyes opened wide in astonishment. No such

doctrine had ever passed through her ears before; and how old Sykes, the friend of her father and mother, the strict chapeller, the authority in his own congregation, could maintain such a doctrine she could not conceive. After a moment of open-mouthed silence she exclaimed—

"So ye're going wi' him!"

"None o' me; but when there's nought to stay for he may go if he likes."

She meditated, still staring at him, and then said with perfect gravity—

"Ye're wrang."

Sarah was a favourite with old Sykes, both on account of her mother's virtues and her own, and he sometimes did her the honour of reasoning with her.

"Sarah, lass," he said, "if a congregation wants help in seeking God they mun bring the mind for it wi' em. No man and no chapel ever helped a careless sinner who had no mind to it. They may go to t' new chapel, and they will get nought by it; and they may leave t' oud 'un, an' they'll lose nought."

"Why for sure," Sarah answered.

"Now then, Sarah, ye'll come wi' us when it's finished, an' sing in it."

"I do believe, Sammy, that's all 'at ever ye want wi' it!" she exclaimed.

Old Sykes burst out laughing.

"Aye, lass, ye've hit it there. That's just what he wants."

"It's not reight, Sammy, it's nought! It's built on sand, an' it will fall."

The Scripture came as naturally as the broad Reptonian to the Puritan dissenter.

"Aye, that's just it, Sammy. It's built on t' top on a fiddle."

Amidst the laughter that followed this sally of old Sykes', Sammy gathered his wits together for an answer. He hit on one that would have been elsewhere very effective.

"Ye're all for making us go straight by Act o' Parliament," he said. "We're none o' us to think for our sens, but to go t' way we're driven. We sud ha' had no chapels at all."

"Go, go, lad," cried his father, "an' when ye're all gone, an' have found any good in it, tell us what it is."

Sammy answered with excessive gravity—

"There's no good in trying to show ye ought. Ye mun bring it wi' ye."

The laugh was turned, and Sarah joined in it; yet she was not convinced.

"There was no bottom in it," she kept saying, "it would never thrive."

She turned in vain to the old man whose principles she thought she knew. He only appeared to "care for none of these things."

"Do ye think," she asked, addressing him with emphatic gesture, "that one thing is as good as another?"

By the help of the intuition that guides those minds that have been thinking together, old Sykes understood her.

"Nay," he said; "there's one thing above all others, but I see nought on 't imang 'em."

In vain Sarah argued, in the firm belief that she was right, and that when the right was fairly before people they ought to yield to it at once. The old man looked on sadly, interested, but not interfering. The young ones tried to mystify her with Scripture quotations and half-laughing quibbles. She left them dissatisfied, and, as usual, told her mother all about it, repeating to her all the arguments that had been so uselessly brought forward already. Her mother agreed with her, as, indeed, it would have been strange if she had not, as the reasoning had been all inspired by herself.

"It is a pity," she said, and Sarah got nothing more.

Her mother endeavoured to inculcate a little toleration, but toleration and zeal find it difficult to live together. Perhaps honest zeal is as much as can be expected from early youth, and patience with those who differ can only come with a little experience.

The week was not out before Sarah had her head full again of things, about which it was absolutely necessary that she should talk to her friend Harriet. So, having got permission, she again went down the lane, and found Harriet alone, as she expected.

"Harriet," she began, "does Bella Somers go to Miss Bell's?"

"Why, Sarah, what does it matter?"

" 'Cause I want to go t' school; an' if Bella Somers goes, why should not I?"

"Sarah, ye'll never be right till ye're as silly as Bella Somers, an' she's fair crazed wi' her mother making her dress up, an' talk like a lady."

"Dressing an' talking like a lady does not make folks crazy. If Bella has any sense she might learn summat 'at would make her a lady."

"Why, what could she learn?"

"I'm not a lady, an' I haven't been at t' school. How can I tell you what ladies does? But them 'at's learned how is better off nor them 'at knows nought. Skilled work is better paid than unskilled, and knowledge is power, so if a man knows more than another, he can do more. That's clear—or a woman either. An' if I knew as much as a lady, I could make as much."

Harriet turned round to watch Sarah tumbling out this confused mass of Mechanics' Institute doctrine, which she herself had only learned a few weeks before.

"If ever I heard such speaks i' my life! Skilled labour! That means thievery, I reckon. Knowledge! Where did ye leeto' such grand words? Know more, an' they'll do more! I'll tell ye what, Sarah. There's nought i' this world like a bit o' hard work, if ye knew all 'at ever was in it!"

"Ye know nought about it! Does Bella Somers go to Miss Bell's?"

"Yes, she does. I see her go past every morning."

Sarah went out, and walked straight home. She talked all the afternoon to her mother about Bella and Miss Bell. "Bella went to t' school. Her mother did not think the Sunday School good enough for *her*. If Miss Bell taught nothing but vain accomplishments, why did the minister send his daughter there? Folk said Miss Bell's was the cheapest school i' t' country-side, considering how much was taught," to all which her mother listened, and only answered now and then, "Why, why, lass!" in the tone and for the purpose with which one might speak to an eager horse.

The week was not out before Sarah's brain was taken possession of by a new idea, and this time it was Harriet that put it into her head.

"Never heed t' new chapel," she said, "nor t' oud un either. There's summat else is up between our Sam and Sydney Wynde, an' your brother John is in it, too. They get together i' t' warehouse, an' they're at it till midnight. Try an' find out what it is they have up."

"I daren't go into your warehouse."

"You mun ask your John."

"He will not tell me."

"Ye mun try."

A little above Sykes's house, and on the same side of the road, the road was diversified by the end of a warehouse, with the crane from the upper story projecting over the footway. The lower doors generally stood open, and Sammy Sykes, his father, and their apprentice, John Miles, or some of them, were often to be seen at work within. After dark, however, the doors were closed, and it needed the courage of a good slider like Sarah to push them open one night at eight o'clock and to grope her way upstairs to the room above. This was almost as dark and dreary as the other. Packs of wool were piled against one end wall, and near the other were a desk, a weighing machine, and a high stool with a candle on it. The three conspirators, whose machinations she had come to inquire into, stood by it. Sydney, with a fiddle beneath his chin, full of energetic instructions and vivacious conversation concerning music and musicians; Sam, with another, listening with business-like gravity; and John, a violincello between his knees, looking more awkward than even a bass player generally does. For John was a youth of more worth than polish, and so conscious of his deficiencies that he always spoke of manners as sour grapes—a thing he would not have upon any account.

"Try again, John. It's the finest piece that ever was played."

(All Sydney's pieces were.) "If you'll only just play it, you'll see. You missed there, and that was flat, and that was wrong altogether, and—"

All three looked round in silent astonishment, while Sarah walked up to the light and stood still by the scales, taking hold of a chain, and looked at the group. The dead stillness she seemed to think quite natural, and observed them all unconcernedly. Soon John began—

"Sarah, whatever are ye comed here for?"

"To see what ye're agate on."

"Why, then, go away again."

"I won't."

"We will n't play a bit till ye're gone."

Sarah blinked at the light and swayed back and forwards by the chain as if lost in the depths of contemplation. After another silence, Sam cried—

"Come, never heed; let's go on."

"We won't go on. She's no business to be here. Sarah, go home and get to your knitting," as the most disagreeable thing he could say.

Sarah appeared not to hear him.

"Come, now; what's the use of waiting?" Sydney asked. "Sammy, just you begin there, and John will come in there, you know."

The music Sydney had chosen was much too difficult for such performers, and they seldom played half-a-dozen bars without their master exclaiming—

"Nay, Sammy"—or John, as the case might be—"you've missed it. There, just begin that again."

Then they began again, and again, and again, failing sometimes here and sometimes there, until at last Sarah could sing the missing or faulty notes, exclaiming—

"That's it, Sammy!"

"You can do it better, I suppose," John growled.

Sydney laid down his bow.

"Sarah, ye mun sing!" he exclaimed, with emphasis. "It's quite a scandalous shame you don't learn to sing!" (With Sydney music was the first, second, and third requisite to form a desirable character.) "Sammy, just let's sing the Old Hundredth Psalm."

"Sydney, we're a fiddling."

"Never mind; there's as grand music to be sung as ever was played."

Any time during the last month he had been persuading his pupils that there was no music on earth equal to what might be produced from the stringed instrument called a fiddle. They had fully believed him, and they believed him now; partly because they knew nothing about it, but chiefly because he believed himself. He proposed to Sarah to sing one of the Psalm tunes that she was accustomed to hear at chapel, and then let her hear what she had never heard before in reasonable perfection—a second voice in harmony with her own. She stopped in astonishment, or, perhaps, to listen to him, for she took the music to be all of his making.

"Go on, Sarah, go on!" they all exclaimed at once, and she went on delighted.

She had plenty of voice, and perfect freedom from embarrassment. She sang a dozen hymns, and they found each one better than the last. Singing was voted much better than fiddling, and was discovered to be much less difficult. They all tried the second and third parts of every tune, and to them all Sarah was indispensable. She was always ready, and the pitch of excitement they got to was something ludicrous. In the midst of their enthusiasm they were all startled by a thundering knock at the door below.

"That's Harriet, I suppose," said Sam. "I told her to come if Tom Saville came."

"What mun we give up for Tom Saville for?"

"He's come to talk about building t' new chapel."

Sarah was disappointed till Sydney whispered to her to come into Sykes's with them, and they would have some more singing later in the evening. So they all went down to the house, where old Sykes was in the arm-chair by the fire, and Harriet standing near it.

A short, broad man in a velveteen coat, with a round head and a little black hair plastered over it, sat on one side of the high cupboard against the opposite wall. He held his hat between his knees, and his head sunk between his high shoulders.

"Now, what do you think, Tom?" said Sam, without sitting down; indeed, without facing the man, but looking into the fire. "Can this chapel be built, think ye? You know what we want, and you know what we've got, and what we are likely to get. You see, we want it cheap. What do you think it will cost us?"

"An' I'll tell ye what, Mr. Samuel, whether you get your chapel or not you ought to get it. You see there's many a one 'at's not contented wi' t' way things is carried on as it is. An' why shouldn't they have a new chapel? There's Mr. Halsy, and there's yourself, Mr. Samuel, and I don't know who is so likely to get up a new chapel if ye like."

Sam blinked into the fire and did not look interested. When the man stopped he merely said—

"What will it cost, Tom?"

"Why, then I'll tell ye what. Ye mun count the cost, as Mr. Halsy would say, an' ye—"

"That's what we want ye to do, Tom. What will it cost?"

"Ye know, Mr. Samuel, ye mun ask somebody to contract for it."

"Why, what if we ask you?"

"Why, then I'll tell ye what. If ye ask me I'll do it as cheap as anybody, an' maybe a bit cheaper. But are you going to give t' job to me?"

"It's for you to give us a price you know."

"Why, then—"

"You're surely going to give us something towards it?" Sam interrupted, impatiently.

"Why, then, I think if I give you some good work in it, it's as much as you can expect—an' cheap work too, mind you."

"Aye, Tom's work is always good," said old Sykes, in a certain tone.

During the whole conversation Sam had stood with his

hands in his pockets and his face to the fire, without ever looking round at the outstretched arm and yellow face that kept gesticulating for his benefit. But now he swung round on his heel and looked both at his father and at Tom. Sydney wheeled his chair round on one leg, and John looked up from his sheet of music.

"Why, what do ye mean by that?" Sydney asked.

"Nay, nought, that's all."

"I don't know what ye mean, Mr. Sykes, but if ye think—"

"There's no 'casion for ye to know. Go ye on talking about t' chapel."

"There's no more to say," said Sam, getting a chair. "Ye can give us a price, Tom. That's what ye should ha' done to-night."

Sydney got up ostentatiously. The arm came out from behind the cupboard stroking the black head.

"Why, I'll tell ye what, Mr. Samuel; ye will n't get no better work, no, or no cheaper work than mine."

He left them and had scarcely closed the door when Sam asked his father what he meant.

"He'll never do for you. He's as slippery a thief as there is i' t' country side."

"He's nobbud just comed into t' country."

"Aye, but he went out on it afore."

"I never heard on him."

"He were born an' bred here. An' he spoilt all t' work 'at he put his hand to. Did ye never hear about his getting 'taties an' getting to t' wrang side o' t' hedge?"

"Wor that Tom Saville?"

"Aye, for sure it wor."

"He'll never come here no more."

"Not he!"

"We're weel shut on him."

Sarah and Harriet had sat on the doorstep leading into the back kitchen and, of course, had heard all the conversation. As soon as the door was closed, Sarah turned round to ask Sammy—

"Are ye really going on wi' t' new chapel?"

"Aye, Sarah, an' ye're going to sing in it."

"It isn't reight on ye Sam, I know it is not."

"Sarah, just let's try that tune again," and he began to sing it.

She began directly, and soon the music was in full swing. Harriet joined. They all got interested until old Sykes interrupted them with, "Now, lads, it's late tonight," and the party broke up.

Sarah and John were accustomed to be told, as if they were still little children, when it was time to go home, and this habit gave a confident ease in the house that added much to their enjoyment. They were often at old Sykes's. Indeed, most of their leisure hours were spent there, and when Sarah answered the invariable question, "Where have you been?" it was always right if she said, "At Sykes's."

But this time there was something different. Her elder sister was seated by the fire at home. Jane Miles was a very respectable personage. She was like Sarah in her ambition to learn the ways of "great folks," but utterly unlike her in the means she took to do it. "Larning" she held in slight esteem. Her first effort had been to go to place, and then by her quickness and civility, and her genuine worship of her superiors, she had risen to a comfortable position. She had learnt besides to wear a bonnet out of doors, and to mince her Repton words in the endeavour to talk English. Sarah could not appreciate her good qualities, and particularly disliked her surface polish. She set her shoulders against the door to shut it and remained against it as if not seeing any special reason for coming farther.

"Eh! Sarah, there you are without your bonnet, and coming in at this time of night!"

"Should I ha' stopped out?"

"Now, Sarah, what's t' use o' talking i' that way? Here you are running about like a common lass, and you might easily keep yourself respectable and look like a lady if you would only go to place."

"I will n't be respectable, an' I will n't go to place."

"She's wanting to go to t' school," said her mother.

"An' what's t' use o' that, I wonder?"

"She wants to be a lady."

"'Tis n't learning makes a lady," Jane exclaimed, who claimed to know a deal more about it than the other two. "You should go to place, Sarah, and see how real ladies does, and then you may learn to be like one."

"When I am a lady I shall look like one. I'll either be t' right thing or nought."

Jane bridled on her chair, pulled on her glove—it was a light coloured discarded glove of Miss Turner's, which had split across the palm, and was drawn together to suit the broader hand of the servant—then, with her head on one side, she said, with a patronizing simper—

"Oh, Sarah! how little you know! You should have seen Miss Amelia when she came home at Easter! and she can do all sorts of things!—not learning, learning is not for ladies!"—this she said with genuine disgust, imitated, like the rest of her speech, from her young mistresses—"but she can play, and sing, and draw to perfection! and speaks so nicely, too!

"What's t' good o' that sort o' laking?" (playing) Sarah exclaimed, speaking as broadly as she knew how.

"What laking?"

"Why drawing an' singing! I can sing mysen."

"Oh, Sarah!" Jane repeated, with her head on one side and a Turner smile on her face.

"What does she do when she is not laking wi' them things?"

Jane did not quite know. She impressed it on her sister that the Miss Turners had no need to work, and was particularly careful to clear them from the disgrace of doing so. Then there was fancy work. Miss Amelia had not done any. She liked going out better, but, no doubt, she would fall back on that inimitable resource when she had finally done with lessons. On inquiry, Sarah found Jane knew nothing whatever about the lessons, what they were, or to what purpose they were learnt.

She stood the cross-questioning very patiently, thinking it betokened an interest in the doings of ladies, that promised well for a change in Sarah's opinions. At last she rose, pulling at her glove and bridling.

"Well, Sarah, I wish you could see Miss Amelia; she's really beautiful."

"I mak nought o' that!"

In this she was sincere. It was part of the stern religion in which she had been brought up, that favour was deceitful and beauty was vain, and it would not have occurred to her that anyone could mention it as a recommendation when discussing a character seriously, and Sarah was always serious, or, at least, always earnest. She "went at it" with her whole heart, mentally pulling to pieces the character Jane had given of the young lady, and she found nothing in it worthy of worship or imitation.

"I reckon ye dunnot rightly know what it is makes a lady," she said, thoughtfully, looking at her sister.

Jane simpered again, and said, "Oh, you foolish child!" and took her leave without finding out that to her own manners was due the greater part of Sarah's objection to her proposals.

Sarah stayed to tell her mother of the grand discovery she had made by forcing the enemy's entrenchments in the warehouse.

"It's t' grandest laking ye ever seed, mother!" she exclaimed; "an' I'm to go again as soon as I can."

"Aye, aye, lass," said the mother; "now it's time for you to go to bed."

The girl took up her candle, and turned round before reaching the door to observe—

"And now, mother, I know how to get on in the world! Just go reight at it when there's ought i' t' gate! See what I've gotten to-night! an' I'll get to go to school yet, mother! I know ye'll let me in a while. And now ye see, mother, I know how to get on in the world!"

"Go thy ways to bed," said the mother, sad and kindly. It

was not her way to interrupt her daughter's confidence by reproof and admonition; these came at another time. The girl
turned round once more—

"I'll go every night when they're agate singing! munnot I,
mother?"

To which the wise woman answered never a word.

Sarah went to her Aunt Jane's next day to tell her triumphant story, but it ended in a lamentation that she could not
get either a single sheet of music or a fiddle. "She had no
brass." Then she asked her aunt what she could do to get some
money.

"Go to place:"

"I can get no money by that. Our Jane spends all her wage,
and gets things given besides, an' says she can't do no other,
cause she mun look respectable."

The last word was uttered in a certain contemptuous tone.

"Go to t' miln then."

"Mother will n't let me."

"Then stay at home and be quiet."

"Ye're allus telling folk to be quiet."

"Do you think you are allus to have what you want, an' do
what you like? Do as other folks does; bite at t' bridle."

"If I never try I shall never get nought. I'll go to school."

"Go to t' school if ye like. Ye'll get nought by that."

But an idea was beginning to develop itself in Sarah's mind
that learning made the lady, or, at least, that it gave the skill
by which wealth was to be won, which made ladyhood possible,
and either the skill or the result thereof, or both together, con-
stituted ladyhood. She blundered out some indistinct expression of this to her aunt, who answered warmly—

"Sarah, never you listen to them that tell you you'll ever
get rich. There's no decent way fit for you to take by which a
woman can earn more than just a living. You must make up
your mind to work close—all day, and every day, and all your
life, and then, if you are sharp and thrifty, you may perhaps
get bread."

A hundred times had Sarah been brought to this conclusion.

The prospect was not encouraging, so she did what most of us do in similar circumstances. She shut her eyes to the evidence, and resolutely refused to believe it. She could not explain whence she got her notion that some other destiny was possible—attainable for her. The fact was that such a notion was as common in Repton as an old proverb, as in most manufacturing towns. That a man's prosperity depended on himself had been so often verified by experience, that even children knew it, and Sarah, without having studied Lindley Murray, believed in his definitions, and thought that if foresight and industry were good for men, they were good for all mankind.

She went often after this to sing with her brother and Sam and Sydney, not into the warehouse, but into the house. Harriet joined them, and soon a few more musically-minded people began to come and help. They all added to the enthusiasm, if not to the progress. Old Sykes sat in the corner chair, and smoked, and held his peace, while they amused themselves. At least, if he spoke at all, it was at such long intervals that the young folks forgot that he might be listening all the while.

CHAPTER III.

HEAVEN LIES ABOUT US IN OUR INFANCY.

"But, Nanny, I want some bread and butter, I do!"

"You must wait till tea is ready, my dear. It is not good for you to eat in that way. Wait till tea is ready."

It was in the kitchen of a Moorland parsonage, about ten miles from Repton, that the child hung about her old nurse, and only left off teasing when she knew the decision was irrevocable.

"Go and walk with papa, dear. He's in the garden."

She set off, hopping two steps on one foot and two on the other, across the matted hall and out at the front door. She pulled papa's hand out of his pocket and, putting her own into it, gravely walked by his side trying to share in his enjoyment, or, at least, to understand what it was.

He was sauntering about the walks of an old-fashioned orchard, flower garden, and kitchen garden all in one. Now and then he looked towards the west, over meadow and woodland, towards the setting sun. He knew and felt, though he could not see it, that widespread moorland lay beyond, and the rolling hills added to the charm of the fertile hollow in which the house was sheltered.

He had lived in it fifty years. His parishioners, like himself, were, more or less, dependent on the land, though he was better off than most of them. He had a few chosen friends among them, and was friendly with them all. Rich and poor looked

to him for advice, or help, or comfort in affliction, and sometimes for company and enlightenment, for he was one of the
very few that had not forgotten the interests and feelings of
cultivated life, while living in a narrow circle. He knew what
was going on, and was able to explain the news that came at
long intervals from outside. The house was made up of large,
low rooms, with lattice windows, and a number of dairy and
farmyard appurtenances, made necessary by the glebe that
gave him more than half his income.

He was content with his position. He loved his friends, and
was interested in his work. He and a few more people practised plain living and high thinking, unknown to the rest of
the world, and strove to spread as much of it as their influence
allowed among the people round them. It has been said that
when the Church of England is disestablished the greatest loss
will be that of a set of men who were gentlemen independently
of money. Mr. Bell was one of those. He and his intimates were
unconsciously acknowledged to be superior to much richer
people among whom he lived. They turned their best side out
when in his company, and he learnt to like them in some
degree, though he found there were wonderful "solutions of
continuity" in their good behaviour.

He looked down at last on his little daughter, somewhat
amused at her silent gravity.

"Look, 'Ria," he said, "at the sun. It is going down to
where the wood touches the green hill. It will set there. It
sets there in spring. I have seen it set there for fifty years, and
it will come there when I am forgotten, and no one lives who
ever heard of me."

She looked at the sun and then at her father, and then
walked on. She had actually taken on some of the feeling of
the older mind by contact with it. At last she asked—

"What shall I be like when I am fifty years old, papa?"

"Why, my child, you will be like an old woman!"

And his thoughts turned from the past to the future, striving to see the one as he saw the other. But it might not be.
He could not follow the child into her coming life. He could

only do as he so often did, strive to give her a guide in the unknown future.

"What will you have to think of when that time comes, my child?"

"I wonder, papa," she said, and walked slowly on.

"So do I. I would I could know, but it is beyond my wisdom, as well as beyond my power. Everyone must dree his own weird; but of this be sure, 'Ria, the thing that will give you most pleasure when that time comes will be the good that you may have done to others. Do you understand that?"

"How can I do good, papa?"

"The time will certainly come when you may do good to someone. Then do it with all your might—always, on all occasions. And remember this. When your own affairs seem past mending, when there seems no hope of gladness in your life, try to help someone else, and light will come."

"But how can I help anyone, papa?"

"If you see no one else to help, it will be that you have selfishly wrapped yourself up in your own affairs until you can see nothing else. It is then that they look darkest."

She was so silent that he stooped to kiss her.

"This is too hard for you, my child. You cannot understand it yet."

"No, papa, it is not too hard. I understand it quite."

And so she did. Children chew such morsels of tough, but interesting, wisdom, until, perhaps years after, they assimilate them somehow; and such food is good for them.

Maria had one little friend besides her little brother, whom, indeed, she rather despised as a companion. Two years difference of age, when the eldest is only nine, make intimacy impossible. The little younger one never recollected yesterday's conversation, and could not carry it on, so she called him stupid. Now, Dora was six months older than herself, and understood her perfectly; and, like herself, Dora was limited in her opportunities for companionship, and the two were much together. Just as 'Ria stoutly maintained her ability to understand her father, Dora's little white face and shaggy hair appeared peeping through the gate, and 'Ria started off to bring her in. The old father smiled. He thought he had made no impression, but he was mistaken. The very seriousness of the subject made it impossible for him to keep to it for long together, but its weight made it one that left its mark. Maria remembered the counsel all her life.

"Dora, Dora, come here, I want to talk to you!"

And she took her down the shady walk under the apple trees, then told her friend that life was not all pleasure, that they would meet with pain, she knew not what, but pain in the coming future, and that then the way was to try to do good to someone.

"You know we must not make an outcry and be selfish, but look round and see. There will always be something to be done. It's mean to cry out. Everyone has pain to bear. Now, that's the way we'll do, won't we, Dora? Say so. We two will always do right."

Dora scowled and listened. She was a thick-set girl, shorter than 'Ria, though older. Her black hair came low on her forehead, and gave her an appearance of scowling defiance, which really she did not feel. She looked at her friend and thought awhile, and said, "Yes, of course we will, 'Ria!" and held up her head in the pride of good resolve. The promise mingled with their thoughts and with their talk, and coloured their future lives.

Dora's mother was a widow, with this little girl for sole interest in this world. She was not poor enough for the child to associate with "common children," and not rich enough to find companions for her among the scattered gentry, who needed carriages to be able to associate with each other at all. She and the Vicar's daughter fraternized naturally, and the two families practised that kind of style that is called parsimonious by the wealthy and simple by those who can afford no other. The "high-thinking" had full welcome in the clergyman's house, and was reverenced as something good, if unattainable, by the widow. The two mammas agreed perfectly, as, indeed, it was easy to do, for Dora's mother, unlike herself, had no distinctive character of her own. She clung to her prop, and would have swayed with it had it swayed at all. As it was, she stood upright, and the whole partnership had the respect of their neighbours, and was looked up to by their inferiors as people who knew the right, and did it.

For five years more the girls continued to indulge in their little plays, their little jokes, and their endless speculations as to the unknown future, and their heroic resolve as to their mode of meeting it. Then something happened; something which made them children no longer, or else being children no longer they took in the new event with the grasp of their full-grown intellects.

The event was this. A man on horseback spoke to the widow in the garden, and then at her invitation hung his horse's bridle on the gate and walked in with her. He was Mr. Woodman, a man known to everyone. He owned the land all round, or nearly. He had shot over it in his younger days, and prevented poachers from shooting. He had done nothing else that anyone remembered. His speech was the local dialect, of which it may be said that he could not have got on without it, and had had no chance of learning any other. He knew of no other pleasures than what he enjoyed himself, and was now elderly, with three stalwart sons leading the same life that their father had done before them, without a thought of change or a belief in the possibility of improvement. A burly, brown, heavy-looking man. He trod his mill-horse round, with age and death before him, and no solace on his pathway to the grave.

It was this man that Mrs. Wells, constrained by that worship of wealth which is the religion of Englishmen, asked into her drawing-room and put on her best manners for. With half an eye she might have seen that his motive for calling was an utter triviality. Perhaps she did, but she asked him to come again sometimes. She would be glad to see him! and he had come again and again, until it became an acknowledged thing that when he came he was to be asked into the drawing-room, and all were to be on their good behaviour.

Dora, hitherto the despot of the house, was scornful, angry, rebellious, and at last absented herself as much as possible. Her mother, unequal to fighting, and without the skill to enforce obedience, still became more and more aware of the necessity of having more respect shown to her visitor. There was constant warfare and constant misery in the house, and the poor woman had no resource but to lament to her new friend that girls were so wayward.

"You know, Mr. Woodman. What can you do?" she said, whining and wondering. "She used to be so good!"

Mr. Woodman evidently thought that he could do something. He would have no such behaviour in his house. He did not descend to particulars, but spoke scornfully of "wimmen" as being poor creatures. He evidently hated the girl, and not without reason, for she did not hide her scorn of him and his pretensions to the treatment due to a gentleman. He would repeat her mother's blame with emphasis, and seemed to think that something ought to come of it. The girl was not brave enough to answer him openly, and, too angry to bear his intermeddling, she would flounce out of the room and stay upstairs, or run over to 'Ria and scold and cry.

"Well, Dora, he is always coming. Why is it worse today?"

"Because, 'Ria, I told mamma he's a nasty man and I hate him! and she told me not to say so, and said he should come, and she would not have me saying so. She said I must speak to him, and I said I would not, and she said I should."

All this was said amidst such sobs and tears that Maria had great difficulty in understanding it. Still more difficult was it to answer, but at last Maria said, very sadly—

"But, Dora, your mamma lets you have your own way in almost everything. Why should not you let her have her friend?"

It was very true that Dora was master at home, but one does not often hear that the possession of power inclines one to give it up now and then.

"Maria, he's detestable! He can't be a friend of mamma's! Smudgy, gruff man! that can talk about nothing, and laughs at what mamma says, and thinks that an answer!"

"But, Dora, your mamma must choose for herself."

"Then I must grieve at it!"

They walked up and down in silence till Dora broke out again—

"It's astonishing! She can't like him. I wonder why she does it? She talks about the oldest family in the neighbourhood, and the old house and the land—*the estate* she calls it—and leads him to talk!"

With a look of disgust, as if stifled by the recollection, Dora walked on. She was broad-built, strong and straight, with pale face, thick eyebrows, and dark hair. When she was angry or disturbed, as now, her face easily took a tragic fierceness that made people think, "That must be a difficult child to manage." Poor mamma was afraid of her when she put it on. But now something made her firm against her daughter and deaf to entreaty, and she persisted in welcoming the stout, elderly representative of "the oldest family in the neighbourhood" who had lately made her acquaintance—her daughter knew neither how nor why.

"He says he never read a book through in his life!" she exclaimed with contempt. "He thought it enough to look for what he wanted; and then he laughed like a pig!"

"Dora, pigs don't laugh."

Dora laughed with the tears on her face.

Maria herself was half crying in sympathy. She strove in vain to find comfort, and at last, taking Dora's hand, she said—

"But, Dora, dear, you must have courage. Perhaps he may be conscientious and kindly, though he is rough."

The alliteration was one of her father's, which she had unconsciously adopted.

"But he's not, I'm sure."

"Dora, how can you know?"

"He told mamma a story once about some cheating or other, which he called a sharp trick, and laughed. I am sure he admired it, and would have done the same, only he's too stupid; and I called out it was a mean, contemptible fraud, and mamma blushed and told me to leave the room, and then she

came and scolded me, and told me to go back again and behave better, and I went and sat, and never spoke till nine
o'clock."

"Does he stay so late?"

"Yes, and would stay longer if mamma would let him."

"How does she send him away?"

"She asks him to stay to supper, and he never will, because
there's no beer. So he goes."

The girls walked on once more. Dora was really to be pitied.
From being the petted tyrant of the small household she had
sunk to a nobody, and had seen her place taken by this dis-
gusting person, who did not even do her the honour to quarrel
with her, but quietly ignored her, except on the occasion of
such outbursts as the one recorded, and then contented himself
with staring at her.

At last Maria put her arm round her.

"But, Dora," she said, "you know what we promised each
other—would be always good."

"Yes, I know; but I am very unhappy, all the same."

"I know; but if you keep right things will mend."

"No, 'Ria, they won't! I know right when I see it, I suppose,
and he is not right. He is a mean clown, he is! And now I
must go. He'll be there now, and when mamma says I ought
not to be out so late he will say, "Yes, it doesn't do for gals
to be oot i' t' dark,' and look as if he had a right to say it."

Then she ran off.

Maria went into the parlour to her father and mother.

"Papa," she said, "is Mr. Woodman going to marry Mrs.
Wells?"

"Marry Mrs. Wells, my dear! What put that into your
head?"

"Because he goes there so often, and stays there till nine
o'clock."

"Mrs. Wells marry again!" said Mrs. Bell. "Marry Mr. Woodman! How can she?"

"She can sure enough if she will."

"And will she?"

"I do not know. Ask Maria."

"It is impossible. She would not think of such a man."

The Vicar knew well enough that the old Squire was bent upon trying matrimony again. With three grown-up sons at home he was solitary and unhappy. Perhaps it was his own fault, but that did not make it easier to bear, so he would try again to bring back the shadow of better times.

But that Mrs. Wells should accept the position confounded Mr. Bell. He had not thought there was danger of such a thing, but if there was— Well, he could do nothing; why should he disturb himself?

Mrs. Bell tried to do more. She waited a day or two for an opportunity, and then found out on reflection that she had seen very little of her friend of late; but it would have been very strange if a week passed over without their meeting and soon the opportunity offered. It is very easy to live a long time with people who always agree with you, and to know nothing of their characters whatever. Mrs. Bell found out to her astonishment that this was her case. To the mild hints as to Mr. Woodman's character and manners, came with overflowing happiness something about "the large estate, you know."

After having been twice or thrice interrupted with this, Mrs. Bell closed her mouth in disgust. She grieved sincerely, but, as far as true communication goes, there was silence between them for evermore. Mrs. Wells knew that they did not approve of Mr. Woodman; she never knew that they condemned herself.

It was true things would go shockingly wrong if those two uncongenial people came together. How could Mr. Bell stand by and see it happen? But how was he to prevent it from happening? He did not even know how to remonstrate, for he did not know the motives that led the widow to make such a fool of herself. And then, seeing she did want to make a fool of herself, how impossible it was to tell her so. She would deserve all she got, he thought, and left it there, or tried to do so; but the painful idea would return in spite of himself that there she was on the edge of a precipice, and he did not raise a hand to warn her. At length it struck him that he had never had a hint of the matter from the lady herself, so he concluded that she had made up her mind not to ask his advice. She knows, then, what it would be, he thought, and let the matter drop. Dora continued to pour out her complaints and her contempt to Maria, and the rest of the two families gradually became estranged. When in due time Mr. Woodman applied to the Vicar for assistance to enter into the holy estate of matrimony, Mr. Bell had nothing to do but in business-like fashion to give him a license and fix a day.

But Mr. Woodman lingered and hesitated, and at last said he had something else to say. He wanted to ask a favour.

"Mrs. Wells thinks—you see the little girl is not altogether pleased, and—Mrs. Wells thought that perhaps it would be best if she was not there. And—she did not like to come herself, you know—t' wimmen's queer about such things, you know"—and then he laughed in the way that Dora called "like a pig"—"but she thought perhaps you and Mrs. Bell would not mind having her for a few days till we were settled."

"Mrs. Wells need not have been afraid to ask me that herself," said the Vicar. "She knows I should have been glad to oblige her."

Woodman went away feeling uncomfortable, and therefore angry, without knowing why; and Dora went to the Vicarage for a few days, a fortnight later, without a formal announcement have been made to her as to when the wedding was to take place. Not the less, both the girls knew the day well enough, and kept out of the way of the church and the road to it."

CHAPTER IV.

AND FADES INTO THE LIGHT OF COMMON DAY.

THE girls spent the few days' interval in alternate anger and tears. Maria admitted the cruelty of the position while recommending patience, and Dora submitted to the teaching while rebelling against the practice of it.

"I won't speak to him when I go," she said. "I will live by myself. He has no right to me, and I won't let him have."

"But, Dora, your mamma will tell you to do what he orders."

Then Dora cried, for she found herself bound hand and foot, and wondered how it could possibly be. She felt herself utterly incapable of the effort that Maria recommended. She would not believe in the possibility of any amelioration. In vain Maria reminded her that he might be a rough jewel, and possibly would turn out to be both kindly and conscientious, and she must not make matters worse by rebellion and provocation. The repetition of this counsel at last frightened Dora.

"They know better than I do what it will be," she said to herself. "What do they fear? Will he beat me? Is it a place where no decency or manners are observed? Even Maria had said to her, "You know, Dora, you have always a refuge here!'—Refuge from what!"

With a deadly chill at her heart, Dora took her way at dusk to the dreaded home. It was three fields off the vicarage, while the old home was only one. And the girl felt as if she would be out of hearing of her friends. "Rough jewel, indeed! and I am in his power!"

The first thing that struck her was the gate hanging off the hinges, and the next, the weed-grown road. Then the front door wanted painting, and the flower-beds were over-grown with weeds. She fairly grasped her mother's hand for comfort, when that lady opened the door. Her mind was still full of that mother's teaching about the style the Woodmans lived in, and the stretch of land round the house—the great estate, as the woman loved to call it. But yet the hall matting was in holes and collections of dust were visible under them. Her mother held fast to her hand, and would not part with it. She took it for a sign of reconciliation, which the daughter by no means intended. In silence she looked at her room, and listened to the explanations that her mother offered as to its not being so comfortable as the one in the old home. She did not see in fact what it was, and her throat swelled too much for her to speak. Again holding her hand, the mother took her down into the sitting-room, where the master was awaiting teatime. She looked at him as they went in, and said, with a deprecating smile—

"Here she is."

The husband looked at her and nodded, but spoke no word. He looked to see whether it was to be peace or war, and not understanding Dora's face of stolid indifference, prepared himself with a scowl for either fate. The resolution made him ill-tempered. He took his place at the tea-table, and the three young men seated round the fire did the same. They had spoken no word to anyone. They were three copies of their father—awkward, sulky, and stupid.

The room was more shabby than the entrance. The carpet was in holes and a window was broken. The paint had not been washed for the last ten years. The side table and the spare chairs were full of litter of various kinds. A glazier had received orders to mend the window, but had not hurried himself to obey the orders of such a slow paying customer. Mrs. Woodman, all ignorant of this, had wondered at the patience of her husband. But she was utterly incapable of supplying the requisite sternness that she thought necessary. That surely was the man's place in the house! It made a part of the utter bewilderment in which she found herself, in which it seemed impossible for anything to go right or to look comfortable.

The young men were a part of this discomfort. They took no notice of anyone, but sat down and accepted the tea and helped themselves to bread and butter. The rest did the same, and the meal began actually without a word spoken. Mrs. Woodman sought and sought for a subject, and found none. No one else tried. A slatternly servant came in and said the mowers wanted to know if they were to go on to-morrow.

"Have they done the field?" asked the master.

"I don't know, sir," she said.

"Have the mowers finished the low field?" he asked again, looking at all his sons in turn.

No one noticed until he said—

"Speak out, some of you, can't you!"

Then they all answered at once, "I know nothing about it," and the master got up in a passion and went to talk to the mowers himself.

No other incident happened. After tea all the four men went out. The mother and daughter were left to themselves, and the former made a slight attempt to imitate the arrangement of the room that they always used to make in the old home, when they settled themselves for a cosy evening. The girl took no part in it. When told, she brought her chair to the table and got some work. After a silence the mother began—

"You see, the young people are vexed at the new wife, and at the new sister. They did not want them. But we must try to make them get used to them. They will find things more comfortable I hope in a little time, and then they will perhaps be more amiable."

She put a little laugh into her conversation to modify the meaning of it. Dora received the explanation with a look of indifference.

"You must mind and be obliging to them you know. We cannot get on unless we are obliging. We are strangers to them, and they did not want us. We came without their will, and we must try to earn our welcome."

Still no answer, and the mother looked round and found herself as solitary as the daughter had felt an hour before.

And so it was. The two might have been strangers for the amount of friendly intercourse they had. The girl was obedient and silent. The mother gave over her attempts to make her position understood, or to secure the co-operation of her daughter. No soul in the house had sympathy with another. At least, if the sons had any among themselves, they gave no signs of it in the presence of other members of the family. They ate and drank in silence, and then took themselves away—where, the women did not know, and as appeared from occasional questions, not often their father either. The master himself had somewhat more to say. He wanted various comforts and small services, and let his displeasure be known if he was not attended to. Dora soon learnt to perform her share of these, for the poor mother thought it best she should put herself forward as useful, were it only to justify her presence. But there was no reconciliation possible. The daughter's determination made such a thing hopeless. She took care at every possible opportunity to show that only necessity compelled her service. Sometimes the mother would get angry, and sometimes grieve. Neither made any impression on the girl, for the parent had lost her respect and the child had no compunction in showing that it was so.

"I get no help from you, Dora, in keeping things straight," the mother said one time after a small domestic storm.

"Why should you expect it?" the girl answered. "You have undertaken the business of your own accord."

The woman became very sad. Each member of the household was utterly alone, and each would have been glad to have been elsewhere. Perhaps the master ought to have been an exception. His wife did her best to make him one. But he had practised too long the habit of storming when anything went wrong, including his own temper, to be able to keep friendly with any mortal thing. He himself remembered too well his own outbursts, and the effect they must have had on the sensitive woman. He soon confined himself to giving orders and saying as little besides as possible.

Moreover, a secret terror soon entered the heart of the weak, well-meaning woman. It became apparent that it was a rule with the master of the house to grumble and get cross whenever he was asked for money, as being the most likely means of preventing, or at least delaying, another application. When his wife first entered the house she was painfully startled by the general shabbiness. She had tried to persuade herself that a woman to keep things in order was all that was wanted. But soon she found that her new relations were troubled by the worst kind of poverty. They were poorer than they wished to appear. With her own small means she had never wanted the requisites for neatness and comfort, but here she could not get a carpenter for the broken doorhandles, or a glazier to the windows, or even a new carpet to replace the ragged one in the principal sitting-room. The half-paid, ill-mannered service she had to supplement herself, and soon saw that that was thought to be her proper place and occupation. Her husband held her bound to make things comfortable by her own skill, and never believed her when she asked for the means to do so. He held her, as he did everyone, as ready to cheat if he allowed her, in order to get money from him. Dora had to perform her share of the day's work.

"It will be better in awhile," her mother said to the girl. But she was chilled to the heart.

Her husband's opinion appeared to agree with hers when she pointed out to him various deficiencies. "It's for you to set that right," he said, playfully. And she thought the matter was left for her to arrange, while he thought that she was bound to make things respectable by her own skill—in fact, to make bricks without straw. Some beginning she made. Some little money she got from him, but this was bound to come to an end, for his notion of the needful was just what could not be done without, and hers was, what she imagined to be suitable to the wealth and standing of a squire with a large estate. She tried patience, reasoning, remonstrance, anger, and found she was as powerless as if she had used an incantation. At last she was forced to the conclusion that he had not the means. She could not explain it, but so it must be. It was sad for her! Day by day the misery deepened. She was coldly despised by her daughter, looked on as a suspected servant by her husband, and now and then insulted by his sons. A fortnight after her marriage a little farther enlightenment sent her down to the pit of despair.

One day a stout overdressed lady appeared at the front door, and servants being scarce and inefficient, Mrs. Woodman herself brought the visitor in.

"Well, now, Mrs. Woodman, I call that kind," said the jolly, good-humoured woman, walking in as if she knew the place. "No ceremony, I see. Of course you don't know me, but I know your husband well enough. We used to play together when we were children, so I thought myself bound to come and be neighbourly to his new wife, though I did not see much of the other one. He was a cut above me in those times. But now you see—of course it might do for you. I dare say you have done a wise thing. You will be company, you know. And of course you have made what you have fast on your own, and then you get a grand name. Woodman is an old name hereabouts—if you care for such things! though he is mortgaged up to his chin. And you see he would not let those lads of his learn anything—trade or profession either—it was beneath them— so there you are, you see! And he is always trying some new scheme or other, and losing money by them, but still, you see"—

Mrs. Greaves—that was her name—always left out the most important part of her communications for people to see, without her showing them.

"But never mind. He's an old acquaintance, and I don't see why we should not be friends. And your girl is about the age of some of mine, I dare say. How old is she, Mrs. Woodman?"

Bewildered by the torrent of enlightenment she had just received, Mrs. Woodman collected herself with difficulty and told her daughter's age, and thanked the woman for her proffer of friendship. It was well she did accept what was offered, for this was almost the only acquaintance she had. Before her marriage she had not many, and they had not belonged to the community in which Mr. Woodman lived. They dropped her on her marriage. The vicar could not be entirely excluded, but he might as well have been, for there was a gulf between them, and never more did Mrs. Woodman hold sweet converse with the vicar's wife about the preserving, and the wickedness of servants, and their unaccountable and detestable proclivity for followers. Dora, it is true, ran through the fields whenever any new provocation stirred her, and made an explosion necessary, and told 'Ria all about it. But as the mother "had no official information" of the fact, and so could pretend not to know it, she had no motive for preventing it, or if she had, she was much too broken-spirited to use her authority.

Mrs. Greaves was a woman of strong health and clear head. She had always known what she wanted, and had never fixed her hopes too high. She had married the miller because she knew she could not expect a better match, and had performed that part of the wife's duty that consists in helping a man to thrive. Her rising family was as rough and as healthy as herself, and she did not teach them polish, for that might come later. "We can't afford to have them brought up at t' boarding-school," she said, "but when they finish, we may happen give them a bit of all that at last." So the girls and boys were equally untamed, and had fists and voices ready, that frightened Dora, and made her submissive at once. She soon decided to have no further communion with them, and then when her mother took her to the house, broke her own resolution, from sheer inability to resist the charm of companionship that she got nowhere else. How much intercourse would there be amongst human beings if they each waited till they found a friend exactly to their minds? And then perhaps those from whom we differ do us most good!

In two years' time Dora had adopted so many of the ways and gestures of the Greaves' that there was little difference to be seen between them. She would have stormed and wept if she had heard anyone say so, but as to outward appearance, so it was. Her dress was more shabby, her hair more untidy, her manners more abrupt than theirs, and her temper much worse. There was no one of her acquaintance whom she did no more or less hate and despise, except her mother, and there was a tinge of both feelings in her manner towards this, her only friend. The girl was, in short, the most disagreeable, ill-mannered, ill-tempered, ugly brat that ever troubled her relations, and all this time she kept her better side open to Maria Bell. They talked over the meanness and vulgarity of those about them, and held themselves aloof in spirit as being not such as they.

Perhaps without this friendship Dora would have forgotten altogether the nobler sentiments that she had unconsciously ceased to practice. She knew none of her faults, nor suspected them. She indulged in a haughty spite against her step-father, which she chiefly showed by never asking him for anything. The absolutely indispensable came through her mother's intercession, and Dora soothed her mind for her shabby dress and ragged linen by repeating that she would never sink so low as to beg of that man. The mother saw the deterioration of her daughter's character with silent sorrow. "Those that cry out get better," say the surgeons in hospitals. Mrs. Woodman never complained any more. Her power of resistance was gone. She grew less and less, physically and mentally drying out, as it were. Except as a third servant, she was of no use or importance to anyone, and as she could not give notice, was not much valued even in that position. Her husband had married her to have a nurse and confidential attendant, and when he began to fear that she would not last out in that capacity, felt himself wronged. The burden of the daughter's maintenance he felt to be heavy. True, the wife's income more than paid for her; but this income died with her, all but a small sum. This sum was his now, to be sure, but then he had the girl;

so he came to the conclusion that he had made a bad bargain, though for the present he was richer than before. As to the bargain, the wife had the worst of it—hopelessly the worst. She saw now that she had thrown away her daughter's little all in the attempt to increase it. She knew her husband well enough to be aware that he would never give up what he had once laid his hands on, and at her death the girl would be penniless. In vain she tried to bring about a more friendly understanding between the two. If Woodman himself could have been brought in some moment of self-forgetfulness to look with kindness on one who had a claim on some of his money, the girl herself would blow away the filmy web of liking before she could profit by it. And the tale of the mortgages was true. The family was so poor that only the bare means of living were left them. How the man had frittered away his money, even the capable Mrs. Greaves could not tell. "You see, my dear," she said, "he wanted to make it more, and did not know how; and kept looking for things that gave high interest. He'll never do anything!" she added, with a spice of contempt, "he was not made for it." And, as in most of her business-like judgments, she was right.

Dora's position with regard to the vicar's family was rather an odd one. She knew she was welcome there, yet she never went farther than the garden in summer, or the little workroom in winter, where she talked exclusively to Maria. The elders seemed to be aware that no confidential conversation could begin so long as they were within hearing, yet they made no effort to stop this singular intercourse. No messages were ever sent between the two families, and it was understood they saw each other no more, but Dora ran across the fields and watched for Maria to come out, and 'Ria would look over the hedge to catch a sight of Dora, and call her in. She always told the substance of the talk to her father or her mother, entering into all Dora's sufferings and anger, and was seldom reproved. "Oh! dear, dear!" mamma would say. "I wish she could have a little more patience. Poor thing! poor thing!"

It was curious to see the two together. Dora, the lesser,

though the elder, broad, firmly set, dark-haired, pale, and scowling; the other, fair, happy, open-eyed, and given to laughing, or rather to smiling, polished and graceful, and always neatly dressed. Neatness had disappeared from Dora's style for long, and mere shabbiness was the prevailing characteristic; rags were frequent with her. But they were fast friends. No one understood them as they understood each other. Their joint affairs were to themselves the most interesting things in the world, and their comments on them could have been uttered to no one else.

"Dora, why did you not come into the garden an hour since?" Maria asked one evening as the untidy girl appeared through the gate at dusk. "Papa would have gone away in a little while. He knows we want to talk."

"I think I will give over coming here altogether," Dora said. "I am better away, where I belong!"

"Dora!"

"I thought so all the time as I watched you. You so quiet and tidy and respectable-looking, and myself—" she looked down at the faded black-brown dress, ragged at the bottom, stained down the front, and, as it happened, with a three-cornered tear on one side.

"Dora! I won't have you say so! Have you got to believe that dress is anything? Are you like Mrs. Greaves?"

"No, I'm not!" Dora said, angrily.

"Yes you are! Here have you come to talk to me ever so many years, and did we ever speak about our dresses, or care what we had on? You had no business to say such things! Are you going to leave me because you are not dressed as well as I am?"

Dora cried.

"But, 'Ria," she said, "you seemed so different from me, as I watched you walking with your father!"

"I am not different!" cried Maria. "I am just like you, and I care more to hear all about you than I care for anything else."

Dora turned sharply round and spoke low.

"Then, 'Ria, you won't forsake me when I get quite poor?"

"Never, Dora!"

"Because it will come! I see it coming. It gets nearer every day, and when it comes, I want to have someone to speak to, to keep me straight, 'Ria! I shall have nobody! Will you keep to me?"

Then 'Ria promised, and the old tale went on. What he had done, what he had said, &c., how mamma said nothing, and would begin a friendly conversation with him ten minutes after being called a useless dawdler, or a stupid good-for-nothing. If she provoked a storm she bent her head to it, quietly accepting her deserts, and then began the provocation again unconsciously. "And when he has stormed enough, then he does what she wants!—sometimes," the girl ended, with an air of surprise.

"Then at least you know the way to get what is needful," Maria said, half laughing.

Dora shook her head, and did not agree.

"It's very little we can get at all," she said, "even with that. 'Ria, you never tell me what your mamma says now."

"No, Dora, she does not say much, though she always asks me what you have said. Oh, Dora, she is so poorly! and it is such a long time!"

"Yes, I know she is," Dora said; "I know through Mrs. Greaves. Somebody said—"

Dora stopped suddenly. Maria turned round in alarm.

"What did they say, Dora?"

"They said—oh, 'Ria, I wish I had never mentioned it."

"Tell me, Dora."

Then they both began to cry. For both knew in their secret hearts what the news was that had to be communicated. That Mrs. Bell was doomed, was a fact known to all the world except her own family, and, indeed, was known to them too whenever they chose to open their ears to the fact. Even Dora, who did not think she had anything to lose, knew now that she was going to lose a friend.

" 'Ria," she said, "you will never leave me, will you? You are all I have."

And 'Ria promised again with truth from the bottom of her heart.

Then sadness swept away all anger, and the forlorn girl went home to the desolate house. She passed in to the little room where her step-father chose to spend his evenings, filling it with smoke, and keeping it silent, except for the sounds of quarrel. Her mamma, as she expected, was there alone, and Dora sat down and took some work in a quietude almost unknown to her. Her mother saw the altered mood by signs invisible to other eyes, and felt comforted. Mentally she crept up to a fellow creature out of the cold solitude of her daily life.

"Mamma," said the girl, "do you know Mrs. Bell is very ill?"

"Yes, dear. You know Mrs. Greaves said so awhile ago. She can't live long, she said."

Then Dora spoke no more, but let the tears flow that had scarcely ceased since she took leave of Maria.

"Are you very sorry, Dora?"

"Yes, mamma."

"Do you often see her?"

"No, mamma."

The mother looked surprised that the girl should care so much.

And again, answering to the unspoken thought, Dora said—

"I shall soon have none left."

Then at last the mother turned again.

"Would you cry when I died, Dora?"

"I have lost you already, mamma," and a shadow came between them.

Each of them knew that they no longer followed each other's thoughts. In silence their minds worked apart, and a feeling of almost anger arose between them. At last the mother rose. She was seeking her pocket handkerchief. Then she found it, and walked from the room. At the door she stopped, turned to her daughter, and facing her, said—

"What I have done, I have done for *you*, Dora," and closed the door after her.

"Now she's gone to cry!" Dora exclaimed, as if someone was there to hear. "And she's brought it all on herself. For me! I will not have it! How could she? I won't have it!" and throwing her work away, she ran out into the darkness, and across the fields to the vicarage. With some difficulty she got hold of Maria at last, and took her into the garden, in the dark.

"Has anything happened?" 'Ria asked in affright.

"No, 'Ria, nothing's happened. But, 'Ria, she says she did it for me!"

"Yes," said Maria. "Mamma and papa said she must have done it for you."

"Oh, why did she not ask me? She did not—she could not think I would have had it if she asked me."

"That was just the reason. She had talked to papa about your desolate position when she died. And papa says no doubt she thought—"

"Mamma! mamma! you should not have done so!"

"But, Dora, she meant well, you see."

"Oh! 'Ria, 'Ria! and I never gave her a word of thanks or pity! She should not have done it!"

"That is quite true, Dora; but did not you know, or at least think?"

"I thought she had got a rage for a fine house and a great estate."

Dora spoke the last words with her usual tone of scorn.

"Was that like your mamma, Dora?"

"No, it was not! Why did you not tell me, 'Ria? You should have told me when you heard me speaking against mamma."

"We could only guess, Dora, and so could you."

"She never told me," repeated the girl, looking mentally back over the long and dreary time since Mr. Woodman first began to trouble the serene atmosphere of their lives. And had her mamma faced it all unconsciously? Had she not been deceived by any will-o'-the-wisp of greatness as her daughter thought, but coolly, intentionally accepted the dreariness of her position. "For my sake!" she kept repeating, and the vexation went deeper at every repetition. "I won't have it!" she said, again and again, but still the fact remained, that so it was.

" 'Ria, what must I do?" she said at last. "I cannot forgive her."

"What have you to forgive, Dora?"

"That she should degrade herself so."

"She did not know so much as she does now, Dora, and she thought that half the vulgarity was owing to the want of a woman to keep up some sort of polish in the daily life."

"Why did she undertake to polish such a creature?"

"For your sake, Dora. She saw but one prospect for you, and it troubled her."

"What was the prospect?"

"Starvation, almost. Thirty pounds a year was all you would have when she was gone."

"And what shall I have now?"

"You will have nothing at all, I think. Your mamma did not make the small sum fast to her own child, and it is your step-father's now. You see women know little of business, and people are careful not to tell them."

"Poor mamma; and so she has lost it all."

"Perhaps not, dear. If you do not provoke Mr. Woodman so often, he may provide for you after all."

"Then I will provoke him every day, and tell him what he has stolen."

"Dora! Dora! you must not. How can you expect him to provide for you if you behave like that?"

"I don't expect it. Don't you say he won't? Why did he deceive mamma if he intended not to do what was just?"

"Dora, you don't consider your mamma."

"I do consider her. She is on my side now. She has been cheated."

"Dora!"

"I will tell her she need not be submissive any more. I will not have the money if she gets it. She shall, at least, not endure all the scolding and do all the work that she does, and lead such a miserable life. We will keep together and defy him.

He can't make us either boil a potato or mend a duster if we don't choose."

In vain Maria tried to quiet her. She could not herself say what the girl ought to do. The submission that was taught as the absolute duty of women would not come to her lips, yet any means of escaping it she could not find.

"Go and take care of your mother," she said at last. "Mind, she has no one but you. It will almost make her happy to have you back."

And Dora went.

The reconciliation did not come about all at once, but gradually. Dora first denounced her step-father until the mother was frightened at her vehemence. She was particularly alarmed at the girl's threat to tell him that she would not take any money from him if he was disposed to give it her. She well knew that if she ever succeeded in disposing her husband to listen to her claims, it would be by putting them as depending entirely on his goodwill, and then slyly intimating that he would avoid the malicious remarks of some people who would think ill of him if he left the girl penniless.

"People will think nothing of the kind," he would repeat, surlily; "they know it's mine."

This was true enough, and Mrs. Woodman had to insinuate a notion of justice that in those days the world had not got. She thought at times she had made an impression on his obtuse mind, and then he would suddenly awake to his own interests and sweep all her arguments away with the assertion of the actual fact. "The girl has nothing, and if she does not behave herself better, she shan't have." And now here was the girl blowing away the whole house of cards and declaring "she would not have it."

Still, things were changed now, and by entreaty the mother persuaded her daughter to keep silence.

And soon the daughter saw that this was the thing most requisite of all. Her mother's weakened frame could no longer bear the alternate violence and contempt of her husband. After a storm she would go to her room to cry by herself. Dora had to follow and console her, and so new and unexpected was this consolation that it was for the time really effective. The girl really thought that under her encouragement her mother would get spirits again and cease to care for the treatment she received. The two would sit together and talk as they used to do in former days; forestalling each other's words and answering each other's thoughts. But it was too late. The old woman's strength was gone, and she sank daily. What matters it going into medical details? She knew she had to die, to be hunted to death by pain, and soon her daughter knew it too. The husband somehow thought he was wronged in having been misled into introducing into his house a woman of so little use. He let the pair alone, grudgingly, but still alone, and they were happier for it. Mrs. Greaves, repulsive, coarse, and interfering as they both thought her, showed herself of great use now. She told Mr. Woodman, roundly, that people would talk if his wife had not this and that, and especially a doctor. Mrs. Woodman objected to this last, but Mrs. Greaves insisted in spite of them both.

"What will people say if your wife dies without a doctor ever having been to the house?" she said, and the argument was suited to the man to whom it was addressed, and the doctor came. And so it was that Mrs. Bell on her sick bed heard that her old friend would not be long in following her, and soon after asked her daughter to bring Dora up to her bedroom some day. Dora did not come so often now across the field. She had found work at home. But yet a time was found, and the girl was introduced, silent and tearful, into the sick chamber. She did not at first know the kindly face she had been familiar with from her childhood. Wan, large-eyed, and shaky, the invalid looked like one bringing a different set of ideas from another world.

"Dora, dear, I have something to say to you. You know your mother has not long to live?"

Dora nodded.

"And then?"

"Oh, I don't know," said Dora.

"Neither do I," said the dying woman. "I strive in vain to see through the darkness. One thing only I know, that there is no light but one. Try to follow it, Dora. Let no hate or anger be your guide. Keep steadily in the narrow path. And—and—I have something more to say. If you would keep right, you must leave that house. Some people would not say so, but do it, Dora. You cannot all at once, but watch for an opportunity. It is very difficult for a woman to do, and all the world will be against you, but try and do it. You must earn your own living and keep from them. Hold fast to that, Dora. You will see the necessity of it more and more."

Mrs. Bell did not know the comfort she was giving to the girl. One approving friend will sometimes keep the mind steady, when on the borders of insanity, from the sheer darkness surrounding it.

"I will do so," Dora said, and Mrs. Bell knew the tone.

"She'll be better than her mother," she said when the girl was gone. "She will work herself out even from this quagmire, in which most people would sink. Do not forsake her, 'Ria."

After nearly four years of marriage Mrs. Woodman died. Her husband thought he was sorry. It is certain he repented him of the step which had brought her into his house. It had not turned out in the least as he intended. He wanted a cheerful, ever-ready nurse, and had transplanted a delicate flower expecting it to brighten his home, unknowing that such flowers can never live in the atmosphere that surrounded him.

During the last twelvemonth Dora had perforce taken her mother's place in the household work, and after her death she went on doing it. No one spoke of her loss. Whatever they felt, each one kept it to himself. If the sons lamented over her melancholy end, or if they triumphed that she was gone, no one knew.

CHAPTER V.

DE PROFUNDIS.

When Dora, shocked by her mother's avowal of her motives, had run over to Maria for the second time in the same evening, she did not return till after ten o'clock at night. Her stepfather accidentally heard her enter the house, and made inquiry, and issued a gruff prohibition to her mother against her going out at such a time. The mother, frightened and confused, said—

"She's only been to the Vicarage. Maria Bell and Dora are great friends."

This information would have justified the girl, and have raised her in the opinion of most people, indeed, it was said, though unconsciously, with that intention. But it had the contrary effect on Mr. Woodman.

"Been to see those folks! They don't think us good enough to come here. See that she does not go there again. I'll not have it."

It ended in Dora only going by stealth. And then the increasing failure and death of Mrs. Bell made a natural break in the interviews. Dora could not thrust herself in at such a time. She would look through her tears out of her own window at the house where the tragedy was enacting, after getting all the information she could as to the fatal progress disease was making. She told her mother every piece of news, but her mother said nothing. The parting had been made long before between the two, and when Dora's mother died, the girl dare not present herself at the Vicarage.

At last, after seeing the funeral go past, and seeing the old man wander down the woodside, she suddenly left the house in open daylight, and Maria met her at the gate as usual.

"Dora," she said, "how different this is to what we thought or expected when we tried to look forward. We thought we would have courage, and not complain because we had something to bear. But how can we bear this? We have no mother, either of us." And the two girls clasped each other round and sobbed. "Where shall we turn to now? There is nothing, and no one can help us!"

"But you have something, 'Ria. You are not like me; you have your father!"

"But father belonged to mother, Dora. He would not talk to me. He thinks I cannot understand, and he tells me nothing."

"But, 'Ria, you have him to care for."

"Well, what can I do?"

"Listen to him."

"I look out that the house is comfortable, as mamma did. I have done it for a long time. But there is nothing else."

"Yes there is. You will see, 'Ria."

The two were very forlorn, though Maria began to see a glimmer of light in Dora's words. She raised her tear-stained face, and looked at the green hillside and the wood meeting it, and resolved to talk to her father and get an answer. There was already comfort in the expectancy.

"Yes, you will get on in peace," Dora said. "But I—" and she burst out afresh. "You know he said I was not to come here any more," she exclaimed.

Maria shrank from the blow, and then all at once making up her mind—

"You must come, Dora. Never mind, you must go on coming."

"Of course I shall, 'Ria," and the two were somewhat consoled by the prospect of the solace. They were both broken down and desolate, and parted in sorrow.

But a new hope had begun in Maria's heart. She never

failed, as the mealtimes came on, and her father took his place in silence, to ask him questions, and to arrange them so as to get an answer. No one can long refuse to talk to an eager listener, and the old man often found that he must perforce give explanations. Then he learnt to ask, How much will she understand of this? and was surprised to find that he had a companion in his daughter, whom he had always considered as a child. The intimacy grew close between them, the more so as her brother Rik left for College. He had only stayed at home so long because of his mother's illness. But now the father would not keep him longer.

The life was not miserable at the vicarage, though there was a habit of sadness about it, but Maria acknowledged that Dora was much worse off than herself.

Dora lived and moved in an acrid atmosphere of isolation. She did the work required of her, and quarrelled with everyone in the doing of it. Personally, she took no pains to keep respectable, or even tidy, in the smallest degree. She had no money, and almost no clothes. As the ragged condition came about gradually, the men were half unconscious of it, and if they observed it, would attribute it to her perversity and idleness.

Mrs. Greaves's practical energy saved her from going about in absolute rags. She one day, after having paid one of her unwelcome visits to the solitary girl, and receiving with leaden indifference all hints that her interference was not wanted, caught Mr. Woodman at the front door, and addressed him in presence of his stepchild.

"George Woodman," she said, "you ought to be ashamed of yourself to let Dora here go about in rags as you do! Why don't you tell her to dress herself better? Just look! She has had this frock these five years I should think! Why do you let her wear it?"

"I've nothing to do with the girl's dress, Mrs. Greaves," he said, looking at the two alternately, as if he did not know which he hated most.

"People will say you have something to do with it," said the woman. "They'll see she has not had a new thing, not even one for mourning. How can you, for shame!"

"Other people" filled a large place in George Woodman's mental horizon, and their opinion was of great use in keeping him decent, as it is to most people without a conscience. He looked at the girl, and asked why she had not a better dress on.

It was an unfortunate question, for she answered quite coolly—

"Because I have none."

"No, I know you have not," said Mrs. Greaves. "Now, she cannot be decently fitted out under five pounds," turning to him. "If there were a woman in the house it would be a shame for it to have gone on so long. People look at her in church. What can they think of ye?"

Mr. Woodman gave her two pounds, and then her objectionable friend told him she must have two dresses besides. She was shameless in begging, and just fit to deal with him, and her manœuvers got a great deal more for the girl than the most submissive asking would ever have done. Dora blushed to receive the money, hated Mrs. Greaves, and still more hated Mr. Woodman.

In her complete isolation she gradually fell back on the amusement. She found books of all kinds in the library that formed part of the style of an old mansion, though the predecessors of the present owner had been as little literary as himself. They were ancient, or at least old. They took her into another world, and she learnt to forget for awhile the grievances of this one. Absorbed in the fate of some old-world hero, she came back to the contemplation of her own affairs from a different side. They looked strange to her. There was nothing exactly like her fate, but there were examples of how an adverse fate should be borne.

"Maria," she said one day, "your mother was right. I must get away from them before I get like them. I was quarrelling to-day with Richard Woodman as if I were his boon companion—just as he does with the men he brings to drink with him

when his father's not coming home that night. I intended
never to quarrel. I thought I would never speak a word but
what was like a lady."

"That's right, Dora," Maria said, energetically. "Hold fast
to your true self. You know you are not one of them. You must
not get like them."

" 'Ria, has everyone, when they grow up, things to do as
difficult as I have? It seems to me I cannot do them! I cannot,
cannot do them!"

"Keep away from them, Dora, and then they won't infect
you."

"But they do, 'Ria!"

Maria looked at her to see if she could observe any change.
But the usual scowl was not there, and in its place was a far-off
look as of someone not living in the actual world around her.
She looked "yonderly," as Yorkshire people say, as if the things
nearest to her did not matter. Then she spoke a sort of book
language, looking at times to see if she was understood. If not,
she took to silence at once, utterly puzzling the people to
whom she talked. But of this last habit Maria saw nothing,
for the thing never happened in her presence. On the other
hand, Dora never talked to anyone else as she did to her friend.
No one else ever saw her fluent, earnest, enthusiastic, talking
by the hour, if she had the opportunity. Truly, Maria thought,
she was changed, but improved by the change; and 'Ria said
in all sincerity—

"No, Dora, you are not like them. You are like yourself, and
nobody else."

"Like no one else! That's what the Greaves girls say, and
they laugh at me for it!"

"Of course they do," Maria said. "How should they appreciate it?"

So Dora was comforted, and kept to her books. They had
not yellow covers nor very wide margins, but they had filled
a wide place in the intellectual world in their time, and her
mind grew to the size of them.

"You always know what no one else does," Miss Greaves

once said to her, rather angrily, when she had known who the Prince of Denmark was.

"Aye, that's just it!" Dora answered, with one of her far-away looks.

"And then you talk like that about it," the other went on, "that no one can tell what you mean."

"That's just it again," Dora said, and turned away.

From the time of Mrs. Bell's death the girls recalled all that the two parents had ever said to them. Dora listened eagerly to the counsels that she had never heard, for her attitude towards her mother in all but the last year of her life had prevented them from ever being offered.

"Your way is easier than mine," she would say to Maria. "You were told to take care of your father. Now, that is something nice and easy to do. But I was always wanted to try if I could not care for Mr. Woodman, and I hated to hear it and even to try. I knew it was for a selfish motive, and it seemed to lower me into the dirt around me to take up such a duty, and I could not persuade mamma to let it alone; I tried sometimes. I was so sorry for her. She was always thinking about me. She used to say what I should do when she was gone, when he was there, and then look at him. Oh, 'Ria, I used to choke, for he never said a word. Is it right, 'Ria, for a woman to do so?"

"Now, Dora, you are asking one of your far-off questions. Was it wrong for your mother to care for you?"

"Are righteous means of helping themselves never to be found for women, and base ones always to be at hand?"

"Dora, your mother was not base."

"No, not by nature."

It was a maze—there comes such a labyrinth to people now and then—a maze from which they see no outlet, yet they cannot cease from seeking one. Their life is too miserable, and misery does not seem a state natural to us—at least to the young.

To Maria her mother's death was as much a blessing as the loss of a friend can be. She was called to a place, important in itself, and peculiarly so to her, for "the care of her father," as her mother had called it, made her kind and thoughtful before her time. The younger brother, too, was a charge, and made her responsible when other girls are requiring or, at least, receiving care, as incapable of standing alone. Then she had a master ever interested, ever forgiving to her failures, ever labouring to impress upon her a sense of a wider principle than that of getting over the present. He gave her a rule to go by that would do for all circumstances, and she would have gone boldly forward without help or guidance in whatever position she might be thrown. "The cold weather shows who has a cloak," says the Italian proverb, and only when the storm comes does it appear who has principles and who has none.

Mrs. Greaves made several efforts to get Mr. Woodman to acknowledge Dora's claim to her mother's money, and she made them in her characteristic way. She bullied and coaxed him alternately. Then she would scold Dora for not forwarding her efforts, and thereupon Dora would behave a little more sulkily than usual to her step-father.

"It's nothing to such a man as you to be generous," Mrs. Greaves would say. "Such a trifle! What can it matter? I wonder how you can make yourself looked down upon by everybody for such a bit of meanness! and you know how much better people would think of you for behaving handsomely."

It was in vain, however. The man made no promise, and did not seem inclined to own to the justice of doing anything; but Mrs. Greaves reserved herself for future efforts.

"If you would but be civil," she said reproachfully to Dora.

"I'm not uncivil," Dora said.

"If you would not look as if the money would burn you to touch it."

"Well, I believe it would," Dora said, quite naturally, looking afar off as if she was wondering why.

Yet Mrs. Greaves was a better friend to Dora than the girl was aware of. She had girls of her own, and pitied both Dora and her mother from the bottom of her heart. What if they were silly? They should be helped all the same. She herself was strong enough to fight her own way, mainly, she would have said, because she confined her attention to her own affairs. She was a model wife in caring for her husband and children, and caring for little else. Their interests were the first thing, and almost the only thing to be studied. As to other things, they might come after, if things went well enough. "Je gelehrter je verkehrter," she would have said if she had known the Swiss proverb, and rather eschewed books, accomplishments, and refinement, as expensive and useless things.

But still, she made up in vigour for her lack of refinement. Many a time her scathing tongue lashed the young men into civility to the helpless girl. Many a time, and with line upon line, she impressed upon her step-father the disgrace of treating her too roughly, or of neglecting her altogether. The man began to have a certain dread of his step-daughter, and yielded perforce to her demands for the needful for housekeeping, though he did it in his own grudging way. Dora would sulk and speak no more when once she had stated what was needful; and then the dinner would appear without potatoes, or even without meat, and, after some loud quarrelling, she would say quietly that there was none. She could not help it.

Mr. Woodman began to be afraid of meeting Mrs. Greaves, too, on the road. She would fall upon him with the words, "George Woodman," and was sure to tell him something that he could not answer, or ask what he could not refuse, and she had her manœuvers, too, which he could neither circumvent nor overcome. She met him one day with the usual words—

"George Woodman, how long am I to keep sending my servant to help in your house?"

The frightened man asked her what she meant.

"Why, have you not seen my Lotty working in your kitchen every day this week?"

Now, though the girl had been there, as Mrs. Greaves said, and had been before his eyes, he had never actually *seen* her, and he asked again—

"Why, what was she there for?"

"Why, how do you think that girl is to get on without help when she has only one servant? You know your 'Liza went away a week since. When are you going to get another?"

The man had not intended getting another, as Mrs. Greaves very well knew. She went on railing at the amount of work to be done where there were four men in the house.

"And you expect it to get done with only one girl and that poor lass."

Another girl came in a week. True, she was a half-starved slip, utterly untaught, but she improved under teaching, and Dora had a sort of friend in her. The little mouse was occasionally able to help the lion, Dora, in unexpected ways.

And the intercourse with the vicarage continued. Mr. Woodman was afraid to repeat his prohibition. Mrs. Greaves did not encourage it. She thought Maria encouraged Dora in going beyond a woman's province, which was exclusively household affairs. Even Dora's perversity she attributed to Maria's influence, and in this she was right. It came from the wider teaching that the girl got from the better influences of books and poetry, and noble-minded people.

"Let Maria Bell go in for them things herself," Mrs. Greaves would say; "maybe she has no need to look after things at home, but Dora should mind something else. The girl ought to think what's to come of her when that old man dies," quite unaware that Dora thought to distraction about what she was to do, not only in the future, but now. She looked in vain for the opportunity that Mrs. Bell had said would come. She thought herself blind and stupid that she could not see it.

"Am I become unworthy to see it?" she asked herself. "Am I grown too like the people I live with? What is it?"

These half insane speeches Maria had to combat, and sometimes began to fear that a fixed idea had taken possession of the tortured brain. But vigorous health and plenty of work kept Dora's mind in order on the whole, though it did not prevent her temper deteriorating to a much greater degree than Maria was ever aware of. At the vicarage the girl would be sprightly, witty, and, above all things, enthusiastic, but no one at her own home ever suspected her of such a thing. If any of the four men, with that happy forgetfulness of their sins that ill-mannered people have, sometimes grew conversational, there was no response whatever. They thought her the most stupid person they had ever seen. The servants were partly of the same mind, but they pitied her, and said it was all the master's fault. She should have more clothes and more gaiety. She had hardly clothes fit to go to church in.

CHAPTER VI.

THE COMMON LOT.

MARIA BELL diligently pursued her many avocations until she found that instead of being in a hopeless condition of isolation, she was, in fact, favoured by fortune to have such a position and such companionship. She kept house with zeal, on the old lines that she had seen followed by her mother for many years. She taught in the Sunday School, and at times visited the poor. Then she had to tell her father of all her doings, and have his opinion and encouragement. Her abilities were taxed, but not overtaxed, and her mind grew, sheltered, but not stifled, to a healthy development. Her father liked to entrust her with occasional matters of business or negotiation, and always listened to every particular of the tale she told afterwards. He wondered at her wit, and was amused at her simplicity, and thought that on the whole there never was so clever and so kindly a girl. He was nearer right than most parents are.

But in four years more this life was ended. Maria and Dora were nearly twenty-two, when a small accident happened. Mr. Bell was thrown out of a gig, and carried home helpless to his death-bed. His son was sent for in haste from college, and the brother and sister watched over him and nursed him for six weeks, until he died.

Then, indeed, Maria felt helpless and forlorn again, and no remedy appeared possible for this bereavement. As she sat by the fire on the winter's day, when her father's coffin had gone out, she thought of him in the ground, never to be warm any more, her tears flowed, and she wiped them away time after time. She tried to think of something else—in vain. She had thought it out many a time in the last few weeks, but now it was gone from her. She would put it off, and ask her father, and so came back again to his grave and the snow above it.

She had let the fire go out as she sat before it, when she heard her brother come in. He came straight into the room and closed the door, and, laying his arm on the back of her chair, put his head on it.

"We're all that's left now, 'Ria. There's only us two."

Then there was another silence, while the tears flowed down. At last, with an effort, Maria asked—

"He never knew, did he, Rik?"

"No, he never knew."

This referred to the savings of his lifetime, which, for some reason, scarcely intelligible to his son and daughter, no longer paid any interest, and perhaps had taken to themselves wings and gone.

"I am glad he did not know, Rik. It may be worse for us, but it saved him some pain."

"Yes, I'm glad."

Now Rik was two years younger than 'Ria, and, though arrived at the manly age of twenty, still retained the habit of turning to her for comfort and for guidance. She, too, roused herself at the accustomed call upon her, and began once more to try to point out their way before them.

"Now, I'll tell you, Rik, what we must do. We must go and live at Repton, and I must find some girls to teach, and you must find something else to do."

"At Repton! Teach! Why Repton? It's where Uncle Turner lives!"

All these objections had occurred to Maria again and again. How strange, how queer, how hopeless it seemed altogether! But, under the spur of necessity, she answered him—

"What else can we do?"

He acknowledged the force of the argument, but asked—

"Why Repton? Why go just there, where Uncle Turner lives?"

They had written to this same uncle to announce their father's death, and had got a very proper letter of condolence, without any inquiry as to those whom the father had left behind. They knew that since their mother's death had been announced to him in the same way four years before no communication had taken place between the two families.

"He will think we want something of him," said the lad, angrily.

"But we will show him we don't," Maria argued. "We will write and say we are going to settle in Repton, and I shall try to keep a school."

"He will be angry."

"What does it matter? We must go somewhere."

"But why there?"

"Mamma was born there, and some people might know her."

"But—but—"

"I know there is not much to hope from that. But where else can we go?"

"Anywhere."

"But where, Rik?"

His mind was a perfect blank as to any place that looked likely to prove a home to them, and he ended by taking up his sister's idea. She, too, had talked herself into the belief that the scheme was feasible, and had got already the germ of a new interest in life. They wrote the letter, and a difficult one it was.

"Shall we say we hope he will not be displeased with our resolution?" Rik asked.

"Why should we care whether he is or not?" Maria said.

"Then we'll just say we are coming as soon as the furniture is sold."

"That will look so abrupt."

"Well, we'll say—"

"Shall we ask if there are any houses that would suit us, or say we shall want a small house?"

"That is just asking him to get one for us."

"Well, then we'll say nothing. No, I'll just say, 'Dear Uncle,— Will you kindly inform us if you know of a small house to let in Repton, as we think of coming to settle there. I shall try to get some day pupils, and Richard, I hope, will be able to find some other employment.' "

They read this over, and it appeared to them both alternately insultingly abrupt and sneakingly civil. Sheer necessity, however, made the thing get done. The letter was sent, and in due time was answered. Mr. Turner could not understand their plans, but hoped he should see them both before they took any farther steps towards settling in Repton.

"We won't go and see him," Rik exclaimed.

"I think we have hardly a reason for refusing his invtation," Maria said. "We have to go to find a house, you know."

Early next morning Dora presented herself, neat, tidy, undemonstrative, and almost silent. She did not condole with Maria, but talked of the last days, and asked quietly for every detail. Then the pair went on to talk of the future. Dora was made acquainted with the circumstances of the family—how the loss of all his savings had been kept from the dying father; how they had, in fact, thought little of them in the presence of death; but how they were resolved now as to what they should do. Rik's prospects of a college education were gone, and his business was to seek employment. They had made up their minds to all with a sort of numbness which prevented them from feeling the disagreeables while under the suffering from the heavy blow of their father's death.

"Now we must wind up and sell up," Maria said, and Dora helped her as long as she dare stay.

Next day she came again, and yet again, and they talked of the past, and tried to talk of the unknown future.

"You will write to me, 'Ria. I must hear. Perhaps you will find a way for me, too. We are shut up here, and see nothing. But once out in the world you may see something more."

She was unconscious that the feeling of confinement that appeared like a wall round her arose from her own ignorance,

and not from her position. We actually see but little with the
bodily eye.

"Dora, did you ever hear of Miss Everard?" Maria asked.

Dora did not know. She might have, but did not remember.

"She was a friend of mamma's, and lives at Repton. I know
nothing more."

"But, then, you know someone!"

"I don't know her. I certainly shall not ask help from her,
though she once came here, long ago, and stayed a week. She
was unhappy, but I don't know what about. I have no claim
upon her whatever."

"What was she like?"

"I can't remember."

And so they strove to pierce the darkness before them.

"You must not feel lost, Dora, when I am gone. You know
you have me all the same. Think of me always, and I will think
of you. We are friends."

She was begging not to be forgotten herself, though she did
not know it. The whole world full of people were nothing to
her. Only Rik and Dora were visibly in it, and the one of
them was disappearing.

"I won't come to-morrow, 'Ria," Dora said, as she kissed
her friend, and turned suddenly round and went away. "I shall
see you in the coach, or at least, I shall know you are there."

And the last night passed, and there was a breakfast gone
through.

"Look, Rik," Maria said, as she put her hand in his arm;
"look at the corner where the wood meets the green hill. It
will set there when I am gone, papa said, and when no one
lives who ever knew me. But we shall not forget it, though we
may never see it again."

Pale and silent they made the journey, and looked up for
the first time when the coach began to descend the hill towards
the long chimney and the black smoke. As they came to the
angle where stood the grocer's shop there was a house, new,
bare, and small, which took Maria's fancy. It stood alone, not

on the lane where all the rest clustered, as if for warmth and company."

"Look, Rik," she said, "that house would do for us."

It had two little rooms and two more above, and a kitchen behind, all small, but not as yet even smoky.

Then they had to dismount, and taking their bag of sandwiches, secured their places for the return journey, and then, looking round, they asked their way to Mr. Turner's.

They went down the lane. Had there been an alternative Maria felt she should have taken it, so unwilling did she feel to face the unknown uncle. Up to this moment she had indulged in the half-formed idea that there must be something better for her to do than to take the course she knew to be crowded by thousands of others who did not themselves thrive in it. Would he point out such a one? Why had he wished to see them before they made up their minds? But then the thousands with whom she should have to compete—

"Them's going to Turner's," she overheard on the road behind her.

It was some distance from the place where she had asked the way, and the words gave her an overpowering idea of the greatness of the uncle whom she should meet.

What would it be to live under the shadow of his presence if his highness should not prove favourably disposed?

"Them's t' gates," said the small escort round them, and watched the strangers walk up the avenue to the great house.

"Why, he lives close to his mill," she said, in astonishment.

"What mill? Has Uncle Turner a mill?"

"He took the mill long ago, before papa and mamma were married. He took it of old Bentley, and people said he was going too fast; but he has gone on since, and I suppose he must be rich now," she added, as she looked at the stately drive and the well-kept garden.

She would have had more courage if she had found only a square piece of ground filled with cabbages and fruit trees, with roses and sweet williams at the corners, as it was in her own home.

"Perhaps he will let us alone, Rik, and then it won't matter."

"I wish he would," the lad exclaimed; "I wish we had never come."

Maria had it on her lips to say "So do I," but the habit of guiding him prevented her, and she answered, sadly—

"We must not make an enemy of him, if we can't have him for a friend. We are not going to ask for assistance; we are going out of courtesy to announce our intention of living here. We could do no less. They might well express astonishment if they found out by accident that we were here and had not let them know."

Yet she herself could not get rid of the feeling that they looked very like humble clients of the great folk, nor could she altogether deny the truth of appearances. They would be thankful for protection and advice, and perhaps, even, of assistance such as Mr. Turner might be able to give them. And should they deprive themselves of it out of foolish pride? She resolved to announce their coming, and then to take her leave pretty quickly, whether any symptoms of interest followed or not.

There was a small lodge among the bushes at the gate, clean, bright-windowed, and cosy-looking, though too much of a toy house for a family to be expected to live in. Then there was a smart servant to open the door, a large entrance hall, a handsome room, a graceful old lady, and an elderly young one.

"Miss Bell?" said the elder, with an air of inquiry, repeating the name.

"Yes, I am Miss Bell, and this is my brother. We are coming to settle here in Repton, and I thought I ought to call and tell you so."

This long speech made it too late for the lady to offer her hand, if she had intended doing so, but she seemed too much taken by surprise. She asked them to be seated, looked lost for a moment, and then rang the bell and sent for Mr. Turner.

"We heard of your loss," she said. "I am very sorry, I am sure. I— Was he long ill?"

"He lived six weeks after his accident."

"Accident! Was it an accident?"

"Yes; the gig was overturned, and his spine was hurt."

As she had written this when she announced the death, Maria began to think it was time to rise and say good morning, but Mr. Turner came in.

Maria looked earnestly at her mother's brother. She had heard of the impression he had made thirty years before, when he came to Repton. The opposite of old Bentley, he had introduced a new manner and style unknown there before. People tried in vain to imitate his bow and smile, and then laughed at him for it.

"He'll none do, you," they said; "he's too uppish."

But he had "done" for thirty years, and for anything people could see would go on for thirty years more. By obstinate insistance he had become a local great man, and from interested motives all the world bowed down to him.

He was much more gracious than his wife, but gracious only. He had a florid politeness by nature that made it impossible for him to be other than demonstratively civil to a woman. He asked how long they were in coming, if they were tired, etc., and then, with some civil circumlocution, what they had come for.

Maria said, without any, that now they must look to earning something, and she knew no other place.

"You know teaching is the only thing a woman can do, and I— There are no pupils to be had at home, and this is the only place I could think of. Mamma was born here."

The reason seemed absurd, and all her plans foolish, even to herself, at the moment.

"Yes," he said, slowly, "I see. But I—I don't know of a suitable house in Repton. There are none large enough for—"

"I should not want a large house for a day school. One good-sized room—"

"A day school! Did you intend beginning a day school in Repton?"

There was so much an air of personal offence in the tone of the question, that Maria got fierce, and said—

"Yes, I did—I do."

"You do!"

"If it were a respectable boarding school, now, we might—my dear, could we not?—could we be of any use?"

"I could not think of taking Amelia away from Miss Forbes."

"I could not think of undertaking the education of Miss Turner," Maria said, hastily. "I intend to get a few little girls to teach reading and writing to. As for a large house, I could not pay the rent of one. It is impossible for me to begin on such a scale."

Mr. Turner looked at her consideringly, and then turned to Rik, who fairly started to find himself addressed.

"Suppose we take a walk round, Mr.—"

Rik stood up, and they left the room.

Maria looked wearily into the fire. Should she endeavour to keep up conversation, and be annoyed by the cold answers she should get, or should she wait in silence till the two men came back again? She wished herself in the house with the green railings. There, at least, no one would set themselves in opposition to her at every step. And she would make it nice. She would put two easy old-fashioned chairs by the fire, and—

"There's Miss Everard coming, mamma," Miss Turner said, and Maria was roused to some languid curiosity to see Miss Everard.

She was a little old woman, with yellow curls and a tense yellow forehead. She wore a black satin dress that had taken its present folds at least a dozen years before, and a black satin bonnet, wonderful to behold, as all bonnets are that are more than three years old, and this was ten. She stood curtseying at the door, and hoping that she did not intrude, until Miss Turner took her in and seated her by the fire. Stammering, uncertain, and apparently unable to take her eyes off Maria, she said she had come—she had heard—Miss Turner had said—that Miss Bell was coming to Repton, and she had seen her go past—at least, she had seen a young lady, and thought—

"You *are* Miss Bell, are you not?" she ended, looking at her.

Maria owned to her name, and asked the old lady how she knew it.

"I knew your mother long ago, my dear, before you were born, and I thought I should like to see you.

Miss Bell was thankful.

"So I took the liberty, Mrs. Turner. I hoped you would have no objections."

"Oh, not at all," Mrs. Turner said, and said it in such a tone that Maria knew she had objections, and that the old lady was disturbed by her abruptness.

She immediately began to make much of the old lady, asking her if it was in Repton she had known mamma, and how long ago. Miss Everard looked distressed, and Miss Bell defiant—all in a quiet, lady-like way, be it understood—and Mrs. Turner and her daughter grew colder than ever.

"And I had something else to talk about, if you will excuse me," Miss Everard went on. "I thought if you settled here, as I heard you talked of doing—"

The feeling that she was offending came over her as she watched Mrs. Turner's face, and, stammering and bewildered, she went on—

"I thought, perhaps, you might want some wine, and"—turning apologetically from one to the other—"and you know you cannot buy it without getting such a quantity! You must get six bottles of each kind—you cannot buy less! Now, I thought, perhaps you are like me—I don't use much—and perhaps you might not want so much at once—"

She was interrupted by Mrs. Turner's cold voice—

"You are rather premature, Miss Everard. It is not settled yet that Miss Bell will come to Repton at all."

"Oh, I beg your pardon. I am very sorry, I am sure."

Miss Bell answered, very distinctly—

"I am much obliged to you, Miss Everard. I think I may want some wine, and if so I shall be glad to join you in buying some, though I don't take it myself. Still, as you say—"

"Oh, then, you do think you will come, after all! If you do I shall be so glad."

Miss Bell felt very much tempted to say, "Yes, certainly I shall," but she kept silence instead. Miss Everard looked more unhappy than ever, and they were all thankful to hear the front door open.

Rik soon appeared, without Mr. Turner, and looking as dark and gloomy as the rest of the company. Miss Bell rose as soon as she caught sight of his face.

"We have troubled you too long, Mrs. Turner," she said. "Now we will wish you good-bye."

Mrs. Turner rose.

"Good-bye, Miss Bell," she said, very stiffly, and her daughter followed suit.

In half-a-minute the pair were out of the house, to their great contentment. Their spirits rose from the mere removal of restraint.

"Now, Rik, we'll go and look at the house to let. Uncle Turner seems to leave me to myself, though he showed some interest in you."

"I wish we'd never come," Rik exclaimed. "I don't call it taking to me to say all the disagreeable things he can to me!"

"What did he say, Rik?"

Maria was trembling again.

"He said I ought not to let you do anything foolish. That I should know it was not fit for you to talk as you did, nor to go, as you talked of doing, seeking for pupils to teach reading and writing to. That once coming down we should never rise into a good position again, and should always be looked down upon. And then he said, 'You see that, don't you?' and I said nothing. So he went on, 'Pray persuade your sister to let that project alone!' So I was forced to answer, and I said, 'What else is there?' He said, 'Oh, things will offer. She is not in immediate want. And then you will have something.' And I said, 'No, there was nothing but what you had said.' 'Well, well,' he said, 'I would give you something for those canal shares. Suppose I gave you—let me see—' Then I said you had decided not to sell them now. Then he tried again to convince me that you must do nothing, or at least he would not say what you could do. Then he turned again to the shares, and kept saying I could not do better than sell them to him. It was so easy to see that was the way out of our difficulties. Then we could live comfortably for a while, and have time to look about us. So I told him we had looked about us, and could see nothing; that there could only be one position worse than ours was, and that would be to have nothing at all to fall back upon, and that was what we should come to if we sold the shares for a low price and spent the money."

Maria was glad her arguments had produced such an impression. He was repeating them almost word for word.

"Then," Rik went on, "he told me he had hoped I had been more of a gentleman than I had proved—that he wondered at me! I ought to know better than to let my sister work in such a way; that working was the man's part, and I ought not to hang on to my own sister. I wish I had never spoken to him," cried Rik, with tears of rage, "and I never will again."

"Never mind, Rik. He said all that to vex you, just because I would not do as he wanted. There's no need to go again. Look, Rik! Here's the house!"

"Who's the owner of this house?" said Rik, suddenly, to a lad passing by.

The boy looked in astonishment at Rik's red face, and then stammered out—

"My father's."

"Who's your father?"

"He's Turner's overlooker."

Maria scarcely kept her countenance at the words.

"Tell us his name," she said, gently, "and where he lives. We want to take the house."

It happened to be twelve o'clock. A stream of people was coming down the road, and to one among them the lad shouted—

"Father, they want to take t' house."

"Who wants?"

The boy nodded his head sideways at the pair. The man came up to them, and asked, in a business-like way, if they wanted to see the house.

"Yes, we want a house," Maria said, embarrassed by the necessity of conducting the negotiation in public, for a number of mill-hands had collected to hear what was going on.

"Will ye come and look at it?" he asked, and led the way, after calling at a cottage for the key.

They looked. It did not take long to do so. Four rooms and a kitchen do not take much looking at to know them thoroughly. Then they stood hesitating a moment, and asked the rent.

"Can't you take less?" Maria stammered.

She knew nothing about it, whether it was dear or cheap, but was afraid to make the final plunge.

The man could not take less, and had no need to do so, for houses were wanted just then; but he pointed out that the house was in good repair and clean, and could be entered immediately. He would open the door for the furniture when she chose to send it, and lock it up when it was unloaded. He did it all in a business-like friendly fashion that helped the girl over the solitary strangeness of her position, and made it seem quite the most natural thing in the world to do. So Maria closed with him and told him some furniture would come tomorrow. As they walked to the coach-office they both began laughing, they scarcely knew what for. There was the distant glimmer of the light of a new home, and being all the light there was it looked cheering. They arranged the furniture in imagination, and almost got fond of the place before they reached the vicarage.

"We have made a beginning," Rik observed.

"So we have," said his sister. "We have no friends, and we have offended our only relation."

At which they both laughed again. They were very busy for two or three days, and then sent away the furniture that the new cottage would hold, or rather more than it would hold comfortably. The house was emptied, the auction held, and the money carefully collected, and then the pair once more mounted the outside of the coach and left their native town. It was busy work arranging, and they were hopeful over it.

Besides, they began to feel unconsciously the warmth of a
thriving place. Scholars were ready, people were friendly, no
one seemed to think they were doing anything extraordinary.
They were both surprised at the run of good luck which followed them. Two of the overlooker's girls were the first pupils.
The wild Reptonians seemed to think—how they got the notion is not known—that Miss Bell was a "real lady," and as
money was going they would all send their children—"for a
quarter at least." Mr. Turner astonished them by announcing
that he had found a place for Rik. It was not in Repton, but
it was a place that might lead to something better. Rik was
sure that he had only done it to get him out of the way, but
as he could not give his suspicions as a reason for refusing it,
he was forced to accept. Maria gave him half their store of
money, he took his departure and the girl was left alone. Her
hands were full of work, and heart full of thankfulness. She
reckoned and re-reckoned, and found she was living—that is,
earning as much or more than she needed to spend. How fortunate it was that she was not sitting in a large empty house,
in debt for the furniture, and looking for pupils that would
not come; thinking of the accumulating rent, and of the day
when she must come to Uncle Turner to explain with fear and
trembling that his plan had not answered. She laughed as she
tried to imagine how he would disclaim all responsibility for
her position. A silent change which she never noticed took
place in her character and disposition. She got courage and
self-confidence, and was braced up to the certainty that she
herself was her own best friend. Full of this feeling she sat
down to write to Dora, and endeavoured to communicate a
little of it to the lonely girl. "Ye mun go right at it," she said
in effect, though not in words, and actually brightened Dora's
life by the description of her success.

　　This was the lady from whom Sarah Miles had set her heart
on receiving instruction. She had been in Repton a twelve-
month when Sarah was introduced to the reader "sliding down
t' hill," and waiting for the opportunity to be taught and
civilized.

CHAPTER VII.

DAYLIGHT TO FIGHT BY.

CHRISTMAS was over with its wholesome merriment and its indigestible food. The day's work was as monotonous as before, and Sarah Miles wondered if ever a change would give her something to hope for and something to do. True, the singing was a great interest, and it grew and grew.

"Eh, mother," she said one day, "I wish I'd plenty o' brass!"

"So does most folks, bairn."

"If I had plenty o' brass I'd buy a fiddle."

"Ye'd buy!"

Her father and John burst out laughing.

"What for shouldn't I?"

"Nay, Sarah! Did ye ever see a lass fiddling?"

"An' what then? Father, why sudn't I?"

"Get the money, bairn."

It is a safeguard against all extravagances to be too poor to indulge in them. And it seems in many cases that the privation does people no harm. We can all of us remember, when we look back, how we longed for such and such a thing. We do not wish for it now; we think it was just as well we never had it. The things we should have been better for are not those we most desired. Perhaps we have thrown these better things away.

So Sarah's brain turned to its old round of activity. She "thought a heap," and was the better for it, let us hope.

She was finishing the "siding up" after dinner, when her mother came downstairs with her "go-to-meeting-gown" on. As Sarah looked at her in astonishment, she said—

"Sarah, put some lump sugar into t' sugar basin, and get t' other cups out. There's Mrs. Somers coming to tea, an' ye mun put your 'other frock' on."

As she spoke she laid on the table the silver spoons that she had brought down with her. Sarah did not rejoice in the prospect of the evening. Mrs. Somers was not amusing to her. She was one of the "old folks," like her father and mother, and old Sykes and old Williams, that had a way of getting together at times, and never saying or doing anything amusing. She hoped to get away, however, and talk to her aunt and Harriet, so she resolved to behave quite properly, and sit silent until she was spoken to. Mrs. Somers was an elderly woman in a scanty silk dress, and thread gloves, thin, angular, and careworn. She had struggled all her life for the good things of this world—for money, influence, respect, and friends. She had no inclination to self-indulgence—no propensity to laziness; yet, whether from want of good fortune, or want of ability, she had never succeeded so far as to think herself entitled to lift her head and look round. One reason was that she had pitched her standard of appearances higher than she could maintain with comfort, and was always stretching her cloth to a wider coat than it would make. Then she spent infinite labour in hiding deficiencies and endeavouring to look as if she had enough. She had quite forgotten how to turn her attention either to her own enjoyment or to other people's feelings. Her face was stamped with the anxious, laborious, trifling character of her mind. Like her figure, it was angular and ugly, and just suited with her large jointed hands, seldom clean, and rough with hard work.

She was very affectionate, apologized for coming late, said she would have come sooner—"But you know, Mrs. Miles, where there's a family there's always something—always! One has never done! I often tell my daughters they will never do as much as their mother! Indeed, they could not do it—they could not!"

To be unequal to much work is a proof of gentility that ill-educated women often like to lay claim to. If not for themselves, at least for their daughters.

Mrs. Miles hoped Mr. Somers was coming to tea. Mrs. Somers was sorry he could not. He was gone to see old Molly Whiteley; she had got him some tea before she left home; he would come for her in the evening. She never allowed her acquaintance to suppose that her husband ever had any time to spare, or that he ever amused himself. In the eyes of his congregation the minister was always getting an uncomfortable meal, or going an uncomfortable errand in a martyr-like fashion. The truth was, the teacher was reacted on by the people taught. His code of the minor moralities at least was given him by his flock, and they exacted a good deal of service from a minister, and a minister's wife too.

"I'm sorry we shall see none of your young folks," Mrs. Miles said, as she sat down before the tray. "Here's our Sarah would have been glad if they had come."

"Oh, thank you, Mrs. Miles," they would have been glad to come, I am sure! But—but they had something to do, and, you see, they are older than your little girl, and perhaps—"

"I'm a month older than Bella," Sarah said, in a way that made her mother look at her.

"Oh, yes, Bella! I had forgotten her. She goes to school, you see."

"Goes to school, does she?" said the hostess.

"Yes, she goes to Miss Bell's. It is a very good school, Mrs. Miles. Miss Bell is quite a lady!" and then, emphatically, "she was a clergyman's daughter, you know! Oh, yes, quite a lady!"

"Is it a very expensive school, Mrs. Somers?"

"Well, not *considering*, you know. My daughter learns the piano, and, of course, that adds up."

"I don't want to learn t' piano," said Sarah.

"Ah, Miss Sarah! you don't know how much it's thought of.

It is really necessary! There is Miss Dunn, now, she is a fellow pupil of my daughter's."

"Miss Dunn goes to Miss Bell's?"

"Yes, Mrs. Miles, and she has learnt for years!"

"I am afraid, then, the school is much above our mark. Sarah cannot have an education like Miss Dunn's."

"Why, mother, she is only going there for one quarter, because they had had scarlet fever at t' boarding school!"

Mrs. Miles looked again at her daughter, and Mrs. Somers went on—

"It really is quite indispensable," she said, with her head on one side. "You can't go anywhere without seeing a piano in the room and being asked to play."

"I don't want to learn t' piano," Sarah said.

Mrs. Somers went on without noticing the interruption.

"Even Mrs. Eldon asked me if my daughter played. Her Sophy is learning."

This was said with emphasis, and an impressive movement of the head.

Mrs. Miles responded in a loud whisper—

"Is she, really!"

Then came more nodding and more confidential whispering.

"Yes, she is indeed; and even her sister takes lessons at home. That Sydney Wynde—" Mrs. Miles nodded—"he teaches her. Now I do think, Mrs. Miles, my daughters are as good as Sophy Eldon!"

"Indeed they are, Mrs. Somers, I should hope."

So the worldly ambition was somehow condoned, and the extravagance of learning the piano forgiven.

"I'm sure I wish I had a grown-up daughter that could play! My two eldest say they're quite ashamed when they go out anywhere. Do you think of your daughter learning, Mrs. Miles?"

This question came because Mrs. Miles kept an impenetrable silence.

"Well, what do you say, Sarah?"

"I don't want to learn t' piano."

"Oh, Miss Sarah! There's nothing in the world looks better for a young lady. Can't you think how much it's thought of, Mrs. Miles? A girl is nothing thought of that can't play."

"I don't want to be thought of."

"But you hear what Mrs. Somers says."

"She'll think differently in a little time," said that lady patronizingly.

"Sarah, you may put your knitting away and go and see Aunt Jane."

Sarah went off in hope, though she would rather have stayed, so long as the present topic lasted. Mrs. Miles went on to ask what Miss Bella Somers learnt besides music. Her mother did not exactly know, but was sure she learnt everything that was necessary. Of course she learnt to read and write, and all that was proper for a girl. But Mrs. Somers thought music was the principal thing. Girls did not need a great deal of learning.

"But you see our Sarah does not care for the piano."

"Oh, but she will do, I'm sure. When she finds how it sets her down not to be able to play, she will wish she had learnt."

Mrs. Miles doubted whether the opinion of casual strangers would have the overpowering effect on Sarah that it appeared to have on Mrs. Somers. But she did not express this opinion.

Sarah meanwhile had found her usual place on the fender by her aunt's fireside, and informed her that her mother and Mrs. Somers were "a talking," and that the minister's wife knew "nought about what lasses learnt at school except to play t' piano."

"Ye 'at's so fond o' singing sud have nought agen that."

"Why it's just laking! Folks doesn't go to t' school just to learn to lake! There's summat better than that, surely."

"It's as good as aught ye'll get among them 'at wants to be ladies. They never nauther learn nought or do nought 'at has any sense in it."

"Aunt Jane, ye know nought about it. They're like to do summat. If they don't do it wi' their hands they do it wi' their heads."

"Sarah, ye may work wi' both your hands an' your head as

hard as any lady i' t' country-side and not earn salt to your porridge."

"How do they get their money then?"

"They never have none but what's given 'em."

Sarah had heard this assertion before, and it always brought on a fit of depression. To undertake to achieve a fortune, though she did not in the least know how to set about doing it, was not too much for her youthful courage; but to wait till it was given! None of her relations, as she well knew, were possessed of wealth to give. But she had heard of people who had made fortunes, and a great many more who proposed that object to themselves. Submission here was not submission to the well-known and inevitable; it was yielding to her own peculiar evil fortune, to contend against which her faculties were given her.

A little girl came to say that her mother said it was time to come home, and on entering the house she found her sister Jane was there once more.

"Well, Sarah, how do you do?" she said, as the girl went in. "Come, shake hands." She was nicely dressed as usual in a shawl and bonnet and kid gloves. She was quite fit to associate with Mrs. Somers and felt herself so, but the style and manner that qualified her to do so separated her from her sister completely. Sarah suspected everything that Jane recommended, and avoided anything resembling her way and behaviour, and saw no earthly reason for the adoption of a foreign accent and even foreign ideas.

Mrs. Miles put some wine on the table. Neither of the old women ever took any except in other people's houses. Then Mr. Somers came and asked very deliberately after the health of every member of the family, and was asked by his wife about Molly Whiteley, and finally inquired of Jane after the health of her young mistresses. They were not members of his congregation, nor had he any acquaintance with them whatever, but both he and his wife showed the greatest interest in them. It made them enter into the minutest details as to their occupations and amusements. Jane was very fluent and a little conceited on the subject, and indulged in a great deal of the foreign dialect that Sarah thought so absurd. Jane was rather proud of the expense, the idleness, and the aimless employments of her young ladies. She spoke much of Miss Amelia, who, it appeared, was still at school, but promised in due time to eclipse her two sisters in beauty and accomplishments.

"In a year's time, Mrs. Somers, you'll see that girl will come out quite the belle of the place."

"The belle! what's that?" said Sarah, abruptly.

"Why, the beauty, child."

"Oh!" said Sarah, in a tone that implied, Is that all? "ye said that afore!" and wondered at the frivolity that could attach importance to so small a matter.

"Yes, and so accomplished! Miss Forbes', where she is at school, is very superior to where Miss Turner and Miss Eliza went."

"And what does she learn?"

"Oh, everything! Drawing and dancing, and I don't know what else, and she plays beautifully." This seemed to Sarah a sorry climax. But the cloud of mystery that enveloped the social heights was not to be raised that night. The minister and his wife took their departure, and Jane after them. There was something to put to rights after they were gone, and then Sarah took her perplexities into the land of dreams. Still the impression remained with her that Miss Amelia Turner must be one of the superior people whom she would like to resemble. The idle accomplishments on which her sister dilated were of course the fringe, or outside, belonging of the character. But what was the foundation of it? and how was it to be obtained? Who was Miss Forbes? who was so much superior to the teachers who had sufficed for Miss Turner and Miss Eliza, and who was, of course, infinitely superior to Miss Bell—the only specimen of the genus accessible to Sarah. Was Miss Bell the right sort at all, or only a spurious article good enough for the Reptonians, who were no judges?

Nothing seemed to come of Mrs. Somers' visit to tea. All things went on as before. There were the same meals to cook, and house to keep clean, and the same recreations after the work. Sarah sang and talked, and asked questions, as was her wont, and spent the evenings at the Sykes's as often as her mother would let her, where she, and John, and Sydney, and at times a few more, tried their hands on every kind of vocal music that came in their way, and often succeeded well enough to give great pleasure both to themselves and their hearers.

But one Monday morning her mother dismissed the pinafore, dressed her in a bonnet, shawl, and gloves, and informed her that she was to go to school, and warned her to be very respectful and attentive.

"Else you know you'll get no good by it, and you willn't have to go any more.

Sarah bore all these preliminaries with patience, and said not a word to all the cautions and commands. As soon as she was free she ran down the lane to overtake Bella Somers, who, as Harriet had said, passed her house every morning.

She walked behind her for a while, studying her dress and appearance. Bella wore a faded green silk frock and frilled white trousers, both somewhat soiled. She had a large over-trimmed bonnet, a pale face, broken-out chin, and a mouthful of toffee. Though only a month younger than Sarah, she was the head less, and the latter wondered at her slow, uncertain gait and stooping forward chin. Suddenly Sarah ranged alongside of her, and asked if she was going to school.

Bella started, looked offended, tried to look dignified, and finally answered—

"Yes, I am."

"So am I."

"Are you going to Miss Bell's?"

"Yes."

There was a pause, and then after a while—

"Are you going to learn music?"

"Learn t' piano? No, I'm not."

Bella recovered her superiority.

"You've never been to school before?" she asked.

"No. What do you do all day?"

"We have lessons to say, and write and dictate."

"And what?"

"Dictate." (By which she meant, write what is dictated to us.) "Oh! you don't know what dictating is!"

"If I did I should not ask you."

"Well, I'll just tell you, and then you'll get on better."

So Bella patronized her to their mutual satisfaction, and was getting almost proud of her *protégé* when they reached the school. She had never patronized anything before. She showed her friend where to hang her shawl and bonnet, and then went in with her. Several girls were lounging about, for Miss Bell was not in the schoolroom.

"Who's that you've got, Bella?" said a tall girl, kneeling on a form in a dowdy frock, open behind.

"I'm the grocer's daughter at the corner," Sarah said, "and you are Sophy Eldon, and you know me well enough."

"The grocer's daughter at the corner!" the sloven repeated, with an insolent air, still staring at her, and flapping a copybook on the table.

"She's never been to school before," said Bella, deprecatingly.

"Not been to school before, hasn't she? Can you read, grocer's daughter?"

"Yes."

"Stand up and read that."

"Sophy Eldon!" cried several girls at once.

"I won't," said Sarah.

"You're civil, anyhow!"

"I'm feared I'm like you, then."

Miss Bell appeared, called her, and showed her a lesson to be learned by heart. Sarah sat down with it, and a parsing class was summoned. Sarah listened with intense curiosity to all that went on. She had formed the idea that the mystery she wished to penetrate might, perhaps, be learnt at school, but not in the lessons. These were given to make the girls appear what they were not—to get like her sister Jane. But parsing was something new to her.

There was some difficulty about placing a new pupil—Miss Dunn. She was the one most interesting to Sarah. Miss Bell told her to stand at the bottom, observing that she would soon find her place. The gulf between Miss Dunn and the rest of the class was marked by a number of trifles. She wore the only print dress in the room, the rest having all better dresses, worn shabby. She was also the only girl whose dress fitted her, and was quite clean. Then she smiled when they laughed. She moved her hand when they jerked their arms, and spoke distinctly and low, while they raised their voices and shouted on the slightest provocation. Her easy, unconscious manner won Sarah's heart, and she was confirmed in her predilection when Miss Dunn quickly rose to the top of the class, showing herself better acquainted with the mystery in hand than any of the rest. She took all her honours with easy good nature, gave a smile to every girl as she passed her, and let no flush or change come on to her round fair face, nor any vehemence into her polished accent. Sophy Eldon was just the opposite to all this, and as her answers were never right except by guess, she was soon at the bottom of the class, and in a very bad temper. When they sat down Sarah found herself next to the slovenly creature, and asked her directly, pointing to Miss Dunn—

"Who's that?"

The cross girl stared, and as this produced no effect on Sarah, she answered at last—

"She won't talk to you. What do you want to know for?"

"Well, what's her name?"

The girl turned to her neighbours, and whispered—

"Here's the new girl wanting to know Miss Dunn's name!"

They both laughed, and the one spoken to leaned over to Sarah and said—

"Miss Dunn's not one of us. She goes to t' boarding school. They're great folks."

"They're no such great folks from what I can see," interrupted the cross girl. "She dresses no better than—"

"Miss Eldon, you are always talking," said Miss Bell. "Miss

Miles, come here and let me see how much you have learnt of your lesson."

"If she goes to school with us she's one of us," Sarah went on.

Sophy poked her with her elbow, asking—

"Don't you hear?"

Then Sarah raised her head, and saw that everyone was looking at her, especially Miss Bell. And now it dawned upon her mind that she was certainly Miss Miles, though she had never before heard the two words put together in her life. She got up and strode across the room in three or four steps, making all the girls titter, while Miss Bell said—

"You should try to walk more quietly, my dear."

"What for?" Sarah asked.

"Do it, my dear. Never mind why."

Sarah considered that if she did not do as she was bid she would probably not be allowed to come to school, so, after a momentary pause, she said, reflectively, "Well," as if consenting to the arrangement. Miss Bell scarcely kept her countenance, and proceeded to ask her how much she had learnt.

"I've lost my place," and she presented the book—shut up.

Miss Bell found the place, and pointed out the lesson, and Sarah went back to her seat; not to the seat she had occupied before, but to the one next Miss Dunn. Miss Eldon gave a poke right and left with her elbows, and raised her eyebrows in her neighbours' faces.

The quiet girl acknowledged her presence by the slightest possible smile. Sarah looked at her book, and over the top of it at Miss Bell, until she saw her busily engaged; then, rousing her neighbour's attention, she asked—

"What's a preposition?"

"A preposition!" said Miss Dunn, with a pause of astonishment. "It's a part of speech."

Sarah considered the answer, and then asked—

"What's a part of speech?"

"It's a word."

"Any word?"

Miss Dunn nodded.

"Then poker is a part of speech?"

"Yes, it's a substantive."

"What's a substantive?"

"Miss Miles, talking is not allowed."

This from Miss Bell.

Sarah looked at her lesson, and in a few minutes asked, quietly—

"What's a substantive?"

"You must learn grammar, and then you'll know."

"What's grammar?"

"You have one in your hand."

For the first time Sarah looked at her book with the intention of learning her lesson. She "went at it" as she had done at the difficult business of entering the warehouse. It did not occur to her to indulge in the peevish exclamations that were rather in fashion among the pupils, such as, "Oh! what a long piece! I'm sure I can never learn it! Miss Bell, may I learn half? It's too much, I declare," and so forth. In due time she astonished Miss Bell by calling out from her seat—

"Please 'm, I know my lesson."

She said it perfectly. Miss Bell was puzzled, and thought it was as well the girl had chosen to learn, as there seemed no way of making her if she had chosen otherwise.

The field whereof Miles' house occupied a corner, was fenced by an unclipped thorn hedge, planted on the top of a high bank. Beneath this hedge, on the grass of the bank, sat most of those girls, friends of Sarah, to whom the reader has been already introduced, together with half-a-dozen more. They had gathered together in spite of the cold to hear her account of the strange place she had been to. She ran forward as soon as she saw them, and, jumping into the dry ditch, sat down facing the assembly.

"Now, Sarah, tell us summat."

"What mun I tell ye?"

"What ha' ye been doing all t' day?"

"Learning lessons."

"An' what's t' use on 'em?"

"I heven't fun' it out yet."

"What are they all like, Sarah?"

"Miss Bell's weel enough, but t' lasses is nought."

"Does Sophy Eldon go?"

"Yes. She was there to day."

"What is she like?"

"She cannot do nought."

"Eh, an' they're as proud as ought 'cause she goes to t' school and learns t' piano!"

"Is that little Wilcox there?"

Sarah did not know, but at last recollected her, a very little girl.

"What sort on a one is Bella Somers?"

"There's nought t' matter wi' her, but she's allus getting called (scolded), and then she roars (cries) and eats toffee."

This was found generally amusing, and so were some other of Sarah's communications—for instance, that she was called Miss Miles. Also that when Miss Bell sent a pupil back or gave rather a long lesson there was generally a burst of tears about it. "Why, they're all great lasses!" they exclaimed. "Sarah, if ye want to be Miss Miles, ye mun be allus 'roaring!' " Altogether the description of the class next above them inspired very little respect, and Sarah had to bear many inquiries as to what she was after to want to be like such folk.

"It isn't roaring, nor sucking toffee, nor playing t' piano 'at makes 'em better off nor we are; an' I want to know what it is."

"It's 'cause they've gotten more brass, for sure."

"An' how do they get it?"

"Nay, Sarah, ye'd puzzle a parson!"

"Then there's wiser folks nor parsons, for there's folks 'at knows."

"Why, ye've only got to cheat right an' left, an' break: (become bankrupt) two or three times, an' then ye'll get on!"

Sarah agreed, but thought there were other ways that answered the purpose better. She really believed that honesty was the best policy. When this is often asserted, though only by those who dislike being cheated, it is not surprising that some people should.

"An' what, then, when ye've gotten it," cried one. "Ye'll ha' to do as they do! My mother wor i' place once, an' she said t' ladies do nought different to what we do, nobbud eat rotten meat, an' twitch theirsens out o' shape!"

"I say, lasses, let's go to Tom Saville's. They're agate about t' new chapel," and all the girls sauntered "down t' loin" (lane).

As Tom's dwelling consisted of only one room, the meeting was held in front of his house, and was open to the public. A small crowd was collected, who came and went, and put in their word as they thought proper.

Sarah knew them all—the women with infants, the lads and lasses, and the few " 'sponsible" men there were among them. One of these took his pipe from his mouth as Sarah came up and asked—

"Who is there wi' ony sense 'at stands up for it?"

"There's old Sykes."

"Not he! There's nobbud t' young un, and he's nought but a lad."

"Why, he's his father to back him. His father lets him tak' his own gate."

"Who is there that's any religion in 'em? All 'at ever they want is a fiddle and a flute! What is there i' them, think ye, 'at a man sud pay down money for them when he goes to worship God?"

"Ye see some on 'em willn't worship without. They'll stay away sooner."

"Let 'em stay! let 'em stay! till they learn to worship rightly."

"How are they to learn if they never come?"

"They mun want to learn first of all."

In that curious phenomenon, an English dissenting congregation—not a large recognized body, but a small split off a split—it is often difficult to arrive at a knowledge of which

among them are the leaders and teachers, and which the followers who receive instruction. The minister is the ostensible
guide, but he lets himself be guided by some of his congregation. They either hold him back or push him forward, or in
some way so arrange matters that movement is only possible
in one direction. The real determining causes of the direction
taken, who shall discover? What makes the first sheep jump
over the fence? Not preaching nor teaching, nor persuasion,
for these are often plentifully used in vain. In the present instance the unknown and unintelligible congeries of motives,
wishes, and discontent found themselves an outlet when old
Saunders, wholly guiltless of any such intention, gave them
leave to stay away from chapel if they chose. And the reason
thenceforward given for secession was, that Will Saunders had
told them they might stay away from chapel if they chose. The
gap was found. One perverse animal had leaped through, and
nothing would stop the rest who wanted to go. Whatever the
reasons might be, personal spite, personal attachment, the hope
of gain, the fear of loss, the fact that everyone had something
to give in these good times, and would like to give an opinion
too. There was a schism in the church under Mr. Somers' min-
istry at Repton; and, as is usual in such cases, each side laid
the blame on the other.

Sarah looked on with vexation; not that she was a warm
supporter of Mr. Somers and his chapel, but that she found
no sincerity in the new. She thought Saunders much more in
the right than Sammy Sykes, and liked Mr. Somers much better than Reuben Halsey. As for Sydney Wynde, he was not a
Reptonian; besides, he was flighty. He certainly added nothing to the credit of the secession.

All this, and more, Sarah talked over while standing at Tom
Saville's door. She heard and approved when Saunders stoutly
refused to have any other music than that of the untaught
human voice, in spite of the triumphant detail of the means
and ability of the seceders. They would raise the cry of persecution if they were not allowed to worship in their own way.
Every mill hand would give a shilling in these times. They

would get some friends in the nearest towns to make a Sabbath collection for them; building new chapels being admittedly a praiseworthy object. They would build on the ground of a man who would lend them money and hold the chapel as security, so that in fact they did not need to raise much. But what availed these arguments against a man who had made up his mind to let them go? All the sheep jumped through the gap one after the other, and, huddled together in the unknown land outside, they were easier to lead than ever.

"Will they build it, think ye?" Sarah asked innocently of Sydney Wynde.

"To be sure they will; and then you can sing in it, Sarah."

"I know that; but who'll sit i' t' singing pew?"

"Why, you, I tell you! What for sudn't you?"

" 'Cause they're going to have some grand singing i' t' new chapel."

"Why, and you're a grand singer—will be if you take pains."

Then Sarah walked home. It was dark when she got in, and she had to explain to her mother what she had been doing.

"An', mother, Sydney Wynde said, I sud maybe sit i' t' new chapel singing pew an' sing!"

"I thought ye did not like t' new chapel, Sarah?"

"I thought they were going to have some grand singers through Halliwell, or somewhere. I never thought we sud just sing wer sens."

Her mother thought of the words, "Unstable as water thou shalt not excel." She had nearly said them, but perhaps they were not quite applicable. It is only those who have done growing that never change their minds. True, the girl was an unprincipled monkey; but then she did not yet very well know what her principles should be.

"Get some through Halliwell! Nay, nay, bairn, it would cost too much!"

"Eh, mother, if I had lots o' brass I'd have all t' grand singers i' t' country!"

"Mind thee thy work. What has ta' done at school?"

Sarah took out her books and showed her mother what she

had to learn, and gave some account of the school, such as she had already given while sitting under the hedge. Then she learnt her lessons until her mother told her it was time to go to bed. Sarah leaned back in her chair and looked into the fire. What a day it had been! How many strange faces she had seen—seen and understood. For she had seen their like before; but Miss Bell and Miss Dunn she had not seen before, and did not understand. In the days to come she would see more of them, and would learn what grammar was, and geography; and she would sing! She would sing no end of grand things at chapel! She had no idea of shirking her labour, having no doubt as to the result.

"Sarah," said her mother, "did not I tell you it was time to go to bed?"

"Eh, mother, I can never be as I was afore!" she said, as she took up her candle.

Which observation Mrs. Miles afterwards repeated to her husband, adding—

"I never did see such a lass as our Sarah; never!"

The father responded—

"Ye're allus thinking she's different to other folks' bairns," being himself in perfect agreement with his wife on this point.

And Sarah slept the sleep of youthful hope. She thought she saw the way before her, and there was daylight to fight by, and she would go right at it.

CHAPTER VIII.

And hope again elastic springs
Unconquered; though she fell,
Still buoyant are her golded wings,
Still strong to beat us well.

"Good news at last, Dora! Going out into the world is like learning to swim. They say that if you put an egg at the bottom of the water and try to get down to it you will be surprised to find how difficult it will be. Now, I have been letting myself go, and to my astonishment I have my feet on solid ground. I got two pupils before I had quite taken the house, and now I have a room full. I am earning my living, Dora, and thinking of the time when I shall have you with me, and both be as busy as possible.

"Never was anyone more forlorn than I was when I walked down 't' loin,' as they call it here, to see Uncle Turner. I did not feel as if I had a right to be there. Now people look up to me as if I had a place in the world. Uncle Turner made me straighten my back without in the least intending it. He took Rik into the garden, and there wanted to persuade him that I was wanting to do a very foolish thing, and that I had better wait for something to turn up. He had before advised me to try a boarding school, and when I explained to him that we had no money to begin with or to pay rent, and no hope of pupils, he turned round to Rik as if I was not worth talking to. He put Rik in a great passion besides.

"I suppose he would say now, if we applied to him, that we had paid no attention to his advice, and must take the consequences of following our own schemes. I can fancy the stiff, stately air he would put on to say it. He is thin and tall, and very gentlemanly—that is, given to bowing and smiling, and gesticulating in a stately way, and looks as if it did not matter what he said to women, if it was only over civil.

"I thought I had seen the last of him when we left his door, but to my surprise he appeared at our little place as soon as I came. He asked if he could see Mr. Richard. I said he was out for the moment—could I tell him anything? He said he had found a place for him, and perhaps he would come up to the counting-house and hear the particulars. I said, 'Of course he could. Might I know what it was?' He looked lofty and said, 'I will explain the matter to Mr. Richard.' Rik went and got the place. It is in a warehouse at Baumforth, and he will get ten shillings a week. Rik is not half grateful. He says he only did it to get him out of the way. He was very doleful. I told him that in a year or two he might be sending for me to keep house for him, for he has hopes that the wage will be raised if he suits. I think if anyone can live on ten shillings a week Rik can, but oh! when will the place get swept and done up? I wish he could have lived here! I gave him half our money. He would not have more, and said he would not spend any; he could do without.

"I do not know if I am silly, building castles in the air! But he has industry and honesty, and people have made fortunes with these two virtues, and nothing else. Men are not like women. They can thrive by these means, while women can't.

"So far I am glorious! I have a room full of pupils. If this goes on I shall be able to send for you, for I will not turn anyone away, and I cannot attend to many more. In the evenings I am dreadfully lonely. If I had not you to write to I don't know what I should do! I must write to you at least once a month. If Mr. Woodman grumbles I will pay the postage beforehand. Rik has written to say he has found a lodging, but he hopes to find a better when he knows more of the town.

He says it is very miserable, but he does not mind it. I wish I knew what to write to him to keep up his spirits. When I have said I have lots of pupils I have written all he will care to hear. There is nothing in my life more.

"Once more I am lonely. At times I don't know what to do with myself. At first I was triumphant. I used to think how much better off I was than I should have been sitting waiting in a large empty house for the pupils that would not come. I wish I could tell it all to papa. I do sometimes fancy he is sitting opposite to me. Then I wish, when I looked out, I could see a girl running across the fields! Oh! Dora, shall we ever be together again? Yet I have made progress since this day month. It is a month to-day since papa went out into the churchyard and came back no more. Is it not sad that every new event seems to take me farther away from him? There will soon be so much that he does not know!

"Now, Dora, remember me, and remember us all, how we used to be together, and remember always our promise to be always good. If it appears to you that I grow cold and forget, remember that I never shall, and that you must still believe in me. I shall not doubt you either. We are friends, though we may never see each other again. Good-bye, Dora. Look forward to the good time."

Not without tears Maria closed her letter, and found perforce some other employment. Work was a blessing to her, as to many others.

When Saturday's holiday had become customary with her, and she had learnt to use it for a Saturday's cleaning, Maria began to find that this, too, was as monotonous as the rest of the week. Her happy hopefulness was disappearing, and the eternal "round of common tasks" was fast becoming repulsive. She cast about for a new source of enjoyment, and found none.

"I am getting absorbed in my own concerns," she said, "until I am getting to be thoroughly dissatisfied. I must think of something else. I will go and see that old woman that wanted me to get some wine. She was mamma's friend. I don't want any, but I can give her some if she can't get any otherwise. We have that, anyhow," for they had brought the little store from the vicarage, and were not likely to use it. "I wonder where she lives!"

To Maria's astonishment, Miss Everard lived in the lodge at Mr. Turner's gate.

"Shall I never be out of the shadow of the Turners?" she said to herself, as she entered them. "I suppose she lives on their charity somehow, or why should she be so afraid of offending them?"

The little old lady opened the door before Maria got to it.

"I am so glad to see you!" she said, with the same anxious politeness that had marked her manner before. "I was afraid you would forget me! I once thought I would call, but then I thought you would be busy, and I thought, 'If she wants me she will come, sooner or later, and if not—' Well, you see, very few people want me, and I do not like to intrude, you know."

"It was very good of you to ask me to come and see you," and Maria looked round the room in order to form some idea of its occupant.

It was silver-clean, as Yorkshire people say. There were two easy chairs—one on each side the fire-place. They had crimson velvet cushions, and the small table standing near one of them had a crimson cloth. This made the room look warm, and the curtains and the bright window lighted it up. All the rest of the furniture was very poor. Some common wooden chairs were ranged against the wall, cupboards of deal were in the corners, two candlesticks and a tea caddy on the chimney-piece, with a pair of snuffers. A silhouette hung over them. The hearth was white, and the fireirons and fire were bright. A recess behind the fire was full of coal, and a book and some work were on the little table. Miss Everard brought a chair from the wall, and seated her visitor before the fire.

Nothing opens the heart like the certainty of a welcome. Maria soon found herself answering Miss Everard's questions with frank confidence. She discussed the pupils, and found Miss Everard knew them all, and their fathers and grandfathers before them. She was able to give very valuable information and very good advice on these subjects to Maria, and they discussed them all to their mutual satisfaction. Maria made the old lady laugh by imitating the style and accent of one of the girls, so that the old lady remarked—

"You talk like your mamma, my dear."

"You knew mamma. You came to see her once. You said you did when I saw you before. Did you know her well?"

"She was my great friend. I knew all her secrets, and she knew mine. I knew about Mr. Bell long before anyone else. Your mamma was a happy woman. Some are not so fortunate. She was a happy woman!"

She looked into the fire, absorbed in her recollections.

"I wonder what mamma was like in those days?"

"She was very quick and sprightly, and yet grave, and looked all the time as if she could not help smiling."

"Yes, that's just mamma! and talking."

"Yes, I tell you we talked!—a quantity! When we had been separated for half a day we had so much to say to each other."

"Papa used to say women ought to be talkers."

Miss Everard laughed.

"So he did! So he did!"

"Did you ever hear him say so?"

"Yes, indeed! We knew him very well."

She sank into her recollections again, and Maria tried to remember what she had heard of Miss Everard. All she knew was that long ago a letter—a long letter, crossed and recrossed—would come now and then, and mamma would say to papa, "From Miss Everard," and Maria had neither known, nor cared to know, any more.

Maria began again after an interval.

"Have you always lived in Repton?"

"Yes, all my life. First at home—where Mr. Turner lives, you know, and then—"

"Where Mr. Turner lives?" Maria exclaimed.

"Yes, in the old house. I was born there. We were a large family, and they are all gone but me. We did not live so quietly then as I do now. We had merry times then. I have known five or six visitors sit down to supper, just, as it were, by accident. We never had stiff parties. And your mamma and I, when we had not seen each other for half a day, we had so much to say to each other; and when she married— Oh, I have heard a great deal about you, although I never saw you. It is four years since your mamma died. Yes, I knew her—well!"

"And you knew papa, too?"

"Yes, in those days. We did not really know much about him, but we could see the difference between him and some people—just the difference between right and wrong. Your mamma was a happy woman."

"Some men are not good," Maria said, thoughtfully. "But how are you to know?"

"You cannot know it, but you can know the difference between them and you, and that ought to be enough."

"Yes."

There was a silence again. Maria wanted to know how Miss Everard had come down from the great house into the lodge, and soon, as is the case when two sit alone together, their thoughts began to run in the same channel, and Miss Everard answered her friend's thought.

"I was the only one left," she said. "John and Charles died like mamma, that is, of consumption, and my sister married and went away, and— Oh, they are all gone, and at last I had the great house to myself, and not too much to keep it up with. Don't you think, my dear, that women ought to learn to be taught something about business?"

Maria looked up for an explanation, for the question was unintelligible to her.

"You see I knew nothing about it, and I know nothing yet, only I think papa spent too much money and we got poorer and poorer. Of course, my brothers and sister took their share, and I suppose there was not much for us all, and I found the house such a burden and expense. I was glad to leave it. I was much happier in a smaller one with only one servant, and then— You see I don't understand it. I wish I knew, and then I should not suspect, and perhaps suspect wrongly. I wish I knew. Then I went to live farther up on the hill, that house near the vicarage, and it was there I began to reflect and make up my mind. In the old house I was getting into a repining habit, in fact, I was always straitened for money. In the smaller house I found out that we really want very little. I was never unhappy there, nor have I been since. If I saw few people it showed me how few real friends I had. Then I thought I must get a little beforehand in the world to provide against misfortune, for I was quite alone, you see, and I saved a little money, but it all went, and I had to come and live here or else I should have got again into that unhappy way of not having money enough, and now here I have saved a trifle. Perhaps I shall not be long ill. When my end comes and I want help, perhaps I shall have enough to bury me and pay all my debts." (She laughed apologetically as if for introducing such a subject.) "I know I cried when first I had a maid to open the door instead of a footman, and now I am quite content to open it myself to the end of my days. 'Man disquieteth himself in vain.' We ought to keep a contented mind, and strive only to wrong no one and owe no man anything."

Maria heartily agreed. She thought people spent money on very useless things sometimes, but—

"Yes, I know there is a 'but.' *Some* money one does want. I am afraid sometimes of being *quite* without. You see, so often I have come to be poorer and poorer. I only wish I may die before I have nothing left. I think I could not bear to live on charity, though, perhaps, you see, I thought once I could not bear to be without a footman, but I wish to keep a contented mind and not to wish for what I am not to have."

There was another silence. Each of the women was striving to brace herself to meet what might be her destiny. Might be. They could not tell. If—and if—they had no friends; and what a cold thing charity was, and how difficult to find at all.

"Did Mr. Turner buy the house?" Maria asked at last.

"No, I let it, and I had the rent; but after a while, as I told you—I don't understand it—he said there was no more rent to pay, except for the mill."

"Was the mill yours too?"

"No, but the ground. Papa let the ground to old Bentley when he was very short of money, and I know he said it would be something when he was gone, and Mr. Turner said he would give me this house rent free, and I should have the ground rent. The great house wanted repairing, and he has made some alterations. I don't understand it, but I hope I shan't come down again, for where should I come to?" She laughed sadly, and looked into the fire.

Suddenly the same thing struck them both. They had talked themselves into absolute darkness without being aware of it.

"Why, here we are in the dark!" Miss Everard exclaimed. "I must shut the shutter."

"Did you and mamma talk like that?" Maria asked, rising.

Miss Everard laughed.

"Yes, indeed we did, my dear! But now I will tell you one thing, for fear you should be frightened. You see there," pointing out of the window. "You see there is something like a man standing there."

"It is a man," Maria said.

"No, it's not, though it looks so much like one."

"But it moves. I saw him move when I came to the window."

"Yes, it moves when you move. It looks just like someone retreating behind the holly. You see it is the round top of the gate-post. The night I first came here I saw it, and thought a man was hiding. I was very frightened. I sat ever so long before I shut the shutters to see if he would go away, and when I came near the window there he was just slinking behind the holly. At last I was forced to go to bed, but I could not sleep; and next night there he was again. So at last I thought I would wait till someone was going past that would hear me scream, and then I would go out and ask him what he was doing there. So out I went, and spoke very loud, and when he did not answer I went up to him directly, for fear the man should be gone that was walking past. . . . And there, you know, there was nothing! . . . Did you ever hear of a belief the Red Indians have?"

Maria looked at her, and forgot her intention of going away.

"They think that when they conquer their enemy all his strength and courage go into themselves. Now, you know, it is really true in a certain sense. I am sure I am more courageous for having got over that fright, just as I was for opening the door myself. I find there is nothing very formidable in it. . . . There are very few things I am afraid of now, only of coming at last to live on charity. I think that would be hard to bear!"

"Yes, that I should dread, too," Maria answered.

They had touched this point before, and again there was a silence, while Miss Everard lighted a candle and closed the shutter. Then she made Maria sit down again.

"Now, you see," she said, "I am very cosy when all is shut up. I have always something to do every day, and at night I sit down, and—and I get on very well with reading and working and such things."

"I hope you will come and see me," Maria said. "We shall be very cosy together."

"Yes, my dear, I shall like to come and see you. I am sure we shall have a deal to say to each other. I shall like to know all your little affairs—all you choose to tell me. Sometimes I might help you, perhaps."

"Yes, indeed, you know all the people hereabouts."

"Yes, of course I do."

It was at the most improper hour of nine o'clock that Miss Bell finally walked up the "Town-Gate" to her own home.

As she entered at the little green gate she recollected the thoughts that had filled her mind as she went out of it. She would gratify the poor old thing by going to see her. She would even give her a bottle of wine or two. As she said she never took any, it would last her for years. "Perhaps," thought the girl, "I shall go and see her once a fortnight or so; it will fill up the Saturday."

Now, she knew that she had made a valuable acquaintance. The frightened, uncertain creature was a pleasant and culti- vated woman as soon as the pressure of the Turners was taken off, and Maria began to hope much from their intercourse, if only Miss Everard was willing.

Miss Everard was, in fact, one in a thousand. She had been brought up in plenty and in idleness, with no definite aim or object in her life. As time went on she had borne her misfortunes with a noble spirit, and had been purified by her adversity. She had begun, it is true, with a very lofty idea of her own position, and the necessity of maintaining it. She had shrunk from opening the door herself as being inconsistent with the dignity of the great house, and many tears had she shed as the necessity of derogating from this dignity had forced itself upon her. But she had come right at last, and saw clearly the only honest way before her. She reduced her expenses courageously, and gave up many a pleasure, and even many a comfort, when she found they made her position uncertain, and threatened to involve her in debt. And through all this bitter trial she complained to none. There was no one, she said, whose business it was to help her, and it was her fault if she was not more capable. Her mind gained strength and her spirit nobleness by the struggle, and Maria found out by degrees that she had a patient, wise, clear-headed friend, whose principles were not less lofty than her own. As this agreement became apparent to each of them they opened out to each other, and by degrees most of the events of their lives became common property. It is a great advantage in dealing with children to know the character of the parents, and this knowledge Miss Everard was able to give. It was mainly through her advice that Maria was enabled to earn the character of a discreet and prudent lady, with a judgment beyond her years.

They once thought it would be pleasanter for them to live together. Then they had dropped the subject from sheer prudence, each one resolving that they would let the other think of it, and wait until she should mention the subject again. At last Maria ventured to touch on it, thinking that perhaps Miss Everard had forgotten it altogether. The old lady was wrapping up for a stormy walk home when Maria said—

"What a pity we can't live together, and then you would not have to walk home."

She was surprised by Miss Everard's look of distress. The old woman positively blushed, and Maria said hastily—

"But perhaps it is better as it is! We could not come and see each other if we were together, you know!"

"No, we could not," Miss Everard began, in great embarrassment. "I am very sorry. I should have liked it so much. But I consulted Mr. Turner, and"—she looked most pitiably ashamed—"I think we will let it alone. I don't like—I have asked him, you know!"

"But I meant for you to come here, not for me to go to his house."

"Yes, but—I have asked him, you know, and I should not like to go against his advice. I think, my dear, we will let it alone, and go on coming to see each other."

Maria puzzled herself about the motive of this advice. Could it be a sheer act of malice, because she herself had not taken his guidance, or did he want to keep Miss Everard under his own control, lest someone should find out for her that she was cheated? It was, in fact, a little of both. If Miss Everard left his house he would have to make the rent out to her in money. And why should she make acquaintance with such an undesirable person as his niece? There was an old opposition, more in feeling than in fact, between himself and Maria's father. "What nonsense!" he thought. "Better stay where she is!" and he put the matter out of his mind.

The gossiping visits still continued, and Maria had a certain malicious pleasure in entering Mr. Turner's gates much oftener than he knew, and keeping up an intimacy in spite of him. She put her foot down firmly in her new position, and went on bravely. Rik wrote to her at long intervals. If a letter had come in less than six weeks she would have looked at it as the herald of misfortune. People in those days were indeed parted when they could not see each other, and their poverty made letters scarce.

Dora's intercourse was rather different, and needs telling.

CHAPTER IX.

LONELY AND HELPLESS.

During Maria's stay at her father's home, Dora was much with her, and many tears and many promises consecrated their friendship. They were both down-hearted as much as it was possible for healthy women to be; no prospect of brighter days was visible.

"If you get on you will tell me," Dora said to her friend; but Maria would not encourage her. Whether either of them could by any means earn a living they did not know.

"If I sink in the deep sea," she said, "why should I call you after me? You at least are on land, though but a barren land."

"Is it in this way," Dora said, "that people, as they grow old, lose their higher feelings, what is called their poetry? Must it be smothered out of them by never being allowed to come to the daylight? I shall never speak of anything good or great when you are gone—never! never! So by-and-bye I shall get like him" (him meant Mr. Woodman), "and raise a loud laugh if I hear of anyone doing anything noble, or even just, that he could escape from doing."

"You will never forget your mother's teaching, Dora?"

"But it is nothing but misery to me to remember it! I cannot bear the contrast. But, Maria—"

"Well, Dora?" for the girl had stopped in embarrassment.

"I have, in secret, a hope left me yet."

"Pray, Dora, tell me what it is."

"You know what your mother said?"

"That you were to get away? Yes."

"I think it is, perhaps, mere cowardice that prevents my walking out of this house and seeking work for myself. Now if you go, you will perhaps find the way for me."

To this Maria repeated her former remark—

"I am going into the deep sea," she said; "how can I ask you to follow me?"

"But somehow, 'Ria, it does not seem so sure that you will be drowned as it would be for me if I ventured."

"I am sure of my duty," Maria said; "perhaps that is the difference."

"If I knew a way to get out of this house, would it not be my duty?"

"Well, I think it would."

After such talks as this, there would come some quiet and consolation into Dora's mind. But when the real parting was accomplished, and the solitude came, her fortitude broke down. She longed so for a word from her friend, that she became almost hysterical when day after day the post brought no letter from her. She went from anger to pity as she thought of the various causes that might have prevented Maria from writing. She would have accused Mr. Woodman of suppressing the letter, but that she herself saw them brought into the house and laid on the breakfast table. In a week after the tearful leave-taking she had lost all measure in her longing, and all reason in her feeling towards her old friend.

She decided she would wait six months and then write, taking a final leave of her. Next day she would wait a fortnight more, and then write an encouraging letter, for she felt sure Maria was in some way amongst breakers, and far too much engaged to have time to write a letter that could give no definite information. At last, after waiting a month, without any decision or definite purpose at all, she sat down and scribbled in hot haste the following, beginning—

My Dear Miss Bell,

"I suppose our childish friendship is at an end. I ought

to have known that it would be, when you got out into the
actual world; everybody told us it would. Do you remember
how sadly mamma smiled when she heard us swearing an eternal friendship? It is over now, and I am left—whatever you
are—without anything in its place; but I will not trouble you
with my misery. You know it, and do not probably wish to be
reminded of unpleasant things. I wish you may be enjoying
happiness now, whatever may be my lot. Lest you should think
that some change must have come over my destiny, I must say
that it has not changed. I have not had a word of communion
with anyone since I saw you. I have to see people, it is true.
Three or four men come in and order me about, and grumble
if they do not get what they want. Now and then I get some
abuse or insult that makes me careful not to speak when I can
help it, and not to be in their company when I can get away.
As this is a farewell letter, I will tell you what my prospects
are, for you to think of when you have time. I sit by myself
till I know myself on the verge of idiocy. I know, too, what I
have so long dreaded, that this is an ordinary fate. Women die
off so sometimes. The first step is, of course, that they sink out
of sight—no one knows what becomes of them. Perhaps they
take to drink, to make the process of dying a little shorter, and,
at least, less painful. I do not wish to trouble you, nor to cast
a shadow over your happiness in your new world; you are still
my very dear friend, and with all my heart I pray God bless
you. Do not write to me any more, for I feel less when I am
not stirred. This is farewell, we must each go our own way
and fulfil our own destiny.

"Your old friend
"DORA."

In eager haste she closed the letter. The postage was then
paid by the receiver, for the fact that she had the money to
produce might have made her pause, but the letter went, and
all she could do was to repent afterwards that she had cost
her poor friend sixpence. She wished she had remembered to
apologize for it, and to remind her that it was the last time.
Maria was very sad when she went down to Miss Everard

with this letter. She related to the new friend the whole history of the old friendship—how they had comforted each other; what they had promised each other; how she had even now written to the one left behind, that she hoped to be able to lift her out of the dark valley into daylight, at least; how it seemed that the help, if it came at all, would not come in time to save her from despair.

Miss Everard listened with breathless interest, and gave her no comfort. Maria could hardly restrain her tears when she heard the old woman confirm all her gloomy prognostics.

"It is so," she said, sadly. "Women do go out of sight. Yes, it is a mysterious dispensation. Is it their own fault? If so, why are they not taught better? Why, why!" she continued. "Questioning is useless; only get it fairly into your head that it is so. No one will think of helping her any more than they would think of taking her up out of her coffin, if they once got her into it."

Now Maria was brave from her own success, she maintained that something could be done.

"Look what I have done in this short time," she said.

And then Miss Everard cut down all her growing hopes by pointing out that she barely earned her living because it was a very good time; that when bad times came she would lose nearly all her pupils, and that to be better than she was now was almost impossible, while occasional adversity was sure.

And though Miss Everard was kind, and proved her interest by entering carefully into the whole business, yet she did not like Dora Wells. She thought her loud, complaining, revengeful, ill-tempered. She had not followed the details of the life that the girl had led now for eight years. She could hardly appreciate with her best endeavours, the effect on the mind of such prolonged suffering. She herself thought she had suffered; yet so little real pain had there been in her life that she had had to draw on the future for what might possibly be to come, and all her self-denial had amounted to this, that she had taught herself to dispense with superfluities. She had done this well, and kept her feelings unwarped by the selfish injustice that makes people in her circumstances think that somehow, or somewhere, they ought to be provided for, and are ill-used in being left to their own fate. But of the constant pressure of actual pain, mental or physical, she knew nothing. She thought Dora very far wrong to "give way" so, and Maria very good and rather foolish in pitying her. In short, she saw the mote in her neighbour's eye, and condemned her accordingly.

Within a week Maria came to her with another letter.

"Now you see it's all right," she said, "she believes me again, she says. Listen—

" 'Your letter lifted me out of the fog of the valley of the shadow of mental death where I habitually live. For a time I was in the clear, and saw all round me. Then I saw you as you are, and cast off all my clinging suspicions of your selfishness, meanness, etc. Now remember whenever I am in my right mind I am your own old friend. Whatever I may write or say, I am.' "

"Maria, my dear, I am afraid for you. You know a friend either drags us up or down." Miss Everard spoke in alarm.

"Then one side must be injured by it," she said; "but it is not so. Friendship does good to both friends."

"Well, that is true too," Miss Everard said, and did not stop to arrange the inconsistency in her own opinions. "But you see you are already somewhat—"

"Somewhat?" Maria repeated after her.

"I don't know how to say it," the old lady said. "Don't you see that what you have just read would be laughed at by everybody?"

"So would truth and justice and all nobility of soul."

"No, no; they would not. There it is where you are like her; and you are wrong."

"But if the faithful few do not laugh at me, what becomes of your argument?"

"I cannot explain to you, my dear; but do not you see that you will soon hate all the world just because no very superior person happens to be within your horizon? Now we should endeavour to keep in that frame of mind in which we can think kindly of everybody—of people as being like ourselves; and not think ourselves superior to other people because they differ from us."

"Whatever our peculiar thoughts may be that other people laugh at, whether they are better than other people's or not, I like to have them; I would only give them up when I was shown they were wrong. They are a great part of my life, so far as I live, beyond the daily cares of poverty."

"Well, my dear, keep all the pleasure you can lay your hands on. I do not say it is wrong, but—I don't like it."

"You think it silly?"

"I think it flighty!"

"It is the chain from Heaven that prevents us from sinking, though we are lowered sometimes very low."

"Now, my dear, don't begin thinking of yourself as an entirely passive agent, who has nothing to do with it, whether she is lowered or pulled up, and then thinking of the everyday duties as the mud into which you are lowered. Daily duties are the earth that we must touch to be strong. It is for you to bear their weight and to ennoble them in the doing."

"That teaching may do for us. But how is Dora to ennoble hers—or rather, how is she to escape her daily suffering?"

"She is to become ennobled by it."

"That was just what I wanted to say to her, and I did not know how."

"She will just accuse you of not caring for her, or not understanding her, and will tell you that your advice may do for yourself that have nothing to bear."

"It is always so," Maria said. "Consolation just gives you the feeling that the speaker knows nothing about suffering, and make you want to scold them."

"Perhaps that is the way it does good. Did you ever notice that when people are frightened the best thing in the world is to put them in a passion?"

Maria laughed.

"There is some good in being in a passion sometimes, certainly," she said. "It keeps one's spirits up. I'll tell Dora so."

"Dora can do it for herself."

"You have not seen her. You do not know her."

"I do not know all about her, but of the ill-temper I am sure."

"Oh, I forgot to tell you of another thing. Mr. Woodman is going to die, she says, at the end of her letter. At least, he is failing, and won't get better."

"Now are you not a couple of selfish creatures? You hear sentence of death pronounced on a man, and almost forget it the next minute. It is scarcely worth recording."

"I don't know how she felt it," Maria said, "but I won't believe she was indifferent. It is not of the first importance to us."

"Will that death make any difference to her when it comes?"

"No, I don't see how it can. She won't get her thirty pounds a year, and—yes, it will. She must either take a place with the stepbrothers, or go and find another."

"And she mentions it as a thing of no importance."

"It is a long way off as yet; he is breaking up, as they say; he can't face the weather, and the doctor says he must not go out; he sits in the little parlour."

"And has that crosspatch for a nurse!"

"Dora is not a crosspatch; she is a very kind and patient nurse."

Had Miss Everard gone and seen Dora in the face she would not have recognized her, so strongly had she convinced herself of the likeness she herself had painted; as it was, the girl was a good symbol of the dilapidated place she lived in, and of the ruined fortunes of its owners. The broken fences, the battered gate, the dirty front, made one pity the people who lived in the large tumbledown house. Inside, matters were worse— the ragged matting had been removed out of the hall, and the place looked like a dirty kitchen floor; more rags met the eye in every carpet, and curtain, and tablecloth; no feminine eyes had been able to point them out in their incipient state, and when they were past mending there was no means of renewing them. With the instinct that makes a sick bird forget to preen itself, the old man had passed over the dilapidations until his eye got used to them. His fortunes had kept pace with his health, and he sank and sank without hope. It is a very simple thing to say that when a man lives beyond his means he will become penniless at the end, but it is much more complicated in the eyes of those who have begun the process; they can borrow, they can sell, there are a hundred ways in which they can mystify themselves when they are eating their cake, and they somehow hope there will be some of it left; then they can swear at their creditors, and soon do that sufficiently to get persuaded that the creditors deserve it; from thence to cheating them is a short step; and the struggle ends in the poor incapable debtor getting the worst of it. Then the poor man can honestly say that if he had all that was owing to him he would be able to pay somebody.

"Poor Mr. Woodman," Mrs. Greaves would say, "he ought never to have tried anything, but now he has not even sense to live on what he has; I thought he would get round again when he gave over speculating, but he is as ill off as ever."

And in the midst of this ruin stood Dora; so silent, sad, and wan that Mrs. Greaves pitied her.

Dora seldom spoke, but always obeyed orders, and did her best with the work. When anything was wanted she would mention the fact at the breakfast table, and Mr. Woodman would bring some silver out of his pocket, or oftener go himself and buy what was needed. He was not a knowing buyer, and the house was not economically managed, in so far as he was manager. Since the bitter winter weather set in he had handed over the money to one or other of his sons, with orders to perform the duty. This was more wasteful still. The old man saw it, and would sometimes storm and sometimes cry, and find no remedy. Dora sometimes pitied him, but she saw clearly there was no remedy. He trusted not a soul, and he had not a soul to trust. True, Dora might have been a faithful friend if she had been treated like one, but he never in his life had had one, and knew not the way of dealing that would make or keep one. Even had his wife lived to perform the part for

which he married her, she would not have been able to do it.
In vain he looked and longed for a friend. Had he by some
magic found one by his side some morning he would have separated himself from him before night by his habit of untrusting
watchfulness.

So he crept towards his grave alone. His poverty increased,
or seemed to increase, with his helplessness, and his isolation
with both. We must all die—alone; yet we like to be attended
to the shores of the dark river, and to think that help is at
hand. But if anyone had spoken to old Woodman of the coming parting he would have accused them, mentally if not in
words, of looking for his empty place.

As for what passed in Dora's mind, he knew as little as anyone else. He thought her occupied in gossip, and in vain endeavours to get hold of some cheap finery. He took credit to
himself for crushing both these tendencies. Then he liked to
see her up to the eyes in work, as she often was, accusing her
of a wish to be always idle. She was certainly not a zealous
worker, nor a tidy housekeeper. It was utterly impossible to
introduce comfort into the house, and she did not attempt it.
She and the servant kept it reasonably clean, and the sticks,
hats, and great-coats got leave to lie where they would, until
their owners moved them somewhere else. This began when
one of the young men asked her insolently, "Where have you
been hiding my great-coat?" She neither sought it nor answered
him, and from that time she never hung it up again.

Mrs. Greaves and the tradespeople who came to the house
thought her a most stupid creature. "She never has a word to
say," they remarked. "I wonder if she's all there!" Some of
them thought not, telling tales of her queer doings. "She went
to church once in her weekday dress," said the servant, "and
said she had forgotten to change it." She would sit in the
garret by herself, and nothing ever came of it. "I thought she
was knitting herself summat or making hersen a new dress
or a tippet—I am sure she needs one—but she were a doing
nought but just reading."

The insanity of reading, Dora was very much given to. It

was the only means by which she lifted from her mind the burden that threatened to break it. But it so isolated her from those about her that public opinion veered slowly round, and instead of thinking that she was illtreated by her step-father, by being so shabbily dressed, people began to think that he was on the whole very charitable in keeping the half-witted creature that had fallen into his hands. It was taken for granted she might be better off if she would, and she shared in the general contempt that settled upon the family. When it began to be rumoured about that they were no longer rich, people troubled themselves no more about Dora's present ills or her hopeless future. No excuse is so convenient, none applies to a greater variety of cases than this—that "It's their own fault." "People should at least do all they can to help themselves before they claim pity from others."

In one thing, Dora's silence was more useful to her than she knew. Mrs. Greaves never knew how heartily Dora detested her. To the solitary, the speaker who cannot enter into their feelings is an enemy. He hurts them at every turn, and it is all the sufferer can do to keep silence when his aching heart is crushed by the hopeless inanity of commonplace conversation. Dora was conscious of the injustice of her hatred. But not the less, it was there, and the girl's idea of happiness was to be where no one would speak to her, or expect to be spoken to.

At times, at long intervals, a letter would come to her from Repton. Then she would remember the mother's teaching, and the early habits long forgotten. And whatsoever things were true and lovely and of good report she would strive to recall and bring back into her daily life. But it was hopeless work. She was more silent than ever while making the vain attempt to remake herself after the long-forgotten model; and no one knew of her endeavours. The servants would notice the far-away look, and the indifference to small annoyances, but could not interpret it; and soon she fell back again into the quarrelsome, perverse, sturdy rebel that she was before.

When Maria received a letter from her she thought that her pity and encouragement had been of no use at all. But she was mistaken. Dora would have sunk infinitely lower without her friendship. She did not finally give up the clinging to the right, and it was Maria who enabled her to do so. We are a little race, we humans! The almighty present fills our eyes, and only with an effort can we see beyond it.

Dora forgot the warning that Mr. Woodman had received, that he must give up his open-air life, and look forward to his coming death. She did not take it as anything but a reminder that he was an old man. She knew that before. But death appeared to her scarcely more near than it had been four years before, when he had followed her mother to her grave. A thing to happen at some indefinite time in the future could not influence her present much. Besides, she did not see how it could alter her fate.

CHAPTER X.

"THEIR WORDS ARE SWEET AS HONEY, BUT THE POISON
OF ASPS IS UNDER THEIR LIPS."

MISS BELL was agreeably disappointed with the behaviour of
her strange pupil. Full of interest and eagerness, she worked
hard, as young people labour at what they like. The idle hours
that generally hinder the progress of day scholars gave her
opportunity to get on the faster; she acquired a large new
vocabulary from books and teaching, as she paid attention
and remembered what she heard. Miss Bell told her a good
deal, all which she made her own, and turned to use as occasion offered. In a few weeks' time all the girls spoke civilly to
her, and many courted her acquaintance. Foremost among
them was Sophy Eldon, as untidy, as loud, and as idle as ever,
but coaxing, affectionate, and false. She got a good deal of
help from Sarah, and some outspoken scoldings besides. At
these she sulked, and would leave her in peace for a day or
two, and then come back again, and get confidential, then
regret it, and quarrel again.

This valuable ally had lately begun to ask Sarah to go home
with her, and threatened to be offended with her frequent
refusals.

"What do you want with me?" Sarah would say; "can't you
talk to me here? You told me long since that your mother and
sister would scarcely like you to go with me, an' then you
thought happen they would let you bring me into t' house,

and now nought will do but I must go. You'll have to tell me
first what for."

To which Sophy would answer—

"You're a nasty, ill-natured thing!" then leave her for a
while and come back and repeat her request.

The reason of her pertinacity may as well be told in order
to make her proceedings intelligible. Sydney Wynde had undertaken to give instruction in singing to Miss Eldon, Sophy's
elder sister. This young lady was found to have a fair voice,
and considerable facility in picking up tunes, and if she could
have been persuaded to learn the accompaniments, would have
been a pleasing performer. It was her master's custom, when
he gave this pupil a lesson, to begin by striking a few chords
on the piano with great vigour and pomposity, to the girl's
great admiration. She used to try to imitate him when he was
gone, but though she struck plenty of notes and made plenty
of noise, she had a suspicion that there was something wrong.
So from this vantage ground, which she was unable to reach,
he used to inspire her with such ideas as he wished to get into
her head.

"What a pity I have not got a lady's voice! a fine voice like
yours, Miss Eldon."

"Oh, Mr. Wynde!"

"Then I could sing second to you, you know."

"Well, so you do."

"Well, I sing bass, but you want a contralto to set off your
voice properly."

"Oh, Mr. Wynde!"

In a minute she asked him—

"Can't Sophy sing second?"

He shook his head.

"Not the right voice."

And he went on playing. In another minute he began—

"I know one too, one that would just do, would make your
high notes sound quite divine."

A little more strumming, and then, as no answer came but
"Oh, Mr. Wynde!" he broke off with—

"But come, it's no use talking, we may as well begin the lesson."

"But who is it, Mr. Wynde?"

"Miss Miles, one of Miss Bell's pupils."

"Can she sing?"

He nodded.

"Not so well as you, of course."

This bouncing fib did not hurt his conscience in the least. He gave her no opening to say any more, but the final result of what he had said was that Miss Eldon and her mother told Sophy to impress upon Sarah the pleasure she would have if she got an invitation some day to go and see Susan and mamma. Sophy's blundering tactics had not got so far as to persuade Sarah that the visit would be a pleasure at all, until she hit by chance upon the argument that Susan wanted to sing with her.

"Why did you not tell me before?" Sarah asked; "we'll go to-night."

And without further asking she crossed the road with Sophy, and went towards the kitchen door. This was not what her companion had intended, she had hoped to bring her in at the front door and show her into the parlour, where there was mahogany furniture and antimacassars, cut paper in the fireplace, and a piano. The kitchen was entered by two steps opening from the street, and was small, dark, and dirty. A stout, middle-aged woman was leaving it by an inner door, but turned back when her daughter said—

"Mother, it's only Sarah Miles."

"Oh, is it you? I was going away to get something on my neck; I look so ugly with a bare neck." Here she tittered.

At this date all young ladies, and those who would not grow old, wore low dresses with a kerchief or chemisette. No one spoke for a few moments, while Sarah looked at Mrs. Eldon. The lady wore curlpapers and a dirty cap, dirty white stockings, and dilapidated stuff shoes.

"We may as well go into the parlour," Sophy said.

"No, indeed," cried her mother, in alarm; "you must do no such a thing."

"Why not?"

"Because there's company there."

This with an air of great importance, and a toss upward and downward of her chin, intended to signify "Don't you ask any more."

Fortunately the parlour door opened at this moment, and a man's voice was heard taking leave. Then the front door opened and shut, and a light step came towards the kitchen.

Sarah wondered at the beauty of the girl when she tripped in. She wore a muslin dress with a white ground and a green leaf upon it, that set off the pinky tinge of her bare arms and neck, and the peach bloom of her cheeks. Soft brown curls waved round her face, and her carmine lips were just breaking into a smile.

"Susan, was that Mr.—"

Susan waved her hand imperiously before her sister's face, so that the finger-tips nearly touched her lips. Sophy was silenced.

"We may as well go into the parlour," said mamma; "Miss Miles would like to hear the piano, I dare say."

"No, I shouldn't," said Sarah, who had never heard any performer on the piano except Miss Bell's pupils. "I should like to hear some singing."

"I'm sure I wonder who's to sing for you, then! I've been singing till I'm tired to death."

The beauty danced back into the parlour, and stood by the open piano. She tried striking chords in Sydney's fashion, but the effect did not improve Sarah's opinion of the instrument. She began to think of going away.

"Perhaps you'll play for us, Miss Miles," Susan said, with an air.

"I can't play."

"Well, I'm too tired of it already," and Miss Eldon sat down.

"I don't want you to play, I want you to sing."

The three looked at each other, and then informed her condescendingly that it was impossible to sing without accompaniment.

"I should not like to do anything so absurd."

"I thought you liked singing?"

"So I do; I like it excessively. Mr. Hill says, mamma, that I shall be quite a performer soon. I can't help getting on, I'm so fond of it."

"Well, I thought you liked singing. But I'll go."

"Very well, Miss Miles. Of course, we don't wonder if you don't like music; you can't be expected to have any taste, you know. You have had no opportunity."

Sophy went back with her through the kitchen, and then rejoined her mother and sister.

"Sophy, whatever did you bring that girl here for?"

"Why, you asked me!"

"You should bring her at proper times—when she's wanted."

"You're not likely to get her when she's wanted, t' way you go on!"

"We can ask her mother to let her come."

"Indeed, but I'm not going to ask her mother anything of the kind," the mother broke in. "I shan't ask for Mally Miles' acquaintance!"

The two had known each other all their lives.

"Why, they all talk to her at school!" Sophy said. "Miss Dunn asked her to go home with her the other day, and she wouldn't go."

"Now, Sophy! To pretend that she was asked there, and would not go!"

"She was, I tell you! believe it or not, as you like."

And yet it was not true. Miss Dunn had wanted something from home during the play-hour, and had asked Sarah to go with her to fetch it. She had refused, because she equally disliked either to walk into the house with her friend or to stand outside.

"They're well enough off. They could dress better if they liked."

"And her sister a servant!"

"She's no need to go to place. She's better than a common servant."

"Well, if we're to keep company with servants! And to be asked to sing to them, too!"

"Why, you asked me to bring her!" Sophy screamed again. "And it would not have cost you so much. You can but play two tunes, and you miss two lines of one of them because they are hard."

"And how much can you play, I wonder! Been a year in the instruction book!"

"Miss Bell says she could learn anything, if she liked. But she won't learn t' piano."

"Vulgar creature! I dare say she won't!"

"And she knows a good many respectable people. She goes to Mr. Sykes'."

"Who's Mr. Sykes, I wonder? A wool-sorter!"

"You think nobody equal to Mr. Hill."

"You're thinking of young Sykes, I suppose."

"Come, come, you may either of you be glad to get young Sykes," said the mother, "so don't be scornful."

Her eldest daughter threw up her chin.

"But, girls, you should get on better than you do. Such work as I had to get that piano for you; and your father grumbled so."

"Father's always grumbling. He'd have us work as if we were mill-girls. What has he been saying?"

"Well, he says we shan't have such good times as we have had. There's many a mill will be standing soon."

"We've nothing to do with the mills."

"No, but you'll find bad times for one is bad times for all."

So with the conviction that she had done her duty to her daughters in the above conversation by her mode of winding it up, Mrs. Eldon left them to themselves. For some days afterwards Sophy let Sarah alone, and then came up to her one afternoon with the message that her mother would be glad to see her to tea next day. She looked quite unconscious of ever having mentioned the subject before, and proportionately surprised when Sarah answered—

"Yes, but I won't go."

"Sarah!"

"What's the matter?"

"You won't go! You ill-natured thing!"

"You took me before, and your sister wouldn't sing nor nought. What's the good of going?"

And no threats or persuasion would move her. In truth, she did not believe half that Sophy said, and unfortunately for Sophy's purpose that half was the wrong one. She doubted the singing altogether.

The task imposed upon Sophy Eldon next day was much more difficult than the one she had already accomplished. She was to bring Sarah at any cost, and if it had required diplomacy to get her to the house the first time, nothing short of falsehood was enough for the second. So Sophy deliberately took her friend's arm on their way to school next morning, prepared to use the necessary weapon.

"Now, Sarah, there's going to be some beautiful music at our house to-night."

"Is there?"

"Yes. Won't it be nice?"

"I don't know."

"Oh, but it will, and if you like you shall come to it. Though you are but a girl, you are my friend, you know. And I will take you in, and nobody will notice you, and we will sit together. Won't we, Sarah?"

"Yes. But I won't go."

"Why, Sarah, what do you mean? You *are* a nasty mean thing! Can't you just come when one asks you?"

"You did not ask me. You said you'd let me."

"I said you should, and then you turn round on me like that. And I just wanted you to see it all!"

"Why, bairn, I don't want to see it, so there's no 'casion to fret!"

For Sophy was crying with passion.

"You don't want! You don't want! And what must I do, then? Sit in the kitchen because you don't want! And mother says I needn't go in because I've nobody to talk to. You nasty mean thing, you! You know very well that I want! That's what you do it for!"

"Sophy, you know you are telling a lot of lies. How could I do it to keep you i' t' kitchen when I did not know your mother wouldn't have you i' t' parlour?"

"Well, but, Sarah, she won't! I know she won't. And I shall have to sit in the kitchen, and they singing!"

"Are they going to sing?"

"Aye, that they are."

"You said so before, and then your sister would not sing a bit."

"Why. I'll tell you, Sarah, our Susan's a nasty proud thing! I'm sure she vexes me many a time. But you'll see she'll sing to-morrow night, and with you, too."

Sarah began to believe her.

"Why, I'll come, then. When do they begin?"

"Oh, you must come to tea."

"I willn't come to tea. I'll come when I have cleaned up."

Accordingly, when she had swept the hearth after tea Sarah put on a checked pinafore in place of her canvas one, and took her way through the darkness to Mrs. Eldon's kitchen-door. An untidy charwoman was looking lost among the tray full of dirty teacups and the plates half-emptied of bread and butter. She stared at Sarah rather stupidly, and repeated after her—

"Sophy, Sophy! Ye mun go in there."

"Fetch her," Sarah urged.

The woman looked at herself and then at Sarah, and finally decided they were neither of them fit to appear.

"Wait while she comes," she said at last, and Sarah saw nothing else for it.

Fortunately Mrs. Eldon came out soon after, and her eldest daughter following her whispered to her in the passage—

"Mother, why is not Sarah Miles coming?"

"Here I am," Sarah cried, and the two stood dumbfounded before her.

"Nay, Sarah, to come like that!"

"What's t' matter?"

"Never dressed yourself nor nought."

"What should I dress mysen for? We allus sing 'dout dressing at Sykes's."

Miss Eldon tossed her head, and her mother, putting her hand on her shoulder, said—

"You just go into the parlour and send Sophy here. Sarah dear," she went on, "we have company. Sophy ought to have told you. You will have to be dressed."

"Then I'll go home again and come sometime else."

"Sarah, you'll do no such thing," cried Sophy, coming in. "Why, child," she continued, taking a survey of her, "what have you come like that for?"

"I've come to sing—an' nought else," she added, her temper rising.

"Sophy," said her mother, "take her upstairs and put her your merino dress on. It will be long, but it will cover her feet; and try and make her—" decent, she was going to say, but left the sentence unfinished.

Shortly after the pair entered the parlour. Sarah wore a blue merino dress, too long for her, and a red bow with long ends fastened in front. She came in resolved to neither speak nor move till the singing began. There were the two Miss Whites sitting stiff and glum, waiting for something to happen.

The Miss Whites were the newly-established milliners of whom Sarah's friends, the Willans', had bought the cap. Sarah was particularly curious about them. She had heard that they had once been better off than they were now. "They were ladies once," was the report concerning them, and Sarah looked askance at them till she had them all by heart, in hopes of finding out what ladyhood was.

She saw two thin, elderly women clad in old-fashioned finery, and looking kindly, feeble, and ceremonious. They were conversing with Mrs. Eldon in this fashion—

Mrs. Eldon was afraid it was a cold night, and the Miss Whites thought it was, too. Then Mrs. Eldon wondered what made the gentlemen so late—

"For you must know we are expecting gentlemen, and I think they want to make themselves of importance, coming so late."

The Miss Whites thought they did, too.

"I always like to have some gentlemen when I have company. It makes it more lively."

The Miss Whites thought it did.

"But I really think they are behaving very badly."

The Miss Whites thought they were. Then came a pause.

"Sarah," said Sophy, flippantly, "why don't you talk?"

" 'Cause I don't want."

"You don't want! Was there ever such a girl?" appealing with a patronizing air of superiority to the Miss Whites.

"You like better to listen, perhaps?" said one of them.

"Yes, ma'am."

"Yet when I was your age I was as fond of talking as anyone."

"What did you do when you were my age?"

"When I was your age, or at least very little older, I should have liked well enough to talk and gad about all·day long."

"But what did you do?"

"Well, sometimes I've visited almost every day in the week."

The three Eldons exclaimed, "Oh, Miss White!" in a tone as if such happiness were almost beyond conception.

"But what did you go for?"

"I never did see such a girl as Sarah. That's just the way she goes on whenever she gets a chance."

"Here's our gentlemen at last," Mrs. Eldon said, and the Miss Whites stiffened themselves a little more.

Mrs. Eldon went forward as the door opened, and Sarah exclaimed as the first man entered—

"Eh, Sammy!"

Sam, who was making his entrance with intense gravity, looked a little fiercer than before. Sydney Wynde, who followed him (it seemed to Sarah that he always did follow him), asked her if she thought they should tell *her* they were coming? The third visitor was a stranger—Mr. Hill, Mrs. Eldon said. This last gentleman rather took Sarah's fancy, his recommendations being an honest outlook and a very awkward manner. The hostesses talked large to him, which he did not appear to understand; but he gave rapt attention to all that fell from Miss Eldon's lips, and tried to respond in kind, in which he altogether failed. Soon the mamma said they ought to have a little music, and called on Susan to begin with "Lightly Waving."

"Well, if I must begin," and Mr. Hill opened the piano and she sat down to it.

"Lightly Waving" is an orthodox young lady's song, having six bars of melody in the first line and four in the second, which are repeated in the third and fourth. The fifth and sixth have a little variety, and the first set of notes is repeated in the seventh and eighth. The "salt" of the song lay in the return to the first melody in the seventh line, and this Miss Eldon had noticed when her master had sung it to her. But, unfortunately, the accompaniment changed with the air, and having spent some labour in mastering the first part, her patience was exhausted, and she came to the decision to play the same set of notes all the way through. This spoilt the one effect that might have been got out of the song, and did not improve Sarah's opinion of the value of a pianoforte.

Then Mrs. Eldon asked Mr. Wynde to favour them.

"Oh, yes, with pleasure. With your assistance, of course," bowing to the last performer. She simpered.

"What shall it be, Mr. Wynde?"

"Well, let me see," striking chords, and rolling his head about inimitably. Then he looked round the room, and called: "Sarah, come up. It's 'The Red Cross Knight.' "

Sam was beckoned too, and the party stood round the piano.

"Blow, Warder, blow thy sounding horn!"

As Sarah sang, the whole company rose and gathered round the piano, as if the summons concerned them. By careful drilling, Miss Eldon's bird-like voice had been trained to sing the first part of the glee. It was altogether well sung and well accompanied. The audience were evidently charmed, and Miss Eldon took the whole credit of the performance to herself.

When the world is all set right, one of the things to be arranged will be the due apportionment of admiration between the song and the singers. At present no one troubles himself to do that correctly, and the performer, especially the pretty one, often gets some praise that was really due to the composer, besides her own fair share. Miss Eldon got it now and was highly delighted with it.

"Oh, what a pity one can't always be singing beautiful songs!" she exclaimed, with rosy cheek and sparkling eyes.

Everyone agreed with her.

"Yes," said Sydney, playing his flourishing chords, "and getting the present company to listen to them."

"Oh, if I had plenty of music I should never want to see a soul."

"Susy's quite a solitary bird," said her mother.

"A bird of solitude are you, Miss Elden?" asked Miss White.

"Quite an owl!" said Sydney, with a grimace. He was half drunk with music and suppressed laughter.

Sarah wondered. His manner had bordered on impertinence before, but now he did not take the trouble to conceal his humour. Then, as if he had done enough for Miss Eldon for one evening, he took the command and ruled things in his own fashion. He was where he liked to be, before a piano with some singers at command, and he suggested, dictated, corrected, scolded, and helped in song after song, until it was unreasonable to go on any longer.

"Sarah, where have you been?" said her mother, according to custom, when she came in rather later than usual.

"At the Eldons."

Mrs. Miles was "siding the table," that is, clearing the table before going to bed, while her husband knocked the ashes out of his last pipe. They both turned round and faced her.

"Been where!"

She repeated her information.

"Whatever sent you there?"

"Sophy would have me go."

"Mind you never enter their house again."

"What for? I shouldn't ha' gone but for Sophy."

"Sarah," said her father, "that house is noan fit for ye, keep ye out o' t' gate."

Mrs. Miles watched keenly over every step and every word of her daughter's life. She held the reins with a strong hand, but it was not her way to let her feel the curb except when it was absolutely necessary. Sarah thought herself free. She knew indeed that she sometimes found a dead wall before her, and that she must try another way. She took it without demur, being generally unconsciously guided by her mother. She never entered the Eldons' house again.

CHAPTER XI.

"Trip on farther, pretty sweeting,
Journeys end in lovers' meeting."

MARIA had begun to feel the effects of the diminished prosperity of the place. There were a few who had never intended to give more than a superficial polish to their girls, which they thought could be acquired in half a year at most. And there were some who never had intended more than to send their children and to trust to Providence for the means of paying. These last were sternly dismissed at the termination of the first quarter by Miss Everard's advice, who knew them all, and was of valuable help to Maria in this as in many other points. She no longer sent flourishing accounts to Dora, and, indeed, was rather ashamed at having done so. Had she not been told by Miss Everard a twelvemonth before that her prosperity was only temporary—that she would have a struggle to live at all? And she had buoyed up the girl with false hopes. She was much relieved by Dora's first answer to the letter avowing her change of fortune. Dora was loving, hopeful, and full of encouragement. It was by her reasoning that Maria perceived that the ill-fortune might be as short-lived as the prosperity, and that she was not sunk into poverty for ever. But her spirits fell. She tried to suit her frame of mind to the real circumstances of her position. And that did not allow of much gaiety of feeling. She must learn to be content with her lot. It was not brilliant, but how few people's was! Well!

"There should be no despair for you,
    While midnight stars are burning,
While flowers are gemmed with evening dew,
    And sunshine gilds the morning."

And she prepared herself to give up what she could not
have, and keep a cheerful mind without it.

In the midst of these thoughts and feelings she had just
made up her mind to a solitary and cheerless life, when an
invitation came from Mrs. Dodds, the Vicar's wife. It was to
tea—"there would be a few friends."

Maria had been there before—indeed, had been welcomed
with kindness and sympathy from her, and admitted to society
as one of the brotherhood, for her father's sake. But this was
an innovation, and Maria thought that would be a sufficient
excuse for refusing the invitation. She could make Mrs. Dodds
understand. All this she told Miss Everard on the evening of
the same day, and was astonished at the warmth of that lady's
condemnation of her reasoning and her decision.

"My dear, you must do no such thing. You want society and
you must take every opportunity of getting it. Never mind
your dress. Never mind if anyone looks at it. You must go."

Maria lifted up her eyes and stammered—

"But I have not the courage. And my conscience would not
be at rest."

Miss Everard looked at her consideringly, and at last appeared to make up her mind.

"Miss Bell," she said, "let me tell you something. You know
in the main what I have gone through, and how I have been
able to fight against destiny. Now let me tell you a mistake I
made."

Maria was interested. She always liked to hear Miss Everard
talk about herself.

"You know I was brought up a member of a large family,
and I had many friends. In fact, I never knew what solitude
was. And when many of them left me, and I left others because I could not entertain them, I began to be much alone.
It was very strange. I found employment, but you know to

women's employment there is no result. Then I began to read, it did well enough, but there was always something wanting; and at last I got into the way of imagining a companion sitting by me, and I made remarks to her. And at last it got to be always your mamma, because, you see, I knew her best. I knew what she would say; and I did not speak loud, for then I marked too well that there was no answer; but I used to talk. And sometimes I have thought that she really put things into my mind that never would have come there if I had not deliberately talked to her."

The old woman looked up as if to say, "Could it really be?"

Then she went on—

"She used to sit in that chair" (pointing to the one opposite), "and I always keep it for her. She is my friend, you know."

Maria remembered that Miss Everard had never offered her the arm-chair. She looked at it almost expecting to see a shadowy figure waiting to be addressed.

"She is my friend; and I tell her everything. I know it is better to talk to real people. But Evelyn and I—"

Maria started at the sound of her mamma's name. She had last heard it from her father long years ago. It was connected with the dead.

"Sometimes I think I should like to call you Evelyn," said the old lady.

"Oh, call me Evelyn!" Maria said, almost in tears. "Call me Evelyn. Then I shall be nearer to you."

"Yes, I will call you Evelyn, and you will answer me. It is better to talk to real people! But it is really true," the old lady went on, "your mamma has put things into my head that I had quite—quite forgotten! Just as she used to do in reality. She was always quick; she remembered everything! It was she who told me to try to make acquaintance with you when you came. When I heard you were coming I told her in the evening, when I was tired of reading. I had not thought of it before, but I started up and said 'I will try.' And I tried," she continued, after a moment, with a trembling voice. "Now, was not that from her? And I have promised her to be your friend.

I know she asked me! For the sake of long ago I will stand by you, Evelyn, as long as I live."

They both sobbed, and Maria thanked her, and then Miss Everard suddenly changed her tone and went on—

"But for all that it is better to talk to real people. One should not get absorbed into another world. So you see, my dear, you must not give over seeing people, for fear of the expense. Go to Mrs. Dodds; never mind being a fright. You must be as you are, and show that you have no means for better clothes, and do not intend to buy anything that you can do without. Let them leave you if they like, but do not you leave them. You may not like the reception you will get, but it will be good for you. And it will be half of it fancy about their not wanting you, or being ashamed of you. There is some sense in the world, never fear! Consider what you will be like after ten years of solitude! There are real griefs enough coming upon us without making much of small ones."

"You think times will get worse?" Maria asked.

"Certainly they will. There is the rest of the time to get over till next harvest."

"Next harvest! Not this one here now!" Maria said, with a face of despair. "More than twelve months!"

"Yes; and then—"

Maria waited.

"There might be another bad season."

"Have you ever seen three bad seasons following?"

"Yes."

"What did the people do?"

"Nothing much; they went into the poorhouse. They bore it, and were discontented; then the time got over, and they forgot it."

"I am thankful that I am not living in a big house and waiting for pupils that don't come; and then having to go and say to Mr. Turner that I could not pay the rent—though I think he would be bound to help me if I had been as obedient to him as he thought I ought."

"I never knew anyone take their responsibilities in that way," Miss Everard said, laughing.

"Well, of course not."

"You see hard times for one means hard times for all. I dread Mr. Turner's mill having nothing to do."

"But he can wait, I suppose."

"But I know my income has always diminished at such times, though that is all I know. I do not see why it should."

Maria thought she ought to make inquiry and insist on information, but the very mention of such a course made the old lady tremble.

"You see," she said, "he might cast me off altogether, and I have no one else. He understands my affairs, and no one else does. You see he gives me this house rent free."

"But perhaps he is keeping back more than the value."

"But, my dear! my dear!" said Miss Everard, in a fright, "I have no reason to say so! I know nothing about it. He said once if things were looked into there might be a heavy charge against me for the repairs done to the house; but he was not going to be exact, and he would continue to pay me something for the ground rent. Then he said another time: 'Don't go too fast, or you may bring down your house about your ears; and then where will you be?' "

"Could not you get someone privately?"

"Don't talk about it, please! Don't talk about it!" she exclaimed, in such evident fear that Maria promised never to mention the matter to a human being.

"What can we do?" the girl said at last, looking up.

"One thing is sure," Miss Everard said—and her clear-headed confidence appeared to return to her when she left the thought of Mr. Turner behind—"repining is the most foolish of mental employments, except complaining. Our business is to keep a contented mind. After all our happiness is much in our own control. We want but little really. And we should not let our minds dwell too much on the possibility that that little may fail us. Thought should lead to action, and then stop. When nothing remains to be done we should set fate at defiance."

Again Maria wondered, "This quiet, frightened old woman was brave enough, it appeared, and I thought of helping and encouraging her!"

"What can I do, do you think?" she asked.

"I do not wish to discourage you, my dear; perhaps things may turn out better than we think."

"But I wish to know! I do not like to be in the dark."

"We are always in the dark, my dear."

"I believe you think me foolish in hoping to save money, and get better off than I am now."

"You do right to try, in any case."

"Though I can't succeed?"

"I don't say you can't succeed. If you did not save you would starve; that is very sure."

Maria thought of the poor of her father's parish, on whom she had so often impressed the duty of saving. Now she saw that if saving did not profit them, the main inducement for making any was gone. They might come to the poorhouse after all, and then whereto the self-denial? They might as well seize what little enjoyment there was to be had.

Perhaps the reaction was wholesome; for the first time for many days she left the subject of her contemplation, and turned away from it.

"Tell me something about mamma," she said. "Where did she live?"

"The house is divided now, and partly pulled down. You can hardly find it. Mr. Turner was manager, or a sort of partner—I don't know what—for old Bentley when he had the mill."

"And mamma lived with him?"

"Yes; it was just down there," nodding, "and I used to run down to the house as soon as I saw Mr. Turner go off to the office. When Mr. Turner married he took the mill. He was always proud, and people said he was going too fast; he should not have gone in for such a large concern; and then to mend it he took the house too, and lived in it. But they have got on well; surely they will continue to do so!"

"You doubt it, I see!"

"Pray don't say such a thing to anybody. It would be very wrong, because I know nothing—nothing whatever!"

There are modes of denying a thing that make it to be suspected, and the possibility of Mr. Turner's ruin, though he had stood for thirty years, entered into Maria's mind.

Maria went home and furbished up her best black dress, and ironed a collar for the evening. She entered the room feeling altogether "low and slow," and was startled into a sort of pained activity by being introduced to Miss Amelia Turner, and bowing to the two elder sisters after her. Mrs. Dodds, having supposed that she had made their acquaintance already, found her a seat, remarking that Miss Amelia was only just come from school, and though she was not yet out—she had only another half year to go—she was big enough to come to a small evening like this. She turned and smiled at Amelia, who smiled cheerfully back again. Maria thought her much superior to the other two, were it only by being much prettier. Besides, she was apparently more good-tempered and more awake, ready for any fun, and ready to make friends with everybody.

As soon as she sat down Maria perceived that she was a fright. Not only was her black dress somewhat brown, but the sleeves were all wrong. They were not half big enough, and her collar, instead of being just large enough to go round her neck, was wide enough to cover her shoulders. Mrs. Dodds had led her to Miss Turner's side, thinking to give her someone to speak to, but thereby making her utterly helpless and silent. On her other side was a Mrs. Overton, who seemed to be a very particular friend of Miss Turner, and the two kept up a half-whispered conversation across her. Mrs. Overton, it is true, seemed not to like this, and gave short answers. Maria gave her credit for disliking the rudeness, but the lady made no effort to put an end to it.

Mrs. Dodds, watchful and uneasy, began to perceive that she had made a great mistake in thinking to oblige the Turners by showing attention to their young cousin. She asked Maria some questions about some of her girls to break off the friendly conversation between the two ladies. Miss Turner, when at last obliged, turned round, and looking at Maria as if she had never seen her before, asked her—

"Oh, so you have begun a school have you?" when she had eyed her sufficiently. "Well, and how do you get on?"

"Not so well as I did at first," Maria said, bluntly.

Miss Turner said—

"Oh!" After a pause she added, "And have you been able to find any society here among us?"

"None at all, except Mrs. Dodds, who is kind enough to take some interest in me."

"I dare say," said Miss Turner, and went no farther.

Maria considered for a while, and thought of remarking that she had been advised not to make friends among the parents of her girls, but Miss Turner interrupted her half-formed remark—

"Then you do not find the mothers of mill girls very interesting?"

"Perhaps I might if I knew them better. There is one, at least, who strikes me as superior; but I do not have much intercourse with her."

"Who is that, Miss Bell?" Mrs. Dodds broke in.

"Mrs. Sugden."

"Oh, Mrs. Sugden. You will know her, Miss Turner. She was servant to your mother once. Her name was—Dear me, what did they call her? She married Jim Sugden, your father's overlooker."

"Oh, I think I remember her. Nancy we used to call her." And then turning round to Maria, "So you are intimate with Mrs. Sugden?"

"I told you I was not," Maria said; "but I think well of her."

Mrs. Dodds hastily called across the room—

"Miss Amelia, we have an old friend of yours coming here to-night, though he seems to put it off till very late."

Amelia, the finished school-girl, duly provided with learning, sat smiling, sensitively pretty, and blushed at the direct assault.

"Indeed, Mrs. Dodds, who is he?"

"Mr. Branksome. Do you remember him?"

"Oh yes, I do! He was always wanting to make me promise to marry him, when I sat on his knee."

There was a general exclamation, and some people thought that he might perhaps try again! She should take care!

"Oh, but I never promised!"

"Perhaps you said something—'ask mamma,' or something of that kind," and the joke was drawn out into very thin gold indeed.

"Branksome? I remember him," Miss Turner said, whose cue it seemed to be very supercilious. "We used to know him, and then, let me see, his father died, and what became of him then? He apprenticed himself to a blacksmith, didn't he, or something of that sort?"

"Matilda!" her sister exclaimed.

"He went to learn engineering," Mrs. Dodds said, severely, "and now he is out of his apprenticeship, and going to set up for himself."

"Oh, then he won't come with a black face?"

And again her sister exclaimed "Matilda!"

"Well, I know there was always something queer about him."

"He has taken a wise step," Mr. Dodds began, seeing that his wife had not succeeded in putting down the sprightly young lady, "in the circumstances in which he was left by his father. Instead of frittering away his money he spent it in paying a high premium in order to learn a trade."

"I say he is queer for all that," Matilda whispered to her friend, Mrs. Overton.

"How queer? What do you mean by 'queer'?"

"Well, queer, you know. He says such queer things."

"What kind of things?"

"Well, once when we were talking about pictures, he suddenly interrupted me to ask if I knew anything of a person called Michael Angelo, and when I asked where he lived he said, 'Up in the skies,' and walked away; and he was little more than a lad then."

When the queer man made his appearance there was a small stir. Mrs. Dodds made some attempt to find him a seat, but he stopped it by saying—

"No, thank you, Mrs. Dodds, I will sit here," and walking quite across the room he seated himself on the sofa beside Amelia. There was a general smile as if that were settled, and Matilda whispered again to her friend, "Now isn't he queer?"

Maria watched him with amusement. He had a vivacious manner, a clear pale complexion, a gnomon of a nose, and a square forehead. From time to time he put his fingers through his hair, as if to remove some obfuscation from his intellects, and from time to time, too, he looked sharply across the room at the three ladies in a row who sat watching him. Miss Turner and Mrs. Overton answered him, but Maria did not consider herself included in the conversation, as he did not know her.

"What is it you are doing, Miss Amelia? Are you knitting something for someone else, or is it for yourself?"

"I'm not knitting, I'm netting, Mr. Branksome, and I don't know who it's for yet," Amelia said.

"Do young ladies learn grammar at school?" he asked.

"Now isn't he queer?" Matilda whispered.

"Of course they do."

Matilda laughed as her contribution to the conversation.

"I'll tell you two pretty colours for a purse—scarlet and white, very little scarlet."

"Oh, but I should not think of carrying a scarlet and white purse."

"Oh, then it's for yourself you are knitting it?"

"I'm not knitting, and I never said so!"

"Never said you were knitting?"

"No, I never said it was for me."

"No, and you did not say who was to have it."

"I won't tell!"

"But really, we must know who is to have it!"

He looked across the room and caught the eye of all the ladies in turn.

"Don't you think so, Mrs. Dodds?"

"Well, I think you are very arbitrary, Mr. Branksome!"

"But who is the scarlet one for—Mr. Branksome?"

"I won't tell."

"Oh, but you must!"

"You are very arbitrary, Miss Amelia!"

All the room laughed. The man put his fingers through his hair, and looked up at the ceiling as if for a fresh absurdity. "He is in his element," thought Maria, and so it seemed. And how he brought out other people's absurdities! Miss Turner asked him for whom the scarlet purse was intended, once more.

"Well," he said, looking up at the ceiling, "suppose you had no purse?"

"Oh, but I have one, Mr. Branksome!"

"Oh, that settles it! Of course, if you have one it can't be supposed that you have not."

"Is not he queer?" Miss Turner whispered again.

Mr. Dodds yawned.

"Are the people full of work about you, Mr. Branksome?" he asked, suddenly.

"Better than hereabouts," was the answer. "They are not starving."

"Well for them," said the clergyman. "But I suppose it will not do them much good, they will spend it all as it comes."

Then all the ladies lamented over the improvidence of the working classes.

"They might have a word to say for themselves if they were here," Mr. Branksome said, sharply.

"Oh, Mr. Branksome, is it not right for them to save? And do they do it?"

"But what is the 'word'?" Mrs. Dodds asked.

Mr. Branksome sat up suddenly.

"Look here, I have worked hard all my life and have no hope but to go on working. I have never been able, and I don't expect to be able, to keep starvation from my door with all I can do. All my life, pleasure and comfort and hope and leisure have passed me by. They have been within sight sometimes, and shall I never taste them?—not for one hour before I die?"

He had clenched his fist unconsciously, and looked, and dropped his hand. The row of ladies were looking open-eyed at him.

"Do you, or would you, act on those feelings, Mr. Branksome?"

"I don't know what I might do if I saw pleasure passing by and knew it would probably never come again."

Tears were in Maria's eyes as she looked full at him, not in the least expecting that he would take notice of her existence. But a moment after he looked her full in the face and her lids fell.

Mrs. Dodds asked Amelia Turner to sing, and she restored the dead level calm that usually reigned. It was a sweet voice and a sweet song, and Maria drooped her head to hide the tears that filled her eyes. Here was a pleasure, and she was leaving it, perhaps never to have the chance of enjoying it again. Should she spend her little means in trying to keep up intercourse with those around her? Was it the last time? She would have liked to ask this man that appeared to know something about it.

As she walked up the lane to her own house she was followed by a man's step until she looked round in self-defence, not against any danger, but against fear. She would rather the man passed her, and stood aside to allow him to do so.

"Shall I see you home, Miss Bell?" said Mr. Branksome's voice, and he offered his arm.

"Oh, thank you, I have only a very short way to go."

"So I know," he said. "I know all about you."

"Really!"

"Yes; I have heard of you ever since you came to Repton. You seem to me to be worthy to hear about, so you must not think me over curious. You have shown great courage and patience, and I have watched you with more interest than you are aware of."

"Indeed! Why me particularly?"

He hesitated.

"Because," he said at last, "I have built my hopes on finding such a woman, and the longer I know her the more the hope grows."

"You know very little about me."

"I know all about you."

"You have imagined half of it."

"Then give me the chance to know you better."

As she did not answer, he asked—

"Is that too much to ask?"

"The thing is impossible," she said.

"How impossible!"

"The customs of the country do not allow it."

"Hang the customs of the country! Did you ever know any rules of that kind that had any sense in them?"

"I intend to abide by them."

"You cannot! You cannot throw away the chance that may bring you the greatest happiness of your life. I speak seriously, it is not conceit!"

It required great charity to believe it anything else. Maria gave no answer.

He bent down to her, pleading gently.

"Let me try, Miss Bell; remember it is not so strange to me as to you. Ever since I came to Repton I have watched you. I thought when I first saw you that you would be my heart's darling, my life-long friend; and I have never seen anything since to make me change my mind. You have kept your quiet way as no one else would do, and every action of yours has been better than others would have done in like case. Now, I will give all the world to win you; let me try. I grant you may well be frightened at such a proposal, but let me try to make your acquaintance! I will never speak a word but in truth and soberness; and I say again, you may have a chance to secure a happiness for life. Perhaps not; we may differ, and you may warn me away. It shall but cost you a wave of your hand and I will go; but, with this prospect before you, is it fair, is it reasonable to talk to me about the customs of the country?"

They stood at the little green gate, and a footstep was heard approaching.

"You are right," she said; "it may be such a chance. But it is not within my reach; it is too far away."

"It shall come nearer to you," he said, stooping to her, and then he went his way.

She took out her key and opened the door, struck a light— for matches were just invented—and with that went upstairs to bed, for she had resolved before leaving the house that it would not be necessary to burn a candle long after her return.

"Why are we so often called upon for a decision?" she asked herself as she lay down. "Here am I again in opposition to the world in general, and must decide which opinion I will follow. Well, I am not sorry I followed my own opinion last time; I think I'll do it again."

She asked Miss Everard next day who and what Mr. Branksome was, and heard that his grandfather—Miss Everard always began a generation or two back—came into the neighbourhood long ago, that the son was a clever man who ruined himself by new inventions, and this one had done a remarkable thing. He had paid away almost all he had as 'prentice fee to a clever engineer, and was just now free from his apprenticeship. "And then," she said, laughing, "he did another. He went to work at a guinea a week! He said he could not afford to wait. And there is nothing doing just now, you know; but when times mend there is no doubt he will get on."

"Get on! get on!" Maria repeated. "But what kind of a man is he? Will the world be benefited by his getting on, or himself only?"

"Judge from what I have told you."

"Well, perhaps it will."

Then the rest of the company was discussed, and Maria described Mr. Branksome's energy in defence of the thriftlessness of the poor.

"Do you know he was half right?" she said; "I have felt it so sometimes. It seems as if our position were not so much in our own power as we are apt to think it is. We may do our best and wisest and fail after all."

CHAPTER XII.

"Quips and cranks and wanton wiles,
Nods and becks and wreathed smiles."

It happened when Sarah had been a year and a half at school that an accidental conversation changed the current of her thoughts and set her imagination a-going again for something to wish for. She had been content and happy with her school work, and the books that Miss Bell occasionally lent her, and with the singing to fill up the evenings and all her spare time. But only on Saturdays and on the few holidays could a real good meeting, from five to nine or thereabouts, be held at Sykes's; and to make the best of this Sarah gave her utmost efforts. When John brought word that Sydney had got some new music and the Flocks's were coming, Sarah went about the living-room that she had to clean like a flitting bird, and was generally at liberty to help Harriet before the afternoon was half over. Harriet, too, began making the house uncomfortable with such energy that old Sykes took himself off immediately after dinner, and Sammy was told he ought to do the same.

"Sammy, ye're i' t' gate," she said, as he stood by the fire and she brought water to put it out.

He moved away, and asked, quietly—

"Worn't Sarah coming to help ye?"

"What are ye doing here?" she said, by way of answer. "Go into t' warehouse."

At this moment Sarah opened the door by putting her two hands against it, and announced herself by exclaiming, "I'm comed!"

Harriet looked round.

"Why, then ye can begin and sweep down. I rubbed t' chairs yesterday."

Sarah began by putting all the chairs into the middle of the floor, inverting one over the other; then she swept the walls and floor, driving Sammy about from place to place.

"What are ye doing here?" she asked, looking at him with a kind of astonishment at such folly; "can't ye go into t' warehouse?"

He moved patiently out of her way, and said nothing.

Then she brought a pail of water, and, kneeling down close to his feet, suddenly flooded the floor all round him.

"Sammy, ye're i' t' gate, I tell ye!"

He went to the table.

"I'se be there i' now."

He turned his feet on to it.

"Sammy!" cried Harriet, "are ye putting your boots o' my clean table?"

He stretched them over the end of it.

"Sarah," he began, quite undisturbed, "I thought now you go t' school ye'd get too proud to clean up!"

"Why, Sammy, ye allus wanted me to go."

"Well."

"No thanks to ye, then, if I don't get proud."

"And what's all this going to t' school for?" he began again.

"I know nought about it. Ladies goes and pays ever so much for it. It mun be like to be worth summat."

"Can they addle ten shillings a week with it all?"

Sarah shook her head and looked thoughtfully into the fire.

"Sarah," said Harriet, "get t' floor washed."

"Well, if ye're so far forward just put t' chairs round for me to wash i' t' middle."

Sam gravely began putting the chairs against the wall.

"Now then, Sarah, what does lasses go t' school for?"

"Sammy, what did ye go t' school for?"

"Why, to learn to addle my living."

"An' what did ye learn?"

"Reading, writing, counting, an' such like."

"Do ye get your living by that?"

"I get my living by wool sorting."

"What does ladies get their living by?"

"Nay nought, bairn. They get's it gi'en."

"Ye talk like Aunt Jane, 'at can never gie 'em a good word. What do they do when nobody gives 'em anything?"

"Starve, I reckon, if they willn't take to washing floors, an' fettling grates, an' such like."

Harriet had lighted the fire and hung the brightened kettle over it, and then began to dust the chairs and arrange the furniture.

"How you have set these chairs!" she exclaimed. "That old one should go behind t' dresser and this by t' door; it's t' brightest i' t' lot."

"Ye mun talk to Sammy; he sided 'em. I reckon he'd never seen 'em afore."

"Men does such things," said Harriet, as if the animal were incorrigible.

Sarah sprinkled sand on the floor, and Harriet set the street door open, according to the universal healthy custom. The house looked fit for the fairies to come and dance in by the flickering firelight. Sarah left them, and sauntered slowly up the "Town Gate" to tea. When she returned with John she found a number of people come to take part in the concert.

"Eh, Sarah, lass," said one of these, "so ye've begun going to t' school."

"Aye," said Nancy's brother Zachariah, "tell us what ye do there, Sarah."

"I've done nought so much," Sarah said. "I've gotten some things to learn."

"And what ha' ye to learn?"

"There's geography."

"An' what's that?"

"Nay, I know nought about it. It's t' names o' all t' places i' t' world, an' where they are."

"An' whatever mun ye learn all that for?"

"Why, I reckon," she said, doubtfully, "if ye wanted to go there, ye know, ye could—"

"When ye want to go tull a spot, ye ask t' way, an' when ye get there, I reckon ye know where it is."

"An' then there's history."

"An' what's history?"

"It's all about t' Romans."

"What, i' t' Bible?"

"Nay, they were a lot o' wild folk, by what I can make out, 'at lived ever so long sin'."

"They could never have nought to do wi' us then?"

"No, so far as I can see."

"An' what do ye want wi' them, then?"

"I know nought about it."

"Sarah, lass, whatever do ye do it for?" This came after a moment of grave reflection. "It's well ye haven't yer living to earn, an' can lake at what ye like!"

"Ye don't know yet what's to come on't," Sarah said.

"Do ye?"

"Nay."

"Ye'll never see ought come on't, and then I reckon ye'll start o' something else."

"Why, I 'st be like!" (meaning I must).

"I think," said Sydney, "that if you let all those things alone, you will have all the more time to enjoy the good things that fall to your share."

"Ye'll never look as far before ye as to-morrow, Sydney," said Sarah. "Ye'd like to have all ye like, and to do nought till you get soft."

"I'd like that sure enough, but I would not get soft. It's doing what they don't like that makes folks soft."

"Sarah means that if we never look forward we shan't do much."

"She's well off o' you to say what she means."

There was a little laughter at this, and Sarah looking up, exclaimed—

"Why shouldn't he explain? He's got more sense than ye!"

She looked round without understanding as the laughter began again, for Sarah was one that never understood an innuendo. Then Sydney took up his fiddle and began to abuse all that respectable class of people who care nothing for music, maintaining that if everyone cared for and appreciated it all the world would go well. Old Sykes laughed at him, and the company generally dissented and even disapproved. Sydney thought this very unjust, for though he disliked work he did not think he lived in a land of cockaigne. He only hoped that he himself might escape the common lot, and, with his share of talent and education, he might certainly have maintained himself without much trouble if he had not indulged in expenses which made his life a series of contentions between his idleness and his honesty, in which it was suspected his honesty was getting the worst of it. What could he do? The necessary was, to him, more than he had, and the idea of altering his definition of the necessary did not occur to him. Those whose poverty had constrained them to work all their lives, and who were incapable of forgetting their habitual fears, took great credit to themselves for the virtue of industry, and thought meanly of Sydney because he did not undertake from choice the labour that for the present he could avoid. To work habitually requires a training from youth upwards, and Sydney did wonders considering how strange the habit was to him.

It was in singing that he regained his superiority. When he whistled and fiddled, and sung, and talked about music and musicians, he was the cock of the walk, and everyone listened to and believed in him. There was no end to the pieces that, under his direction, they tried to sing and play, and,—if the pleasure they gave to themselves was a criterion,—with perfect success. At every pause a conversation began, which seemed to have accumulated during the singing. Question and answer, repartee and rejoinder, flew about among the dancing notes without confusion or discordance. They pronounced each new piece "grand," and immediately began something else.

A cloud at times passed over their merry talks of late. Some-one would accidentally mention that So-and-so was out of work, and then there would be a talk as to his family, and if any members of it were working. Often they were, but latterly this was no longer so. Then there were mills that had stopped working, and others that were going to do so, and others working half time. The looms stood idle in the cottages. The cloth could not be sold. All the low country was under water. There was no chance of a harvest, and people were burning ricks i' t' farming country; the poorhouse was full, and the people starving that would not take refuge there.

Sarah knew that Miss Bell's pupils had dwindled away to half-a-dozen, and that the number would be still further diminished at Christmas. In their own house at home their mother talked of being ashamed of any expenditure for luxury or pleasure. Their custom diminished, and they were not sorry, for it was chiefly on credit. Old Miles knew not in many in-stances how long he might have to wait for his money. Sarah had begun to quarrel with Sydney's everlasting optimism, which she saw arose from a wish to ignore all unpleasant sub-jects rather than a belief in the coming compensation. The certainty that such seasons had passed before comforted them not. A twelve-month was too long to look forward to.

Sarah's gloom was not on her own account. She knew that her father, as well as old Sykes and a few more, were able to stand such a bad time; but she was of too sympathetic a nature to be able, like Sydney, to shut her eyes to what was going on around her, and especially to the future prospect. Above all, it disturbed her to find that among the elders there was no reference to any future means of improvement. "They'll ha' to bide it," was all they could say, and they said it with gloomy faces.

Everyone's thoughts were, more or less, occupied with the same thing—how the people were to get bread for the next twelve months. The assembled singers feared not for themselves, but for the neighbours and friends who would pinch and starve around them.

"Well, Sarah, what are ye a-thinking of?" old Sykes said, in one of the pauses aforesaid.

"She's thinking o' t' bad times," Sammy answered for her, "aren't ye, Sarah?"

"What 'casion ha' ye to think o' t' bad times?" Harriet asked. "Ye can go to school through it all."

"There's summat they hev' to learn at school about a woman and a box," Sarah said, tumbling out her words, as usual, without any attempt at arrangement; "but I don't think they learn much how to cure the evils of life with it all. Seems to me that all 'at them wise folk does is just to talk about 'em, an' then say how well somebody or other has said it before."

"Evils of life! Sarah, lass, just tell us what ye're after."

"Jove gave a box to a woman with all the evils of life in it, and with hope at the bottom."

There was a pause.

"Now, I think we may bear all the evils of life if we have hope that we can mend them, but not without."

Another pause. Then someone said—

"Well?"

"Well, I think hope is pretty well all we have in the world."

"Why, Sarah, you're fair down. Have you no hope, I wonder? What is 't ye want?"

"Do ye never want nought, Sydney?"

"An' so ye've no hope! an' ye think ye're worse off than other folk?"

"I said nought about other folks. I think I'm ill off."

Old Sykes took his pipe out of his mouth—he did not often do it, and began—

"Sarah, ye're a fine lass, but just take a word of my advice. The world is full of good things, but there's very little for each one of us; and to want more than falls to our lot, is to get hold of the worst evil your old woman had in her box."

"Seems to me if you are to wish for nought, there's no hope. There's nought in the world but all it's evils."

"Seems to me," said Sydney, "if ye'd pitch yer old woman out o' t' door, box and all, ye'd be better without her. What's t' use o' hoping for what ye cannot get so long as there's something to be had, an' all handy," and he took up his fiddle.

They laughed, but Sarah could not leave the subject.

"Did ye never wish for nought 'at ye could not get?" she said. "Ye wanted a chapel once. Ha' ye gotten it?"

The laugh was more general now, for the walls of the new chapel, just risen above ground, were familiar to them all, standing neglected and ruinous looking.

"T' will's good enough to build it, as good as ever it wor. If t' hard times had not come we should ha' been agate now."

"Aye, there's allus summat."

"Ye get that o' Miss Bell, Sarah. "Ye uppery folk has never no pluck. If we had had a place built for us, an' t' parson's wage beside, we should get on a deal better, for sure. They want nought for their worship, doesn't t' church folk, nobbud folk to go to it."

"There's folk goes to it."

"Aye, for sure there is; about t' quarter o' t' folk i' Repton reckon to belong to 'em, an' not t' half on 'em gets inside t' church doors, an' then t' parson wants a new church to reclaim the worse than heathen in these benighted districts!"

The sudden lapse into dictionary words and well-pronounced English produced an effect quite indescribable.

"Well, do you reckon there will be anything so much more Christian i' your new chapel?"

"If our minister goes about slandering his neighbours i' that fashion, we'll sack him before t' week's out."

"It caps me what ye want a minister at all for! It's never to teach ye ought! If he told ye ye did ought wrong, ye'd sack him!"

"If we were Church folk, we'd never go near him at all!"

"Aye, aye!" said his father, "t' one's much like t' other."

"What are ye starting o' running down t' chapellers for? I've heard ye say many a time 'at Christianity would never ha' been known i' t' country if it had not been for t' chapellers o' one sort an' another."

"I've known men who have borne witness to the truth when there were few to do it—aye, and suffered for it, too. And I believe the seed they sowed has flourished and come to good. And now when every man has got his Bible, and can preach what he likes, without let or hindrance, up starts a young jackanapes wi' a fiddle, an' another at things he can sing, an' they mun get agate to teach folks religion."

"T' oud times is allus t' the best wi' ye. I wonder what we shall come down to afore ye die!"

"I cannot tell ye, but this is sure—it needs hard work to get up, but we go down o' wer sens."

Thus it was that half unconsciously there was kept alive among the young people a notion of something higher than riches, something better than success. They appeared to care little about it; it was, perhaps, sometimes rather in their way, but, had they come to doubt of this higher life, they would have found a light gone out of their world. After such an evening there was little pleasure for Sarah in sitting opposite to the Miss Whites and exchanging scraps of news, about which neither of them cared a pin. There was a nobler tone in the conversation at old Sykes's than either at the milliner's or the minister's. Amidst all the outspoken fun and idle laughter in the sanded kitchen there was a scorn of meanness, an Ithuriel spear for detecting falsehood, and a sense of brotherhood in the truth.

Sarah's youth and hope rebelled utterly against the decision of the elders as to her future destiny. What! There might be little for each one, as old Sykes had said, but why should it be a sin to ask for more? The worst evil of all! No, no, it could not be! There were those in the world who had more, who had money "to lake wi'," and plenty of it. Why should she sit down in poverty, and give up hope for ever? Could one but learn how!

She had hoped much from Miss Bell and the school. But now she began to see that Miss Bell was as ignorant as herself.

Most of her pupils were gone, and Sarah saw the signs of pinching and poverty in the mistress's house.

It had become a custom between Sarah and her teacher to have a talk after the rest of the pupils were gone home in the afternoon; and at these times Sarah would question Miss Bell as to the use of learning.

"Are you no wiser than you were two years ago?" Miss Bell asked, somewhat puzzled by her pupil's questioning.

"Why, for sure I should be," Sarah exclaimed, recalling to mind the child that thought the best use for money was to enable her to "slide down t' hill," without having to wash the kitchen floor first. "I should be, but—"

"But what?"

"I am not wise enough for what I have to do and to go through."

Miss Bell pondered.

"No," she said, "none of us are. But you have learnt to value wisdom, and with age you will get more."

"Where?" Sarah asked, emphatically, as if she would fetch it that moment if she only knew where from.

"By reading wise books and thinking for yourself," the teacher answered, and thought her reply was not worth much.

Sarah took it in, however.

"Of course," she said, "it is not to be got all at once. I must try."

And with that she said good-night to Miss Bell; and this lady took her frequent evening walk, and told Miss Everard of the girl's oddity.

Sarah went home, and thought over her past life as she walked. She saw with what labour and care and self-privation she had been shielded from the common lot of poverty—how her mother and father had worked and saved for thirty years that she and their other children might have enough. They had won so much that even now famine did not come near them. Sarah's own lot, with which she felt so discontented, was one of the best among all the class that she knew. Was there anything more to be done by learning? She could not see it. But, again, her mother had wished her to learn; there must, therefore, be something in it.

Maria had another subject of conversation with her friend the same evening. It had occurred to her that, with all her caution, she had actually made the same mistake that Mr. Turner himself had recommended to her to make. She had taken a house much beyond her means.

"I really only want two rooms," she said, "and here I have five! I ought to sell some of the furniture, and take a smaller house." But Miss Everard was so much disturbed by the proposal that the two came to no conclusion. The old leaven still lurked in Miss Everard's heart. She was ashamed by the exposure of poverty that would be made by selling old furniture. Maria hesitated, and promised to wait yet awhile.

Her doubt was put an end to by the appearance of her landlord the same evening. Maria saw him coming, and thought: "Why, I have paid my rent. He thinks, perhaps, that I shall not be able to pay it next term, and he will be in time."

She opened the door for him.

"No, he would not come in. He had just a word to say." He stammered a little, and then said: "These were hard times. No doubt but she would feel them so as well as others; that houses were cheaper now, but he hoped she was not thinking of leaving. He was come to lower the rent; he did not want her to leave. Of course, half rent was better than none. He did not mean that it would always be so. But now, you see, I am glad to get anything. I'll let you as cheap a house as you can find anywhere."

Maria had difficulty in keeping back a burst of tears. She said she should be very glad not to leave, and then he suddenly turned round and took himself off, for it was not his habit to spend his time in useless talk. Maria mentioned her good fortune to Miss Everard, who said it was not unusual for landlords to lower the rents of cottages in hard times. "You see they are all going into smaller houses, and two families into one house, and even for that they will put off paying the rent, knowing very well they will not be turned out. They will, perhaps, pay in better times."

Well might Maria echo Sarah's remark that she was not wise enough for what she had to do and to go through. For while her prospects looked so dark a brighter path lay smiling within her view. Might she take it or not? She recoiled utterly from taking advice on the subject. "It is for me and me only," she thought, "and I must decide alone."

Mr. Branksome had written not long after the visit to Mrs. Dodds.

"I told you I did not care a pin for the customs of the country. But for fear I might grieve you, or cause you pain in any way, I have resolved to abide by them. I intend you to make my acquaintance by letter, and I promise you to be as sincere as I know how. In this, the most important matter of my life, I dare not be other.

"I have watched you for long. I went to Mrs. Dodds' because you were to be there; and I thought from what I knew of you that you were the woman I am seeking for, whose thoughts and principles would so far suit me that I could build my hopes upon them. I intend to learn how far we differ, and how far we can tolerate each other. To me this is the most important matter of my life, and, I venture to say, to you too.

"I beg of you to answer me. If you cannot let me entertain a hope, and signify that I should leave you in peace, I will do it. Only in obedience to a wave of your hand I will step out of your way. But do not, pray do not, turn from me for such childish reasons as the customs of the country, or any other dictates of senseless custom. I venture to say the thing concerns you. It is the most important of your life. Consider it so, and you will not hastily decline to give me my opportunity. If it is not, I will accept dismissal."

Maria took a pen, and answered while the impression of his absolute sincerity was still upon her.

"You are right. It is the most important question of my life. I grant your request, and promise you sincerity."

Then he began to write to her, giving an account of himself. How he had no relations, being an only son; how in his child-hood he had known the worst kind of poverty—that which must hide itself; and how he had always resolved, as soon as he was his own master, he would submit to no such fetters. In the long isolation of his boyhood he had brooded over the future, while his father, morose and solitary, had suffered and kept silence; how they spent their lives in the vain attempt to keep a secret that everybody knew, and how at last when his father died, glad to be rid of the weary burden of life, he threw it off at once, and stood a free man, but almost penni-less when he had paid his apprentice fee. That time was over, and perhaps now there was a prospect. Perhaps,—he could not tell yet, but he believed in honesty and industry. He asked for his lady's opinion. Might he have one approving voice to carry in his heart while he waited in the darkness?

She studied all his letters. She wrote always her approval, or her sympathy, or her pity for his present anxieties. She had no opinion to give as to his prospects, but was sure that he was in the right way so far as honest industry was concerned.

She said little of her own lot, but took it for granted that his future looked brighter than her own. So they went on, each keenly noting the other's admissions and innuendoes. The man saw plainly the suspicion that lurked behind her civility, and did not resent it. Perhaps he even approved of it, and would not have had her otherwise.

CHAPTER XIII.

IN THE VALLEY OF THE SHADOW.

As Christmas came nearer the young folks began to look forward to a merry-making of some sort, and the elders to throw cold water on all projects. There could be no such thing as merry-making even for those who had the means. People were afraid to show their comforts or to appear at their ease. Mrs. Miles had given leave for a quiet meeting at her house to sing hymns and such like. She had reduced the style of living before the end of the year. The family ate oatcake instead of wheaten bread, and spared the butter to it. For them there was no fear of want, but there was the general poverty. "I dare not be seen eating Christmas cake," she said, and her husband agreed. He had resolved to give over trusting a month before Christmas in order that people might not find themselves pulled up too suddenly. He laid in no stock and let his bare shelves be seen, and most of his business now was to stand behind his counter and say "No" to his customers.

He came into the house from the shop in a moment of leisure and sat wearily down, wondering how long it would last. In a few minutes a knock on the counter summoned him back again, and he rose unwillingly to go.

"It's a woman! Go thee, lass," he said, turning back again; "go thee, lass," and his wife went.

"Mrs. Miles, can I have a bit o' meal?"

It was Mrs. Willans.

"Nay, I cannot, Peggy. T' master says there's to be no more trust."

"I wouldn't ha' asked you, but our Pal will get some wage to-night. She has but two days' work i' t' week now an' to lake four. But you know she cannot go to it if she's to clam while Monday, Tuesday." (Monday was Christmas Day.) "An' t' master's gone beyond Baumforth ten miles, 'cause somebody telled him there's some work to be had there. An' ye know if he gets it we's t' ha' summat to eat—an' summat to pay for it wi'," she added, as Mrs. Miles stood immovable.

The two women faced each other for a minute. They had known each other all their lives, through many changes and many sorrows. Then Mrs. Miles turned round, while Peggy watched her with wide-open eyes.

"I wonder what's to become on us all?" Mrs. Miles murmured, as she took up the broken plate that served for a scoop, and brought it full of oatmeal to the counter. Mrs. Willans hastily spread out her apron.

'Say ye nought about it," she whispered.

Peggy nodded her head, with quivering lips, and hurried out. Then Mrs. Miles shut the shop door and retreated to the fireside. Sarah, who had seen the whole transaction through the door ajar, sat down too, scared and silent.

Mrs. Willans went across to her own house. It was nearly empty, and she was alone in it. Her two eldest daughters had tried the experiment of going to place. They knew nothing of the work they would have to do and did not intend to adopt the profession permanently, but they were willing to work hard and to bear all the scolding that their inefficiency was sure to bring upon them. Most of the furniture was gone. They had lived on it and on the two days' wage that their remaining daughter had earned until now. Now there was little left to sell, and the house mother was driven to her last expedient. The truth was, she hoped nothing from her husband's journey, and, therefore, would not delay till his return, for then her plea would be gone. He had made many such, and she had always encouraged him to go on the slightest hope presenting itself. It was a relief somehow, now there was nothing to come home to. She took off her apron and put it, with the meal in it, on the window sill, where it was hidden by the table. Then she went out to look for her husband and daughter.

It was dusk when the man came home, and his wife saw by his face that he had got nothing. She followed him silently into the house, where he sat down by the dying fire.

"There's nought," he said, looking at her. " 'T wor all goan afore I got there."

She looked out of the window. The man got up again.

"Ye've gotten some meal," he said, looking sharply round.

She turned round and faced him, but said nothing.

He smelt like a dog, and then going straight to the table laid his hand on it at once.

"Ye sall n't have it while t' lass come home. Ye may have it between ye when she comes."

For a moment he looked wolfishly at her and then went wearily back to his chair. Then he crouched over the dying fire and shook with cold, and perhaps despair. Neither of them noticed Sarah coming in until she said—

"Ye've been to—"

"Aye."

"Ha' ye gotten ought?"

"Nay, nought."

Bitter anger was in his heart, he knew not against what or whom. The girl was half aware of it, and soon sidled out of the house. She did not enter the shop, nor yet the house door, but went past them into the yard, where she filled a basket with coals, and set it on the wall, while she climbed over. Then carrying it into Willans' house she announced, in a business-like manner—

"Please, mother's sent ye some coals," and proceeded to put some pieces carefully on the fire, and to empty the basket into the skep that stood near.

The old man neither spoke nor moved. Sarah had intended sitting down again, but she was afraid of him. He stooped towards the fire, holding his palms to it. The melted snow had run from his well-worn shoes into the chinks between the flag-stones. His parched and blackened lips were drawn apart from his clenched teeth, and the grizzled hair and half-grown beard made the sunk cheeks look white. Mrs. Willans touched her as she went past, saying—

"Thou'rt a good lass, Sarah," and Sarah hung her head and escaped to her own home.

Twenty times she looked out to see if Peggy Willans had lighted a candle, which she knew would not be done till her daughter came home. Wages were often paid in those days in the evening and the shops were open till Sunday morning. "They'll get something to eat then," she repeated to herself, for she knew the oatmeal would make porridge for all three. It was near eight o'clock before she heard the Willans' door open and saw the light she looked for. Then she sat by the fire more contentedly.

The family sat with little interruption from customers through the dreary evening. Earlier than usual Miles told his wife that he might as well put up the shutters, for the light was burning for nought. Just as he rose to do it they were startled by a knock at the house door, and the moment after it was opened and Pal Willans stood on the mat.

"Please, mother says will ye come to father? He's taken bad and we've been for t' doctor."

She stood looking at them, unable to say more.

"For t' doctor, heve ye?" and old Miles got up.

A doctor in such a house at such a time was as sure a signal of death as an undertaker. He left them without a word more.

"Sarah, go ye to bed," said her mother, to which she answered with surprise—

"Nay, mother."

"Well, put t' candle out then."

And so they sat till midnight. John, half sleepy, half sulky, told them from time to time details of want and hardship amongst the neighbours, or some signs of evil in the distance.

"They're setting t' stacks a-fire again i' t' farming country," he said; " 'cause they've nought to eat they think other folks sall n't have."

"Why, what good can that do?"

"How sud they know? There's summat wrong somewhere. An' let them 'at's taken t' job of overlooking find it out."

"I reckon they don't know so much more nor we do."

"They're keen enough o' hindering other folks fro' melling out. They sud do it reight their sens."

"Why, would ye be melling out?"

"I couldn't do war nor they do."

"Who is it 'at does it, John? and what do they do?"

This was a child's question—past answering.

None of them thought of eating, though it got to be eight hours since their last meal. Their real hunger gave vividness to the tales of privation they were discussing. And their cold and gloom seemed to enwrap the world. An hour after midnight a footfall passes the window and the house-father opened the door. His wife looked at him. The two young ones stood up.

"He's goan," he said, and sat gloomily down.

"You might ha' sent for me. But I reckon there were nought to do?"

"There were lots o' folk; there's allus too many."

"What were t' matter? Did t' doctor say?"

"Cramp in his inside. I reckon ye know it wor t' want o' summat to eat."

"She came an' got some meal this afternoon."

This was a consolation to both of them.

"Happen t' lass got it and t' oud woman."

"Nay, she'd ha' none. She can clam like a dog."

"He were allus a hard-working man! He's worked all his life, and couldn't get on, an' this is t' end on it! And we were lads together! There's surely summat wrong when such as he wor cannot live."

Sarah looked at him with surprise. She had never heard her father blame the unknown authorities of the land before. It was always the people's own fault if they did not thrive.

"What's wrong, father? And why don't they put it right?"

"Aye, why don't they, bairn!"

"I'st never be a bairn again," Sarah repeated, when she laid her head on her pillow.

She had lived so far in a world in which were many pleasant things, and where more were to be had for the earning. Now she opened her eyes and saw that work, lifelong work, was the destiny of nearly all mankind, and possible starvation besides.

"Is this all that life has for us?" she questioned. "To fight hard as long as we can, and then lie down and die? If we get a trifle in a good time, then comes a bad one and takes it all away."

She remembered how in the days long past, when she was a child—about two years ago—she had said to the old man now lying dead in the next house that when she was a woman she would work hard, and save up her money and get rich, and the quiet laugh with which he had answered, "Aye, do bairn!" Now the wisdom of recklessness was revealed to her, the bold indifference that says, "Why not take what we can get, before we lose it? To-day is ours, and we can do nothing for to-morrow."

When, after a sound night's rest, she came down too late for chapel, the same train of thought was still afloat in the house. A neighbour was standing by the table where Mrs. Miles was washing the breakfast cups. Her father sat by the fire. Even John was not gone to chapel.

"They laid him out about three o'clock this morning," her father was saying. "He's above six feet, and was as able and honest a man as there is i' t' town. Allus wor. Whose ever fault it is that such a man cannot live, they've summat to answer for. A body might as well turn reckless as to bring up bairns to such a life!"

When all the people were gone to chapel, Sarah went across the road. The house was swept and tidy. Mrs. Willans and another woman sat at the round table, and within the closed curtains of the bed lay the house-father. The strange length of the figure, the upturned feet, made him appear to belong already to another world. The women uncovered the face. The lips were still parted, and the teeth still clenched. But Sarah thought she had never before seen the old man's face at rest. She let the tears follow each other down her cheeks, and walked away without a word.

"How was it you were not at chapel, none o' you?" old Sykes asked in the evening.

Sarah told him the night's history, and then asked him how it was that some people could get rich, while some people could not live?

He thought it was because some people took more pains.

"We all take pains. We do nought else but work from morn till night, when we can get it to do."

"Aye, sure enough we do. I'm none o' them that lays all t' blame o' all 'at goes wrong on t' Government, but I think it's a hard case when a man cannot live by working."

"Is it Government that hinders them?"

"Aye, for sure it is!" Sam broke in. "They've done all for theirsens, an' nought for nobody else this many a year. Think o' reckoning 'at we're to send members to Parliament 'to deliberate for the good of the people' "—Sam pronounced these dictionary words with scornful emphasis—"and sending them from places where there are no people! There's many a spot where there are happen two, happen twenty, and they'll start up and send their two members to Parliament! And many a town with a hundred thousand folk in it has nought to say tull 't."

"And what ha' they done it so for?"

"Don't ye see, they can easier manage twenty folk nor a hundred thousand; an' then they've nobody to ask no questions, nor to say nought tull 'em. They can do what they like."

"An' will all t' towns, big an' little, ha' to make up their mind afore it can be mended?"

"Aye, an' their agate on't, too."

"An' how long will it be? Till I am an old woman?"

"Aye," said the old man, despondently, "how long will it be, Sarah?"

"I'll go to place," she said, following out a train of ideas that everyone understood.

"Aye, that's right, Sarah! Look ye to doing your own work. I cannot say that you can live by working, but I'm sure you cannot live without it. Look you out for something to do."

"There's better things than going to place, though," said Sam.

"What is there, Sammy?"

"Why, there's singing."

"How can folk get anything by singing?"

"There's plenty o' folk gets a good deal. There's Miss Raines, at Baumfurth, 'at was at t' Miln five years since, an' now she's half a lady."

"How did she frame?"

"She learnt, for sure."

"It'll take a lot o' brass to learn!"

"Sure enough it will."

"I'll go to place," she repeated, thoughtfully.

She has reached the age, or at least the time, when she stood face to face with the great problem of existence, how was she to live? She had hitherto expected that it would be enough when the time came to do as other people did. But it appeared that other people sometimes died of hunger. She began to have a great respect for the forethought and kindness that had secured for her oatcake on the creel, and a roof over her head. It was not everyone who could do so much for their children.

"Ye'll ha' given over trusting i' t' shop, Sarah?" old Sykes asks, watching her gloomy face.

"Aye, father says we munnot trust no more."

"Aye, right enough."

"An' t' folks is clamming!"

"An' ye'll ha' to clam too, if you trust 'em all."

Monday was Christmas Day, and the corpse in the Willans' house was but like the visible representative of the misery in most of the others. Mrs. Miles went down to the Sykes's in the dark on Sunday evening, and said quietly—

"Ye'll come up to morn. We mud as well be together," to

which the old man agreed, and Sammy, resolved not to have a mourning meeting, gave a hint to Sydney to find his way on some excuse with his fiddle.

There was at least the appearance of mirth inside the house which he entered on Monday night from the slush and snow outside. Mrs. Miles sat in her corner; the other elders were near the fire; Sarah and Harriet at their usual place in the window-seat, with sheets of music in their hands; John and Sammy sat in the middle of the floor, and several voices were heard at once.

Sydney advanced gravely, hat in hand, and shook hands with his hostess, which ceremony ended the company manners for the evening. It came to be understood the young folks were to have their own way in their own fashion, and when he had nodded to the two old men, Sydney walked up to the young ones asking—

"Now, what have you picked out?"

"This, an' this, an' that to begin with."

"What is it you're going to give us to begin with?" asked old Miles.

" 'Christians Awake.' "

"Aye, that's right; but cannot ye sing 'Vital Spark?' "

"Aye, for sure! We'll sing 'em all."

And so they did, and some of them twice over. Then they asked Sydney for more, and he sang song after song, or rather scrap after scrap—some comic, some pathetic—which were praised or damned as unceremoniously as if he were a theatrical performer.

"Ye've no patience at all," he said. "If you'd only listen it comes out grand!"

"It isn't grand, man. It's right faal!"—foul meaning ugly.

"Why, then, I've got one of my own. Will you have that?"

They all voted by acclamation for that.

"Why, then, don't run it down before you've heard it. It's a bit o' your sort," he added, nodding to old Sykes.

"Why, then it's a reight 'un," he responded. He expected some comic thing that would ridicule his serious preaching,

and prepared to take it in good part. After a proper amount
of coughing and tuning, Sydney began, looking him in the
face with warning gravity—

> "What'll you do when you come to be old?"

A general burst of laughter interrupted him. The words
and the look were an exact copy.

"Why, how can you listen if you laugh like that! Go on
again, Sidney."

> "What'll you do when you come to be old?
>   Fiddle and sing?
> I'll walk with a crutch when I can't go without,
> If I haven't a lodging I can't be turned out,
>   And I'll always fiddle and sing!"

"That's noan o' me," said old Sykes, amidst the laughter
that would not be silenced at the end of the verse.

"That's ye," said Sydney, emphatically. "And this is—"
He nodded towards old Miles.

> "What'll ye do when you're hampered wi' debt?
>   Fiddle and sing?
> I'll leave my old debts standing out in the cold,
> And as for the new ones I'll let them get old,
>   And I'll always fiddle and sing!"

"That's ye, Sydney! That's just ye!"
"Nought o't sort! This is me:—

> "What'll ye do when your money runs short?
>   Fiddle and sing?
> I'll call on my friends and be happy together,
> If we can't help ourselves we can help one another,
>   And always fiddle and sing!"

"That's ye, sure enough."
"Have ye nought for Sammy?" somebody asked.
Sydney turned towards him.

> "What'll ye do when ye're left to your sen?
>   Fiddle and sing?
> I'll choose my own gate like a sensible man,

> And then frame and get it as fast as I can,
> And I'll always fiddle and sing!"

Amid the talk and laughter that followed, old Miles looked anxiously at his wife. They had both heard footsteps and murmurs beneath the window, and both understood that the people outside were probably without much food or fire at home. They grew half-ashamed of their mirth, and at the first pause Mrs. Miles addressed them—

"Now, lads, I've nought again a bit o' laughing, but I think when there's so many folk 'at's nought to laugh at, in these hard times, maybe we have had enough of it. An' somebody lying dead i' t' next house an' all. So just give us a hymn or two, not to make so much noise."

"We've done all t' hymns."

"Let's go down to Aunt Jane's and sing 'em all over again?"

"Aye, away wi' ye! let's be shut on ye!"

So the troop turned out, headed by Sarah, who had made the proposal, and took the middle of the road, for the causeway was narrow and the night dark.

"Aunt Jane, we're comed to sing ye a song."

"That's right, Sarah! Come in all on ye."

The silent house was in trim order and "silver clean." Aunt Jane sat by the table with her Bible before her. As there were only two more chairs no one thought of sitting down, but ranged themselves in a row facing the old woman.

"It's him 'at's made it," Sarah explained, pointing to Sydney; "and there's a verse for everybody."

So Sydney had the triumph of drawing a laugh from the old woman, who seldom laughed. The very sight made the young ones uproarious again. When at last there were no more jokes to be made, Sarah announced that she had got another verse.

"I made it mysen coming down t' loine," she said.

Sydney played and she sang.

> "What'll ye do in a house o' your own?
> Fiddle and sing?
> I'll make a good fire, and I'll put on the pot;

> If there's nought to put in it I cannot help that.
> I can always fiddle and sing!"

The praise was not stinted to this effort either. When it subsided Sydney looked at Sam in a way that made Sarah say—

"Now, Sydney, you've got some more."

"Well, there is some more, to be sure," and he whispered to Sam, who fell behind, and laid his hand on the door latch.

> "What'll ye do at the end o' your days?
> Fiddle and sing?
> We must all of us leave it, whatever we do!
> Never mind!—in the heaven that I go to,
> We'll always fiddle and sing!"

"But ye willn't sing that song here! ye graceless lot!" and Aunt Jane got up and looked about for a weapon of offence; but the words were scarcely uttered when Sam flung wide the door, and the whole laughing troop were in the street. As she went to shut it she heard Sarah's ringing voice about the laughter—

> "Never mind!—in the heaven that I go to,
> We'll always fiddle and sing!"

They were in far too high spirits to think of going home again; and when somebody exclaimed "Let's go to Nancy Flocks," the whole company turned round at once and set off in the new direction. It was only a mile off, and though the night was as dark as pitch and as cold as ice, it did not rain. They sang something—not hymns—to shorten the way; and, finishing the last as they stood before the door, it was opened for them.

"We're comed to sing ye summat."

"Aunt Jane's turned us out!"

"We're like to give you a stave."

"We want ye to help us to tune up a bit."

If the reader has paid proper attention he ought to be able to assign these sentences to their proper speakers.

Perhaps—for it is not certain—Zachariah Flocks was master of the house. But, besides his wife and baby, there sat by the fireside his brother and sister, for though these two had another house of their own, they spent most of their time—the

one in helping the wife, the other in enjoying the society and
comfort made by the women together. The brothers were good
singers, and Sarah and Harriet always liked them to come and
to hear their own voices above the tremendous noise they
made. These people now made them welcome, and there was
some furious music. Sydney's composition found great acceptance, though it soon became recognized among them that the
principal merit lay in the words. These raised roars of laughter, in the midst of which baby woke up and joined—to another tune. His father took him up and hushed him without
success, the mother held out her arms for him.

"Sit ye down, lass," said the father, "I'm bahn to hug (carry)
him mysen," and, as the child squalled, he roared at him in
a tremendous bass—

> "Never mind!—in the heaven that I go to,
> We'll always have plenty o' this!"

A version which brought out more uproarious merriment and
more squalling. Then the mother got up with a will of her
own in her face, a thing which so astonished her husband that
he yielded up the infant at once, saying penitently—

"There, then."

The girls got up, observing that it would never be quiet
while they were in the house. So they said good-night, Sam
explaining that they were like to go back for t' oud man, an'
take him home wi' 'em.

They went more silently homeward. The spree was over,
and it was sleepy time. But when they were near the house,
Sarah, who was first, faced round and said—

"Let's go into Willans'!"

"What, wi' t' coffin i' t' house?"

"Aye, and sing, 'Vital Spark.' "

Without a word they turned, went up to the door and
knocked.

"Please we're come to ask if we may sing 'Vital Spark of
Heavenly Flame,' if ye please."

It was not Mrs. Willans who had opened the door, but a

neighbour woman, and she turned round to ask the widow, and then invited them in. The room was in the chillest order, with a modicum of fire in the grate, not sufficient to keep the cold from the door, but the visitation had attracted help to the house. Some friends had undertaken to beg of the mill-owners and charitable people, and whatever the pressure on their own finances at such a time of trouble, they had not refused a shilling or two for such a case. Mrs. Willans was in decent mourning, some of the furniture was come back again. Through the opening of the drawn curtains the coffin was visible beneath the white sheet. The large mushroom top of the single candle cast a shadow like a presence on the whitened ceiling. The party ranged themselves in a row before the window; the men, holding their hats on their hips, stood straight and silent for a moment before they began. Singing much within the capacity of their voices, and accustomed to sing together, the music appeared to be absolutely spontaneous, and the words were spoken as by one voice, only at the line—

"Lend, lend your wings; I mount, I fly!"

they raised their heads a little, and increased the volume of sound, as they could hardly help doing. The widow, with her face in her hands, sobbed without restraint. The singing ended, and there was silence for a moment.

"We wish you good-night, Mrs. Willans, good-night, good-night, good-night," and the party disappeared and closed the door.

They all entered the opposite house in silence and sat down.

"Ye've been singing 'Vital Spark' over there?" Mrs. Miles asked.

Someone said "Aye."

"That wor reight."

'And where else ha' ye been?" old Miles asked, with forced gaiety.

"We've been to Aunt Jane's, an' Nancy Flocks', an' we've sung lots o' things: 'Sound the Loud Timbrel,' an' 'Hallelujah,' an' 'Glorious Apollo,' an' 'Amen,' an' plenty more."

"An' I reckon they had to turn you out?"

"Nay, not so bad as that, but t' bairn started o' roaring (crying), and so we were like to go."

"Why, for sure."

Then old Sykes rose, and good-nights were interchanged, the holiday was over, and Sarah laid her head on her pillow thinking there were fearful things in the world, but she would have courage yet. It is a question whether we are wise in sheltering children so carefully from the knowledge of suffering or misfortune. Their buoyant youth can bear it, and it brings wisdom with it that nothing else can give.

The conversation of the elders had been gloomy enough. They had known more than the young ones, and they saw little hope. Besides the certain evils of want, there were unknown dangers to be feared from the remedies proposed. It is as easy as talking now to say that if there were no restrictions to prevent it, the labour of the starving people would bring them bread from all the world; everybody understands all about it, or thinks he does, but in those days the egg had not been broken, and it seemed the most difficult thing in the world to make it stand on end.

The only thing apparent to the anxious watchers at that moment was the imminent danger of anarchy from the determination of large numbers to have a change of some sort. Every authority was questioned, and from questioning to resisting there is but a step. True, it was no one's intention to make it, but it was doubtful at that time if discussion would be permitted, and as people were determined to discuss, rebellion seemed inevitable. Add to this all the deteriorating influences of poverty, the increase of vice and crime, the class hatred, the fierce self-assertion that poverty makes necessary, and it will be owned that to well-doing and well-wishing people the future looked fearfully dark.

But with the history of these times, this tale has little to do, and the state of the country is only mentioned because it overshadowed the opening life of "Miss Miles."

CHAPTER XIV.

THE TUMULT OF THE PEOPLE.

To most people of these younger days, it will seem as if the description of misery and famine here given was exaggerated and sensational, but the older generation will recollect well enough how often such times came half a century ago, when a bad harvest could bring poverty to the most careful and industrious, and for the greater number there was no prospect but the workhouse, or actual famine. There was a time when one-sixth of the population of Leeds were "on the rates," when small thefts of food were severely punished on the express ground that the severity was necessary, to protect property from the starving people; when few people could thrive and not many keep their position, and for women to earn their living was almost impossible; when the phrase, "relapsing fever," was invented, or became common, for an illness that arose oftenest from want, and when the cases in the Edinburgh Hospital, usually about two hundred or two hundred and fifty a year, rose to over three thousand. These poor people would go home cured, and return again in a few months, ill of the same complaint. In all classes was the same poverty, the same hopelessness.

And now when March, cold and biting, was come and gone, and spring seemed to have forgotten to bring summer with her, when there seemed little prospect of a good harvest, and no hope of a better trade, old Sykes sat in the gloaming by his fireside alone, and thought sadly of the present, and the probable future. As usual the presence of misery brought back into prominence the recollections of other times equally miserable, and the spots of sunshine were hidden by the gloom. How often had he seen the like, and though his lifelong exertions had put him and his family beyond reach of famine, would it always be so? Would they struggle as successfully as he had done? "Our life is but labour in vain," he said, almost aloud.

> "Alas for love if this be all!
> And nought beyond, O earth."

Then he thought of his hopes and his consolation: he had prayed and struggled for the right; would they hold fast to it as he had done? He had striven to give them the one thing needful, but the brotherhood that had stood by each other had passed away. At first, by the help of a little persecution, and a little social ostracism, they were kept together; but now some were dead and some were fallen away, and the very few remaining faithful had learnt that the tares were not to be separated from the wheat till his good time. They could not refuse their countenance to those who made profession, but neither could they give their intimacy to those with whom they had little in common, and they withdrew in silence and let the world go by. Their chapel had been superseded by a larger one, and their assembly by one held together by a thousand motives, who justified themselves and condemned their neighbours with confident authority, worshipped the letter instead of the spirit, paid their tithe of mint and cummin, and knew of nothing else that they had to do. The old leaders hoped that he would not leave himself without a witness in Israel, and trusted there was still faith in the land, though they themselves saw little of it. They did not wish to dictate. They would go with anyone who was striving for the right, not one mile only, but twain. To his own master he standeth or falleth.

"All t' low country is under water," he heard, as some one passed the door. And soon there followed the sound most pleasant to a father's ear—the children's feet. His stalwart son crossed the threshold, followed by a small troop of young men like himself. Sarah and Harriet came quietly behind, conscious that the only way of hearing anything of what was going on was to remain themselves unnoticed.

"Come in, lads, come in," Sam cried; and seizing the poker he struck the coals into a blaze, and crouching on his heels with his shoulder to the light, he displayed a newspaper and held it up before the fire light. As people passed the open door he now and then called one or two who joined the discussion on the usual topic.

"Eh! what ha' ye got there? What have they to say about it?"

"Dunnot ye mell on it?" said old Sykes.

"But we're like to mell on it! As if a body could help melling on't! What are we all coming to?"

"Just ye listen here, I've seen folk shot down i' t' street for coming together, an' ta'en away and hanged for less than that. Keep ye quiet, I tell ye."

Sam held up his newspaper to the fire light and began to read:—

"We should be very sorry to think that all respect for law, and all intention to uphold it, was lost to the people of England. We prefer to believe that we have too many timid, or at least over-cautious, men among our rulers, who start at the sound of danger, or look forward too far into the future for the possible consequences of what they have to do. For what do these people tell us? What are we required to believe in order that our statesmanship may win their approbation? They would have us alter the very framework of our constitution at the bidding of a crowd of wild, ignorant men, whose very language is scarcely English, whose poverty has prevented them from acquiring even an outside varnish of civilization. These men are going to hold meetings forsooth, or rather they have done so, and will do it again; and having met, they will be harangued by certain demagogues and would-be rebels (they have already made alliance with the arch-traitor O'Connel, though they hate above all things both his countrymen and their religion), and will signify that they desire to take part in the government of the country."

"That's ye lads 'at isn't varnished wi' civilization!"

"The old boroughs of England that were rich and civilized when Liverpool was a marsh, and Manchester a village, are to lose their rights in favour of places peopled by a collection of vagabonds gathered from all quarters for the sake of work and wages."

"Where did ye come thro', lads?"

"We are not blaming them for herding together. Let them seek work and do it, and by all means let them have their wages for it when done! To them, as to other Englishmen, are given the blessings of peace and security, of equal laws and free institutions. But let them not meddle with the roof that shelters them, lest they pull it about their ears, or rather—for we cannot afford to let them try the experiment—lest they learn the penalties of riot and rebellion."

"There ye are, lads. Ye've free institutions, but yet munnot meet nor mak' no speeches."

"We must speak plainly. Hesitation and cowardice are going to leave us at the mercy of the brute force of the country: nay, wily politicians are preaching that it is our duty to yield to it. They have such a large population! and for this excellent reason half-a-dozen spinners or weavers or what not are to come from Leeds, and Manchester, and Halifax and join the counsels of the nation! They, or at most their fathers (grandfathers there are none), have scraped together a little money, so they take off their aprons and propose to employ themselves in law-making.

"Once more we protest against the folly, the wickedness of the arguments to which we have referred. As we have shown, the parts of England that are most populous are not, therefore, to govern the country. That they have made money is even a still worse reason. Ignorance with a swagger in it is, if possible, worse, more objectionable, than ignorance without it. If the money-grubbers wax fat and kick, let them be kept under with a tighter rein and a stronger arm. Let us not be told that we are to go to destruction because they are minded to take the reins."

"There's for ye, lads."

"It seems we've gotten nauther sense nor conscience! It's all by favour that they let us work for our living. If we've ought to say, there mun be a tighter hand and a stronger arm."

"I wonder which is t' strongest?"

"We may happen try."

"Whatever ye do, lads, keep ye quiet. Ye'll rue, every man on ye, if there's a hand raised!"

"Aye, for sure. If we had not more respect for law than them that says we've none, we could raise fire through one end o' t' country to t' other."

Old Sykes stood up and told them all to go to bed, not without fear that the discussion had already gone too far. Harriet followed Sarah out and joined her on the road.

"Sarah," she said, "there's t' grand meeting going to come off; they're agoing to all t' places round about. Our Sam's been to Baumforth an' all over, an' they're all to meet at t' top o' Swanston Moor. An' they do say," she added, doubtfully, "that if they're all i' one mind they can get what they want."

"An' what do they want?"

"There's folk coming to make speeches an' tell 'em."

"What did not they tell 'em for at Baumforth?"

"I know nought about that."

"Then they're just going to get a lot o' folks together an' get agate talking! I think nought on 't."

"But, Sarah, Sam says there's to be a band o' music thro every town 'at's got one, an' flags, an' everything."

"When do they start?" Sarah asked, "and which way do they go?"

"They're all going to t' top o' Swanston Moor, and Repton will march"—imitating Sam, who imitated the authorities—"in time to meet Broughton and Swanston at the cross roads, each with their band and banners."

She looked at Sarah, and saw the infection had taken.

"Say ye nought about it. What day is it to be?"

"Why, to-morn, for sure."

"Say ye nought about it. When they get reight throng we can do what we like."

Her father and mother were talking when she entered the house. They held their peace as she came in, and she did not ask the subject of their discussion.

Next morning Sarah looked up the street and down, and saw there was something unusual afoot. Small knots of people were talking on the road, strange men stood at the doors of public-houses; now and then a flag was waved and disappeared again. Sarah re-entered the house with an air of childish indifference and said not a word about anything.

Tantara! tantara! rang through the street as she was washing the breakfast cups. The towel shook in her hands, for she knew that "Repton was marching." She let the train go by without so much as looking out of the window. Her father went out at the house door and her mother went into the shop; then Sarah quietly took the bread and butter into the milk-house and went out at the back door into the yard. Thence she climbed over the wall into the field, and was soon under the high thorn hedge that separated it from the road. She crept between two ancient stems and watched the band, the men, and finally the rabble of boys, women, and girls that followed.

"Now, lasses!" she shouted, jumping down the bank.

"Eh, Sarah!" was the greeting she received from all, each one anxious for countenance and sympathy.

She ranged in line, and marched to the music like the rest. There was a sharp morning and a merry wind, and the tramp of men before them gave them a sense of power, as if they themselves were making all the noise.

There was a sudden stop of both march and music; the women parted right and left to see what was the matter. Looking forward towards the head of the column Sarah saw Sammy Sykes on horseback, his horse wet with foam from hard riding,

and his face dark with dust and fatigue. He was talking to
the men at the head of the column, and waved it forwards as
Sarah looked.

"Now, order, lads; order afore all things. Dunnot shout
when anybody's speaking, and strike up when ye come up wi'
Broughton and Swanston. And— Sarah, whatever are ye doing
here? Get ye away home wi' ye!"

"Go home yer sen, Sammy," and raising her curled hands
to her mouth she blew a loud tantara-ra-rara that made the
men look round and raise a shout of laughter.

Sam's face flushed with vexation.

"Now, order, lasses, order!" he cried, with angry gestures.
"Shout when other folks does. Cannot ye be content wi' that?"

"Aye, aye, Sammy, we know! Nobody mun speak but ye!"

Sammy swore—at no one in particular. Then he turned his
horse round back towards Sarah, and stooping down whispered
to her—

"Sarah, keep ye wi' t' Repton folk."

"Go ye home, Sam, and wash your face."

The women's attempt at marching had thrown them so
much in the rear that they gave over laughing and shouting
and took to running to regain their position. Then the music
ceased and they trudged on in silence. Soon a whisper ran
through the crowd, though why they should whisper no one
knew. There was a burst of music to the right and an answering burst from before, and another from the left, and then
the shout of a multitude that overpowered it all. Broughton
and Swanston had joined. Somewhat awed, if not frightened,
the boys and women hung back on the outskirts of the crowd,
and ran on in eager silence more interested than ever. As they
went up the hill the women with infants and the younger
children dropped behind and were left. When they reached
the moor the boys gathered furze branches and waved them,
shouting, "Hurrah lads, hurrah lasses!" The morning air, the
breathless exertion, the echoing crowd before them made them
wild. They would have been ready to leap off the end of the
world. The broad hill-top was capped with a dense mass of

men murmuring, struggling, and shouting, and above them, seen against the sky, were a dozen or more who seemed to be standing on the shoulders of the rest. All faces were turned towards them. As Sarah came up she was subdued by the earnest looks around her. Whispers ran through the crowd and a long hush went over it like a wind. Stooping under the elbows of the motionless men she made her way into the midst of them. She heard a murmur before her and an answer from those around her. Raising her head to look she saw a thin, anxious-looking man almost in rags, facing the looks of all the rest, and repeating to them what he had heard from those before.

"English workmen are the best workmen in the world; they have the most sense and they can work the hardest. And what for? Was it right their earnings should go?"

"Aye, aye, aye!" burst from the men around her. "A fair day's wage for a fair day's work! We want no more."

"Whisht, lads; whisht!" and they were silent again. Sarah raised her head to look at the man. He had no coat nor hat, and stood with folded arms and his back to them, now listening, now and then turning round to retail what he had heard. Beyond them Sarah caught sight of the people on the platform, one of whom was gesticulating and apparently speaking, though not a sound reached her.

"What are ye doing here, lass?" said a man, grasping her arm. "Keep ye at t' outside."

"Aye, aye: keep ye at t' outside, lass," and quickly passing from hand to hand she found herself in the open air, baffled and rueful. She wandered round among the scattered groups until she perceived that the main crowd had somewhat altered its position and that there were comparatively few behind the platform, all having pressed forward to the front of it. Creeping up as near as possible on this vacant side, she saw the four waggons on which the speakers stood, and could distinguish their gestures. Still she heard not a word, and there appeared to be no organized means of communication on this side. She pushed forward until close to the waggons, and then stooping crept beneath them. She heard a loud but inarticulate voice above her, and an answering "Hear, hear" that burst in front and rolled outwards till it died away. There was a moment's silence, and then the speech went on. Desperate with curiosity, Sarah crept from under the shelter of the waggons and came suddenly within the scope of the voice.

"Are honest men to toil like this to keep up the rents of the landlords? Is it to be tolerated that a base aristocracy should make laws for their own profit, and take the bread that you've worked for out of your mouths? Are the men that have done this still to control the legislation of the country?

> "Know ye not,
> Who would be free themselves must strike the blow!"

A shout answered him that shook the ground. Turning cautiously and raising her head, Sarah caught sight of the speaker, with folded arms and closed lips watching the wave of excitement that he had just set in motion. In his large head and shoulders, his square jaw and defiant, uncivilized face, Sarah recognized something akin to her own people, which she understood. "That's one of them that can do it," she thought, referring to the problem of life in general.

A strong hand was laid on her shoulder.

"Get thee out o' t' gate, lass, be sharp!" and she was pressed down under the waggons again. Creeping out on the vacant side she drew the hair from her hot cheeks, and found herself face to face with three Repton girls.

"Eh! Sarah, ha' ye been in there? Wornt ye flayed?" (frightened).

"What are they talking about?" she asked, in return.

" 'Bout Church rates," said one.

"They're going to petition," said another.

"They sud petition for somebody to find out why there is not enough to eat," said another.

"Oh! I say, lasses, let's go home," said a fourth.

Sarah entertained the proposition, but unwillingly. She

looked at the eager, surging crowd, at the silent clouds above them, and the wide rolling hills spread out all round. But then she was hungry, and there was nothing more to be heard. Suddenly a Repton girl came up with a loaf in her hand, exclaiming, "Look here, lasses, who'll ha' some bread?"

The non-Reptonians stepped back instinctively, whilst the four or five fortunate acquaintances pulled the loaf in pieces and began to ask for water. Someone said there was water in the beck in the wood over yonder, and the troop set off. There was a wall to climb and hazel bushes to push through, and again some of the girls raised a cry to go home. "We're lost! we're lost!" they said, sobbing, as they crept through the high underwood. "Keep on down t' hill," Sarah urged, "we're like to come to summat." At the bottom the bushes had been cleared away in order to remove some felled timber, and the lopped trunks lay here and there on the ground. In spite of the leafless season, the sheltered place, the glancing water, the spiky green of the young grass made them all happy. As they sat munching their bread they were soon all laughing without knowing why, except that one of them picked up a chip and offered it to her neighbour, asking in mincing tones, "Would you like some roast beef to your bread? Oh! do take a small piece!" And all the others began to do the like.

"Nay, ye cannot make a fine speak! Sarah can do 't! Sarah, just do Mrs. Eldon a bit."

"I say, I wish you'd do them folks 'at's speeching just now!"

"Aye, do Sarah, lass!"

"I think nought on 't," said Sarah. "If they'd tell ye summat they'd be something like."

"Never heed. Just do 'em, Sarah."

Sarah jumped on to a tree trunk, and, facing her audience, began—

"King, Lords, and Commons—"

"Nay, that isn't it. It's 'Gentlemen.'"

"I tell you it's them that has it to do! Miss Bell says so."

"It's allus 'Miss Bell'! It sud be 'Gentlemen'!"

"Keep agate, Sarah! Never heed which on 'em it is!"

"King, Lords, and Commons—You that has everything that you want and can do what you like! Of all t' petitions 'at ever you got, this should come first an' get done! We want helping, and this is what for: We work all day and every day. We begin before we're grown up and we never leave off till we die. We know nothing about nothing, and we'll do anything in the world 'at ever you tell us just for two things—for bread to eat, and hope for to-morrow! We're oft short o' bread, and there's little hope in the world; an' if ye can't do better than this we mud as weel do for wer sens."

"Eh! Sarah, ye can go on!"

She had raised her clenched fist in the face of the authorities. All the girls applauded. She herself thought well of her speech, particularly of the last idea, and was quite unconscious that she had only picked it up half an hour before.

"Look," she said, "at that grass; how straight up it grows! Let's build a house round it!"

It was a square yard or two of level ground by the waterside. Near it were some elder bushes, with their thick buds just burst. They gathered boughs of them, and enclosed the bit of level with a fence about a foot high. Then they found slender willow twigs of a pale yellow green, and set them round too, so that they bent over the enclosure, and laid white and coloured shining stones from the brook on the grass inside. It was grand, they all declared, and sought for more gay things to deck it with. A cluster of bright-coloured fungus was set in the middle, and some early buttercups hung in the angles of the elder branches. They got quite an affection for it, and began to lament that the men moving the tree trunks must tread it down. But as the sun got low the colours grew dim, and they left it at last.

They had some difficulty in getting out of the wood, as they went right and left round the hazel bushes; some of them began to cry and say they were lost. The sun was set, and it was almost dark. They had to climb the wall at a different place to where they had entered, and on the broad road there were fresh exclamations.

"Now, then, we are lost! Whatever is to come on us?"

"Come on home, to be sure," Sarah cried, not herself knowing where it was; but she saw men standing at a little distance, and went on boldly.

Scattered groups were listening to speeches where the serried crowds had stood in the morning. At last they caught sight of the waggons, and knew the points of the compass again. It was grey, dark, and desolate. Why is it that where men have been is so much more desolate than where there is no trace of them?

"I'm sure," said one, "there were enough men here this morning to do whatever they liked. All 'at's ever done in the world is done by men, and here were men plenty!"

"Aye, but if they did not know what to do?"

"They might ha' done summat!" which opinion of a fish in a frying-pan was fast becoming common in the class the speaker belonged to.

The sharp wind made them wrap their arms in their pinafores as they took to the road. It would have been dark but for the full moon lately risen behind thick flying clouds.

"Let's run, lasses," someone said, as they left the moor, and the valley lay dark below them. They set off down the middle of the road; but soon they found that there were heaps of dried mud that had been laid at intervals near the hedge, and it seemed to them much easier to run over all these than to keep on the smooth, so as they leaped forward from each little elevation they quickened their speed.

"Look there," said Sarah, "there's a star! It's scattering behind a cloud! It wants to get out o' t' gate. An' there's another! Go on," she cried, shaking her fist at them, "an' say we're coming!" Then she leaped forward faster than ever.

"Sarah, whisht, lass!" said several, in a low voice; "ye munnot talk so."

They had a kind of idea that it was irreverent.

Where the road turned down the valley to Repton, a high garden wall with evergreens above it depressed the gloom, and they gathered closer together and walked quietly.

"Couldn't all them men together ha' done summat?" one of them asked.

"It isn't men; it's sense 'at does things," Sarah answered.

"Why, do you think poor folks has no sense?"

"Why, then, it isn't sense; it's knowledge."

"There you are, wi' your fine words! What's t' good o' speaking different to other folk?"

" 'Cause I've something different to say."

"Aye, I'll be bun (bound) for ye. When ye get agate ye're allus a bit out o' your head!"

The lights of the Repton houses were in sight. It was enough to give a home feeling to the hungry and weary group. Sarah was one of the first that left them. She walked into her home with her mind too full to remember at the moment that she was a culprit, guilty of serious transgression. Her mother sat by the fire, as usual. There was a single candle burning on the table, and the firelight danced on the furniture—as usual! Sarah walked leisurely to the hearth, and turning round surveyed it all. It had never looked so to her before. Was it like *that* it looked to other people?—so small, so crowded! A lot of old dingy things that people could do either with or without, that she never thought of all day long, and certainly never wanted! What was there here to compare with the call of music, the thunder of marching men, the half-revealed mysteries of statesmanship, or even with the amusement of "biggin' a bower" by the waterside, and flying home in company of the elfin moonlight and demon shadows? She remembered how she had dusted the chairs every day, and made a point always of putting each chair in the place of the next adjoining one, so that, as there were six chairs, they all travelled round the room in a week. She had been pleased with this, and had thought it a fortunate arrangement of Providence that the number of days and the number of chairs should suit. Could she ever care for such a thing again?

"Sarah," said her mother, after a silence which she had meant should be impressive, "do you think it right to spend your whole day in such idleness? Ye'll make decent folks ashamed of you, running all t' day long after ye dunnot know what, an' what's naught to you! How could you fashion to do so?"

Sarah turned and looked at her mother as she had done at the chairs, with grave, considering face.

"How can it be naught to me?" she said. "Is it naught to me whether other folks starves or thrives, or lives or dies? Am I never so much as to ask ought about it? It is summat to me! An' if summat isn't done we mun do it wersens," and with this she walked into the milk-house, took a piece of bread in her hand, and went off to bed.

Anxious and weary, the house-father came back late in the night.

"Thank God there's been no bloodshed," he said. "I thought once there would have been. But they held their tongues, so 'twas as good as being all of one mind."

"Ye didn't see our Sarah there, I reckon?"

"See our Sarah at t' top o' Swanston Moor!"

"Aye, she's been there all t' day. I'm sure I don't know what I'm to do wi' t' lass! An' when I tell her to mind her own work, 'at she's nought to do wi' you, she looks at me as if she had never seen me afore, and says she has summat to do wi' it, for if nobody does nought we mun do it wersens!"

Old Miles suddenly raised his hand to keep his pipe in his mouth, while his face relaxed into a broad smile.

"Well done, Sarah, lass."

"Ye call it well done, John Miles, 'at your own daughter should be running out wi' all sorts o' folk all t' day long!"

"Why, why, lass, never heed! She'll mend o' that. She'll tak' after her mother, ye'll see."

"But I'm sure I never did such a thing i' all my life!"

"Why, lass, why! it'll all come right, ye'll see. She's none so bad, isn't our Sarah!"

With which consolation she had to rest content. She did it the more easily, as it was secretly her own opinion.

The next morning all the excitement and confusion in Sarah's mind yielded to the desire for the accustomed pleasure of telling her mother all about it. She sidled about her, helping to light the fire and skim the milk, and get the breakfast ready, seeking an opportunity that nothing but her own consciousness prevented her from taking. At last, when, after breakfast, her father and brother had left the house, she took her courage in both hands and exclaimed, without any preface whatever—

"Eh, mother, but it wor grand yesterday!"

And for the life of her the mother could not help responding—

"Wor it, lass?"

So she heard the whole history of her daughter's proceedings, which was at least an indispensable preliminary to setting things right. Then she told her she must never do such a thing again.

"I tell you, Sarah, I will not have it, not never, at no rate."

Very few times in her life had Sarah been checked so sharply. She tossed her head half-restive, half-frightened. But Mrs. Miles had the uncommon wisdom to stop when she had said enough, and her daughter, not knowing what else to do, soon trotted quietly along the road appointed for her, and took it for her own.

She did not escape many expressions of astonishment from her friends at her outrageous proceedings.

"Ye 'at's been to t' school, and wants to be a lady, to start off i' that fashion! Why nobody like ye never did nought o' t' kind. Ye can never set yersen up no more!"

Luckily, monster meetings don't take place very often, or Sarah would have been strongly tempted to set these advisers at defiance, and most of all her sister Jane. Jane seemed to think her escapade a ground for continual iteration of her favourite teaching.

"Ye'll never learn how to behave, Sarah, till ye've been to place. It isn't schooling 'at ye want. Book learning isn't for girls. Ye want to learn how to behave."

For years Jane had preached this doctrine, but without knowing what impression it had made on her mother. On Sarah there was certainly none, but Mrs. Miles was not in the habit of declaring herself except by her actions.

"You should see how young ladies does, and then you'll learn. Why, Miss Turner sometimes does not go out by the week together, and never gets browned one bit. She has the whitest hands you ever saw, and she works beautiful," Jane went on, tempted by the attention Sarah was giving, and which the Turners had never inspired before. "You should see that cap she worked for Mrs. Overton's baby."

"Can't Mrs. Overton work caps for her own bairns?"

"Of course she could, but she won't let her baby wear caps. She says it's not the fashion now."

"Couldn't she tell her afore?"

"Afore what?"

"Afore she'd worked it?"

"She knew nothing about it."

"An' her 'at had done it, worn't she ashamed on hersen?"

Sarah always adopted her worst English when talking to Jane, and her dialect always grew particularly awkward when her sister held forth on polite life and behaviour. This made Jane mince all the more. She explained with great dignity that Miss Turner was not obliged to count the time she spent in working.

"Why, Miss Turner is working another one just now and it's to be given away."

"An' them 'at's to have it does not want it?"

"Oh, but they will be delighted with it."

"Couldn't they buy nought 'at 'ud do?"

"Of course they could, but it would not be the same thing."

"'T 'ud maybe be a deal better."

To which Jane simpered and said, with Turnerian accent—

"You foolish girl!"

"An' t' next one, what does she do?"

"Miss Eliza? Oh, she does a great deal about the house. Her mamma says she is a born housekeeper. The most useful one of the family."

"An' isn't t' others o' no use? An' aren't they shamed o' theirsens?"

"Ashamed!" said Jane, with immense dignity. "It's not their place to work like common people."

Sarah looked at her sister meditatively for a little while and then said—

"It caps (astonishes) me that they aren't stalled (tired) just wi' doing nought! What does t' youngest do?"

"Oh, Miss Amelia has not long left school. She is the most accomplished of them all, and her mamma calls her the belle of the family. Miss Turner used to be considered very pretty, but Miss Amelia beats her far away."

"But what does she do?"

"She goes on with her studies; she has had a first rate education. She has been to Miss Forbes'. Neither Miss Turner nor Miss Eliza went to Miss Forbes'. I've heard Mrs. Turner say she wished they had. Miss Forbes' school is the best school anywhere, and they are all very proud of her, I can tell you. Even Mr. Fred and Mr. Charles will go out with her. Why, Mr. Fred went making calls with her the other day!" and Jane stretched her neck forward and lifted her eyebrows. Then primming her mouth she said, mincing, "I foresee we shall have much more visiting in future than we have had. Indeed, Mrs. Turner has told me she is looking for another servant, because there will be more to do. Now, Sarah, there's a chance for you!"

In vain Sarah meditated. She could not see the concatenation of ideas that yet evidently hung together somehow. Amelia was the best educated and the handsomest, and the conclusion was, "there would be more visiting than there used to be."

"Well, I think I'll go," she said, thoughtfully, wondering if she could live in the same house with ladies, and find their doings as unintelligible as she did now.

When the door at which she had pushed so long suddenly gave way before her, Jane almost fell on her face with surprise. Even her mother looked at Sarah for a moment.

"Do you mean it, Sarah?"

"For sure I do."

"It's t' best thing you've said this many a day, Sarah," said her sister.

"Happen it is; happen it is not. I'se see when I've tried."

If her truant day on the moor had called forth remark, this step in an opposite direction did not retrieve her character.

"You that's going to be a lady!" was as good an objection to this move as to the last, so that Sarah wondered what mode of activity was open to ladies, when they could neither work nor play.

"Ye sud stick to one thing, Sarah, and not start o' learning all sorts, and then running wild all at once, an' then topping up wi' going to place."

"I'm going to try to be like our Jane," Sarah said, mincing so as to make them all laugh.

"Ye'll ha' summat to say for yersen whoever ye're like."

"An' ye can't bide that, 'cause ye've gotten nought yersen."

This was her last passage of arms with Sammy before leaving home. Jane proposed her to Mrs. Turner and sent her word she might come on trial, or rather on inspection.

CHAPTER XV.

OUT INTO THE WORLD.

THOUGH Sarah's new whim to go to place excited so much astonishment, she knew that she had the entire approval of both father and mother. It was their teaching, probably, that had unconsciously led her to take it. They were not obliged to send her out to maintain herself, they could, in fact, have lived without working themselves, but nothing could be farther from their habits and ideas than that their children should cease working on that account. If any better employment had offered itself for Sarah they would have directed her attention to it; as it was they would have laughed at the notion of losing dignity by work of any kind. If dignity could not take care of itself they would let it go. At worst, taking up an inferior trade was but "reculer pour mieux sauter"—a thing quite in accordance with their practical, sterling character. So Mrs. Miles gave the girl some instructions as to her dress and behaviour, and Sarah felt herself quite equal to the occasion. She was thinking all the while of quite other matters. Her duties seemed to her easy enough, but of small importance compared with the discoveries she should make when once within the gate of Paradise. As to what she should discover, how could she tell? If she had known it, she need not have sought! People pass their youth in that way! Forward! Where to? To what purpose, they know not; but forwards!

She observed the bright window of the lodge and the trim

gravel walk to the kitchen door, and then went with Jane into
the drawing-room to be introduced to her new mistress. She
let Jane go first to give her time to look round. The room
seemed to her enormously large, and the elderly young lady,
by a window in the distance, with some tanglement of thread
in her hands, seemed to be living in quite another country
to the old one, sitting by the fire doing nothing. Sarah studied
the younger one intently. She had a thin, sallow face, with
dark hair laid smoothly down each side of it; a somewhat
peevish mouth, and a slightly frowning brow, as if her head
ached, which it often did.

"This is my sister, ma'am," Jane said to the old lady, and
Sarah turned to examine her. She was very pretty. One small
hand was on the arm of the chair, and one foot appeared on
the stool. The lace round her wrists and neck deepened the
black of her satin dress, and softened the outline of the faded
features. The sadness of age was on her face as she sat looking
at the fire, and letting the girls stand a moment unnoticed.
Then she turned and said—

"Is it, Jane? What is her name?"

"Sarah, ma'am."

"Has she been out before?"

"No, ma'am."

"Oh, well, you can find her something to do till Miss Eliza
comes in."

"Yes, 'm."

And Jane went out and Sarah followed. They had not
reached the kitchen before Sarah began—

"Jane, wor that working or laking 'at she were agate on?

"Now, hush, Sarah! they'll hear ye!"

To which Sarah answered—

"An' what were they looking so faal for?" (faal—foul, means
both ill-tempered and ugly).

Jane hushed her again, and finally could give no information as to why her mistresses were "faal." Sarah had to take
patience, and to hope the veneration would come in time.

"I knew you would have to wait till Miss Eliza came in: she

always looks after things. The others know nothing about it. To be sure, Miss Amelia says she is going to learn. They will do some shopping now while they are out. But I fancy she will do more at calling with her brother than shopping with Miss Eliza."

Then Jane had to explain what calling was, and why the brothers went with her in the one case and not in the other. Sarah listened patiently, and drew her own conclusions, only affrighting her sister occasionally by irreverent questions. Jane's worship for the superior class was so sincere and so unreasoning that she took all as right that they chose to do. She was, therefore, very ill-provided with reasons for their proceedings, and was all the more touchy when Sarah required them.

"Sarah, you know nought about it!" she exclaimed at last; "ye must learn, and give over asking questions."

"I reckon t' young men's learning a trade?" said Sarah, by way of answer.

"The young gentlemen are with their father in the office," Jane said, with dignity. "There they are!" she went on, meaning the ladies. "They will be upstairs presently; straighten your hair, and mind you say 'Yes, 'm,' when you are spoken to!"

They heard the young ladies go into the drawing-room, and then come upstairs. Sarah watched them pass into their own room, but could not get a sight of Miss Amelia's face. As to the other one, she was not a very interesting person. House-keeping came by nature, and Sarah would have trusted herself to do it without learning. But what qualities, what gifts, natural or acquired, must Miss Amelia have to be the flower of the flock?

She heard them talk as they took off their walking gear.

"I shall go now and practice," said the younger; "I want to do some reading before dinner."

"Dear me! what a fuss you make over your reading! Why should you read at all?"

"Miss Forbes said I ought."

Amelia left the room, and Sarah stood where she could see her full front face as she came along the passage. She was a straight, lithe girl, rosy, fair, and smiling. She held her walking boots clear of her dress and passed with a level eye and purpose-like expression. The features were not absolutely regular, yet she was pretty. Sarah determined there and then to have some long talks with her, if by any means it might be accomplished. She went back to her work slowly, thinking how it was to be done.

"Miss Amelia says she is not going to dress much," Jane informed her; "she is going to wear quite simple things. But I guess how that will be; she will have to dress, I know! There's something ordered already, though she was not quite pleased, I saw."

Miss Eliza came in with a pair of sheets and a business-like face.

"Jane, is that your sister? Very well, you can keep her to help you, for there is the best bed to be got ready, and here are the sheets; and you must put water and towels in the blue-room, too, for anyone that wants. You need not uncover the curtains," etc., etc.

"Yes 'm! yes 'm!" Jane kept repeating, which was very civil of her, as she knew every item of the work to be done when a visitor came to the house, or evening visitors were expected.

"Mr. Thelwal will likely stay some time with us," Eliza went on; "and the house must be kept nice while he is here. The front door step must be washed before breakfast, and the gentlemen's slippers must not be left in the breakfast-room all the morning. And mind you have a clean apron on when you go to the door; and don't leave the kitchen door open when you answer the bell. Has your sister been used to waiting?"

"No, ma'am, she has never been out."

"You must let her help you at dinner, and you"—turning to Sarah—"what is your name?"

"Sarah, 'm."

"You must take notice and try to learn. Listen to what mamma says, and watch what is wanted."

This suited Sarah exactly, and Miss Eliza thought her a very willing, intelligent girl to answer so readily. In the next few days Sarah picked up the art of waiting at table, and making herself useful in a comfortable manner.

When Sarah Miles proposed to herself to make the new start in life she was not unqualified to produce a favourable impression on anyone wanting her services. Strong and straight, open-eyed and observing, quick and pleasant in intercourse, she would get on well with anyone, and be valuable to an active mistress. Besides all these qualities, she had many more of greater worth. She had been brought up in the strictest practice of a religious morality, with something of the self-denying self-control of Calvinism superadded. In fact, she had never known any other teaching, and very little of any other practice. With the minutest watchfulness her mother had guarded her from coarse brutality and cunning rognery, and the girl really believed that the world was full of people who were honestly fighting against poverty to the best of their ability. Some cases of lapse there were, of course, but she was rather of opinion that these people should be forgiven, and start afresh. Perhaps if they had been helped they would not have been backsliders. She knew how constantly among their own little community—not the whole numbers of the over-grown chapel, but the remnant that had stood the brunt of persecution—the weak were helped and encouraged. She knew that now there was serious help given to many, and among her elders it was acknowledged that their poor had a claim on those that were better off. She knew how, years ago, the father and mother of the thriving Flocks family had died, if not of absolute starvation, yet of poverty and its consequences; and how their brethren in the faith had stood round them, and helped them in the fight for life; how the young men, scarcely come to years of discretion, had been advised and trusted, and how their work had been successful. They had taken a colliery, and worked it chiefly themselves. The coal was near the surface, and the whole undertaking on a small scale. Nancy had been banksman, and the two brothers had worked below. It was not possible that such honesty and energy could fail. They were astonished themselves at the certainty and abundance of the reward of their labour, and were not ungrateful. Long since they had returned the money lent, and enlarged their concern. They were still of the faithful few, and contributed in their turn to the maintenance of their poorer brethren. They never thought it needful to polish their manner, or to alter their speech. Indeed, this last refinement would only have made them unintelligible to their neighbours. They made no change in their manner of living, except that there was always plenty to eat in the house. One of them got married, but they were still most of their time together, and seemed to want no other company.

They had enemies, to be sure, these kindly, quiet people. The sect they belonged to was out of favour, and looked on with evil eye. They were socially ostracized, a thing which did them a great deal of good, by cleansing them of all time-serving hypocrites. But thriving became a characteristic of the sect, as it does of all industrious, economical communities. Then their prosperity began, and the crowding votaries had to build a new chapel. A large barn of a place it was, and held more than half the inhabitants of Repton. And after this triumph began their decay, though they little thought it. They dictated to others, and quarrelled among themselves, and the elders who had passed through the fire gradually withdrew. They clung to their old friends, and were slow to condemn anyone, but there was sadness in their silence. They were acknowledged leaders, pillars of the chapel, but they did not govern the congregation, nor were things conducted according to their judgment.

The history of the people she lived amongst was thus well known to Sarah; and it made her more thoughtful, and indeed wiser, than most girls are at sixteen. She was brought up with the elders, and took naturally to their mode of thinking. But no harshness had ever checked her in her pleasures, for no unlicensed pleasure was ever permitted to approach her. She thought herself as free as air, because the steps she had to take were made pleasant to her, and she chose them because she liked them. Her open nature, and her utter confidence, made her mother aware of every thought in her head, and every feeling in her heart.

But it is difficult to describe the absolute ignorance in which the girl lived as to the class above her, and this ignorance was intensified by her refusal to believe in the few indications she received from Jane of the actual mode of existence going on in the great house, and the inferences that might be drawn from it. They who could put down a shilling whenever they wanted, she observed, who went about in silk dresses on occasion, who indulged in expenses of all kinds, that did not appear to be either useful or necessary; above all, who spent their lives in doing nothing—how different their lives must be to any she had known! And wherein lay the difference? What did they do, and think, and feel? And thus with the truth before her she persisted in seeking it elsewhere. She had often heard that wealth did not give happiness, that the rich had their troubles as well as the poor, that sorrow was the lot of man, that if we knew all there was as much happiness among the poor as the rich, etc., etc. But all this doctrine her vigorous vitality refused to accept. She hoped and believed that she could augment her stock of happiness by her own exertions, and utterly, though unconsciously, rejected the opinion that where we were put there we had to remain, and "therewith to be content."

It was this state of darkness that made her ask in wonder why her new mistresses looked so "faal." They had apparently everything they wanted, though they could only amuse themselves by sitting in a parlour and doing nothing!

She was rather more interested in Miss Amelia, and the beginning of her conversations gave her hope of something better. Amelia assumed at once the position of instructor, which the more wealthy classes almost invariably take up towards their inferiors. She earnestly informed Sarah that one ought always to speak the truth, to be industrious and frugal, etc., etc. Sarah listened approvingly, having all these commonplaces bred in the bone, and looked anxiously for something more. She finally concluded that there was a settled determination on Amelia's part not to communicate the rest of her learning. An absurd and obstinate belief took possession of her that there was something to be found out. She watched the family life going on before her without seeing any signs of what it was, and learning more and more every day that the people before her were commonplace and even vulgar souls. Amelia was an exception, it was true, and to Amelia she softened and fraternized unconsciously. She was the only one who habitually used the words "It is right," or "It is not right," as a reason. She alone was industrious, kindly, and, above all, cheerful; and, indeed, her cheerfulness brightened the house much more than Sarah knew. Her active will had more influence than fairly belonged to her position of youngest daughter and quasi school-girl. Even the young men let her have her way, and Sarah wondered at the position she took.

It was some days later than was expected that Jane called Sarah to the window to see the visitor coming with Mr. Turner up the garden to the front door.

Sarah studied the pair carefully as they came near. At first she admired Mr. Turner exceedingly, and was taken by surprise. She had seen him often. His usual look was one of lordly indifference, or of careworn abstraction. Now he was smiling, attentive, almost officious to the younger man. But his gracious bow, his occasional glance into the face of the stranger, had a most unpleasant effect on Sarah, who had never seen an old man so servilely civil to a young one before. Still more disagreeable was the younger man himself. Stylish, or rather foppish, sunk-eyed, weary, indifferent, he barely answered the earnest efforts to amuse him, and Sarah could only wonder that Mr. Turner did not leave him to himself.

Of course, the news was told at once in the kitchen, and the stranger was much discussed. The cook knew them well enough; there were two of them, an old one and a young one. This was the young one. He had been before. Yes; he was an admirer of Miss Amelia even when she was at school, and he would be again, she was sure. They would see. She knew well enough there would be plenty of gaiety; there would be a party, she was sure. Sarah asked what a party was, but made nothing of the information.

"Shall I fasten your dress, Miss Amelia?" Sarah asked, taking care to be in the way when the dress would need fastening; for in those days, as the dresses were all fastened behind, no lady could hook her own.

"Yes, Sarah, do."

And then would begin a conversation, for with the instinct of a talker Sarah would listen and never disagree; and Amelia, quite unconscious of the management, would teach, and explain, and inculcate as became a superior who had never learnt that silence is not always agreement. She talked of economy and simplicity in dress, and of the frivolity of the business altogether. She urged economy as if Sarah had never heard the name of it, and of receding quietude of demeanour, till Sarah, who had heard of such things all her lifetime, could have answered in her sleep. But more than this she did not learn. The practising, and the reading, and the French were to go on, and the early rising was added thereto; but nothing more could she get. She knew not how to formulate a question, and dare not have asked it if she had.

Her hopes were renewed when the party sat down at six o'clock to an elaborate tea. A late dinner was unheard of in Repton. They did their best to be merry, but only succeeded in showing that it was an effort to be so. Sarah wondered at the company manners of the two young gentlemen, but Jane told her that Mr. Fred and Mr. Charles could be fine gentlemen when they liked. Amelia opened out like a flower, and, encouraged on all hands, chatted, smiled, and sparkled, happy herself, and the cause of happiness in others. Sarah saw, as a looker-on always sees, more of the game than the players, more of the drift of the business in hand. To the rest of the company she was a pretty child, and they made her talk, content with any answer they might get. She, on the other hand, was—

if one could see the tragedy that underlies our amusements—
terribly in earnest. She was defending her conduct and her
principles with all her heart, and continued amiable and merry
only because she thought she was convincing the whole circle.

"So you'll be bound to get up at six o'clock every morning
because Miss Forbes said you ought?"

"It is not that, Fred, and I am not bound to get up just at
six. You know very well it is right to get up soon, and Miss
Forbes was right to tell me to do so."

"Quite right, Milly," said her father. "I wish Miss Forbes
would tell Fred so, and make him do it."

Amelia's eyes sparkled at her father's approbation, and she
saw not the irony of his remark.

"Miss Forbes is a great friend of yours, Miss Amelia?"

"She is the lady I was at school with, and she is very nice,
and Fred always laughs at me because I like her."

"Miss Forbes' school is certainly the best in our neighbourhood," said mamma, "and Amelia was her favourite pupil."

"No, mamma, I was not a favourite; Miss Forbes had no
favourites. She said she never would; it would not be just."

The last word, and the emphasis with which she pronounced
it, caused a general smile; the girl was so in earnest.

"Who'll hear your lesson for you, Milly?" Fred asked her.
"You will have to go over once a week to say them."

"If you make sure you know a thing there is nothing gained
by repeating it aloud," Amelia informed him, with dignity.
"And, besides, I am not going to learn lessons; I am going to
read."

For a moment her good humour faltered at the laughter
her declaration called forth. Her face cleared, however, when
Mr. Thelwal remarked—

"I think that a very good resolution, Miss Amelia. Have you
fixed upon a course of reading?"

"I—I know some books that I intend to read."

"You will read history, probably?"

"Yes, and French, and poetry, and Sir Walter Scott's novels."

"Have you read 'The Lay of the Last Minstrel?' "

"No, but I am going to when I have finished 'The Excursion.' "

"Do you know 'The Ancient Mariner?' "

"No; who is it by?"

The rest kept silence when Mr. Thelwal got so confidential with Amelia. They, too, seemed to understand each other, but no one else would have thought of mentioning poetry or novels to Mr. Thelwal. Yet he talked of them seriously, and as if he had read them all. Reading was not the fashion at the Turners', but now everyone who could recollect the name of a popular work mentioned it and passed an opinion thereon. Amelia, flushed and interested, spoke with confident warmth about all she knew, and asked eagerly about what was new to her. When tea was over she found a small table, and set to work vigorously copying music. Mr. Thelwal took a seat by her, and asked if it was for a friend.

"No, it was not; but it was very useful to copy music. Miss Forbes recommended her to do so."

Mr. Thelwal praised Miss Forbes and Miss Forbes' pupil, and took interest in her copying, and discussed her favourite pieces, and did not weary of her childish energy of phrase, while she worked away, reverent and happy, now and then catching Thelwal's eye as she looked up when he agreed with her opinion or roused her curiosity. Everyone left them to themselves, though everyone heard all they said. The brothers took up something to read and yawned over it; Miss Turner took her work and let the corners of her mouth drop gradually down; Miss Eliza was busy elsewhere; and Mrs. Turner, in her easy-chair, did nothing, as usual.

And many things Amelia and Thelwal talked of during the evenings of the next fortnight. The tone was given to the conversation by Amelia, though she herself had not the slightest idea of it. Sarah could see that he followed her lead and agreed with her opinions, sometimes with a covert sneer, which she wondered the elders did not detect, or, if they did, did not put an end to it.

"Of course," he would say, when Amelia reminded him that so and so "would not be right," and would reform his conversation accordingly.

Sarah grew angry in defence of the girl, and more angry with the mother, who looked silently on. Was it possible they could not see? The man sat there agreeing and disagreeing with absolute indifference to the truth. Amelia would look up suddenly when he contradicted himself, or propounded some careless or godless notion; and he seemed to make her look up very often. Then he would answer, quietly, "Why, yes, so we should, Miss Amelia," and go on again.

And what was he there for? Why had he come into the house? Was this the business, or was there some other? Was Mr. Turner bound to give him a daughter to amuse his idle time? for they all agreed in helping him to his amusement. Amelia herself began to think at last that she was calling back to his memory the half-forgotten principles that he really owned to, but somehow forgot now and then. It was the woman's duty, she told her mamma, and she performed it with a peculiar zeal. It ennobled her in her own eyes and certainly made her better, and more resolved to be worthy of her position of mentor.

"But one should not laugh at other people's misfortunes," Amelia said, when Thelwal had related how a young gentleman came to grief in consequence of a plot that Mr. Thelwal himself had laid for him.

"Well, but he was such a fool," that gentleman answered.

"Still less should one laugh at a fool; he can't help it, you know."

"Not laugh at a fool!"

She looked up at him quickly.

"No; do you think we should?" with perfect gravity.

"Well, no, perhaps not," seeing that she insisted.

She looked at him again, smiling.

"You know you should not," she said, and forgave him.

Sarah got deeply interested, though she heard but little. The simple rules of duty, and the earnestness with which they were laid down, charmed her heart. Their minds were in the same stage of development, and, perhaps, too, of the same natural tendencies. A noble line of duty attracted them, and they laid down the law, both to themselves and others, with confident certainty. Something of this unconscious feeling made a friendship between them. Amelia "took to" Sarah, and always found something to say to her; while Sarah developed a talent as lady's maid that surprised her sister, and made her declare that "she never could understand our Sarah, never!"

"Our Sarah" had a private opinion that she and Miss Amelia were the only two sensible people in the house, and that no one else in it knew what they were living for. The young men were her special detestation, the rest only merited her contempt; but Fred and Charles were actively bad. Their gentlemanly manners were not for home consumption, and when only their relations were present they revealed themselves as ill-tempered, selfish, and sensual. Their talk with their guest never reverted to any duty or to any principle whatever, and made such a contrast to that of Amelia that Sarah wondered why they did not interrupt her with a flat contradiction now and then. They submitted to their father and bullied their mother, and made it evident that they thought nothing of the two elder sisters because they were not pretty. Amelia they looked down upon, but tolerated. As time went on they began to show their impatience to their visitor whenever their father was not present, for if they indulged in it when he was there he would look at them and, perhaps, reprimand them in a frightened tone that was beyond Sarah's comprehension. Then they sulked with their father, and would not help him; she could see that, though without knowing what they should have done. Mrs. Turner laboured to keep peace, and altogether failed; the young men would not forego their indolence and their ill-temper. The old lady and the visitor, on the other hand, were on the best of terms, and would talk futile politeness to each other by the hour, and, it is to be hoped, found some satisfaction in doing so. No one else did, for the forms and the reality were clashing in the house and the atmosphere was unwholesome. Only Amelia seemed able to resist its influence, and she lived in a heaven of her own.

Night after night the mode of spending the evening was the same. In the morning the men left the house, and were understood to be very busy all day. Sometimes they would come in to dinner, and sometimes not; but they nearly always spent the evening in the drawing-room, in the very quiet amusement of listening to the conversation of two speakers; and Sarah was not the only one who took it for granted that a courtship and the conclusion thereto had been arranged beforehand.

" 'The Ancient Mariner!' " Amelia had repeated next morning. "I wonder what it is? I mean is it a poem or a play, or what?"

"Ask Mr. Thelwal," Miss Turner said, and thought that enough.

"But I want to know how to get it. Papa, how could I get 'The Ancient Mariner?' "

She spoke confidently, as one whose difficulties were always smoothed away as soon as she mentioned them.

" 'Ancient Mariner!' " he said. "What's that?"

"I don't know exactly. Mr. Thelwal asked me if I had read it."

She had learnt somehow that Mr. Thelwal was almost as important as herself in the household.

"Did he?" Mr. Turner said, and nothing more.

For Amelia this was a reproof. She blushed, and was silent.

But she had not quite given up her wish. She asked her friends privately, and as they knew nothing about it, she asked himself, and got some information on the subject. Yet it appeared he had never read it, and could not tell her much.

With all this talking Sarah heard of her wish, and told her "The Ancient Mariner" was in Coleridge's works. She had seen it. Amelia stared.

"What do you know about it?" she said, and then heard some account of Miss Bell.

"Miss Bell was a real lady," Sarah answered, "and she kept a school up the lane. Her mother used to live in Repton. She was Mr. Turner's sister."

Amelia very soon asked her mother why they none of them went to see Miss Bell. She had something of Sarah Miles' energetic faculty of making herself troublesome.

To the question her mother answered—

"My dear!"

"Well, mamma, she's our cousin, and she's quite respectable, is not she?"

"We don't want to keep up acquaintance with all the riff-raff in the country," Matilda said, with an air of disgust. "Respectable, indeed!"

"But why is she riff-raff?"

"Because she chose to make herself so! She keeps a dame school. You have seen her. It was that woman at Mrs. Dodds', with the big collar."

Amelia remembered the "woman," and remembered, too, that her dress was old-fashioned and shabby beyond belief. She hesitated and began to be ashamed. In a few minutes she sucked in a dose of the morality of the house. She felt she could not have ventured to walk into the drawing-room with such a figure. She resolved to compromise, and to be good to Miss Bell when occasion offered.

The alarm of the female Turners at the idea of associating with anyone beneath them was not unnatural. When Mr. Turner married his penniless wife, he was just on the edge of the class he wished to belong to. He had to strive hard and watch carefully over his dignity that no mistake might be made as to his position. His wife helped him, and thought the result in a great measure due to her own exertions. She had carefully brought up her daughters to be, first of all, genteel. Matilda had fully answered her expectations in this respect. She was, or had been, pretty, long-fingered, and feeble in health. She had never showed any wish for work or activity of any kind. Out-door exercise was then unknown for girls, but Matilda had learnt the use of the globes and poonah painting, and would have practised potichomania if it had been invented. Eliza redeemed the credit of the family as to common sense but she was stout and freckled, and to hear herself called "like her Aunt Bankes" sometimes made her cry, for Aunt Bankes was understood to occupy a very inferior position to her sister, Mrs. Turner. Eliza won herself a position by the activity that Miss Turner refused to be guilty of.

But Amelia was the flower of the flock, as Jane had said. She was as pretty as Matilda, and as sensible as Eliza, and she had been to a school to which her mother had vainly wished to send her sisters. Miss Forbes had a high character through a wide circle, though Mrs. Turner could not tell exactly why, and certainly Amelia brought home a set of opinions that were not in vogue in the Turner house. When she talked to Mr. Thelwal, her mother listened as to something new, and might well believe them born for each other. She could hardly follow them, as they talked about mental cultivation and mental training, refined taste and true greatness, etc., etc. That affair, at least, was going on well, she thought, if nothing else did, for it began to be clear to her that nothing else was doing so. The sons grew more cross and ill-mannered than ever, and the father more down-hearted.

His wife had begun in the last few days to talk about a matter that annoyed him excessively. She wanted to give a party.

"Not a grand ball, you know, but a little party, with some dancing. We have the room. Why should we not use it?"

"It will cost more than the room," her husband said, wearily.

"Oh, but it need not cost much."

"I have something else to think of than giving parties."

Thus baffled she took to stratagem. She mentioned in Mr. Thelwal's presence that they had but few amusements to offer him, but yet she hoped that before he left them she should be able to give him a small entertainment. The husband saw that to refuse his consent would be an insult to his guest. So the matter was taken out of his hands. A day was fixed, and Mr. Thelwal, while saying that he was due in London, said he should be very happy to join it.

The one who expected most from the affair was Sarah Miles. To her it was not merely the gathering together of a score or so of people to spend the evening, it was the mysterious rites of gentlefolks visiting, which Sarah had often heard of, and could never even guess at. It should be something grand, she thought, as she noticed the preparations. As for Jane's answers to her questions, she simply refused to believe them. Play a bit! and sing a bit! and talk! they could do all that, she said, without all this disturbance. There must be something else; there must be some mode of enjoying the evening that was peculiar to themselves, and she set herself to discover it in spite of fate. She thought the prepared drawing-room grand, with its uncovered furniture, its scattered lights, and gay pictures. When they were all assembled and tea was handed round, and she had to follow her sister with a tray, she thought the sight was splendid. The many coloured dresses, the varied positions, and the murmur of talk, made her think it was a little paradise where the people were waiting till some noble spectacle should begin. But a nearer inspection did not improve her opinion of the party, for, as has often been said, you could not enjoy even Heaven unless you were fit for it, and Sarah was not trained to enjoy a Repton small party. Why did they sit all round, and look as if there were "nought agate?" she asked. And why did they wear such enormous sleeves that they had to go in sideways through a doorway? She thought the white stockings rather pretty, with black sandals crossed and recrossed over the instep, but why had the shoes so little toe to them that she wondered how they were kept on? The dresses were short enough to show the whole height of the sandal, and were kept on in the same mysterious way as the shoes, merely hanging by the narrowest possible edge on the shoulders. Perhaps the best part of the costume was a coronet of hair round the head, but the whole of it produced an absurd effect. Every fashion does to those unused to it, be it that they have not known it, or that they have got used to others since.

With the faces she was more disappointed than with the

dresses. This, too, was the fault of her deficient education, for no one can understand the face of another class. A European cannot read that of a savage, nor even can a man of one nation read that of another till use has taught him their meaning. But the conversation was the worst of all. It was trivial, exaggerated, and generally affected. She heard some broken sentences, and found the same thing repeated half-a-dozen times. On the whole it was very like that of the Miss Whites and Mrs. Eldon.

Mr. Turner stood with his feet on his native hearthrug, and his face she understood. He was courteous, sprightly, and entertaining. Two or three gentlemen stood round him, looking as if they were afraid to sit down lest they too should be struck with the palsy that kept the rest almost motionless and almost silent.

"Well, no," he was saying; "we have some cultivation among us, though. The Yorkshire people are decidedly musical."

He was looking with a gracious smile at Mr. Thelwal, who answered—

"Yes, I suppose so. I have heard so, at least," and then seemed to forget the subject almost before he had finished the sentence.

Mr. Turner had, as it were, to begin again.

"We have some very respectable chorus singers, I assure you," to which the two neighbours responded, readily—

"Oh, yes, indeed!" and Mr. Thelwal echoed, seeing it was necessary—

"Oh, yes, I daresay."

Then he walked off rather suddenly. Sarah saw Mr. Turner's face darken at his sudden departure, and then brighten again as he saw where he went. It was straight to Miss Amelia, with a cool confidence that no other man in the room would have shown. For when everyone is doing their utmost not to attract attention, a man walking across the room makes as great a splash as a stone thrown into a bucket of water.

Miss Amelia was doing her utmost to entertain an old lady, who was looking at her with a smiling kind of wonder. She spoke about "The Excursion"—she had just been reading it—to which the lady, who was not listening very attentively, asked—

"And where did you go to, my dear?"

Then Amelia got on to history.

"About Cyrus, you know. I think him such an interesting character."

"Do you really, my dear?"

"Yes, and he had such a nice education. Don't you think so? To draw the bow, and to speak the truth."

"Well, yes, my dear; as to speaking the truth, at least."

"But don't you think there is rather a contradiction there, Miss Amelia?"

It was Mr. Thelwal broke in, and a laugh from two or three more gentlemen made Amelia's cheeks flush.

"No, Mr. Thelwal, there is no contradiction; it does not mean what you think. It means literally to draw the bow, to learn to shoot arrows, you know."

"Oh, I understand," he said, bowing. "Yes, I see; then it does not contradict the other half of his bringing up?"

Amelia was disappointed, half conscious, not that she was absolutely laughed at, but treated like a child; yet she thought her conversation, or at least its subject, was interesting enough. There is nothing that the young idea just shooting detests more than the cold water sometimes thrown on it by the old idea full grown. A dislike to Mr. Thelwal sank deep into Sarah's heart when she heard his answer, scarcely veiling the mockery of his tone.

Yet Amelia spent a pleasant evening, and at two o'clock in the morning, when Sarah was helping them to disrobe, she and Eliza were very talkative.

"Really some of the people were very nice," Amelia exclaimed; "but that Mrs. Dodds, one would think some people know nothing at all. One wonders if they can read!"

"Amelia, I wish you would give over with your reading and your information, it's not for ladies to be literary; people don't like it, you silly thing!"

"Some people like it, and so do I; Mr. Thelwal is very well informed."

Eliza smiled and let her alone.

There was a lazy house next morning; Mrs. Turner did not come down to breakfast. The young men scarcely spoke, but left it to their father to entertain the visitor, who gave himself no trouble to hide his sleepiness and *ennui*. As soon as they rose from table, the two left the house together; the old man attentive and obsequious, the young one careless and even hasty.

There was a busy kitchen that morning; Sarah was kept downstairs to help to put things away. In the middle of the morning her sister ran hastily down, and opening a drawer in the dresser took out a clean apron and put it on.

"There's Mrs. Overton's carriage coming," she exclaimed, in apology.

Miss Eliza left the kitchen and Sarah sidled after her sister, who went to open the door. This was the "cut above Turners" that she was anxious to see. Mrs. Overton had not come to the party, as the cook had prophesied. Why was she come now? Cook must be mistaken in her motives, though right as to the fact.

Sarah saw nothing, however, but a shawl and bonnet, as Jane showed the visitor into the drawing-room, and Miss Eliza followed her, having taken a look at her dress upstairs.

But by-and-bye, Mrs. Overton came out again, and Sarah took another look. The stately lady passed slowly from the drawing-room followed by the whole family of female Turners. A description of her dress would give very little account of the effect it produced to the surrounding people; she had on Mrs. Gamp's bonnet, that being the year it was invented; a mass of dark ringlets hung from within it down below the chin, her shawl was a "Paisley long," that is a scarf, fully four yards long and two wide. This was doubled into a square and then a corner was folded down, and it was worn so that the lower corner touched the heels. A slight intimation of a waist was given by drawing it in at the elbows, and the whole thing was, at that time, the height of grace and gentility.

"I am so sorry I could not come," she was saying, as she walked to the door.

"Oh, so are we all; so sorry."

As all her mistresses stood with their backs to her, Sarah stepped forward and had a full view of the stranger as she turned round and shook hands with them all, before entering her carriage. She had a smile, gracious as Mr. Turner's, and rather like it; a creamy pale face with dark ringlets on either side, and heavy eyelids that she raised slowly, as, seated in the carriage, she put two fingers with reticent gesture on the window-ledge and bowed her last adieu.

"Decidedly a cut above Turners," Sarah thought, as she retreated to the kitchen; but why she thought so she knew not. "She is much prettier than any of them," she said, and strove in vain to puzzle out the meaning of her face. In this she failed altogether, for the reason aforesaid.

Not long after Mrs. Overton drove off, Mr. Turner came in at the front door. It was not his custom to do so in the middle of the morning, and Sarah remarked it the more as he was alone, and she had got used to see him always attending on Mr. Thelwal. Mrs. Turner had rung for coals, and Jane willingly let Sarah carry them in.

Mr. Turner was standing on the hearthrug, and his voice stopped as Sarah opened the door. She left him standing, and within two minutes heard him go out again at the hall door. Then the bell rung again.

"Sarah," said her mistress, faintly, "Jane can take the sheets off the best bed, for Mr. Thelwal won't sleep there any more; he's gone. And, Sarah"—she fumbled with trembling hands for her pocket and brought out her purse—"and Sarah, we shall have no more visiting now, so you will not be wanted any more. Here's your wages. You have done very well."

The dumbfoundered girl hesitated a moment, and then advanced and took the money.

"You can go at once, Sarah," said the old lady, and the girl curtsied and went out.

Eliza looked as much lost as herself when she told her news in the kitchen, and said—

"You need not make the custard, cook, we shall have enough without," and leaving the forced meat she was engaged in, she took off her apron and went into the drawing-room.

"I knew it was not for long," Jane remarked; "but there's something up now. Why are you to leave before the best bed is made up again, and no covers put on the chairs, nor nothing?"

The same unaccountable gloom seemed to Sarah to follow her as she walked up the "Towngate" on her way home. People lounged at their doors as they had done all the winter for want of work. At the corner shop stood three or four elderly women, her mother being one. Now for the elderly women to turn out there must be something uncommon happening, and when her mother stood idle, outside her own door, Sarah almost took fright. Still more was she puzzled when the first person who perceived her exclaimed in excited fashion—

"And there's Sarah, I declare!"

"Now, Sarah, what are ye come for?" said her mother, sharply.

"T' missis sent me. She said they did not want me no more."

"What have ye been doing, Sarah? Aren't ye ashamed to come home just to-day?"

"I'm like to come when I am sent. What's to-day 'at I mun-not come to-day?"

"Dunnot ye know 'at Turner's is banked?" (bankrupt).

Sarah looked blankly from one to another; the stoppage of a mill is a serious misfortune in a small place. Well might Turner and his affairs be the theme of conversation in every house, or rather at every house door in Repton. At length Sarah held out the money which she had brought home, in her hand.

"Mun I tak' it back?"

Mrs. Miles considered a moment and asked what her mistress had said.

"She said t' company was gone, and they did not want me no more, an' I had been a good lass, an' there were my wage."

"Nay, I think ye'll ha' to keep it."

After dark Sarah stole down, scared and silent, to the Sykes's house. They were all there, equally silent, and scarcely greeted her as she sat down. At last they asked her what she would do now. It was all up with her going to place.

"Folks has to do summat i' these times. Mun I never start o' nought till there is not a bit o' cake o' t' creel."

"That's your mother all over," said old Sykes, with a half laugh.

He seldom spoke, and when he did Sarah held his words not to be worth much. She thought the wisdom was her own.

"Ye'll ha' to wait awhile for that," said Sammy. "Your father lived afore you."

"But whatever will the Turner lasses do?"

She then entered into a description of the Turner lasses and their surroundings, and left an impression of pity on her hearers that she was herself surprised at.

"What will they do?" she repeated, and Sammy answered with a spice of contempt—

"Nought."

Sarah looked at him awhile in silence.

"It's ye 'at knows nought about it," she said at last.

"What do ye say they'll do?"

"How should I know? They mun do summat."

"Ye may take my word for it, they'll never do nought beyond fettling up, an' then they'll have a lass to help them, maybe two."

"What, them three lasses?"

"Aye. An' if there were other three to help them they'd all do nought."

There was a melancholy pause again; each one thought of the misery in the great house, and found no hope and no remedy. Sarah ended it by saying—

"Thank God I'm not a lady!" which roused a general exclamation.

"They are worse off than we are if they cannot do nought to help themselves."

"Aye, it's t' oud man 'll have it all to do."

"Has he ought left, think ye?" old Sykes asked of his son. "They say Thelwal's is right mad at him. It's them 'at's done it."

"What do you mean?—'at's banked him?" Sarah asked.

"Aye. What have they done it for?"

" 'Cause they wanted their money, I reckon. They say young Thelwal came down to see how things stood, an' more he saw, an' worse he liked it. T' oud man would not let on 'bout anything 'at he could keep out o' sight, an' allus tried to put him off wi' summat, an' it made him right mad."

"What had he to do wi' him 'at he mud tell him ought?"

"He bought wool on 'em, lass, an' never paid for it."

Sarah thought of the patient civility of the old man and the idle ill-temper of the young ones, and kept a reverent silence before the misery that was revealed to her. Yet she hated the position and the mode of action into which the poor man appeared to be forced.

"Was there no other help? Could not the young ones do their share? What was all their learning for? Miss Amelia has had the best teaching, and she was so clever! Miss Bell says ye may get wise through books an' ye mun read books! So far as I can see, they tell ye nought but what does not concern ye, or else what ye knew afore. An' this is good, an' that is good, because it's so like nature! Why, how do they now know, when they have to learn what nature is by reading it? But they allus reckon to know it at sight afore ever they read it. And then they read what another man has said about it, an' then another man writes about 'em both, an' happen another about all three. An' when ye have read 'em all ye're eddicated and cultivated, an' ye stand there as helpless as a blind kitten! Eh! but them lasses is ill-off!"

"Aye," said Sammy, "an' more folks than them."

He walked to the window with his fingers in his waistcoat

pocket and looked out into the silent lane where the children used to play.

His warehouse was empty; there was nothing doing, and he and his father were not bankrupt only because his father's habits made him limit his expenditure within bounds that would now be thought ridiculous. To earn nothing for one or two years was what the Sykes' purse could stand. But it was a dreary outlook, for the young man had promised himself to do so much better than those that went before him.

He turned away from the window as the candle was lighted.

"Now, lasses, let's sing a bit!"

CHAPTER XVI.

"Wir menschen werden wunderbar geprüft.
Wir konnten's nicht ertragen hät' uns nicht,
Dir schöne leichtsinn die natur verliehen."

STUNNED and feeble when she learnt the full extent of the misfortune that had befallen Repton, and its consequences to herself, Maria sat down to write to Dora and make her acquainted with the destruction of all the hopes that they had begun to indulge of being together.

"Here ends my first attempt at getting a living," she began, and then went on to explain the reason. After the explanation she went on, "I have lost my last pupil and the house is empty, except when the two little Miss Dodds come for their music lesson. I have been expecting this some time, and have in a certain degree got used to the contemplation thereof. Certainly I have gained in wisdom since I left my father's house. I ignorantly thought that my life would be filled with work and with slow reward of work, promising me competence for old age. I thought I could, by careful economy, advance and increase the distance between me and utter poverty, and then I could bring you out of prison to do the same. Now I see my fate is to hang on the borders of want, sometimes, perhaps, taking a plunge downwards and sometimes rising on the wave, clinging fiercely to a straw or two. True, I have a reserve put by for a rainy day, but the question is, must it slowly disappear, only being of use to put off the catastrophe for a little while? I could live two years or more without begging. Would it be as well that this little store came to an end? I should then sooner come to a conclusion about my prospects. As it is, I must soon begin to eat off the end of it, and when the good times come, shall I begin to make it good again? In three years I have had some fairly good times, and I have not gathered together the means of living one! My present prospects are to stint myself to the border of want till I lose my health and courage, and then to die slowly for want of the means of renewing them.

"I am so far wiser than when I began, that I do not consider my case exceptional. There is terrible distress here, and as far as I can learn, everywhere else. There are people here, and not a few, in a state of famine. There is a great deal of illness, for which food is the only cure, and that cannot be had. If there were any comfort in that common topic of consolation— that there are other people much worse off than I am—I have it in plenty. I am really one of the most fortunate. I have no children to starve before my eyes, no immediate prospect of starvation myself. Thank God, therefore.

> " 'There should be no despair for you
>   While midnight stars are burning,
> While flowers are gemmed by evening dew,
>   And sunshine gilds the morning.'

"So I will bate no jot of heart or hope, but take the common lot and keep a cheerful mind.

"There is another thing that may almost be called a hope. Remember my mother's words, 'You may think it is impossible, but the time will come when there will be an opportunity given, then take it. Hold fast to it and grasp it with all your might!' Now, if there is to be a chance for you, so also there must be for me, and I shall certainly hold fast to it. Neither storm nor cold shall make me lose my grasp.

"So write to me, and remember that to lose my friend is not, like the rest, a thing I could face at all."

Then Maria leaned back in her chair and took up a letter from Mr. Branksome. This individual had begun to puzzle her exceedingly. She had been forced to acknowledge that he might become a mighty factor in her future life—or, he might not. And latterly she had begun to see that she was to him more than he to her. She almost began to think with Miss Turner that he was "a queer man! Was not he now?" How he had contrived to fall in love she could not imagine. He knew absolutely nothing of her, except her parentage and her poverty. "If I had been a beauty now, or had done anything heroic!" she thought. "Why, queer as he is, I understand him better than he does me. Ought I to tell him not to trifle longer with his own happiness, but leave me and take someone more accessible and more likely?" But a sudden shock came over her as she thought of his doing so, and she felt that if truth and openness could secure him, she would give them to the utmost. Her mind rested on him, and only his want of steadiness could make her tremble.

"I thought I knew my own mind, and could keep to it," said the queer individual; "but now I see that I have been wavering and changeable, compared to what I am now. No question or hesitation troubles me. So long as I can think or move, my life will be spent in pressing forward to my prize. I began these letters with the intention of laying before you myself; but just now I pause to express to you the anxiety I fear about your personal position. I dare not interfere. I dare not offer help, though I doubt you are suffering much. This time will go by, but I have felt the pressure, and wonder how you will feel it! I will not say I have a right to know, but I beg of you to tell me.

"I have watched you constantly ever since you came to Repton, more than three years ago. I have seen you with quiet heroism take your own way, neither turning aside to ask for pity, nor to brave opposition. I know how Mr. Turner wanted to thwart you. I know how you throve, in spite of him. You went about your work as if he were not there; and you have been, since then, a light and warmth to this half-savage community. Your mere presence has done more good than you are aware of. Your quiet goings out and comings in have held up to the place a picture of goodness and refinement that many will feel, or ought to feel, thankful for. Do not turn weary! Surely you will find means to go on! Though how, I know not. But I dread most of all to hear of your entertaining the idea of trying your fortune elsewhere! You do not know how much you would lose by going where you are totally unknown. You do not know how your spotless character and daily kindness have won you the reverence of people little given to reverence anything. Here you are on a sort of pedestal, as you ought to be, and sooner or later you will find the benefit of it.

"This is very useless comfort! It will not send you one pupil more; but let the consciousness of watching care be round you. It is a pleasant feeling, and it cannot be but that I shall find some means or other of making my good wishes effective. Some time or other I shall see the chance of helping you. Stay by me, Maria. You will come to see it wise to do so."

Maria was taken by surprise by the picture of herself as a heroine. Of course she had gone on her way quietly. Why, or how should she make a noise? She had tried to earn her bread as best she could. If this were heroism, how many heroes there were in Repton—in this uncivilized place that she was supposed to honour and enlighten by the fact of living there! She laughed at the extravagance, even while she was pleased and comforted by it. And she told her lover that she had determined to stay in Repton; not so much to shed the light of civilization there, as because the landlord had lowered her rent, and also because of the expense of moving.

"I do not recognize myself in your poetic description of me. I am plodding on my dreary way; at present through mud and mire—perhaps to something better; perhaps to sink beneath it. In neither case have I time to think of the world in general, or to undertake that my life shall meet with their approbation. The praise or blame of other people cannot determine my course, even though it should make them worship me. You put me in a wrong position, and, I doubt, mistake my character. If I am as far mistaken in your character as you are in mine—"

She would not finish the sentence. Her mind refused to dwell on the possible conclusion of their dream. No, she would be utterly sincere with him, and, surely, she would know if he failed in sincerity. Was there not a touchstone in sincerity that made her able to recognize the like?

She took up the letter again. The last sentence of it was—

"I wish you would show some slight interest in me—just so much as to ask how I am! as much as you did the first time you saw me, and looked across at me when any new absurdity was uttered. Don't pity me, but take some interest in me! It does not matter that I am not thriving. I make no complaint, but I should like to know if you are able to tell me that you are better pleased with my prosperity than my starvation. If you go so far as to ask a question, let it be sincere; and however you decide, or however you may feel, may you go on and prosper."

As Maria sat alone reading this, and wondering how in the world Branksome came to fall in love with her, she quietly did the same thing herself. "It is certain," she thought, "he has not chosen me for money or position, or anything else. There must be some similarity of feeling and character." She took up the pen and wrote without connecting the sentence with what had gone before.

"Sincerely I ask you to tell me something about yourself and your affairs. I wish to know them. I cannot judge of you without knowing them. I am interested, too, in your good fortune and in your happiness. I would contribute to it if I knew how. Perhaps the best thing for me to do would be to beg of you to leave me alone and seek someone more accessible, and whom you know better than you do me; but I will wait and see. Surely we can learn enough of each other to see if we are too uncongenial to be friends. I beg of you sincerity, as you do of me."

She found herself getting stilted and unreal, and finished the letter in haste. It was enough. The correspondence went on briskly and happily after that, and Maria astonished her friends by the quietness with which she took all her misfortunes and anxiety.

When your own troubles are too much for you it is often that you have forgotten those of other people. Maria thought of this when with some compunction she locked her door and took her way down to Miss Everard's at dusk.

"I will not make much of it," she said to herself, as she entered Mr. Turner's gates. "I will talk cheerily, and at least hide my sorrows if I cannot forget them."

She forgot them the moment she entered the house. The feeble voice that answered her knock made her eager to see the speaker. Miss Everard sat by the fire without going eagerly to welcome her.

"I thought you would come," she said; "though I do not see what good it does, Maria! It is come at last! There is no help any more!"

"Have I actually been so absorbed in my own griefs as to forget that this poor creature is much worse off than I?" Maria asked herself. "What can I say to her?" She sat down in silence, and Miss Everard looked into the fire.

"It is come at last," she said again. "I have looked for it long! I did not mind getting poorer and poorer if anything was left at last."

"I thought you would suffer!" Maria exclaimed.

"Yes, I shall suffer. I do not see how I am to get any rent, even the ground-rent for the mill. No one will take it now, nor the house either."

"Will they leave the house?"

"They must, it seems to me. How can they pay for it? But, indeed, they have paid nothing and no one lately."

Then they talked over the fate of the Turners. Miss Everard recalled the time when the young man first came to Repton.

"He was from Baumforth, you know. I don't know what his father was, but he was such a handsome young man; and he claimed to consort with the first people in the neighbourhood. We used to wonder why, for he was just employed somehow

in Bentley's office. We never found out how. He said he was
not a partner; and when someone said 'You are a clerk, then,'
he said 'No.' He was something, however, for a while, and then
old Bentley gave up the mill, and he took it. We were all
astonished. Papa knew all about it. And then he brought his
sister, and took a small house down there, that house that is
now nearly pulled down. And I used to go and see her there.
We were great friends; and then he brought home a wife!"
Miss Everard laid her open palms on her knee, and paused a
moment as if she had not even yet got over the astonishment
this had created. "And she was as handsome as he was. People
used to say they were the handsomest couple in Repton. But
everybody said he was going too fast; but he never heeded,
but took the house we lived in as soon as I went out of it. To
be sure, it was some years after his marriage; and then people
had given over prophesying about his going too fast. Everyone
thought he was firmly established. And now—all at once—"

She laid her palms on her knees again in silent wonder at
the fate that was come at last.

"He's old to begin again," Maria remarked.

"Ah, he is; and the sons are no help to him."

"But they're old enough."

"So they are; but it was well known that they were worth
nothing. The old father wanted to keep up their dignity, so
he would not stint them in money, so they went on as they
liked."

"And now they're gone!" Maria said.

Miss Everard did not know, but said they were no loss either
to their father or to the place. "He will have fewer to keep,"
she thought.

Maria reflected awhile as to whether she could ask Miss
Everard anything more about her chance of getting anything
amongst the creditors; but how should the old lady know? She
had never known anything of her own fortunes or her own
prospects. And now they were more involved than ever; besides, Maria saw that the weight was lifted off her mind for a
moment, and she would not be the one to replace it. She was

grieved, therefore, when Miss Everard said quietly, as if only finishing a sentence begun before—

"I do not like charity; but it seems to come very near."

Maria had no answer to give. They parted quietly, and she promised to come again soon.

"At least we can do that, now I have nothing else to do."

There was another person who visited Miss Bell during these weary times. Sarah Miles was curious to know how ladies behaved in such difficulties. Her real liking for her teacher made her visits not impertinent. She spoke respectfully, and listened to the instruction received. It was, as she herself said, little to the purpose. Miss Bell was in utter darkness as to the way to improve her own fortunes, and could give no help to others. She inculcated patience, economy, uprightness, and such like, and maintained that well-taught women were better off than ignorant ones. "Wisdom comes of knowledge," she would say, "and wisdom will guide you through the world better than either courage or cunning." Sarah doubted, but the conversations did good to both sides.

There was never a formal invitation. They met accidentally, and stood at the little green gate in summer, or by the fireside in winter, and talked. Ice would have shot over the brimming news and comment if Sarah had been asked to sit down. But much was said and much learnt for all that. Sarah would sometimes take back a book which had been lent her, and often got another to take away. On this occasion there was too much to tell for them to think of books. Sarah mentioned one item after another as they struck her fancy, and Miss Bell listened pityingly to the tale. Sarah referred to her everlasting question, but in vain. Such as Miss Bell had, she gave. What could she do more?

"There's someone coming," Sarah said, hearing the gate click. "It's Sugden. He's come to tell you t' mill's to start o' Monday. Turner's going on again."

Whenever Sarah grew excited she reverted to her vernacular.

Miss Bell did not understand her. She went to the door, and

was informed that as the mill was going to work again his girls should come back on Monday.

"I would not have taken them away, but I did not know how long we should ha' to lake," he said. "And there's more than mine will be coming, too," he added, with the fellow feeling that fellow suffering produces.

It was scarcely consistent with the dignity of a reasoning creature that Maria should be so suddenly lifted out of the slough of despond by the news she had just heard. For, in truth, it amounted to this: That she had no more control over her own good or ill-luck than a little child. Her prosperity had left her, and it had come back again. No effort of hers had had anything to do with it, and the prospect of a life-long see-saw between want and well-being was still the same. But yet her spirits rose. She thought life was worth living, and it was a pleasant thing to behold the sun. She wrote more cheery letters to Dora, and to her brother. She wrote, too, to Branksome, so that the sheets sent and received had to be crossed and re-crossed. The pair seldom saw each other, though they could see each other half a mile off. There seemed to her a glory round his name, and she—she did not fall in love, she walked into it with her eyes open. We all know how it's done! Each side dressed up an image deprived of half its earthly nature, and of the residue they made a god! And each believed in the homage of the other.

It seemed as if the previous stagnation had disappeared with the failure. The mill was full of work, and the town of activity. Maria raised her eyes, and saw the clouds were gone, and had left as little trace as if they had never been. She reminded Miss Everard of the saying that our worst troubles are those that never come. Miss Everard explained that hers were certainly so. "For you know I could have waited half a year at least, and by that time I might have got some rent."

Sarah was the only one dissatisfied in the new state of things. She had lost her place. There was no longer the school to interest her. She grew almost peevish under the monotony of

her accustomed work, and began to talk with Sammy, or anyone else that would listen to her, about the possibilities of
learning something, or trying something else.

Sydney told her she might learn to sing. Now, singing was
not in favour in the Puritan household in which Sarah had
been brought up, and in which she had acquired the unconscious morality by which we usually guide ourselves. But now,
under the pressure of temptation, she began to dally with the
evil thing.

"But what's t' use o' singing?" she asked.

"To get money, bairn!" Sammy exclaimed.

And, encouraged by his evident familiarity with the subject,
she went on—

"How does folks get money by it?"

"Singing at concerts and such like."

"But them's grand singers!"

"So may ye be a grand singer."

This same question had entered into the minds of the elders,
and under pressure of the general anxiety they had begun to
consider whether there were not a means of providing for their
daughter better than the uncertain work at a mill, or poorly
paid hardships of household service.

"She must follow things that are lovely and of good report,"
they said. "It is better to be poor and righteous than rich and
forgotten of God." With this feeling they began to listen to
the hints of Sammy and of Sydney Wynde. When Miss Bell
had assured them that their daughter had really a remarkable
voice they thought farther of the matter; and their eyes being
opened to the advantages of being able to earn a little more,
they took in the new possibility. There was really less of self-
interest in the change than goes to help most people's conver-
sions. Their minds were really large enough to receive a new
idea, though not without severe criticism; and they began to
make inquiry, and to familiarize themselves with the idea of
work as a singer.

CHAPTER XVII.

HOPE AGAIN ELASTIC SPRINGS.

WHAT is it that makes a new idea come into people's heads—a new idea on a subject whereon they have perhaps thought long and earnestly for days or weeks? We have perhaps a hard nut to crack, and see no way of doing it. We turn it over and over, and find no one side more impressible than another. We settle a hundred times that there is nothing to be done with it, but yet we go on looking at it, and trying to find a weak place where we may make an attempt. We turn in despair away, and then from nowhere comes the solution that we have sought so long. Some unconscious cerebration, or other new name for an unknown thing, brings out the new light we sought so long and painfully in vain.

When within a week Mr. Turner had seen his sons depart, and his workmen all gone, and walked up and down the path between his office and his house in weary silence, such an idea came to him, and he turned sharply round and went out at the garden gate. He took the way up the village, to the door of Sykes' house, and knocked. By good fortune there was no one in except the members of the family. The tea was over, and they sat in the gathering darkness talking idly. The two young ones, used to seeing some of their many friends at this time, called out both at once "Come in." Slowly the door opened, and the old man showed his anxious face in the firelight.

"Is Mr. Sykes— This is Mr. Sykes' house, is it not?"

The two men stood up in reverence. Old Sykes went forward; Sam brought a chair; Harriet disappeared into the kitchen, as her custom was. Not that she heard any the less what went on, or was supposed to do so, but her presence might be a constraint.

"Mr. Sykes," Mr. Turner began, sinking into a chair as if he had need of it, "I wish to consult you; I think you a man of judgment, Mr. Sykes. I—you know I have lost my sons, that is, my sons have left me—that is, they thought they would not be a burden on the family in our present circumstances. They have gone." He found he could not mend the matter, and tried another subject. "You see, Mr. Sykes, I thought once I should struggle through; I did, indeed. If I had had more capital I could just now go on again. I know I could. Now, Mr. Sykes, I will just ask your opinion as a man of sense and knowledge. I have orders that I could execute if I had money now. But how am I to pay wages? You know one must have something to go on with until things come round a little. I will not hide anything from you, Mr. Sykes. If I had a thousand pounds I could go on. Yes, and thrive as well as ever I did. Now, Mr. Sykes, if I had your son in place of mine, and you could advance us a thousand pounds, it would be the making of us both. It would start us fair. I am an old man. My sons do not like the business. I can really say your son might do well in it. I will show you all about it; I will not hide anything from you."

One flash of the eye passed between Sam and his father. No one would have seen it if they had watched them, but the overwrought senses of the old bankrupt took it in. He turned to the young man, and pointed out to him that he would soon master the part of the business of which he was as yet ignorant; that it was a chance; that he, Sammy, must look before him. Why should not he be a mill owner in the years to come?

"I know you are an industrious man, Mr. Samuel, and if you have the strength, I have the knowledge, and you might acquire it! Will you come up to me to-morrow, and I will explain to you all the circumstances and the conditions of partnership? I wish you to understand everything, Mr. Sykes."

To this they agreed. Mr. Turner took his departure, and Harriet came out of the back kitchen flushed and wondering.

"Will ye go, father?"

"Why, lass, we're like to go."

"Will ye do what he wants ye?"

"We mun see, bairn."

Mr. Turner succeeded in making his new friends believe that the scheme was feasible. They weighed it well and consulted with the rest of the brotherhood. They were well acquainted with the actual working of a cloth mill, and saw the opportunity of learning the part of the business that they knew nothing about. Sam became a partner, and he, or rather his father, advanced a thousand pounds. Mr. Turner, true to his nature, expressed a wish that the Sykes' name should not appear as a member of the new firm. Sam was not ambitious as to the honours of the alliance; indeed, he thought less of it than Mr. Turner would have quite liked. He looked to the reality, and saw an opening for work and its reward. The Sykes' believed in industry and economy, and considered that "prestige," name and fame, so far as they were purchased by keeping up a style, were mere pitfalls wherein to sink, when without them they might have kept their heads above water.

When Eliza Turner, with stony face and voice scarcely audible, had told Jane that she need not make the best bed again, and that there would be enough for dinner without the custard, she went into the drawing-room and stood without speaking a word before her mother. In the dim, undecided way in which most women see the powers that are weaving their destiny; she had known that Mr. Thelwal was a power to be propitiated, and knew that if he was angry misfortune would befall them all. She waited for an explanation, and, as her mother's tears prevented it from being intelligible, she had to make it out by questions.

Thelwal was gone. He would not do what was wanted. He was very cruel. He might have had more mercy.

"But what was wanted of him?" Eliza asked.

"More time! That was what was wanted of him. He was asked to wait. Your papa asked him—begged of him—and he won't!"

A new flood of tears made Eliza understand that the waiting was most important, and that Thelwal's impatience was ruin.

"But, mamma, is there no one else than Thelwal?"

Mamma was angry. She wanted her daughters to understand that the ruin was come, not merely coming. She asked her crossly who she thought would be likely to lend her father a thousand pounds, and then turned her temper into lamentation over her poor daughters, and the evil fortune that had befallen her in her old age.

Eliza tried to get some information as to what would come next, but Mrs. Turner knew no more than herself, and at last Eliza went into the kitchen to see that some dinner was got ready. That, at least, must be prepared and eaten. She had the relief that comes from employment under her misfortune. The elders thought she had a coarse nature and less feeling than they had, and was just fit for her position. Eliza's "coarseness" had conduced much to Matilda's gentility. The elder sister could sit in full-dressed dignity often when there was more work than the servants could accomplish, because her sister's more active disposition led her to undertake it. Thus she was looked down upon and leaned against at the same time, and had some degree of authority in the house through it all. After having "put the dinner forward," she went into the cold drawing-room where Amelia was practising and called her to come into the breakfast-room to hear the news. For Eliza saw that it would hurt her father to have to tell it to her alone, or even to know that she had not been told.

"I don't know where to put my head," her mother said, and the elders echoed—

"No, indeed, we cannot show our faces now."

"But what for?" Amelia cried. "Papa has done nothing wrong. We have only lost our money."

"Only!" was echoed three times over with a sort of laugh.

"Well, I don't mean to say it is nothing. It's a great deal. But, mamma, dear"—and she knelt down at her mother's knee—"mamma, dear, I am sure we can manage to earn enough to make you comfortable—you and papa. We will find some way of working; there must be plenty of ways. Look how many trades there are in the world!"

"My poor child," said her mother, sobbing on her neck, "you little know."

"Milly, dear, don't talk in that way; that is just what grieves mamma most of all," Matilda said.

"What is?" said Amelia, astonished. "There is nothing in working—but you need not work, mamma," she added. "Eliza, can't we work for mamma?"

"We must do what we can," Eliza said. "But do not talk so; you don't understand."

"No, my dear, don't talk so; it will grieve your papa, too."

"But, mamma, don't be grieved for us; we shall like it."

"Milly, give over," Matilda said, angrily. And, at last, seeing she was, as she thought, quite misunderstood, Amelia held her peace. She promised herself to begin again when her father came in, feeling sure he would understand and see the evident necessity of people who had no money beginning to work.

"You must not be so down-hearted," she told them all. "We shall get bread and comforts for mamma and papa, and what does the rest matter? Our souls are our own all the same, and our pleasures may be."

Matilda twisted herself round as if she were tired of such nonsense.

Eliza called Amelia away into the store-room and asked if they could not do with one servant now.

"You know we shall see no company now, and need not have more than one sitting-room fire, and so on."

Amelia jumped into agreement at once, promising to do everything necessary. The two arranged to talk about it when papa came in.

"And then we must ask him what we had best do to earn something," Amelia added.

"Now don't you speak about that," Eliza said; "you don't understand it."

"No, to be sure I don't. That's the reason why I shall ask advice. I will make papa understand that we are not sorry to work, but are quite ready to begin, and shall be quite as happy as we have been till now, and then he won't be so grieved, you know."

The three came in in due time and sat down to dinner.

Mr. Turner soon laid down his knife and fork, and putting his elbow on the table and his head in his hands, looked at his plate.

Mrs. Turner cried, and the girls fumbled with their dinner somehow. The young men made short work of it, and then walked out. Eliza and Amelia helped to clear the table that the servant might be as little in the room as possible. Then the door was shut and Amelia thought that now her time was come and she would comfort papa.

He was still sitting with his elbow on the table. She went up to him with the confidence of a favourite, and tried to take his hand away from his face.

"Papa, dear, I want to talk to you. It's not so very bad after all. We need not starve, if you *have* lost your money."

"My poor child," said the old man, ten years older than he was a few days ago, "my poor child, what am I to do with you?"

"I'm going to do for you, papa, as is but right when you have done so long for me. We will consider what we can do. We must work at something, you know. We will consult with you and mamma, and you will tell us how to do."

"Poor thing, poor thing!" said her father, stroking her cheek, "there's no consulting to be done, we must just wait till—"

"Till when, papa?"

"Till things are a little bit settled." He knew not himself how this was to be.

She was baffled again, how or why she did not understand. But some time they must explain, then all would be right, and she would have some scope for her activity, and papa would see.

At tea time there was another meeting. The father talked with his sons and they mentioned Thelwal's name. He would do, or not do, something, she did not understand what.

"Not he," said one.

"Nay, but he might."

"Not he," said the father, with bitterness.

"But, papa," Amelia broke in, "I am sure Mr. Thelwal will help you if he can. I am sure he will do what is right. Why is he gone away?"

Then Mrs. Turner explained that Mr. Thelwal was just the greatest enemy papa had, and was doing him all the mischief he could.

"But, papa, you did not think so a little while ago. You were very friendly with him, and I am sure he is a good man."

"Good man enough to ruin us," said the eldest son. "Are you going to stand up for the man that has ruined your father?"

Then Amelia broke down, for the foundations of her world were loosened. Was there no truth on earth? Were men all base? And did no one but herself believe in the difference between right and wrong? Oh, but this man must be more base than others, for he had professed more. He, her father's enemy, how dare he talk of friendship to her? She scorned his falsehood. She could never speak to him with decent civility again.

She had rather a contempt for herself for having been cheated, for having listened and believed. True, they had but agreed about the necessity of doing one's duty, and being kindly to everyone, but then that was everything, and Amelia had found fellowship and trust in the stranger and made him kin in her heart.

So the house lost its one bit of sunshine. The girl still looked forward to the time when she should begin to be the help of the family, she knew not how; but the spring was gone. Was the world worth living in if all men were like that?

Then it was announced to the womenkind that they need not make any change in their way of living, for some mysterious reason it was not wise to do so. Of course they should not see much company just now, but they need not show off as if they were ruined.

This was in answer to a proposal of Amelia's that they should do with one servant.

"I don't want to show off anything," she said; "I only want to do my work."

"Do it then, and be quiet," her father said, so sternly that the very thought of mentioning "work" again brought a pain and fear to her heart. Fear, she knew not of what, or why, and yet the feeling that she must do it made her miserable. So ever and ever when the pain she felt roused her to think, she swung between two opposite poles, and could not fix on either to hold fast by. Should she face her father's anger, and press upon him the necessity of—she knew not what—he must tell her what, or should she dare to throw aside the rule by which she had hoped to guide her life? She was poor, she must earn her living. Nothing was clearer. When they spoke of other people they never doubted a moment about this. Why then should she hesitate? "I shall never be happy till I am working!" she felt with all her heart. It was the remedy for all the small evils of her life that now began to crowd round her. Someone would slight them in the street, and then Amelia would say "That is because we are doing nothing," or someone would invite them as usual, and then they must refuse. "We ought to be doing something instead of visiting," she thought. Or the inevitable renewals of clothing would be discussed, and one guinea must do the work of two, and then would come, "If we were only earning something!" As these exclamations always brought forth a burst of anger from those who chanced to hear them, the girl soon learned to keep them to herself. "But it was pain and grief to her."

She turned to Eliza, recollecting her proposal to do with one servant, and represented that perhaps something might be found more profitable than doing servants' work. Eliza turned round and gave her a "setting down," as she called it. She said Amelia was the most cruel girl she had ever known; that she might see if she had a bit of feeling that nothing grieved papa so much as to talk about wanting money. "He does what he can! Can't you let him alone? He has enough to bear."

Whatever the other women of the Turner family could not accomplish, or did not like the trouble of doing, was reserved for Eliza to attempt. "Eliza, try what you can do," the mother would say, and Eliza would try. It was in this way that she was commissioned to silence Amelia, and in this way she did it. "She was hard-hearted," and the confident daughter became a trembling slave. She never gave an opinion, or proposed a change. Her father took her conduct as a silent reproach, and thought her unthankful and selfish. "I do what I can for you," he would say sometimes, *a propos* to nothing and to no one in particular. Amelia shrunk and said nothing.

A life of hard work and self-denial is, or may be, one of the noblest lives on earth. But self-denial without effort is mere mockery, good for no human soul. The more zealously it is followed the more it destroys the human faculty and feeling. And now the Turner women began the process of destroying their faculties and feelings in obedience to the unwritten law of appearances. They could not go out for want of suitable clothes, they could not invite friends, lest they should see the nakedness of the land. They began to make a difference between the days when Mr. Turner dined at home and when he did not. In every detail the sap of enjoyment was taken out, by the necessity of counting the cost. There never was a laugh in the house, it might somehow cost money!

Under this rule the young men soon took themselves off. They had quarrelled with the father repeatedly, even during the time of difficulty, when Mr. Thelwal was still in the house, and now found the means of maintaining themselves elsewhere. Amelia asked where it was, and what they did. One was gone to Manchester, and one somewhere, they had forgotten the name of the place. They were doing—"O, I don't know what it is, some commission thing or other." The old father took the blow in silence. Perhaps he was better without them. They would not be stinted in their customary expenditure, and their work was not of the best. The women felt only the diminished household expense.

One day the father came into the house with a different look. He had lately acquired the habit of being somewhat stern and distant, as if on the look-out for some slight or offence. This look had not left him, but there was superadded an air of dignity that he had of late forgotten. He sat down to dinner like a master without a word of any kind. Dinner was half over before he looked round and said, pompously—

"At last I am able to say that things are arranged."

They looked up, afraid to ask what things; for if it were their things it would offend him not to know, and if it were some other matter he would be angry at their eternal reference to their own affairs.

After all he was as much offended by their silence as he could have been by any answer he could have got.

"I have arranged things with our most grasping creditor," he went on, "and we go on again as before. But it has been a difficult matter, and I shall have to struggle hard. We must not launch out into useless expenses; we must get on quietly."

Then the mother promised to do all that they could, and was thankful. The girls held their peace, except the unfortunate Amelia, who innocently asked—

"Who is the most grasping creditor, papa?"

There was a general outburst of "Oh, Amelia!" while her father scowled.

In the girl's fright she did not exactly know how she learnt that the grasping creditor was Thelwal, and she saw that here, too, she was looked on as an unfeeling fool.

"Mr. Thelwal has behaved very ill to your papa," Mrs. Turner said, with severity, and then no one spoke any more about the matter.

The fact that they were "going on" did not make much difference to them; money was as scarce as ever.

Mr. Turner hoped that now at least his home would grow cheerful again, but the pride of his heart, his youngest daughter, remained cold as before. She could never more come confidently to her father, and, between coaxing and confidence, tell him her plans, her hopes, her good intentions. She had been called hard-hearted, and was no longer confident of welcome. She dared not try to explain herself; she would not look as if she was better pleased because they had more money. She would rather have had less, if only to show how little she cared. The other girls would ask for at least this or that, "just to look *something;* not as if we never had anything." The poor man was struggling too hard to listen; he was, in fact, as poor as ever, and only so far was his condition improved that he had hopes of being richer at some future time. Then he had as little notion, as men generally have, how much was really necessary for the household expenses. He did not know that his family were suffering from real discomforts; part of their privations were hid from him, part they underwent voluntarily in order to have money for bits of ostentation that he saw and did not value. He certainly would not go any farther in spending, since there was enough for that! The proverbial effects of poverty soon appeared in the Turner household. The women quarrelled about the disposal of the small means at their command, and they all showed themselves rather displeased with the husband and father for his stinginess.

"We might have something just for that!" they agreed, after a refusal made, not over civilly, to a suggestion of theirs.

"I know he gets his dinner at the best hotel at Baumforth every time he goes," Matilda said, "and we may go without getting any dinner at all. We must get our dresses made here, and look like sights all the summer!"

Amelia's young enthusiasm and her quixotic notions would have enabled her to go without dress altogether, and she made some comment in that spirit to her sister, and got for it another "sitting down." By this time every item of her life was either repulsive or burdensome to her. She was sick of "appearances," sick of quarrelling, and, above all, sick of the misconception that attended everything she did, every word she spoke. To her the evil one seemed to be guiding the household, and to have with him seven other spirits worse than himself.

She went wearily about her day's work, and sank in the evenings into total inertia. Eliza was busy and cross, Matilda whined and grumbled, the house-mother watched painfully lest anything should be said or done to vex the master, who sat like a stranger at his own fireside. They had become a "fortuitous concourse of atoms," and the pet, the hope of the family, was the most isolated atom of them all.

CHAPTER XVIII.

FORGET THE THINGS WHICH ARE BEHIND, AND PRESS FORWORD TO THOSE THAT ARE BEFORE.

WE all feel sure at times that if we were allowed a free hand we could carve out for ourselves a magnificent destiny; we would work and fight, and deny ourselves, and do whatever was necessary, and we would succeed. Only now and then comes the gloomy certainty that there are difficulties that we cannot overcome, and that only under favourable circumstances can we find the "leave to toil" that Burns thought it so hard to have to beg.

As this certainty became clear to Sarah, her character changed considerably; she was too courageous not to look forward, however gloomy the prospect before her, and too well off in her present position to feel deeply the possible future. She asked of everybody, as she had done of the Miss Whites when she made their acquaintance at the Eldons, "What did you do when you were young? What employments were possible for you?" She was eager to see new people and new things, and to go to new places.

> "Sicherlich es muss das beste
> Irgendwo zu finden seyn."

She got gloomy and impatient when nothing happened, for surely something ought to happen. So far things had happened,

something had come to widen her horizon, to increase her
knowledge, and her power to contend with fortune. She
scowled when people told her she was well off; she could not
answer them, nor name the unknown thing that was to come
and give her a step forward. "How can I tell," says the man
in a dungeon, "what there is outside?" You may talk of storm
and wind, but you stay outside. You never put yourselves inside so long as you can put one foot before another and walk
away! None of them knew what she meant, not even Miss Bell,
to whom she tried to explain it.

"Sarah," said her mother at last, "your father an' me's been
thinking that perhaps you might learn singing; you've gotten
a voice, an' maybe it might help you to addle your living. It
may be a state of temptation, but ye will meet wi' that everywhere, and it's your place to stand firm, not to shirk your work
because of that. There's more temptation in idleness than in
work, anywhere, an' if ye see best you can always come home
again, ye know. You're old enough now to start for yoursen."

It had come then— the thing that had more power to move
her than anything else in the world. As to danger, caution,
harm to come of it, she dreaded nothing. Could not she take
care? She would be industrious, and she would succeed, and
she would win. A glorious halo veiled and mystified the things
she saw before her, but that they were worth the winning she
was sure.

She had learnt from her elders a habit, probably derived
from their puritan ancestry, of veiling her deepest feelings.
They would no more have thought of a gushing demonstration
than they would have thought of going without clothes; so the
girl stood still until her heart went down again out of her
throat, and then said—

"Yes, mother."

"Now there's a man at Baumforth 'at 'll teach ye, an' ye'll
ha' to live wi' Mrs. Gracehurst. Ye know Mrs. Gracehurst?"

Sarah knew her well enough, though she had not seen her
for some time. She was one of the "oud folk" who visited her
mother sometimes, and from whose presence Sarah had always

slipped away as soon as opportunity offered, so that now she found, to her great regret, that she was quite unable to form any idea of what this woman was like.

"Will it be better than going to t' miln?" she asked.

"That's as ye get on, Sarah. There's nought for nobody without pains, so get all your things mended up, ye'll ha' to go next week, an' mind ye do as ye're bid when ye get there. Mrs. Gracehurst keeps a school, an' ye'll ha' to fettle up an' mense about same as ye do here, an' to go to your singing besides."

And on Monday morning Sarah stood by the little table with a bundle in her hand. She was dressed in a bonnet and shawl, which made her feel as if she was going to chapel. Her mother came out of the shop to say a last word.

"Now, Sarah, mind and do as you're bid, an' learn all you can, and you'll come home on Saturday nights, you know; and mind you come by daylight."

Something in the earnestness with which her mother repeated her instructions and put her hand on her shoulder sent a cold shiver through Sarah. This was indeed a parting!

"Mother, I'm coming back o' t' Saturday?" she said, with a start.

"Aye, for sure, lass!"

Sarah blushed, smiled, and taking up her bundle, walked out at the door.

She had never been at Baumforth, but it was the nearest town, and everybody in Repton who went anywhere, went there; so it seemed to a Reptonian impossible to miss the way. It was not six miles off, and the road could not possibly be confounded with any of the lanes that branched off from it. After an hour's walk, Sarah came to a more crowded country and a denser atmosphere. The houses, almost all of one class, consisted, like those in Repton, of a "house and a chamer," the idea of two lodging-rooms not having yet entered the operative mind; but unlike Repton houses, they were agglomerated into rows, or at least into pairs. They were all of brick, with the one window facing the road, either painted dark or made so by the smoke. The road and footway were black, being mended with cinders, and the swarms of children who played on them were black too. As the rows of houses got more continuous, Sarah began to look for the number of the one that was to be her home.

"There it is," she said, aloud, as she saw a troop of children issuing out by an open door into the street, and a tall, angular woman standing in the doorway looking up and down. Sarah hurried on to speak to her before she went into the house again.

"You're Mrs. Gracehurst?" she said.

"Yes, and I know who you are," was the answer, and the two looked at each other for a moment.

Sarah thought the woman like Miss Turner; she had the same look of superficial peevishness, and the same real sorrow beneath it; but Miss Turner would have been shocked to hear of the likeness. This woman's dress was even cynical in its poverty. A black gown so flat in its folds, so ragged in the sleeves, and in the gathers, and round the bottom, and so brown all over, could only be worn by a woman who had deliberately given up the intention of looking as well as she could.

"I thought you would have been here sooner," she said; "but it's just as well the children are gone," and she led her through the schoolroom into the kitchen, for the house had no passage and only one room upstairs.

Then she strode about the kitchen, getting some knives and forks out of a drawer, some salt and cold meat out of a cupboard, and dipping a jug into a pail of water that stood on the sink.

"Just see if the potatoes are enough," she said, and Sarah felt comforted by the home-feeling that the accustomed action brought with it.

"They'll be five minutes yet," she said.

"Why, then, take your things upstairs; there's t' bottom drawer emptied for you to put them in."

The odd pair sat down to their dinner of cold meat and potatoes. Mrs. Gracehurst did not indulge in conversation, and Sarah had nothing to say. After dinner Sarah prepared to wash up and tidy the room; the children came back, and the woman left her to herself. She spent as long as she could finishing off, for she felt really afraid of the first interview with the master. At last she was forced to put on her bonnet and shawl again, which garments seemed to have the power of taking all her natural pluck out of her.

"If I could only have her to go with me," she thought, as she came downstairs, and she slowly opened the schoolroom door with the intention of proposing to wait till Mrs. Gracehurst could go with her.

"I'm going," she said, hesitating.

"Why, you might have been ready long ago," Mrs. Gracehurst said, looking sharply round; "be sharp, lass," and Sarah found it would be as easy to face the master alone as to ask Mrs. Gracehurst to go with her.

She tried to get some directions, or advice, or information, beyond that conveyed in the opinion given during dinner, that "he was a queer one," but all she got was, "Go thy ways, lass," interjected between the spelling of two syllables.

So she went her ways and found out the house by inquiry. The front door and the room door close to it were opened; Sarah saw a number of children on the floor, a woman sitting by the table mending stockings, and the master of the house standing by the window smoking a long pipe. When she knocked no one moved, but several voices cried, "Come in." She came in, and asked if this was Mr. Holroyd's?

She knew it was, but shyness, like fear, makes us all deceitful.

The woman said, "Yes; was she wanting something?"

"Please I'm Sarah Miles, and I'm come to learn to sing."

She spoke to Mr. Holroyd himself, and stood facing him. He kept his pipe in his mouth, and stood meditatively looking at her in silence. The woman raised her head and looked too, and then dropped her eyes on her work again. After waiting a minute, Sarah looked him in the face in a manner which said, "Now will you answer?"

He took out his pipe and said—

"So you are come to learn to sing?"

"Yes."

He put his pipe in again, and Sarah waited another minute, still under inspection. At last he went to the fire, knocked the ashes out of his pipe, and laid it carefully on the chimney-piece; then he motioned to her to go into the next room. The door was open—open doors were the fashion of the house—and she went in. There was a piece of grey carpet in the middle of the stone floor, a piano on one side, some chairs against the wall, and a table piled with music before the window. He sat down to the piano, and, after playing a few chords, began—

"Now, can you sing this, think you?" drumming on one note.

Sarah sung it.

"Sing it louder; sing it louder, louder, louder."

After singing her loudest for a little while, Sarah stopped.

He took his hands off the keys, and resting his knuckles on his knees, faced round towards her and asked—

"What are you stopping for?"

"Must I go on?"

"It's all the same to me."

As he drummed on the note again Sarah went on, and sang both long and loudly for some twenty minutes. He changed the note again and again, and she went on, as she would have called it, 'raughting," without being able to see the sense or profit of such a proceeding. Then he put his hands on his knees again and asked—

"So you've come to learn to sing?"

"Yes."

"I don't see why you shouldn't. Come to-morrow morning," and he walked away.

Sarah stood for a moment taking counsel with herself, and then followed him. Her hesitation came from her asking herself, "Is he in his right mind?" and she decided, not in the affirmative, but that she would see farther. Had she ever seen insanity she would have known there was nothing of it about him. He was a man of large build, with the strength of man-

hood about his head and shoulders, and the signs of incipient
age upon his face. He had a humorous lip, a melancholy eye,
a mass of long light hair on his large head, all in disorder, like
his clothes. His hands were seldom clean, for it was his custom
when he hesitated to poke a finger into his pipe—perhaps for
an idea. He went to the chimney-piece, where he had left it,
calling to Sarah as she went out—

"Come at ten o'clock."

The murmur of instruction was still going on when Sarah
got back to her new home, glad and triumphant that she had
got through the ordeal. She set the kettle on, swept the hearth,
and peeping out at the back door saw a pump, and filled the
bucket afresh. She longed sadly for someone to talk to, and
when, after another hour, Mrs. Gracehurst came in she gave
such a spirited account of her lesson that the grim woman
fairly smiled. She did not interrupt her work, however, but
began on a black dress that looked much more respectable than
her own.

"Is that your Sunday gown?" Sarah asked.

"It's noan o' mine. Ye've nought to do, Sarah, ye mud as
well help me to mend it up. I'm doing it for Mrs. Whitehead;
he's been to mend a pane of glass." (*He,* in this connection,
always means the husband of the person last spoken of.) "We
mun find new sleeves somewhere. I reckon she'll have to do
with a breadth less i' t' skirt. I never reckon to go to bed before eight o'clock, 'cept Sundays. Tak hod o' that."

And at "that" they worked till bedtime.

At dawn next morning Sarah looked out on the smoky street
and the mean houses, and reviewed her position. She was entirely satisfied with it. Mending up and cleaning up had always
been her employment, and she found nothing to object to in
it. Meagre diet and homely surroundings were familiar to her,
and brought no depression with them, and there was now a
rosy light on the horizon that had not been there before. She
went on her way contented and energetic; she would learn,
learn, learn. Since that was what she had to do, something
should come of it; so she prepared to work with a will.

Little more than a week passed when something happened. As she was "siding" the tea-things one afternoon and Mrs. Gracehurst was arranging the schoolroom, Sarah saw two girls a little older than herself come in and begin a whispered conversation with her. According to her somewhat perverse nature, the woman answered their question aloud—

"Aye, she's i' t' house." And then, "Sarah, here's two lasses comed to see you."

Sarah came forward to scrutinize them. She had seen them before, not at the singing-master's, but near it, and more than once. There were half-a-dozen girls who seemed to be often in the neighbourhood, generally with music in their hands, and always going in twos and threes. They were better dressed than Sarah, and in the passing glance that is sufficient for the purpose had decided that she was their inferior, and had let her know it.

One of her visitors, round-faced and rosy, pushed the other forward as they came into the house. This other was different, and in both her own opinion and that of her companion was a much more important personage. She was very pretty, though owing to her town-bred languor and pallor, she did not make a pleasant impression on Sarah. Her features were nothing in particular, and people might be very like her without being pretty at all—without having just that shade of brown hair that matched so well with her creamy skin, and just the red, pouting lips that suited both. She had curls, too—a quantity of ringlets of which she was very conscious, leaning her head sometimes this way, sometimes that, so that they swung a little off her cheek, like Mrs. Overton's. Her face and air told of nothing but *ennui* and the longing for a sensation, and, perhaps, of her inability to provide for herself in that respect.

"These lasses learns wi' Holroyd as weel as you," Mrs. Gracehurst explained; "I reckon they're comed to talk to you about him."

"We've seen you going to your lessons; you go at ten o'clock. Oh, isn't he a funny man?"

Sarah laughed, and owned that she had often resolved not

to "mind what he said, but just then he would say something sensible."

"What do you call sensible?"

"Something about singing."

"He does not always talk sense about singing, though."

"He seems to know a deal about it."

"He tells Miss Raines she knows nothing about singing, and there has she been to many and many a concert!"

"Are you Miss Raines?" Sarah asked, turning to the ringlets.

The girl bent her head, and waved her curls to signify yes.

"I've heard of you, but I thought you were a grand singer."

"So she is a grand singer," said the round face, stoutly. "If I'd been her and could get ten shillings a night I'd never have begun taking lessons again."

"What did you do it for?" Sarah asked.

Miss Raines turned her head and waved her curls, and said—

"Mr. Walsh thought it advisable. He said I should take a higher position."

"Who's Mr. Walsh?"

But to this she bridled, and, putting her head on the other side, she drew herself up and minced—

"A friend of mine."

The round face, whose name was Woodhead, asked Sarah what she could sing. They discussed their favourites, and hummed tunes and talked and laughed till at length the visitors found it was time to go. As soon as they were gone, Sarah asked Mrs. Gracehurst who Mr. Walsh was.

"He's a fellow 'at makes a fool on her," she said. "She thinks a rare deal on him. It's allus Mr. Walsh, Mr. Walsh! Tommy Walsh wor never no Mister while (till) she kirstened him!"

"What does he do?"

"He plays t' big fiddle, and he reckons to get up concerts an' t' like o' that. Him an' Holroyd's fit to fight allus, an' they're nauther on 'em worth sixpence. Nauther on 'em. Ye may have their own word for it, t' oan o' t' other!"

Sarah laughed, and asked what Tommy Walsh could have to do with Miss Raines.

"Why, it wor him 'at started her o' singing, and set her up so she couldn't stand straight ever sin!"

"What did she do afore?"

"Went to t' miln like other folk."

"It's better singing nor going to t' miln."

"She willn't addle so much wi' singing. She never sings so oft as once a week, an' she needn't give up going to t' miln for that."

"No, for sure," said Sarah, emphatically, whose whole training and education taught her better than to discount fair prospects before they were actually realized.

Sarah thought the subject finished, but Mrs. Gracehurst had still to speak her mind on the late visitors.

'They're all a pack of gaumless lasses," she went on. "They're just fit to be made fools on, if they could nobbud find somebody to do it for 'em. They'll believe ought 'at anybody tells 'em, 'specially if it is not true!"

Sarah laughed again, deprecatingly, and implied that she thought the old woman too severe.

"Ye'll see if it isn't so. A man can allus talk best when he sticks at naught, an' that's just what they like."

"You're like Aunt Jane."

"Your Aunt Jane's got a bit o' sense."

"But it's better singing nor going to t' miln, if they addle more brass. Miss Raines can get—"

"Miss Raines! There's no Miss about it! She's just a mill lass. It's Lizzie Raines an' Lizzie Woodhead, I tell ye."

"They may call themselves what they like, I reckon?"

"It wouldn't matter if they did not think better o' themselves wi' t' oan name nor t' other. It's them lads 'at's putten it into their heads."

"What lads?"

"A lot o' fiddlers 'at they've gotten together through (from) nobody knows where. T' half on 'em does not belong to Baumforth."

Mrs. Gracehurst had the very common opinion that her own country and her own town were the best places in the world to belong to, and found good reason for despising anyone in the fact of their having been born elsewhere.

"There's that Walsh, but he's aboon forty year old. Sydney Wynde's one of 'em, 'at goes to your house."

Sarah recalled the flourishing *attitude of falsehood* that Sydney Wynde often assumed, and that he generally thought good enough for girls, and for Sarah in particular.

"Everybody doesn't reel it right off like Sydney," she said.

"Like draws to like. But I'm right glad ye see through him."

But this was owing to no perspicuity of Sarah's; at least, not much. At the age when she made his acquaintance Sydney had not thought it worth while to drape and attitudinize before her. She had seen him more than once pay broad compliments to people whom he held in contempt, particularly women.

"I know well enough what ye mean," she said. "But they've no 'casion to believe it. Does Mr. Walsh do t' same?"

"It's all for his sen what he does. He talks tull her for what he can get. He nobbud pays her ten shilling a time, and I've heard say 'at if she'd just learn summat an' tak' a bit o' pains she'd get two or three pound."

"Would he pay me summat, do you think, when I had learnt a bit?"

"He'll pay ye as little as ever he can help."

"Why, in course he will."

"If you're worth five pounds you may trust him to offer you twenty shillings."

From this hour a scheme ran in Sarah's head. She would learn diligently, and she would let Mr. Walsh hear her sing. Ten shillings would be more than she had ever earned in her life. Twenty would be wealth. The offer of five pounds a night she reckoned as being only in dreamland, where the rainbow comes down to earth, but where no one ever finds it.

In committing her daughter to the care of her old friend Mrs. Gracehurst, it is doubtful if Mrs. Miles knew the character of the girls who would be her natural companions in Baumforth. Mrs. Gracehurst herself knew them, and did her best to counteract the effects of their silly depravity respecting love and love affairs. Sarah herself recoiled from the strange creatures when she began to make their nearer acquaintance. Not yet seventeen, and, little as she knew it, protected from indiscriminate conversations, she simply stared when one girl after another confided to her that someone admired her, or, indeed, that the world in general always "looked at her," the last word being said with a tone of wonder which made Sarah answer, "Why, ye need not mind 'em." She soon found that this was not the sort of reception such news ought to meet with. It ought to rouse a keen interest, and to lead to endless whispers and laughing remarks. Soon she found out that the girls would insist on the importance of their communications, and say to her—

"Whatever shall I do? I can't keep him off, I declare."

Then Sarah would gravely ask—

"Do you want to keep him off, or to keep him on?"

"Oh, I don't know! And there's another"—another whispered name—"he always speaks to me."

And Sarah found that two or three, or half a dozen, were found more interesting than one, and would go home laughing and tell Mrs. Gracehurst that So-and-so was fair out of her head.

Mrs. Gracehurst would take the opportunity to reiterate her opinion as to courting in general. She told Sarah that none of the young men were worth a rush, and that she would be like them if she listened to them.

"They never gets agate wi' me," said Sarah, simply.

"Happen ye believe it all."

"Nay, there's nought to believe."

After doubting Mrs. Gracehurst's opinion, and putting aside the constant proofs of it which came before her eyes, Sarah began to believe it, or at least to doubt every word she heard when a mixed conversation was going on. Then she got angry with the trifling, and at last took a settled dislike to the men and women both. "They are just fit for one another," she thought, "and either of them fit for that Thelwal at Repton." Thelwal was, and always had been since she had made his acquaintance, the incarnation of evil to Sarah, and any likeness to him was enough to lose her favour for ever.

The round-faced, rosy girl, Miss Woodhead, who was really an affectionate girl, and in want of a friend, told her that some of the young men had been asking about her. She thought it a good deed to tell her so. Sarah merely said—

"Why, I'm nought to them!"

"Oh, but they think a great deal of you!"

"An' they're nought to me," she added, with a commencement of a frown that made Miss Woodhead drop the subject.

Sarah bridled with anger at the mere idea that any young fool should begin talking to her as the whole set were in the habit of talking to some of the girls. It is true that she heard of the follies chiefly from those who listened to them, and treasured them up for repetition; and Sarah had often noticed that the same tale was never told twice exactly in the same manner. "But they need not begin wi' me," she said, angrily, without exactly explaining to herself why the habit was so very detestable.

She missed her home. She felt it a cold and treacherous world, and thought Repton was a much happier place than Baumforth. There she expanded and opened her flower leaves, which no one at Baumforth ever saw. Her reticence and suspicions pleased Mrs. Gracehurst, who took credit to herself, as indeed was her due. Her father and mother were pleased, on the other hand, to see her keep her outspoken candour. They never asked for it, being too wise, but they were not the less anxious on that account. They never heard that the frequent inquiries of the Repton youth concerning her had roused the jealousy of the girls, and that she had made herself enemies unconsciously, for which she cared nothing at all, not even when a spice of calumny was added to the ill will of the tribe.

So the time passed on, through the winter and through the summer following, and Sarah began to be impatient again for a change.

And a short time after something occurred to keep up her

hopes. She plodded conscientiously with Mr. Holroyd, doing whatever she was bid. She generally thought it silly, and it was almost always unintelligible. Indeed, the idea passed through her mind that she would ask him some day if she might not give over "raughting,' and take and learn summat. Fortunately she learnt of the girls to whom Miss Woodhead and Miss Raines introduced her that they too had all to go through the same discipline. So she contented herself with watching for some sign that her master was satisfied with her performances. She watched in vain, so far as he was concerned, but she learnt from them that he never had the slightest hesitation in telling any girl of her failure or incompetence. "He can set anybody down!" all the girls agreed; and, indeed, his readiness in doing so was one main reason why, with very superior skill in his profession, he had to content himself with a very inferior class of pupils. With genuine music lovers Holroyd was a great favourite; fashionable pretenders would not tolerate him at all.

Sarah had never been "set down," and a small indication of success came to encourage her. After the lesson was over one day, as she prepared to leave, Mr. Holroyd told her to wait a bit; he had not done with her. He left her standing by the piano, and went into the house, took a look out of the window, and then sat down by the fire, taking his pipe off the chimney-piece first. Sarah changed her place a little so as to keep him in sight, but she knew better than to do more, or inquire further. For a good ten minutes she stood silent, and then saw half a dozen of her new acquaintances pass the window and enter the house. They were greeted with—

"Now, what are ye come for?"

"Now, Mr. Holroyd, you told us to come!"

"I told you to come at eleven o'clock for a singing lesson. What do you want now, at this time of day?"

"Well, Mr. Holroyd, it's only ten minutes past. Do be good, now, and don't scold. We'll do as well as ever we can."

"Then you'll do better than you've ever done before. When did you make up your minds to that?"

"To what, Mr. Holroyd?"

"To do as well as you can. Not that it's much you can do."

"Oh, Mr. Holroyd!" and a general laugh.

They were to have some practice in part singing; and as the lesson went on Sarah was astonished at the incompetence and carelessness of the girls. The instruction which she had picked up as if it were gold, carefully and in driblets, was set before them and almost always neglected. Besides the errors and deficiencies of which they were unconscious, they were continually committing faults that they knew of. They had no end of bad habits, each of which was pitilessly corrected by Mr. Holroyd, every time it appeared, and each of which might be expected to appear again, when the opportunity offered. In fact, he evidently watched for each of them, well knowing when it would come.

"Oh, dear, Mr. Holroyd, do give us something nice to sing, and then one could take more pains!"

"As if you could sing anything nice!"

"Do just try us, Mr. Holroyd. Now I'm sure you don't keep Miss Miles singing at one stupid thing for half-an-hour together."

"Miss Miles has got more sense than you."

From which Sarah gathered that she had been held up as a model to the others. She quickly said that Mr. Holroyd had never let her sing a song at all so far. Holroyd's eyes twinkled with fun at the discomfiture of the idle, babbling girls. He told them if they were not content they should have nothing but sol-faing for the next hour, and so got a little practice out of them.

The part singing was a great additional interest to Sarah, and it served to increase her intimacy with her fellow pupils. Since her sliding days she had always liked to be in the midst of companions, giving and receiving excitement, and generally foremost amongst them. She did not succeed so well with her new friends as with the old ones. They were different. As we branch out in life we part company for ever with those with whom we were once enfolded in one protecting sheath, and not only from them, but from all others. The farther we grow the wider is our solitude. Never can man or woman enjoy the perfect sympathy that they gave and received in childhood. True, they are akin; they spring from the same stock, but they reach out in different ways.

So Sarah looked on in silent wonder and disappointment, while the girls talked of their dress, their hair, and their acquaintances, and sung snatches of melody taught by them to each other, missing or spoiling the difficult parts of every song they tried. They were the daughters of clerks and shopkeepers, and even mill hands, whose means were not sufficient to secure a more fashionable teacher, and they were reasonably proud of their position as pupils, for Mr. Holroyd would unhesitatingly refuse to teach a girl who had not both ear and voice. So taking the fact of their admission as evidence of their superiority they took little pains to advance farther.

As the autumn came on a new subject came into favour. It appeared to Sarah that every girl she knew either was herself interested, or had a friend interested, or knew someone who had a friend interested in some kind of public musical performance. Who the singers were, what could they do, how much they got—all was discussed incessantly. Miss Raines enjoyed this season exceedingly. Since she had been offered a small payment by some blundering, straightforward *entrepreneur,* she had become more difficult to please, and, as her voice was really remarkable, and her notions of payment were rather primitive, she often got her demands. She had great hopes of her own future, and, considering the quality of her voice, they would not have been unreasonable, if she had shown any industry. But she was possessed by the feminine idea that her fortune was to come to her, not to be made by her, and had all the faults and inefficiency that come of habitual waiting. As yet no one appreciated her so highly as Tommy Walsh, and she thought well of him accordingly. He generally gave a concert or two during the winter, played at a great many, and negotiated for performers at a great many more, out of which he somehow made his living. He and Mr. Holroyd were sworn foes. Walsh said his enemy knew nothing of manners, and Holroyd, that Walsh knew nothing of music.

Mr. Holroyd, too, gave a concert every winter. He was a great favourite with about half the professional people, and could command some good performers, and gave good music. In the previous winter he had asked Miss Raines to sing a short piece, in which she had been well drilled, and the honour was such that she had been indocile ever since. There were many speculations among the girls as to whether the scoldings they got when they met twice a week to practise together were not preparatory to a proposition that they should all sing in the next concert; and when this was acknowledged to be improbable, whether any of them would. They all shared with Sarah in a wish to exhibit their proficiency, and most of them added to the wish the sincere belief that it only needed to be exhibited to meet with more appreciation than they got from their master. There was even a talk of some of them offering their services as fellow professionals. They discussed the matter often with the immense amount of talk which they gave to everything they took in hand, and repeatedly uttered innuendoes on the subject, which the master gave no signs of understanding. At last they arranged a conversation beforehand, in which it was accidentally mentioned. He snubbed them unmercifully before the proposal was finished, and Miss Raines, as soon as she was out of the house, declared herself insulted. There was a small indignation meeting at the house-corner, and when the fact that they were very angry had been sufficiently dilated on, Sarah struck in with—

"Never mind, lasses, let's do it without asking him anything about it."

"You don't understand," Miss Raines said, condescendingly.

"Yes, I do, well enough."

The girls all began to laugh.

"How can you sing at his concert and he not know?"

"Well enough we can. He won't know till we start off, and then folk will think it's all right, and he can't stop us."

"Eh! Sarah Miles, ye are a lass."

When the plan was kneaded into shape it was this: Sam and Sydney, whom she had to introduce to them as Mr. Sykes and Mr. Wynde, were to supply the men's voices, and assist in the practising. The female performers were to be admitted among the audience and to ascend the platform from the front, while the gentlemen found their way in from behind. As soon as Mr. Holroyd's programme was known, they would choose where their piece was to be interpolated. It must be near the end, they all agreed, and then its failure would not spoil much, "and then we can slip off home, right away," they said.

"We mun do it right," Sarah said. "We'll do it first-rate an' say we did it out of compliment."

So on the following Saturday Sarah was entrusted with the business of securing the co-operation of the bass voices. Sam and Sydney and John Miles all avowed their readiness to practise with them anything they liked, and promised to find a fourth voice by the day of meeting, but when this was settled the whole negotiation was broken off by Sarah's declaring that if they began more than one piece she would quit the whole concern.

"Why, Sarah, what have you against singing? You have lived so long wi' Mrs. Gracehurst that you've gotten like her."

"If you begin anything else they'll soon tire of practising, they'll go on and on all night, but you'll never get 'em back to that."

So it was agreed that the chosen piece was to be learnt first; the men keeping their intentions secret as to what they would do besides.

Sarah was rather astonished by the first results of her proposal. It was eagerly accepted, a madrigal chosen, and a night fixed for the first meeting in Mrs. Gracehurst's schoolroom. The girls all appeared "donned," that is, in their best dresses, with, moreover, some gaiety of adornment added, which would not be quite proper on Sunday. Sarah asked what they had done that for. They replied by asking how they could do any other, and looking at each other with such confidence of unanimous support that she had to drop that subject. The next annoyance was that "'t lads," as she called them, had done the same. She refrained from asking them why. Sydney was in high feather, and with great flourish introduced Mr. Moss, a little fat man with smiling face and red hair. He flourished, too, and the whole four proceeded to talk about anything in the world but the chosen piece. The thing was produced out of Sydney's pocket, but he began by asking Miss Raines if she knew of nothing better. There was so-and-so, and—"

"Ye said that was the best, Sydney, so start."

"Well, but there are others. I once heard you sing, Miss Raines, at a concert."

"I've only sung once in a part-song," she said.

And then came a long discussion as to when it was. There were fulsome compliments from Sydney and Mr. Moss, and all the girls were soon chattering away at full steam. Sometimes they returned to the business of the evening, but as they began by supposing that the girls knew their parts, and the girls knew nothing about them, they were shy of trying, and mentally resolved to put off the attempt till they had practised it a little.

At eight o'clock Mrs. Gracehurst put her head in from the kitchen and said—

"Now, lads, it's time ye were off. Ye sud hae come sooner."

There was blank dismay among the whole dozen.

Sarah quietly informed Sammy that if they did so again she would help no more.

"Did so! did how?" Sammy asked.

She threw her hand towards the door, by way of answer, and spoke to no one as they went out.

When next Saturday evening the confederates met at old Sykes', they asked her if they should come to practise.

"Aye!" she said, "if ye think ye can."

"Can! what for can't we?"

"Ye can try."

And with this ungracious permission they came. Some work was done, and the girls in some degree broken in. They pronounced Sarah worse than Holroyd, but obeyed her nevertheless.

Under Sarah's despotic guidance something was learnt at the next meeting. With some difficulty Sarah succeeded in making them repeat and repeat until they got the certainty that would enable them to overcome their shyness and be confident in their own powers. Fault after fault was eliminated, and sometimes the thing was very well sung. Sarah began to be grateful to the lads for making the long distance from Repton to Baumforth so often, not knowing how far a man, "auf Freiers fuss," will wander. It even became a custom to practise diligently for a time, and then strike work deliberately and introduce something else. But there was no gainsaying Mrs. Gracehurst's peremptory "Now then, lads," and the party broke up punctually at eight o'clock. Sydney would try a little blarney, telling her how much obliged to her they were, etc., etc. But all he got would be "Aye, aye, now ye mun go."

"More than t' hauf on't is nought but idle talk," she would observe as she closed the door.

And Sarah answered—

"Aye, that Sydney Wynde and that other red-haired chap never can stop their fond talk!" (Fond, meaning foolish.)

"Aye, Sam and John were none so far behind."

"Nay, our Sammy never tells no lies."

"Our Sammy! Who's our Sammy, I wonder?"

"Why, Sammy Sykes, for sure. Sykes's and us has allus been thick."

"Our Sammy!" the old woman repeated.

And for the first time in her life Sarah began to think it odd that she should have acquired the habit of speaking so.

The whole team was restless and disorderly, and needed a strong hand to get any work out of them. They would whisper together whenever there was a moment's interval. And Sydney would begin with an ostentatious civility that was like stroking Sarah's fur the wrong way—

"Now, Miss Miles, do you not think we have sung this piece often enough for one night?"

"Oh! I am sure we have," the rest would chime in. "Do let us try something else."

And Sarah would pull them up sharp with—

"Will ye or willn't ye? Ye mun either do it or drop it. There's noan so much time left. So now say!"

"Oh, we can come every night if you like," all the men said at once. "We shall have time enough."

"If ye come ye'll ha' to sing," Sarah answered, and there was rather better behaviour for a little time. And though they had no patience or perseverance, they accomplished the little they had to do. By constant pressure Sarah secured a good deal of practising, which, all being spent on one short madrigal, produced a remarkable effect, and each part grew to be as clear as a bell and as distinct as speech. Sarah secured this result by dint of constant urging, aided by tact and diplomacy. Sometimes the second voices were to sing their part again because the first had sung theirs so often; sometimes because three times was lucky, and again because four was an even number, and just once more, and then again, because there was a mistake that last time, until by constant repetition the voices were so sure that nothing could shake them. They grumbled, yawned, and interrupted in vain, till the men thought they had given a fair share of work for their amusement, and then they were unmanageable, and sung anything but what they ought, until Mrs. Gracehurst knocked at the door with her "Now, lads!"

Nothing less could have overcome the trepidation of the performers as the day drew near. They thought the piece nought, that folks would say that they were "impident lasses," that they should forget what came next "reight i' t' middle on 't, that Mr. Holroyd would interrupt them, and that in any of these cases they should never get over it as long as they lived. Sam or Sydney had an answer to these terrors which Sarah soon learnt of them.

"Well then, lasses, let's drop it," she would say, a proposal that was always negatived unanimously.

Only the day before the concert could they learn the programme, and pitch upon the place where their own piece was to be interpolated. They put it last but one, making it the last piece of vocal music performed. Once the whole plot had very nearly fallen through on the question of dress. Miss Raines thought they all ought to wear white muslin, but as no one was provided with it except herself she submitted perforce to something else. So the girls put on their best frocks, and smoothed their hair, and looked much better than they would have done if they had adopted a style they were unused to.

The platform reached across the end of the concert room, and behind it was a door for the performers. Close to the wall on each side the male conspirators contrived two steps by which the girls could ascend it. They were among the audience, but not in front, and when the door had closed on the retreating performers of the last piece but one, a voice was heard among the audience, exclaiming—

"Hullo, what now!"

In dead silence eight girls ascended the steps, while the four men leaped up in front. With all eyes upon them they ranged themselves in line. Miss Raines leaned forward and caught Sydney's eye; he described some mystic flourish with his right hand, and at once the twelve voices started.

"Down in a flowery vale," etc.

It had never been so well sung in Baumforth before. Unconsciously, from long practice, their voices harmonized exactly, the suppressed excitement kept them up to pitch, and gave them the quality which sets the human organ above all other musical instruments. As the verse came to an end, Mr. Holroyd's shaggy head and broad shoulders appeared behind the singers. His hand held a long pipe in his mouth, and his eyes danced beneath their thick brows. As they finished, he raised his hand and pipe shouting—

"Encore, I say!"

The girls started in fright. The audience shouted with laughter, and echoed the encore. After some whispering, the piece was sung again, and then the girls descended and hurried out of the room. Chattering and laughing they made their way to Mrs. Gracehurst's to talk it over. They explained to her how they had thought they never could get up those steps, how they could not get into line, how they scarcely knew what they were doing, and how they started when they heard the shout behind them!

"Did not you see him open the door?" asked Sydney.

"No; how could we? We were overthrong" (busy).

"Now, ye see," Sarah said next day, "Sammy doesn't tell no lies like t' other folk."

"Why, why, lass, ye know all about it, dunnot ye?"

"Why, I know that."

"There never wor a man yet 'at couldn't lake wi' t' lasses if they'd nobbud let 'em," Mrs. Gracehurst repeated.

"Ye never seed Sammy Sykes mak' a fool on a lass same as that Mr. Moss and Sydney carries on wi' Miss Raines."

"They just carry on as far as ye'll let 'em, sure enough they willn't go no farder."

"He doesn't carry on, I tell ye!"

"He knows better than to say what ye willn't believe."

This persistence in Sarah arose in fact from awakened suspicion. She did believe all Sammy said, and approved of all he did. Now she began to think that his sayings and doings were perhaps modified for her eyes and ears. Was he different to other people? or was his object merely to persuade her to the things he wanted, and to let her think they were both a "pleasuring" together? She saw well enough that the men had had a grand spree with the girls, and did not intend to let the acquaintance drop. Was Sammy Sykes one of them? Or was he with her? On reflection, she saw that it was unreasonable to expect that he would give up the girl's acquaintance because the singing was over; but she was one among the half-dozen whom it pleased the men to laugh at. This, too, could not be answered.

"He wants ye to sing at his new chapel, if ever he gets it finished," Mrs. Gracehurst had said at another time.

"Yes, of course he does," Sarah had said; "we're both going to sing."

"Aye, why then it's all right," the old woman had answered, in a dry sarcastic way, that made Sarah think that she knew it was all wrong.

The more she pondered the more clearly she saw that since Sammy would never tell her anything but what he knew she would believe, she could never know whether he spoke the truth or not. "It's all nought," she said a dozen times, and then began thinking again, as if the question were not settled.

She had hoped for some result to follow from the madrigal, but it seemed to her to make no difference whatever. She watched closely for some indication that Mr. Holroyd's estimate of her powers was raised by her performance, and saw none. She concluded she was a long way from the ten shillings a night. Would she perhaps never get to it at all? Was she incurably inferior, so that pains and labour could not compensate for her want of talent? If so, she had better go home and find some other employment. She thought that, sooner or later, she must ask Mr. Holroyd's opinion about it. Not yet, for she knew very well she would lower herself in his opinion by such impatience; but some time. So with the plodding industry that was hers both by inheritance and training, she went on through the winter, and then, as no one seemed to expect anything else, through the following summer, and began to look to what another concert season might bring forth in the way of improvement and opportunity; and now the question was decided for her without any action on her part.

Coming home one afternoon as usual, about half-an-hour before the school "laused," she found to her great surprise the children gone, and the room empty. She went forward, talking as she went, asking Mrs. Gracehurst why the children were gone so soon, but the old woman was not in the house, and in her stead sat, leaning over the fire, a lank, ill-dressed man, who turned round when she entered, with a defiant look, but spoke not a word. Though under-sized, his lankness made him look tall; he held his bony, flat-sided head forward on his shoulders, and his mouth was the foremost part of it. The two faced each other for a moment, and Sarah's face, too, took a defiant expression, merely from seeing the one before her; then she heard a noise above, and went upstairs. She found Mrs. Gracehurst stooping over her (Sarah's) drawer, which she had nearly emptied.

"There's a man sitting i' t' kitchen," she said.

"Aye, I know," the woman answered, without raising her head.

"What's agate?" Sarah asked, after a pause, watching her throwing all the clothes into an apron and tying the corners together in haste.

"Ye're a going home, here's your things, all 'at you want just now; you may get t' other after, and tell your mother I sent you."

Sarah took the bundle, but stood still. Mrs. Gracehurst took her by the arm and turned her round to the door.

"It's all right. Say I sent ye."

Sarah slowly descended the stairs and met the eyes of the man by the fire. She gave a defiant toss as she went by; she was ready for war, not expecting anything but words, and having a tongue of her own.

"What ha' ye gotten there?" he asked, glowering at her bundle.

"It's her clothes," Mrs. Gracehurst called out hastily from the stairs.

And now Sarah took fright. Without her understanding why, the submissive explanation impressed her with fear. She went out of the kitchen, turning round in the passage for a last look. She saw Mrs. Gracehurst walk across the kitchen floor to the fire, and take the kettle lid off. Then she went to the sink for water. The bucket was empty, and Sarah saw her sling it on her arm and go out at the door just as Sarah closed the front one. She loitered, well knowing that Mrs. Gracehurst would come and speak to her. As she put her arm through her bundle at the front door, and prepared to walk away, the woman's hand was on her shoulder.

"Here, give this to your mother," she said, holding a grey woollen sock, tightly tied up. "Now, tak' care on it; there's money in it."

"Aye, I'll give it her," Sarah said, with a lost look, and waiting to hear more.

"Now go your ways," was all she got, as the old woman pushed her on, and left her.

Long as she had been used to the woman's abrupt and angular manner, it never struck her so much as now. It was just herself; it was twice herself.

As Mrs. Miles went into the shop that evening at dusk, she took a look, according to custom, up the street and down the street, observing the passers-by, all of whose faces and most of whose business she knew. But there was something that took her by surprise. Her daughter was coming up the lane, though it was neither Saturday nor a holiday. The mother stood in some perplexity waiting to speak to her.

"Eh, mother, she's sent me home."

"What's t' matter, lass?"

"I know nought about it. She just sent me off all in a minute, an' she said I were to give you this; an' there's money in it."

Her mother held out her hand for it, and took it without surprise.

"What, he's comed again, then, is he?" and she turned into the house.

"Who's comed again, mother?"

"Why, her husband, bairn."

Mrs. Miles did not leave her own house very often. She had a shorter way of communicating with her friends. Watching through the shop window she soon saw the person she wanted, and called to him as he passed the door. If she did not see the right person, she was sure to see one or other of his neighbours, or someone who passed his house on their way to their work. By this means she let Zachariah Flocks know that she wanted to speak with him, and before seven o'clock he strolled into the shop, on his way home.

"Zack," she said, without any preface, "he's comed again."

"I guessed as much when I seed your Sarah."

"She'll be over here in a day or two, you may be sure, and ye mun tak' her in."

Zack nodded.

"I would tak' her in here, but he'd be sure to come here for her."

"If he comes near our house, I'll give him my clog."

"Ye munnot let him see her; and ask him for t' brass to pay for her dinner."

"Noan a bad idea," he said. "But if he shows his face here we'll hunt him out o' t' town."

He turned round and walked out as a customer walked in.

Before night Mrs. Gracehurst appeared, sharper, sourer, more haggard than ever. She knocked at the house door, and as there was no one in the house had to knock several times. When at last Mrs. Miles opened the door, she stood at a little distance, and asked—

"Happen ye dunnot want onybody 'at's turned out of their own house?" and stood as if prepared to walk off as soon as the answer came, or rather sooner if it was long in coming.

"Come in, Susy, lass, come in," Mrs. Miles answered, taking her hand.

She came in, sat down on the nearest chair, and burst into tears. In the course of an hour she was comforted, warmed, and fed, and restored to her habitual fighting condition. Then she took her departure, and settled herself with Nancy Flocks, and was made welcome.

She was one of the old chapellers whose conduct had entitled her to belong to the brotherhood, and to get help from them. All the world knew of her wrongs, and of the way in which she was helped over them. Everyone approved, for the state of the law in this respect was below the common standard of morality in Repton. In a week she went back again, private information having reached her that her husband was gone.

She found the house door open and a friend on guard, and laughed, even she, at the account of the way in which the man had been got rid of.

"We watched him day and night," said the woman, "till he took a chair out to t' pop-shop, an' then my husband says to him, 'Let that alone,' an' he says, 'Ye've nought to do wi' it.' An' then he telled him all t' furniture belonged to him. An' then ye sud ha' seen him! He banged down t' chair an' started o' swearing! An' then my husband says, 'If ye break my chairs I'll ha' ye up!' An' then he set off, an' we never seed him since."

"He did not get his dinner yesterday?" said the wife.

"Nay, I reckon he had eaten all 'at there was i' t' house afore; an' there's nought else gone."

She was mistaken, however; the water-bucket was gone. It was found at the nearest pawn-shop, and redeemed by the wife. Then things returned to their old rut. The scholars came back, and Mrs. Gracehurst congratulated herself that she had escaped with little damage. Things had been worse in former days; the drunkard had brought her to poverty, beaten her as long as he dare, and then deserted her. It was not for long, for there was still something in the house he had left. When he had cleared it out he went off again, only to come again when a few comforts had been gathered together by the struggling wife. At last means had been devised for her protection, and she was comparatively free. True, he could come when he liked, but as, when he asked for something to eat, her only answer was to ask him for money, he went and found other means of living and drinking.

CHAPTER XIX.

IN TWO MINDS.

It was not till Sarah had been at home a few days that she found out how completely she had turned a corner during her two years' life in Baumforth. She had left her home a brave, self-confident girl, and she returned to it a reserved, cautious, almost suspicious woman.

"Eh, mother," she said, "it's grand to be at home," as she washed the tea-things at night.

"I say, wife," said the father from his chimney-corner, "does ta remember there was once a little lass wi' her head all curls, 'at used to run about t' house floor, an' used to keep her tongue agate till tha' said tha'd never seen such a lass i' all t' world, never! And then the bairn asked, 'How big is all t' world, mammy?'"

The mother laughed at the recollection, and Sarah called out from the milk-house—

"I allus like to know all about it."

And the old pair recognized that they stood in the presence of an intellect that must be satisfied, or deceived, as the case might be.

Outside, the case was different; she never went down the lane without meeting with half-a-dozen acquaintances who saluted her with a smile of surprise, not being used to see her except at chapel, and "Eh, Sarah lass, ye are growed," which was not true, but which somehow expressed the change which had taken place in her appearance and her dress. She wore a long-sleeved frock and an apron, which seemed, in Repton, ridiculously small in comparison with the customary Repton wrap. Her hair was smooth, and her face grave. Sometimes she smiled very effectively, and always held her head high and her mouth closed. Of this last peculiarity she was quite unconscious, and so knew nothing of the effect it produced. Her speech was more English, owing to her intercourse with strangers, and from this she must have acquired her unaccustomed reticence and gravity; she herself felt the restraint, but never more could she indulge in the outspoken sincerity of former days. She no longer expected her hearers either to agree with or to differ from her, but looked almost of course for an abounding assent to everything she said. With an underlying contempt, almost visible, while she had constantly fought against Mrs. Gracehurst's misanthropy, it had produced its effect nevertheless, and what she had witnessed among the girls had deepened the impression and embittered her feelings. She alternately despised the girls and hated the falsehood, if not the men who uttered it.

But she was the daughter of one of the most thriving men in the place; old Miles took a high position among his own class, both from his character and from the comfortable competence resulting therefrom. On all hands she was treated civilly, and everyone sought her acquaintance. Her sister grew proud of her, and boasted of her to her mistresses.

In her own home she thawed considerably. The Sykes' had allus been thick with the Miles', and the same might be said of the Flocks', and with these, either at the Sykes' or in her father's house, she disputed with Sam and Sydney, and told all the oddities of Mrs. Gracehurst's house, and when she won a laugh, even from the elders, her eyes sparkled with triumph.

"There were never ought like them lasses and them lads," she said, pointing to the three young men sitting opposite to her, while Zack and Nancy watched and laughed.

She described their tones and their dictionary English, and it raised more laughter than she expected or understood, and she stopped at once.

"An' what do ye think Miss Raines did t' last concert?" she went on, after a minute.

They did not know.

"Tommy Walsh wanted her to sing 'Bid me Discourse' at his concert, an' said he'd teach her a bit, but she thought he'd make her go through with it as he always does, taking a line at a time, an' making her sing it till she were stalled; but she thought she'd never thoil, so she took it to Holroyd and asked leave to sing it to him a two or three times, an' he stared at her like a pot-cat, an' never spoke, an' took it out of her hand an' laid it down, an' never took it up again."

The men laughed heartily, and declared they could "just see Holroyd."

"She's reight fond (foolish), is t' lass," John opined.

Then Sarah's skeleton suddenly rose by her side. How differently had they spoken last time they had seen her, when, with everlasting bows and smiles, they had praised her singing and everything else about her.

"All lasses aren't like her," she said.

" 'Cause they haven't all t' chance."

"If anyone started o' telling me such lies I'd soon set 'em down."

John spoke once more out of the depths of his young experience.

"Ye'd think it was all true."

"It takes a fool to set a man off at that game," Sarah said, "and another to let him go on."

Old Sykes noticed a different accent, of bitter energy, that he had never heard in her voice before. The girl spoke with all the confidence of the young, that they will never be found doing anything either wrong or foolish; but her courage was gone. Was it possible John was right? Was she herself one of the fools, and were they all ready to laugh at her, as they did at Lizzie Raines?

She passed the company over in her mind, looking, as she did so, in every separate face as if she had never seen it before. There was the old man who seldom spoke, and never contradicted her, but whose words were always true. Was it possible that he cared nothing for her opinions, or even for herself? There had always been a comforting sense of safety in his presence, but was it only the safety that a kitten has, when people watch its gambols because they find them amusing?

Then there was Sydney Wynde. She had no difficulty in setting him down at once as worthless. With her he never had much weight, and now she called to mind how he had turned her to his own purposes as he would. She remembered the times when she had detected untruthfulness, inconsistency, hints of doubtful morality. Above all, she remembered how, through him, she was led into visiting the only people whose acquaintance her father and mother had forbidden her to cultivate. She remembered the look with which he had met the question, and remembered, too, that he had not a single word to say in favour of his friends. She herself would have flared up and defended them, or have owned their deficiencies; he did neither, he was like a thief found out, that sneaked away silently.

"I'd keep decent company if I were ye," Nancy Flocks had said, and he was neither offended nor angry.

But why was Sammy led by him? It is comforting to the sorrowing relations, when a poor, foolish youth has transgressed, to hear that it was because he was so easily led. He was so amiable! but to Sarah's instinct, as to that of the rest of the world, this beautiful quality of being easily led is the one damning fault that will ruin a man. To Sarah it did not look like a virtue at all, for, as she saw, a man is easily led where he wants to go, and nowhere else. Sam had wanted the chapel, he had wanted the evening's pleasure at the Eldons', he had enjoyed the noisy fun and the secret mockery in Mrs. Gracehurst's schoolroom. He had never been upright nor downright, as Sarah had all along maintained. She had seen through him no more than Miss Raines had seen through the other rattle pates. Sam's conduct ought to have been different. He ought to have pronounced a wrathful condemnation of their behaviour, and somehow have put a stop to it. A man should be ashamed, she thought, to lend himself to such unworthy falsehood, and she found nothing unreasonable in exacting such lofty morality. She saw, too, that public opinion was not with her, that no one scouted the laughers, but laughed with them. Sarah had always believed in good folk and bad folk; those whom she trusted she trusted absolutely, and all others she relegated into the outer world, where it did not matter what they were or what they did. In this warm heaven she had lived since her infancy, and now it was fading into the light of common day! The grey, cold world was all before her, but there was in it no place of rest!

One day, while in this gloomy frame of mind, she walked past the milliners' shop, and one of the Miss Whites called her in.

"Your sister Jane is here," she said; "won't you come in and talk to her?"

Now the sister was an excuse only, for the Miss Whites would call anyone in for the sake of a gossip whenever they had nothing else to do, and Jane had no greater pleasure in life than telling and hearing some new thing.

Jane Miles had stayed with the Turners at first, because it would have been disgraceful to leave them in their extremity, and afterwards because her wages were continued at the old rate, and, though the Miss Turners had, unknown to their father, dismissed one servant, they themselves had done the extra work. The sons, the most troublesome part of the household, were gone. The women each spared the servant's labour, so Jane, trusted and important, did the marketing and the disagreeable work outside, because the young ladies did not like to show themselves. They imagined that by this means they kept things secret. The only result of their arrangement was that they gave their servant an outlet for all the news of their concerns that the whole village cared to hear. It had become a custom with her to call at the milliners', both to hear the news and to give such detail as she had concerning the state of affairs at the great house, and so it happened that the very means taken by the family to isolate themselves resulted in giving weekly information of every pinching expedient to the world in general.

The party at the Miss Whites' were discussing Sarah herself when she came in. They were agreed as to how much she was improved—what a voice she had! And how Mr. Holroyd had told her he should want her for his next concert, and how other people had done the same, how that scamp Sydney had pronounced in her favour, though he never gives her a good word when he can help it.

"If only she would give up that idea of singing in the new chapel," Jane said, with disgust. "How can she rise in the world if she is to keep herself down with singing at them places?"

For Jane had fully imbibed the idea from her young mistresses that Dissent was low, and that the best thing Sarah could do was to get rid of it herself, and to stifle the fact that her parents were guilty of it.

"Young Mr. Sykes has a good deal of influence over her," Miss White observed, in the manner of a question.

"Oh, I don't know," Jane said, bridling; "there's many a one thinks much of our Sarah, and she cares for none of them."

"Is that true, Miss Sarah?" Miss White said, as she came in.

"Is what true?"

"That though many people admire you, you care for none of them?"

"Nay, it's nought to me," she answered, indifferently.

"I would not care for any of them," Jane said. "Don't you be led by anyone, Sarah; they'll only laugh at you when you have done what they want."

Jane spoke with direct reference to Sam and his chapel, but she did not care if Sarah acquired a general distrustfulness that would retard the time of her final settlement in life, until her advancing fortunes had removed her to a higher position.

"What can anybody want?" Sarah asked, as gruffly as if she would fight them if the answer were not satisfactory.

They smiled simultaneously, and then, seeing clearly that this was not satisfactory, Miss White insinuated that—

"Perhaps young Mr. Sykes might think he could get her to sing in the new chapel."

"Well, so I am going to do," she said.

"He's got you to do it!" they all exclaimed in chorus.

"Why for sure he has. What for shouldn't I?"

"Oh, Miss Sarah!"

"Well?"

"I did not know things were so far gone," her sister said, with a vexed air.

"Gone! Where to?—and what about?"

"I suppose it's all made up between you," Jane said. "If ye go together so far ye'll ha' to go together all t' way through."

"Ye're talking stuff. There's no going together at all in it."

"Why, then there ought to be; an' ye'd far better not sing at chapel if there's nought to come on't. But I expect he'll do as he likes, an' then laugh at ye when he's done."

"Sammy Sykes is a decent man," Sarah said, seriously offended.

And the women saw that joking would not do. They came to exactly the wrong conclusion as to the relations between him and Sarah Miles. When they accepted the conclusion that nothing was to be said against Sam, in Sarah's presence, they understood that he was too well grounded in her affections for there to be room for an insinuation to get in between them. Miss White was very sure that Mr. Sykes was a very agreeable young man, that she herself knew nothing against him; to which Jane added—

"Aye, he had as good a tongue of his own as any man, she dare be bound."

"But, Sarah, ye know nought about men," she added, with emphasis, and the two other old maids agreed with her.

"They'll flatter ye up to ought if ye listen to them."

"Sammy doesn't flatter," Sarah said.

"Of couse he does not talk such stuff to you as he would to Miss Raines. But he can find how to take you, it seems, when he wants ought."

"He has nobud to ask for it," she said angrily.

They laughed again.

There is no accusation so provoking as that which is made by innuendo, because there is no disproving it. Sarah was ashamed of herself for being provoked, and walked out indignantly.

Yet the Miss Whites were not the only people who seemed to know something. Everyone behaved in a manner somewhat different. Even old Sykes, she thought, was not so free as before, when she joined the evening party once more, to sing and rattle—for talking their intercourse could hardly be called. Sydney, too, actually spoke respectfully to her, and once, though rather in joke, called her Miss Miles. It was hard to quarrel with this, yet Sarah saw with vexation that her childhood was gone, and her audacious freedom with it. They discussed Miss Raines while Sarah watched them narrowly, but only saw some good-humoured laughter at her ridiculous folly. They opined that she was well off in having Tom Walsh to persuade her to learn something, for if she were to venture to produce a song without his correction and instruction, she would fail in it to a certainty. Then they sang, and Harriet profited in some degree by Sarah's teaching. But their sheet anchor was practice. They sang, with liking and appreciation, many things, and sang them, when once they had mastered them, again and again. They had found that they were welcome in almost any house in Repton if they would but come together, and in other places, too, where they began to make a little money among a people really musical and not particular.

These were happy times. Nothing pleased Sarah better than to have "some grand singing" with them all, and never to remember that there might be another side to the picture—that perhaps the men-folk, as she called them, were not friends, but managers, who spoke her fair for purposes of their own. She wavered between two opinions, and held fast by neither. The thing that best suited her temperament would have been to walk up to Sammy and ask him if he was a friend or a trickster; but she saw that this style of question would not do. It must be, "Are ye a courting on me, to get me to sing for ye?" and for this even Sarah was too shy. "He never flatters me up, nor nought," she said; "he never talks as Sydney and that young Moss would talk by the hour together to them lasses. If he is not upright and downright, where is he ought else?" This she could not answer, and it seemed to follow that the answer was nowhere.

Sarah kept repeating these vigorous assertions to herself because she had begun to doubt; besides, being herself quite ignorant that she was at all impressed by Sammy as a lover, she could not come to the only reasonable conclusion in which she might have rested content, whatever Sammy's conduct had been or might be. "It's nought to me," she had repeated again and again, but could not prove it by leaving the subject. No sooner had she said it than she began again to go over the proofs that Sam was—all right.

Again the spectre rose at her side.

One day, as she walked thoughtfully down the lane, she was stopped by a tall figure standing in her way. Looking up, she saw a long, lanky, loose-jointed woman, with such ribbons, lockets, scarf, flounces, and many coloured clothes that Sarah eyed her from head to foot in wonder.

"Well, I declare! So you don't know me! Well I never!"

"Sophy Elden!" she exclaimed at last, looking her over once more, and then there was a pause.

Sarah thought, of course, that Sophy had stopped her for a purpose, but the fact was that Sophy had no purpose beyond the ever-present desire for a gossip, and perhaps for a little mischief.

"Well, you are improved," she said at last, and then, putting her head on one side, asked affectedly, "And when is it to be?"

"Now, ye mun talk reight if ye talk to me!"

This was a way she had found effective before, in putting an end to Sophy's innuendoes.

"Ah, well, you won't tell, I see; but we all know well enough he's been to see you oft enough at Baumforth."

"Who's been to see me?"

"Why, young Mr. Sykes; you need not look so innocent!"

"Why, so he has! At least, he's been to the house where I was."

"Oh! you sly thing."

"There's no sly about it; an' I willn't have you say so."

"Oh! then you own?" Sophy began, standing back a little.

"Own what?" Sarah asked, looking her in the face.

Miss Sophy was taken by surprise by Sarah's anger. She herself would have smirked and been pleased at such an imputation, whether founded or not. She sidled off, exclaiming—

"Oh! very well, Miss Miles. You choose to tell me nothing, so I need not tell you. I know what I know."

"Happen ye do, an' happen ye don't."

And Sarah walked off in disgust.

Sophy called after her—

"I see, now, why you would never let our Susy come to your singing parties! Oh! you sly thing."

Sarah knew not how little the talk of such people is attended to. She took Sophy's account of her proceedings as a true picture of public opinion on the subject. She was regarded by the community as having frequented the Sykes's house for a far-fetched purpose of her own, and of being willing to sing in the chapel as a part of a scheme that she was anxious to carry out. Then it must be that Sammy thought he had her at command, merely by keeping up hopes that he never intended to gratify; and she was seized with a violent desire never to do what he asked of her any more—just because he wanted it; she knew she had always done it, and her belief in the slow justice of time failed her utterly, and she had as good an inclination to make her slanderer eat her words as ever a ruffler with a sword by his side.

Once more she got into the sunlight when, her mother's consent having been gained, the singers came to spend an hour at Miles's, and to settle the pieces to be sung at the chapel opening. Under her mother's wing everything must be right; and yet the skeleton had left its mark. She was full of gloom and bitterness as she sat with Harriet in the window-seat in her father's house, waiting for the coming of the rest.

"What are ye a-thinking on, Sarah?" Harriet asked; "ye're uncommon solid to-night."

John joked her about the pinafore long since discarded.

"Mrs. Gracehurst made me," she said, indifferently.

"An' ye think summat o' yersen, nowadays," John remarked, putting his head on one side; "ye sud get some curls, Sarah."

John's instinct did not approve of Miss Raines.

"I never could be such a fool as Miss Raines," she said.

"She's as solid as ought," she heard repeated in front of her, and looked at the speaker in order to understand him better.

The speaker was Sydney Wynde, who looked as if he saw something new in her face.

She felt herself getting confused and angry, and suddenly rose to shake off the impression of isolation.

"Let us see what we are to sing," she said, and moving Sammy's hat out of the way; "Sammy, how long is it since you've taken to wearing your hat o' warter's? It's allus i' t' gate."

"Why, ever sin' he were partner wi' Turner. Did ye never know that?"

"Partner wi' Turner! When was he a partner?"

"Why, these two years and more."

"Partner wi' Turner!"

It was really true that Sarah, being often away, had never heard of the partnership; owing to Turner's sensitive pride the matter was not much talked of. It was taken for granted that Sarah knew, though no one ever told her.

"Ye never told me," she said to the company in general.

"Nay, whoever thought on't?"

"Why, for sure ye had no 'casion! I've nought to do with it," she said, and began to talk vigorously about the pieces to be performed, and led the conversation into its accustomed channel.

There was a general feeling of a rock ahead, against which they might come to grief, and all sides laboured to keep up the flow of mirth that generally spouted out of itself.

"Now we'st do it, shan't we, mother?" Sammy said; "there's

many a one will come thro' t' whistling shop to hear Sarah sing."

"T' singing's well enough," Mrs. Miles opined, "but I wish there were a little more religion with it. What did ye build t' chapel for?"

Had Sammy been upright and downright, like Sarah, he would have said, "To sing in it," but he urged instead that they were like to have a place of their own when Mr. Somers would not do what they wanted.

Sarah noticed the equivocation; she knew there had always been an incoherence between Sammy's words and his intentions with regard to the chapel.

"Will ye bring a true heart and a right spirit with you when ye come to worship?" Mrs. Miles asked; "if not, ye know—He will not be inquired of by you."

When Mrs. Miles began "a-preaching like," and using Scripture language, every one yielded; it would have been going "clean agin Scripture" to do otherwise.

Sydney came to the rescue with an interruption.

"Now, Sammy," he said, "ye're like to make a speech to t' lasses; that's what ye brought yer hat for! Here, put it on."

"Well, a body's like to say summat," and he looked at Sydney with a grimace of almost contempt for the business he was undertaking.

Sarah stood by the table, and caught sight of it, while Sam and John began a mocking laugh. The girl's face turned to stone.

"Are ye, Sammy?" she said, with a small wrinkle in her forehead, and a look as if she would not put the snuffers down until she got an answer.

"What ails ye, Sarah?" Harriet asked, as Sammy began to stammer.

"I care nought about it," she said; "ye may speechify as much as you like."

"What dunnot ye care about?"

"I care nought about it," she repeated, and, passing round

the outside of the circle, walked into the shop, and closed the door after her.

The thing can hardly be made more intelligible to the reader than it was to the spectators. Impressed with the idea that she was a kitten to be played with, Sarah was provoked to see the very string dangled before her eyes. Three scoffers at once was too much for her pride.

After a minute's silence, Sydney took Sam by the arm, whispering—

"Go after her, lad."

Sarah went as far as the counter, and, stooping over it, propped her forehead on her hands. Here was all the fabric of her future crumbled before her. 'Twas there that she had garnered up her heart. She knew it now, when her idol fell to pieces before her eyes. Where was she, and what was left of her former existence? Nothing but the recollection that she had been such a fool! Only anger bore her up under the weight of her self-contempt.

Sydney Wynde had never understood Sarah. He lived in the belief that there was nothing to understand in her. He could not possibly have chosen a worse ambassador than Sam, and Sarah's wrath rose higher when she heard his foot on the floor.

Sam left the door ajar in order to see where she was. Then he advanced to the other side of the counter, opposite to her.

"What ails ye, Sarah?" he said, stooping down to her.

She started back, and Sam heard the feet walking round the counter and going to the shop door. She unbolted and opened it. Sam strode up to her as she stood on the threshold, and, stooping down to her, he put his arm round her waist. It was the first liberty he had ever taken, and Sarah started back as he put his face close to hers, and with her clenched fist struck him between the eyes, sending his head back against the stone door-post. He caught at it to save himself, as he dropped on his knees. When the flash was gone out of his eyes, he gathered himself up again, and saw her stately shoulders against the horizon passing the house door. He watched her enter the milk-

house, and knew she would appear no more that night. Then
he put his hands in his pockets and went home.

When the bewildered party in the house heard the shop
door open they exclaimed. John peeped in and said, wondering—

"They're off! Both on 'em!"

"They'll come back, I know," someone hoped.

But in a minute the mother heard her daughter's step in
the room above, and said—

"Nay, she's up there."

It was thought useless for them to wait longer, and they took
their departure.

After this evening's amusement there was as much manœu-
vring and diplomacy between the two families as would have
got together a European Congress. Napoleon Sydney thought
his prestige involved in carrying through a splendid performance at the chapel opening, and the federation for that purpose having burst asunder, he set himself to bring the pieces
together again. It was not in accordance with his mental constitution to address himself to Sarah, though this would have
shortened the business considerably. He applied first to John
Miles to appeal to his mother, who, it was well known, was the
only one who could do anything with Sarah. But Mrs. Miles
refused to waste her precious influence on so small a matter.
She thought the chapel would get opened somehow, and, if
not, it was no harm. At last Sydney convinced Sam that it was
his business to make it up with Sarah, whatever it was. Sammy
did not even know what it was, and did not feel disposed to
inquire. But at last, as the week was coming to an end, and the
opening was advertised for Sunday next, he resolved to have
it out with her. Sarah, who though before as accessible as daylight, was now never to be seen, and he had to walk into the
shop and ask her mother for her.

"She's i' t' house," Mrs. Miles said, and he lifted the counter
flap and went in.

She was finishing washing the tea-things after breakfast.

"Now, Sarah," and "Now, Sammy," they said respectively,

and then there was a pause. Sarah got a duster, and prepared to move the chairs round according to custom. Sam studied her, but found her face unintelligible. She plodded on as if there were nothing in the world to think of but chair-dusting. With a feeble pulse and a hopeless face she thought of her prospects, her friends, her hopes of employment; and whatever the subject was, it always led up to Sammy Sykes, and then she let it drop with a recoil of pain. Such a recoil the sight of him had given her, and she tried to turn her attention to her work, and forget there was anything else in the world to think of.

Sam strained his senses to observe her. He thought her sulky, yet he had not the slightest idea of what could have made her so. It was not her way. Should he ask her what was wrong? But what if she said there was nought wrong? He was horribly afraid of such an answer, for how was he to get any farther? In the midst of his hesitation she quietly said—

"Sammy!"

He could scarcely avoid a start.

"Sammy, ye know what mother's let ye come in here for?"

"I came because I wanted," he said, looking straight into her eyes.

"An' it wor better ye did not."

"I do not think so."

"She thought ye meant well by me, but ye mean nought o' t' kind."

"I never meant ye ought else, Sarah."

"Ye meant to turn me whichever way ye liked, an' then to laugh at me for going."

"I never meant—"

He stopped, for she turned fiercely on him.

"I seed ye," she said. "If ye had waited just a bit, just while ye'd gotten out o' t' house, I might ha' gone on believing ye. But ye couldn't, and now ye need try no more."

"But what's gone wrong, Sarah? Ye thought better o' me awhile ago."

"I thought like a fool."

"Did ye?"

"I thought ye were o' my side. Happen ye wor till somebody laughed at me. Then ye knew nought better than to get behind 'em and snigger."

"I allus was on your side, Sarah. I was allus ready to help ye."

"Help yoursen, Sammy. Ye'll help noan o' me. I knew well enough 'at mony a one would laugh at me for singing at t' chapel, and then I thought ye'd stand by me. More fool me! Ye held yer tongue, and set faces an' sniggered wi' Sydney Wynde. Go ye wi' a crowd, Sammy, an' get into t' middle on 't. But never try to take care o' me. I'll trouble noan o' ye when I want helping."

A flash of light illuminated his confusion as she recalled the grimace. He had partly yielded to Sydney's opinion, and tried to think that "t' lasses" were not of so much importance in this or any other business. They were to be talked over, to be sure, but it was easily done. Sarah finished, and set down the last chair, and went to the window, let down the blind, and began to clean it. Sam watched her flushed and scornful face, but could not frame his answer even now that he partially understood the charge. Should he own to it? Should he deny that he had any particular meaning in his setting faces? Either would be false in a way. He was guilty, but his guilt was so trivial that he could neither defend it nor own that he was to blame. At last he said, in anger—

"I did laugh, Sarah! And what o' that? I worn't again ye!"

"An I've nought again ye, Sammy. Ye'll do for a fair-weather friend."

He stood up and walked to the door.

"I'm as good a man as ye are a woman, Sarah. An' I can stick by my friends in all weathers. I did leave ye to yoursen. I might ha' done different. If I had known ye cared, happen I should ha' done. I can stand up for my friends as well as another man. I did shirk it once, maybe, just once!"

As he opened the door he looked at her, and saw the tears running down her face. He stopped in sudden truimph, and she faced him at once.

"Just when ye were wanted, Sammy."

He came up to her.

"Did ye want me, Sarah? Ye allus go yer own gate, and care for nobody. I knew nought on 't! Is there ony fairness, think ye, in setting a man down like that for not speaking his mind? I might ha' done it, I know, an' I did not. But for all that, Sarah, I'm worth having for a friend, an' ye'll do well to think so."

He was gone.

Strong in the belief that " all was over between them," Sarah had spoken her mind, and showed her feeling more than she had deliberately intended doing. Now, his words had made such an impression on her that she had reverted to the same state of doubt in which she had lived for the last fortnight. She could not set him down as she had meant to do, for he stood straight, as one that is sure of his footing. What should she do? How should she meet him? O! if she could get away!

The week was nearly over, and the opening performance was still in doubt. Sam's granted prayer in the shape of the new chapel seemed likely to become the curse of his life. He would have rather bitten his tongue out than have asked her to sing in it.

Sydney once more had an idea. He suggested that Harriet was the proper person to manage Sarah. She should ask her what she would do. So Sam proposed it to her in this reasonable fashion—

"Harriet, what has ye and Sarah quarrelled for?"

"Nay, Sammy, I know nought about it."

"Go an' ask her if she's going to sing at t' chapel next Sunday."

Harriet was wise in her generation, and said not a word, but went.

She sauntered up and down before Sarah's door, and could not enter. The things about which she talked to Sarah came of themselves, and the occasion also. But at last Sarah, either by design or by chance, came to the door, and Harriet came to her.

"Eh, Sarah, I've done cleaning afore ye to-day. I'd done by noon."

"Had you?" Sarah said, indifferently.

Harriet hesitated again. She was afraid of spoiling all by an injudicious word. She did not know exactly the state of matters between her brother and Sarah, nor what to take for granted. At last she began—

"Are ye going to chapel to-morrow, Sarah?"

This was at least a harmless question, though the two girls had been to chapel every Sunday hitherto without ever thinking it necessary to make a previous agreement about it.

"Why, for sure," Sarah said.

Harriet was more puzzled than ever, until Sarah, raising her hand, said—

"It's t' other way now, ye know!"

The way to the old chapel lay "down the town," and to the new one "up the town."

"Aye, for sure," Harriet said in her turn; and, fearful of spoiling matters by an imprudent word, she ran home again, and told the result of her negotiation. So that was settled.

The opening came off successfully. Though no one deserted the whistling shop this first Sunday, there were plenty of people with itching ears, who even paid something at the collection to hear the singing. They were not worse than their neighbours. Is it not thought a legitimate means of attracting people to divine service to give them something else as well? Sarah did not stay to hear the amount of the collection, nor did she inquire about it afterwards. She walked home like a model of propriety, never letting the strangers or others see her and Sammy Sykes together.

He knew nothing of the reason that influenced her. He was almost in the dark as to all the reasons she might have for her new style of proceeding, and whenever this is the case with him a man always says: "There's no dealing wi' women—if they had a bit o' reason in 'em!"

He gave her the music for the next Sunday, and made no remark and heard none from her. They met no more. He

would not seek her. There was for the time no more practising, nor evening merriment. No one asked questions, and
no one interfered. Everyone thought "they would come right
when they bethought 'em."

Harriet Sykes lost more by this than anyone. The evenings
when the house was full were her holidays of enjoyment. She
was prevented by her responsible position from leaving the
place much, and depended on the news and conversation that
other people brought to her. She resolved to make Sarah come
back again to the old habits, and watched her opportunity of
trying her powers. Sarah was not difficult to address. Harriet
did not expect a quarrel, or even a scolding, if she should ask
her to come, but still she did not think that would break the
ice that had shot over the connection. If she spoke to Sarah
she got an answer, and no more. Sarah would look at her as
if with an effort to try and recollect who she was. She never
asked a question, never proposed a visit, never made a remark
that showed that she remembered the last time of meeting.

After considerable study Harriet armed herself with patience
and resolved by one means or other to get Sarah into the house,
and keep her there long enough to make some little conversation almost impossible to avoid. So she called her as she passed,
and made her come in—the usual way of getting into talk at
Repton—and told her she had done cleaning, or she had not,
'tis no matter which, and then asked how Sarah herself was
getting on.

Sarah sat down on the fender, and then, as if the comfortable place had thawed her intellects, she began—

"Harriet, I wish I could get right away from here."

"Do you want to go back to Baumforth?"

"No. Farther than Baumforth. Somewhere right away."

"Why, whatever for? And have no one to come and go,
and talk to?"

"I don't want anyone to talk to."

"What do you want, then?"

"I want to go away."

"What sort of a place do you want, Sarah?"

"Any sort. Somewhere a long way off."

Harriet was washing the dishes; she went on for a little while, and then said—

"I should not like to be so far off."

"I wonder what you see here. There's nought to have and nought to look for. We might as well lie awake in our graves."

"Nay, Sarah, you fair frighten a body. What's come to you that nothing pleases you?"

"What is there to please me? Do you see ought to please you?"

"Why, everybody likes best where they were born and bred."

"Aye, till they change their mind."

"I know you have changed your mind, Sarah, but I don't know what for. Ye want to get out o' t' gate and see no more of us, but I willn't have it so. We've known each other too long for that. Your folk an' us has allus been friends, ever sin t' day 'at mother's coffin went out o' this house. I remember weel enough t' day after I stood looking out o' t' window, an' father an' Sammy had goan into t' warehouse an' left me by mysen, an' I were fair lost. An' father had goan out t' night afore when he an' Sam came home fro' t' funeral, an' I had sat by t' fire by mysen till I were fair flayed, an' when they sat off again i' t' morning I hallacked about an' couldn't do nought. I thought I'd never thoil to sweep t' hearth, nor fettle up, for there were nobody there, an' nobody cared what I did, nor what became of me. An' I stood staring out o' t' window, an' I seed your mother go by, an' then she came in at t' door an' put her hand on my shoulder, an' she says 'It's oonly (lonely), isn't it, lass?' "

Harriet suited the action to the word, putting her hand on Sarah's shoulder, and looking into her face.

She said the words with such pathos that the tears rose to the eyes of both the girls.

"An' then she went on, 'Aye, I know it is. Your father came to us last night, an' he said it was like as if all were goan when t' wife were goan, an' I were fair capped, for I had never thought he cared half so much.' An' then she said, 'Ye see he's nought left but ye, but ye mun let him see it isn't all gone. Ye mun just mense up a bit an' set things straight, an' look to him a bit as yer mother did, an' let him see it isn't all gone.'

"An' as soon as she was gone, I started an' cleaned up an' blackleaded as if it were Saturday. An' I whitened t' hearth i' t' afternoon, 'cause he did not come home to dinner 'cause of it being market day, an' I brought t' armchair down, 'at had been upstairs ever sin mother were ill, an' I set t' tray ready for t' tea. An' when he came in he sat him down as if he had forgotten all about it, and then he looked up an' says, 'Now then,' for I stood, 'cause I did not know where to sit. Then he waked up and looked, an' says, 'Sit ye there, Harriet'—that was in mother's place—'sit ye there, an' give us some tea,' an' then I started o' roaring an' covered my face wi' my apron, an' Sammy laid his head on his arms at t' top o' t' table, an' nobody said nought, an' then father turned his chair to t' table, an' he says, 'We sorrow not as those who have no hope. Ye mun mind that. Now Harriet, lass, put down thy apron and give us our tea,' an' when we'd gotten our tea I took t' candle over to t' little table at t' other side, by his own chair, as mother allus did, in case he wanted to write or ought o' that, an' when he went across t' hearth he put his hand on my shoulder, an' he said I were his lass, an' I telled him we mud have some new blinds for upstairs, for t' oud uns were fair done, mother had said so, an' he says, 'Why, then, we mun have 'em,' an' he's allus gi'en me ought 'at ever I asked for ever sin, an' I never asked for nought but what were right 'at I know on. An' your mother's been here mony and mony a time, an' she's telled me mony an' mony a thing, an' she never set hersen up nor nought, for all I were such a bairn, an' so it isn't to say that ye an' us is to fratch an' have nought to say to one another, cause I willn't have it so."

Carried away by her own eloquence, Harriet stood before Sarah with a plate and towel in hand, as if defying her to say it should be otherwise.

"Ye've no 'casion to look at me as if ye had never seen me before, 'cause I tell you it mun be as I say."

And Sarah continued to look at her and to wonder. Harriet turned to her work again. All the history of her life passed before Sarah's mind since she was a girl sliding down the hill. She recollected very well the time of Mrs. Sykes's death, and how her mother had been often there. It was a way the old folks had to see one another occasionally, and, as Sarah expressed it, "to talk their talks." She knew that her mother had encouraged her to go and see Harriet, and at times to help her with the work of the house. She remembered the time when she had told her mother of her storming the citadel of the warehouse, when Sam and Sydney and her own brother had ensconced themselves there out of the way of feminine interruption. She recollected how her mother had gone down and spoken with old Sykes the next day, and how the singers had met in the house ever since. She had heard that it was old Sykes's wish, and understood now the whole transaction from beginning to end. She wondered at his patience. She knew how she had chattered forth her likings and her opinions, not thinking or not caring that he was there. He would smoke through it all, never interfering save at rare times when the fun grew "fast and furious," and he would say, "Now, now, lads, come now," and they would "come," and the place would be kept worthy of his daughter's home, and of his wife's memory.

And her mother, she had been often there, as Harriet said. She had kept the girl straight, kindly and quietly, performing the duty as to a "brother in the faith." She had carefully brought up the young people, who themselves knew and understood nothing about it, in the way they should go, and Sarah recognized now that she had lived from childhood in "the best society" in Repton.

There is, perhaps, no judgment so little liable to be wrong as that passed by grown-up children upon their parents. No one knows them so thoroughly. By their intimate knowledge and their grown-up powers of judging, they are able to tell how much temper or selfishness has entered into the treatment they have received. They understand the care of which in childhood they knew nothing, and they understand, too, the

failings that have gone with it. So judging, Sarah looked back
on the last six years, and suddenly exclaimed—

"My mother's t' best lass i' all Repton."

"I've nought agin that," said Harriet.

Without a word Sarah went quietly home. Harriet knew
that she had given up the idea that the world was not worth
living in. Slowly Sarah began to see that the society in which
her mother had permitted her to live could not be altogether
bad. There must surely be faith and truth in it. She ceased to
look longingly at the horizon, and to wonder whether there
was another kind of people over there, and if she could become a denizen among them. True, she had lost the mainstay
of her happiness. She saw that it was Sammy's opinion that
had sufficed to give her courage during the tedious hours of
work, that came like wine to her heart, when even work was
wanting, and she knew not where to turn. She had not known
till now how much he stood for in her mental economy, and
had difficulty in finding her place without him.

But yet life had a savour in it. And Sarah washed pots and
dusted chairs, and moved them round, and felt a comfort in
being under the old roof and surrounded by the old protection.
Gradually the singing meetings began again, ostensibly for the
sake of settling what was to be sung at chapel. Yet it was not
as before. It seemed to Sarah that they were like the scattered
brands of a former fire, which Harriet had gathered together,
hoping in vain that a little warmth would come again from
their juxtaposition. But the hearth remained cold. Sometimes
a spark flashed between Sam and Sarah, but it was one of
anger, hatred, and malice. Harriet would put her foot on it
at once, and it disappeared. The two were rather ashamed of
their ill-temper, but would come to no better terms.

Sam would willingly have paid her a good price for singing
in the chapel, but that was negatived by the whole band of
performers. He talked, however, of some remuneration when
they should be more able to pay it. No one seconded him, and
the allusion only served to provoke Sarah.

CHAPTER XX.

"Are the white hours for ever fled,
That used to bless the cheerful day?"

WHEN, two years ago, Mr. Turner had succeeded in getting on his feet again, by the help of Sykes' money, the only people who did not benefit by the arrangement were, his own family. From sheer necessity, as well as from utter ignorance of what was really needed in a house like theirs, he always kept them short of money, and with this reminder ever before them they could never shake off the sense of disgrace and failure that depressed their spirits and spoilt their temper. Such was their state of ignorance that they would have blushed less for a theft, or a fraud, that had been successful, than they did now for stinted means. They were not at one as to the way in which they should take their position. Amelia was the crook in their lot, whose awkward maunderings added much to the burdens they had to bear.

She had brought home certain ideas from school that her relations could neither understand nor tolerate. She would talk on all occasions of work not being degrading, of luxury not being necessary to a happy life, of the approbation of their own consciences being sufficient to support them when cleaning stoves and blacking boots, and would coolly propose when the money question was discussed to dismiss the servant and dine in the kitchen, and then in some way to earn her dinner.

It must be owned that she was provoking. They could not understand it, but she was a failure somehow. Her mother wondered how she came to have such a daughter. She would have liked to visit her vexation on Miss Forbes, for having turned out such a specimen; but alas, she remembered that she was no longer a power that could denounce or recommend anyone.

But why was the girl so different from all the rest? Mrs. Turner, as she sat by the fire, which she did most of her time, reviewed the history of her children, and the hopes connected with them; how Matilda had been the darling of her heart, because she was pretty; how Eliza had derogated from the dignity of her station, and would sometimes reproduce the opinions and sentiments of Aunt Bankes, whom she seldom saw, in a way most provoking to her mother, for Aunt Bankes had kept the station she was born in, that Mrs. Turner had risen out of and strove to forget. She had married her cousin, who farmed his own land, and they had remained primitive people, hearty and honest, but not genteel.

But for the youngest darling, born in the purple, who had seen no stint in the house, and who innocently thought that her family had lived in affluence for generations at least, for her the mother had hoped for something better. She had had the benefit of a renowned school, that the elders could only look on from a distance. How was it?—how on earth was it!—that this one should show such vulgar notions, that she would talk quite coolly of selling muffins or taking in plain sewing, and answer, when reproved, "Well, mamma, I only mean if we cannot do anything better, but what is there better?"

She was a failure. Her word was seldom listened to; her opinion never followed. They ceased to care for her wishes. She found herself sinking by swift degrees from being the petted favourite, to being one always in the way, who must learn perforce to efface herself, to avoid being always run down. Then the girl began to think her own thoughts, and to comfort herself with her own approbation, in the way recommended by the moral teachers of the time. True, her own happiness involved the idea of other people's inferiority. The two became so constantly connected that it was necessary to believe herself superior; the feeling told on her temper and on her courtesy with baleful effect, and the life of the household was not made pleasanter by it.

Now to be content with the approbation of one's own conscience is surely a very Christian frame of mind, but reader, did you ever try it? Were you ever quite at your ease with all the world against you, not merely some one person, or even many, but the whole world?

Did you ever try not to fall out of your armchair? Did you ever grasp the arms in terror, and strive with all the might of your trembling limbs to keep yourself in the middle of it? You have never done this because you thought it would be impossible almost to fall out if you tried. Yet this is what you would do if, looking round, you saw that the earth was gone, sunk far away beneath you, and your fall would be fearful.

Perhaps you have had a difference with some people, but this is only having a precipice on one side. You have only lost the land in one direction, but to stand upright, and to stand alone, is not given to many, nor possible for long. In weariness or in terror, we all descend to the warm earth where we were born, and whence comes our strength. The air up in the solitudes above is too exhausting for our lungs, and we lie down in weariness, or faint with exhaustion after breathing it awhile.

So Amelia trifled with her conscience, at one time acknowledging its dictates as commonplace morality, at another neglecting its simple teaching. She grew to be constantly ashamed of herself, first for not maintaining her own opinions until she brought people to see the truth of them, and then for the scorn she met with for trying to do so.

"Now, mamma, I have nearly done this," she said, one morning, "and I shall have some time to myself."

She had grown so frightened of the possible consequences of introducing her own schemes, that she had always to create an opening for the subject.

"What do you want with time to yourself, child? What you are doing is for yourself."

"This is only to wear; I want time to earn something."

This answer was prepared beforehand. Her brain whirled too much for her to take things as they came. She already hung down her head and took a deprecating tone, but the storm she had evoked was much wilder than she had expected. Her father started up and clashed down the newspaper on the table.

"If you had taught your daughters their proper place and duties, Mrs. Turner, they would know better than to insult their father."

He walked out and slammed the door.

"Amelia," her mother began, "why can't you hold your tongue about your nonsense when your father is here? You torment us enough when he is away. Why am I to be scolded for your foolish fancies?" and Mrs. Turner began to cry, as she was getting the habit of doing at every trouble.

Amelia, blind and breathless, still held to her programme; she was in the fight and must fight on.

"What have I said?" she asked. "I only said I should have time to—"

"Now do hold your tongue," Eliza exclaimed, "and don't go on making it worse."

"Why should I hold my tongue?"

"Because you don't know what you are talking of," Matilda exclaimed.

Her mother rose with solemnity.

"Amelia, you must *not* talk in that way. You make your father so angry. Do! do! let us have some peace!"

She sat down again and took out her pocket handkerchief, and Amelia was beaten. She could not go on quarrelling, since what she was fighting for was to bring other people to her mind, not to rouse their opposition. She dropped her head and remained silent.

"I wonder how you can do so," whined Matilda; "you know we have not much peace or pleasure left, and here, when father comes in and wants a bit of quiet, you cannot do but begin saying what vexes him. Do learn some sense, and don't think yourself the wisest person in the world."

And Matilda began to cry like her mother; she often did. Eliza saw Amelia's tears dropping on her work, and in a broken, but angry voice, began scolding them all round.

"What was the use of crying?" she asked. "There was no sense in it. Why could not they go on quietly, and make the best of things, and Amelia not be so stupid? There was nothing to cry for that she could see."

So Amelia came down from her lofty heights and strove to find comfort in the warm world below.

And soon the mother began to lament, not only over the moral delinquencies, but over the failing health of her youngest daughter. The united strength of the three had stifled all the wild notions that she had begun to put forth, but they were all three conscious that the perversity was not crushed out of her, but only held down for the moment. If she would only give up those outrageous ideas, there was nothing the mother would not do to bring back again the sprightly girl, the willing help, the admired of all, and the hope of father and mother. But now, faded in health, broken in temper, too weak to work, too sad to talk, what was to be done with her? Could she be got to the seaside? There would be a furious fight for the money, and little hope of any good result, so she let the idea drop for want of energy to fight against probability, and without hope. These commonplace remedies would fail in their effect.

Meanwhile Amelia got into the way of spending most of her time upstairs. Sometimes she went there to cry after a quarrel or a scolding. Sometimes she was tired, without knowing why. She never came down to breakfast, and always went early to bed, and at last bethought herself to make some use of these long, long hours. She got out her desk, and began a letter to her former friend and teacher, Miss Forbes.

"MY DEAR MISS FORBES,

"Do you remember me, and how I used to make you promise not to forget me? You said I should forget you first, or should have other friends. Though I have been so long without writing to you, I have neither forgotten you nor changed my mind. I often wish you were here, that I might talk to you, and ask your advice. I do assure you I sometimes need it very much. Oh! how I wish I was at school again, where I could always ask you what to do. You must not think this flattery, dear Miss Forbes, for indeed it is not. You know you promised always to advise me in the best way you could. Now I do very much want advice. Dear Miss Forbes, I hope you won't think me selfish in writing about nothing but myself, after so long an interval of silence, but the remembrance of your kindness gives me courage to ask of you what I would not, dare not, ask of anyone else in the world. You must know, dear Miss Forbes, that we are—"

The two last words were erased, and she went on—
"That I find I must—"
These shared the same fate.
"That papa has—"
After drawing her pen through these, Amelia threw it down, and began to walk about the room. "I don't know what to do," she said, almost aloud. "What must I do? What must I say? How can she help me? It's just going a-begging!" She walked on with her chin in the shawl she had wrapped round her. "If I must beg, why must I go to her? She has nothing to spare. I don't even know what to ask her for." At last she turned again to the table. "There is no other chance," she said aloud, and took up her pen again.

"Dear Miss Forbes,

"I have resolved to write to you because I am very unhappy. You said once you would be glad to help me, and I don't know how to help myself. I have nothing to live on; none of us have. We can't pay our debts. We can't get half of what we want, and what we do get we promise to pay for and don't. You used to say if we did our duty we should always have some comfort. Now, I think we cannot be doing right to go on as we do, for there is no comfort—none. It is dark all round me, darkest of all before me, and I must try to change,

I am so unhappy. Forgive me for writing to you in this exaggerated way, but it is not exaggerated, it is the truth. Now, my dear Miss Forbes, ought I not to begin to earn something, when I cannot live without? And what must I do? It is for this I write to you. Will you advise me how to begin? Perhaps if you recommended it mamma would let me—"

"Oh, no!" she said, quickly erasing the last sentence. "If she thinks mamma is against it she will do nothing."

"I'll do anything you tell me that will enable me to get my living, either now or by-and-bye. Ought I not to do it, dear Miss Forbes?

"I am too unhappy to write any more, but I beg of you to answer my letter soon.

> "Your affectionate pupil,
> "AMELIA TURNER."

She copied this, and sealed and sent it with fear and trembling. It was a first step, and she knew not how to take a second, and between fear and hope she became at times almost incapable of attention to anything. No answer came by return of post, and she grew angry and contemptuous towards her idolized teacher. But the next day Eliza called her down. "There was a letter."

Amelia threw down what was in her hand, and ran downstairs. Her mother and sisters were all there, but not her father. An open letter was in her mother's hand, and dark displeasure was in the faces of all three.

"Well, Amelia! here's Miss Forbes proposing to take you as under-governess."

And the lady extended her hand and drew back her head like Mrs. Dombey the second.

"Oh, mamma! do let me go."

"Upon my word!" and she drew back her head still further. "Really, Amelia!"

"Now, is not that shameful? As if we had not enough to bear without your helping to disgrace us!"

Amelia looked in terror from one to the other as they

passed their judgments upon her. Afterwards, when alone, she thought of answers to all this, but for the present she was simply annihilated. She had never been opposed to anyone in her life till lately, and knew not how to take the attitude. Her face betrayed more and more her sense of utter defeat as her mamma went on.

"How could you think of publishing your poor papa's misfortunes in such a way, Amelia?" And Amelia blushed with shame. "As if other people's insults were not enough, you must show him up to strangers because he can't provide you with everything you please to want. Other people have something to bear as well as you, and why are *you* to make mischief? If your papa knew of that letter! Amelia, you will make the house so that we can't live in it if you go on so!"

The storm came to a sudden end as Mr. Turner's foot was heard on the stairs, and Amelia slunk away with stifled tears and a whirling brain. She fancied for a moment that she might find a door of escape if she could only see the letter. But she never saw it, and never knew even whether it was addressed to her or not. And now she had a new wound. Mrs. Turner knew well the impression that the words "Poor papa" would make on her daughter. It is frightful to a child to hear of pity to her father. Hate she can bear for him, and return for him double-fold, but pity is intolerable. She had taken her father's part with natural warmth when she heard of insult or discourtesy towards him, which she often did, for the unfortunate not only feel and treasure up the scorn which they really meet with, but a great deal more which they only imagine. Often had the evening been spent in listening to his account of the slights and insults that he had received, till Amelia thought the world was peopled with unfeeling or malignant demons, and she had discovered the defects in his armour to enemies such as these. With bitter tears she paced the room, looking far and near for a remedy for this added sorrow. But neither for this nor her own could she see any help but one, and that one she was forbidden even to think about. If she could only right herself in her own eyes, and look the world in the face free from debt and dependence! But she knew she was bound hand and foot while the scorn of her enemies eat at her vitals.

The letter was addressed to Mrs. Turner, and was apparently not at all calculated to raise such a storm. The writer had heard some time ago of Mr. Turner's misfortunes, with much regret. She had hoped they were by this time a thing of the past. She had been grieved exceedingly to hear through Miss Amelia that it was not so. She was quite willing to do all in her power to assist Miss Amelia, and, having the highest opinion of her talents and principles, she had no doubt that when she got a little experience her energy would be valuable. Would Mrs. Turner allow Miss Amelia to pay her (Miss Forbes) a visit. If she would, Miss Forbes would find pleasure in smoothing the difficulties that stood in the way of a beginner. Miss Amelia would make a valuable and efficient teacher, and Miss Forbes had no doubt that she would soon meet with a fair share of success.

"She will do nothing of the kind," the writer said, as she folded her letter. "But I cannot help it. I can do no other way."

She was not surprised when she received no answer. She knew she was offending when she wrote. Yet, as she said, she could do no other way. She had alienated Amelia too, for which she cared more. But Amelia had not risen to the dignity of being an independent personage. She could have no friends. She could no more steer her own course than a log on the waves. Of the causes of her present poverty she knew no more than the reader knows. Some people—nearly everybody, Amelia thought—had done her father wrong. She was never told how or why, still less why he was so defenceless and helpless under it. Indeed, such was her state of ignorance that she never thought of asking the question, though she pondered to the verge of insanity about the means there might be of escaping from it.

When Sarah came home from Baumforth, and it was understood that she was going to stay there, Jane was naturally much occupied with the improvement that had taken place in her personal appearance, and also in her accomplishments and prospects, and could not be expected to refrain from making her a subject of conversation with the young ladies.

"She is going to be a great singer; she can get ten shillings a time now, and she will get more if she goes on. Ever so many people have asked about her. Even Mr. Holroyd says she will go far, and he never says much. She is going to get a lot of money and be a lady, is our Sarah."

No one saw Amelia's face when this announcement was made. She had learnt to keep her thoughts to herself, but she pondered on the news.

But soon she saw that it came to nothing; she had not the voice, and the discovery caused her so much disappointment that she was almost ill with it. Still her thoughts always turned to Sarah. Sarah had found a way, because she had tried and had been helped. Could she help Amelia? Were the means known in Sarah's class of getting work and getting wages? Why, of course they were. To that they were brought up. Why not do as they did?

She was now an acknowledged invalid. Her wishes were attended to on this account, though her opinion was, if possible, less valued or listened to than ever. The efforts of the family were directed to making her eat and walk about, and take interest, like other people. She seldom did it. She would trail about, doing something, she knew and cared not what. When told, she would go and sit down in the breakfast-room, now the living-room of the whole family. There she fiddled with some work, which she seldom finished. She did not listen when others talked, and seldom spoke herself, and never gave any sign of caring whether the world was coming to an end or not. Her mother lamented over every lapse of intelligence or energy, and was almost thankful when the girl began on any subject to show a will of her own. And now she began to evince a feeble, uncertain hankering after Sarah Miles. She should like to see her, to talk to her. Sarah Miles was always civil, she would be civil now.

"Why, whatever can you have to say to her?"

"Why, talk to her. You talk to people, why should not I?"

"But what about?"

"Why, about—anything. About old times."

Amelia is not the first woman who has set her heart on something apparently unaccountable in the same circumstances. Men who try to govern women should distrust, above all things, "the unaccountable."

On one occasion when Amelia began on the subject, Matilda exclaimed, with a burst of peevishness, that it was always Sarah Miles, morning, noon, and night, and Amelia suddenly burst into tears, and asked why she was never to have anything she wanted.

It was a display she did not often make. Indeed, she acquired so perfectly the habit of concealing her feelings that no one knew what she really cared for, or to what extent; but her weakened nerves were taken unawares, and she betrayed herself. The mother looked anxiously at her, and said—

"Let her alone, it's her not being well, I have seen it this long time. Eliza, why should you not go and ask Sarah Miles to come up some day?"

So Jane got leave to go home and say that they would like to see Sarah again—that Miss Amelia wanted to see how she was getting on. Jane performed her office faithfully, and Sarah walked up to the great house rather puzzled as to what Amelia could want with her.

When she presented herself at the kitchen door, Miss Eliza was at work, and looked at her without recognizing her. She inquired for Miss Amelia.

"Miss Amelia! You want Miss Amelia?"

There was a slight assumption of offence in the tone as if the lady were asking, "What do you want with Miss Amelia?"

"She sent for me," Sarah said, as if it did not matter to her whether she saw Miss Amelia or not.

"Oh, you are Sarah Miles; come in, and I'll see about it."

She went to her mother; she suspected Amelia of wishing to be guilty of some impropriety or other, that would disgrace the family.

"Now, mother, is she to see her? What can it matter whether she sees her or not? It is some fancy or other she has got. What can Sarah Miles do for her?"

"I'll speak to Sarah first," said the mother. "Let her go into the drawing-room."

Sarah was sent into the drawing-room, and stood there looking round for some little time. It was there she had first seen Mrs. Turner and Miss Matilda. How warm and elegant, and dignified the large room had looked—how refined the ladies in it. Now it was cold and damp, the curtains and chairs covered with brown holland, and cheerless in the extreme, not having had a fire in all the winter.

When Mrs. Turner came in she looked as faded as her fortunes, shivering in a dressing-gown and a shawl. She attempted the dignified, as Sarah made a respectful curtsy and asked for Miss Amelia.

"Sarah," the lady began, without preface, "my daughter wished to see you. I had no objections, but I must caution you about what you say to her. You must not encourage any fancies, it would not do for her to indulge any, about doing—many things—things that you might do, for instance; it is impossible—quite impossible."

Sarah opened her mouth to ask for some explanation. "What sort of things?" she would have said, but Mrs. Turner gave her no opportunity.

"She is different to you, you know; she has been brought up a lady, and her duty is to behave like one. Endeavour to impress it upon her that nothing is to be gained by sacrificing her position. Her business ought to be to make the house cheerful by being cheerful herself, and a comfort to her father and mother. Tell her this; now you can go."

It was the rising tendency to question and object that brought the orders to such a sudden conclusion. The girl hesitated a moment; she thought she could scarcely go without expressing something of her own opinion. It would not be upright and downright, and like herself, to do so; but as Mrs. Turner began to move away, she was forced to go too.

"Miss Amelia is in the breakfast-room," Mrs. Turner said, as she walked out, and Sarah went to the door and knocked.

She heard someone say "Come in," and she came in, but at first she thought the room was empty. Then she saw a woman sitting on a footstool near the fender, who looked like an untidy servant, but was too idle. Her hair was ruffled, her dress dirty, and her whole attitude sunk and hopeless in the extreme. At last Sarah said—

"I came to see Miss Amelia."

The woman looked, and said—

"Oh, yes, come in."

Then Sarah walked towards the fire and recognized her young mistress.

"Oh, Miss Amelia," she said, "I did not know you; I thought—"

She was on the point of bursting into tears. Was this what ladies did in presence of misfortune? Was this how they suffered?

Amelia looked at her with vacant face; she had an earthy grey complexion, a small thick-ended pug nose, a stoop in the shoulders, with the chin coming vacantly forward.

"You wished to see me, Miss Amelia," Sarah said, when she had collected her ideas.

"Well, I did; I don't know that it is of any use, though. I thought perhaps—Sarah, what are you doing now?"

"I am at home now, Miss Amelia."

"Ah! you are at home, but what are you going to do? Sarah, how well you look! What are you—what do you look forward to, Sarah? What will you be? What will you do in the time to come?"

Sarah's first thought was that time to come was eternity, then taking it as the immediate future, she scarce knew how to answer the question; she began a sentence or two and could finish none.

"Sarah," said Miss Amelia, "I'll tell you why I sent for you. You earn your living in some way or other, I suppose—or at

least you will have to do so when your father dies. Now what
is there that *I* could do? You ought to know."

"Oh, there should be plenty of things that you could do,
Miss Amelia."

"But what? *But what,* Sarah?"

The girl had raised her head with flashing eyes, like a cat
pouncing on the long-watched-for mouse; but now Sarah stammered; she dare not propose to the young lady the poor ill-
paid trades that were open to her.

"But what, Sarah? You see I am in prison, I can do nothing."

"Oh, Miss Amelia, how are you in prison? You can go where
you like, and do what you like."

"No I can't, I'm in prison; they would not let me."

"Well, people must always do as their fathers and mothers
tell them, but they are not prisoners for that; Miss Turner and
Miss Eliza are not prisoners, why should you be different to
them?"

Amelia laid her head on her hands and did not raise it again
while Sarah stayed.

"Aye, there it is; I am different to them, it's my fault, I suppose; I cannot help it. I am different, and I am in prison. You
may go away, Sarah, you cannot help me; I shall never get
what I want, never as long as I live; never. You may go
away."

Sarah stood in silent pity. Except Miss Amelia, Sarah had
never liked the Turners; she hated them now. But the bare
idea of the helpless girl trying the hardships of a life of labour,
with evidently failing health and peevish temper, frightened
her.

"It's very hard work," she said stammering; "an' there's not
much at the end of it."

"Is there any work at all?" Amelia said from between her
hands.

"Yes, Miss Amelia, you might—"

"I might?"

"If Aunt Jane would let you lodge with her and cook for

yourself, and take in work—dressmaking and such like—you might be able to live."

"Could I?"

"I am pretty sure you could."

"But," this seemed to Amelia like walking over a precipice— "but how could I?"

'Aunt Jane's just an old woman, you know, an' you would just have to sit by the fire and sew. You're a good hand at sewing, I know. Shall I ask Aunt Jane?"

It was long since Amelia had heard a word of praise; still longer since such hopes had beckoned her. The mere physical effect of her quickened pulse on her weak nerves set her laughing hysterically, while, with the tears running between her fingers that still covered her face, she said—

"Can I?"

"Yes, Miss Amelia. Shall I ask Aunt Jane?"

"Yes, oh, yes; if you would do it for me!"

"Yes, I'll do it, Miss Amelia," and she turned to go.

"Oh, stay! Don't go yet, please."

Then Sarah stood still, and, seeing that Amelia did not speak, asked if there was anything else. But Amelia only wished to become familiar with the new idea, and knew not how to frame a question about it.

"I don't know what to say," she repeated. "Must you go?"

"Yes, Miss Amelia, I will go and ask Aunt Jane."

She was unconsciously taking the position of leader, and Amelia was yielding to the easy pressure.

"Go, then. Good-bye."

Sarah lingered for a moment, trying to say something comforting, then curtsied, and said "Good-morning." Passing through the kitchen she saw Mrs. Turner and Eliza. Both looked at her as if intending to speak, but she made the quickest possible curtsy and walked fast out at the door.

She went straight to Aunt Jane's, and her face made her aunt ask her "what ailed her now?"

She gave an account of her visit, and of the proposal she herself had made.

"T' lass is i' t' reight on 't," said Aunt Jane. "What for sudn't they try to addle summat? But for all that she'll never do nought."

"What for shouldn't she do nought? She can do 't well enough."

" 'Cause she'll tak' after her mother; an' her mother's a fooil, an' allus war."

"If she starts again telling me what I mun do an' what I mun say, I'll set her down," Sarah exclaimed.

"I've nought again that, but childer mun do as they're bid. It is but reight."

"An' is it reight o' their fathers an' mothers to lead 'em wrong? Folks belongs to themselves, an' not to other folk. T' lass is fair pining for want o' summat, and they mun set themselves i' t' gate!"

Sarah persuaded her aunt to let Amelia Turner share her bed and board in the hope that she would be able to bear her share of the small outlay for which they were both to live. She was more kind-hearted in doing this than Sarah knew, and less sanguine of success. She was aware of the difficulties in the way, and, besides, had the most contemptible opinion of the capacity and energy of ladies.

"There is not one on 'em can earn ten shillings i' t' week," she would say with scorn; "they do nought every bit o' t' day but tak' care o' theirsens, an' then they cannot do it."

It was settled, however, that Sarah should carry the good news to Miss Amelia next morning that there was a home for her at hand.

"An' ye'll go round to a two or three houses an' tell 'em 'at she's wanting work, an' she's a right good hand."

"Nay, I think I'll wait while (till) I see her," the aunt said, drily, and Sarah was forced to be content.

She took her way joyously to the house next morning, as became the bearer of good news. As she came up to the kitchen door she met Miss Eliza in a canvas apron bearing a pailful of dirty water, and looking unmistakably angry at being thus taken by surprise.

"Please, 'm, could I speak to Miss Amelia?"

"Speak! Miss Amelia!"

"Yes."

Sarah was taken by surprise to find the condescending kindness all gone so suddenly, and Miss Eliza was still more so to see that her haughty anger made no impression whatever.

"Amelia, what does this girl want? Come and speak to her."

Amelia, who had caught sight of her, was just preparing to run away. She came forward with bent head, flushing crimson, and began a stammering speech; the first half of which was an inquiry what Sarah wanted, and the second a formal "good-morning." Then she stepped out, and began to sidle away from the door.

Sarah followed her.

"Please, Miss Amelia, you can come to Aunt Jane's as soon as you like. She's ready for you. We'll find plenty of work for you. Aunt Jane'll go out this afternoon and tell folk—"

"Oh, where is she going? She must not! I don't want her! What will she say to the people?"

"She'll say ye want some sewing, an' ye're a good hand."

"She mustn't! she mustn't! Whatever will papa say?" and Amelia burst into tears.

Sarah stood looking at her in wonder and confusion, and at last observed in a half-penitent manner—

"Ye asked me, Miss Amelia. I thought you wanted it."

"I believe I did say something about it, but you misunderstood me."

The tears were suddenly dried, and Amelia looked much as her mother had done when the day before she stood opposite to Sarah in the dreary, fireless room.

"We had an application once," she said, raising her head and drooping her eyelids; "someone had heard we wanted work, and papa was so angry! But really our time is so much occupied! I really must beg of you not to use my name. I am really not thinking of offering myself as a work-woman."

Sarah stared and waited. There must be some explanation, she thought. Miss Amelia seemed to find her astonishment unpleasant, and commenced a dignified movement towards the house.

'Then you won't come to my aunt's?" Sarah asked.

Miss Amelia turned slowly round.

"Let me beg of you, Sarah, not to allow your aunt to use my name in seeking for work of any kind."

Another pause of astonishment, and then Sarah curtsied.

"Good-morning, Miss Amelia."

"Good-morning," Amelia answered, and Sarah was quickly outside the gate.

Lest anyone should think that something had been said or done to make Amelia change her mind, it must be said that there was no cause whatever for her doing so, except her own fatuity. Sarah had found her yesterday seated up aloft in the atmosphere of dignified enlightenment, and intending to be guided by pure ideas of right; but this morning she had come down for a little warmth and companionship to the grovelling lower regions. She spoke as she thought on both occasions, but her mind was too weak to carry out either course of conduct. She could not bear the misery of suffering, but she dared not face the hardships of activity. She would have complained in any position, and have turned away from any remedy.

Yet, had Sarah undertaken the task, she could have brought back the opinions and feelings of yesterday in five minutes' time. The poor girl wavered when she saw Sarah's astonishment, and was ready to turn round. The slight accent of scorn with which her former servant wished her good-morning went to her heart. She stood looking after her till her face was wet with tears, and thought, as she wearily entered the house, "There goes my last hope." When the visit was talked over in the evening, and the rest wondered what attraction there was that Amelia should have wanted to see her, Amelia kept silence and cried. Then Eliza scolded. Why should people give way so? They had enough to bear without crying at a trifle like that. "Indeed, I can't see what there was at all to cry for!"

It was just that—no one could see it—that made Amelia's hopelessness. She had lost the power of speech. Like one sinking under water, she felt there were no means of calling for help. She must go down. Her mother sighed and watched her, but knew no remedy, and was often inclined to quarrel with her because none could be found.

Aunt Jane was less astonished at this history than Sarah expected.

"Well, I shan't have to go, then, seeking work for her, an' I shall miss telling a few lies, for I don't believe nought about her being a good hand; ye say so, but I never seed a lady yet 'at wor a good hand at ought whatever!"

Aunt Jane would not pity Amelia, maintaining that she was no worse off than other folk.

"Some folks likes to lake," she said, "an' they mun tak' t' consequences."

The Sykes's, too, refused to take Amelia's part. "Them Turner women" they took in the lump, and would not separate Amelia from them. It is true, Sarah did not tell her story well. She did not know herself how she had acquired the knowledge of the deep gulf between Amelia and the rest of them.

"They like doing nought—such folk allus did. Ye need never expect no other on 'em."

Sarah left the house in violent anger. She thought the whole household unfeeling and callous, whereas they only did not feel because they did not know. Sarah thought that it was because she was only a woman, and it was right to make use of women so long as they served a purpose, and then to let them drop. She had fixed her eyes on Sammy in a manner past his comprehension, as she thought—

"So ye would do with me, if it suited ye."

She never considered how imperfectly he was acquainted with the circumstances, scarcely knew how she herself had learnt them, and she only could judge now that Amelia was thrown down, crushed, and broken, and not a word of even commiseration given her as she reached out her despairing hands.

'Am I like that?" she asked, in scorn, and she began to see how little control she had over her own fortunes. "Will they throw me down like that, and tread on me if I stand in their way?"

This poor, rejected thing was to Sarah a human soul of infinitely higher temper than those into whose power she had fallen. Sarah knew her to be upright and full of kindness and enthusiasm for the right, and brave beyond common in facing the hard struggle into which she was thrown. Their unconscious mental kinship had made Sarah trust her utterly, and in fact she had looked to her with straining curiosity and interest as the one sole specimen that could show her by example what were the unknown duties of ladies.

Was this the destiny of ladies? Was there, in fact, nothing but selfish cruelty at the bottom of all the care lavished on them? She rebelled utterly against her destiny. Henceforth she would suspect everyone, and trust none. She would stiffen herself against all guidance, not openly, but constantly.

This fierce decision lasted until she got to work again in her own home; then her mother's quiet orders, and the pleasant custom of the old routine, brought back the old, trustful frame of mind. All the world was as before, and all her resolutions were forgotten. But the ground whereon she had built her structure of happiness was shaken, and a few more such shocks would make it crumble down.

CHAPTER XXI.

AN EVIL GENIUS.

ANOTHER incident happened to show to Sarah that the glory of her childhood was fading; the world she had believed in was disappearing, and what was left was a dangerous, unknown desert. Was there any firm ground in it at all?—any place of safety?

She met on the road that evil genius, Sophy Eldon. The two had not seen each other lately; Sarah thought she knew why. It was Sophy's custom to take offence and ignore Sarah altogether, until "she bethought her," and then to renew the acquaintance as if it had never been interrupted. This time, however, Sarah saw at the distance of several yards that Sophy was decidedly ill-tempered, and yet was resolved to speak. She stood before Sarah, stopping the way, and exclaimed—

"Well, now that you have broken poor Susan's heart I hope you are content, Sarah Miles."

"Do just talk a bit o' sense, Sophy. What's up now?"

"You know how our Susan cared for Mr. Hill. She knew him long before your Harriet Sykes did! It was at our house Sammy Sykes first made acquaintance with him. An' now you've gotten him away from her!"

"Who's her? An' where have I hugged him to?" Sarah asked, with quiet scorn (hugged meaning carried.)

"You know well enough, Sarah."

"Tell no lies, Sophy."

"Why, then, how is it they are to be married?"

"Who's to be married?"

"Harriet Sykes and Mr. Hill."

Sarah almost burst into tears.

"It is not true," she said, but the words were a question, not a contradiction.

"It is true," Sophy said, and walked away with the comfortable feeling that she had succeeded in setting Sarah and Harriet by the ears, for she saw well enough that the news was unknown to Sarah, and was a cause of grief to her.

That she should not know! That Harriet, like Sammy, should make a stranger of her in all serious matters! "Would she so much as tell me when she got a new apron? I'm nought to noan on 'em." And then that Harriet should have accepted the advances of a man no better than the rest of them! Had she not seen Mr. Hill worshipping at the shrine of the most contemptible woman Sarah knew?

In a whirl of anger and pain Sarah turned round and walked straight in upon Harriet without a moment's warning. Harriet, looking her in the face, thought—

"She is come to have it out. I wonder what it is?"

Sarah had thought first to state that she did not wish to penetrate farther into Harriet's secrets than the latter wished her to know, and then she would complain that Sophy Eldon knew more than she (Sarah) did. But when she began there appeared to her a certain inconsistency in these two items, so she resolved to congratulate Harriet, and then walk out as if all had been said that was needful.

"I've come to wish you joy, Harriet," she said, walking to the table where Harriet was preparing dinner.

"Eh, Sarah, lass, have ye fun' it out?"

"Why, I were like when all t' town knows! Sophy Eldon told me. I reckon she's noan t' only one. If ye did not happen to want me to know, ye sud ha' telled her not to tell."

"I'd ha' told ye mysen; but ye never gave a body t' chance."

Sarah stood convicted. Unless Harriet had sought her out

she would not have had the opportunity of communicating the news. She began to think she had played a part as senseless as any petted girl of the dozen whose acquaintance she had made at Miss Bell's.

"I am a reight fool!" she said. "How was it I never fun' it out?"

Then she heard how Sammy had made Mr. Hill's acquaintance, and he had soon found an object more worthy of worship than Susy Eldon.

"They had been friends," Harriet said. "If James—"

"Who's James?" Sarah asked.

"James Hill," Harriet explained, as if in wonder that anybody could possibly not know. "An' if he had been ought of a singer Sam would have taken him to Baumforth to learn 'Down in a Flowery Vale.' But he never could sing a bit; but he used to say he liked to hear it, an' he came most nights when there were ought agate."

"An' oft enough beside, I'll be bun!" Sarah said.

"Well, ye know—"

"What is he like?" Sarah asked. "Has he ony decency or honesty about him?"

To which Harriet responded—

"Sarah!"

"Why, they haven't, all of them."

"Do ye know ought against him?"

"Ye're like to know better than I do. I never seed him mysen since he were making a fool on hisself wi' that Susy Eldon."

"Why, he told me himself that he would have been such a fool as to marry her if she had not been such a fool hersen. So ye see two fools cannot hit it," she added, with a happy laugh, that showed that she had no doubts to contend with.

"Well, happen it's all right," Sarah said, as she walked to the door."

"Aye, for sure it's all right. And, Sarah, I've done ye no wrong."

"No, Harriet. An', Harriet, I'm sorry ye're going."

The two began to cry.

"What for do ye allus keep out o' t' gate, Sarah? It's ye 'at's goan."

Sarah saw it was so. It was she that had gone. Without refusing to come to the house, she knew she was the cause that there were no more meetings.

"Come again as ye used to do. What for sudn't ye come on Saturday?"

Sarah agreed to come on Saturday, and Harriet set to work to make it a happy meeting. To this end she knew of nothing better than to get together a number of singers and mutual friends, including James, and trusting to numbers and natural spirits to break down the crust of reserve that had gathered over the two families. Sydney and his fiddle made at least two, and Zack and Nancy, and a few more, filled the house, and made anything but heartiness impossible.

Sarah had lately acquired a feeling of shyness with regard to old Sykes. How could he like or tolerate such a houseful?— and what would he think of it when it came together? But all went on as it had done a hundred times before.

"Why, Sarah," Zachariah exclaimed, "ye've kept yersen out o' sight o' latly."

"Happen ye never looked for me, Zack. What for sud ye?"

In a kindly way they all began to accuse her of forsaking them. They "thought happen she was starting o' setting up for a lady," at which Sarah burst into such a fit of laughter that the house echoed with the response.

But between Sam and Sarah there was no reconciliation. Sarah had always known that Sydney had a low opinion of women, including herself, and now she credited Sam with the same. They were in her eyes both equally false when either of them spoke her fair. She would blink with half-closed eyes into the fire, and start a new subject as soon as their sentence was finished. Sam at last began to imply that the present conditions of the chapel singing were never intended to be permanent.

"We never offered ye ought for it, Sarah," he said. "But when we get right agate—"

"I never asked ye for ought, Sammy."

"No, no," said the whole party at once, "we all sing for nought, dun not we, Sarah?"

"Why, for sure."

"For sure we cannot help it just now," Sam said, "but happen we may some day."

"Ye can turn me off when ye like," Sarah observed.

"Aye, an' ye can go when ye like," Sam responded.

It was said as if in joke, but it was a bitter joke. Harriet half cried. Sydney brought out his fiddle.

The silence had lasted long enough to bring out that palsy of the intellect that comes of painfully seeking something to say, when there came the thin wail of the violin. It was drawn out till Nancy exclaimed—

"Listen, t' fiddle's started a-roaring!" (crying.)

There was a burst of laughter, and Sydney assured them all that it would "roar" till they began singing. So they got up and brought out the music. Sam pocketed his pipe, and took his sheet, and sang as he was bid. Neither he nor Sarah noticed each other. Sarah was sprightly, Sam was sulky. Painfully they laboured through several old favourites and took the flavour out of them all. Then Nancy and Zack found it was time to be going. Nobody said nay, and they went, and the others followed.

So the heaven that had lain about her in her infancy was succeeded to Sarah by the light of common day, and she found it cold and gloomy. As for the evenings at Sykes's, she almost cried at the idea of the house without Harriet in it. The picture of the white fire-lit floor, of the quiet old man, and the laughing merry party looked to her like heaven, and she saw it moving farther and farther away from her, while on her ear lingered the sound, "No more—no more! we return no more!"

As she entered the house by the shop door a woman with her arms wrapped in her apron followed her in, and, walking up to Mrs. Miles, half whispered to her—

"There's that faal beggar through London comed again."

Mrs. Miles said—

"Is he!" and a look of gloom and anxiety came over the faces of both.

"Aye, I seed him," and the visitor walked out again.

"Who is it, mother?" Sarah asked.

"Why, Thelwal, for sure!"

"Why, what does that matter?"

"Why, Sarah, did ye ever hear o' ony good come on 't when he came?"

"Nay, I never did," she said, heartily.

"No, nor ever will."

"But what's he come for now?"

"Who knows?"

The girl perceived that her mother knew more than she chose to tell, and with closed lips she entered the house. She recognized that she was "out of it" and must stand alone; she would learn to do so, and not to intrude where she was not wanted. And then, when she had made good her footing—why, then, it was a desolate world.

The dilemma into which Sarah and Sammy had fallen with regard to the chapel was arranged in a most unexpected way.

One day, a day just like any other day, with nothing to mark it as one on which anything unusual should happen, Mr. Dodds, the Vicar of Repton, walked into the grocer's shop while Mrs. Miles stood behind the counter arranging for the evening sales.

Now Mr. Dodds had certainly never been there before. The two who now stood face to face had lived in Repton all their lives. They had known of each other's existence, but had never acknowledged it to each other before; they were, in common parlance, sworn enemies, and though the Vicar would never be so ill-bred as to show a sign of enmity, and Mrs. Miles had striven with all her might to forgive her enemies, as became a Christian, it had not seemed possible to either of them to get any farther. Whether the clergyman, in the hot days of his youth, had really injured the chapel property, which he detested so much, was never proved, but true it was that to have done so would have met with small blame from his party and his friends. In Mr. Dodds' youth the best Christians in the place were hooted and ostracized because they did not belong to the dominant Church. The social ostracism was as severe as Mr. Dodds and his friends could make it; and as their numbers were small the victory was complete.

And now, after thirty or forty years of ill-will, comes this man with his naturally somewhat pompous politeness, and takes off his clerical hat to her in her own shop and asks after her daughter Sarah.

"I have heard, Mrs. Miles, that she has a very fine voice, and is able to earn something by her singing. Now, if that is the case, I could find her some employment in that way—quite unexceptionable employment, I think."

Mrs. Miles, who could not take her eyes off the man for astonishment, raised the counter-flap, and said—

"She's in the house; you can ask her," and the reverend gentleman passed through and disappeared.

"Good morning. Miss Miles," and Sarah, turning half round so as to get a full view of him, scowled more decidedly than her mother.

"Good morning," she said, at last.

He cared not a whit.

"I have heard much of your fine voice, Miss Miles. Is it true that you are willing to sing—that you do sing in public?"

"I sing at chapel," she said, defiantly.

"Would you have any objections to sing in church?" he asked, and while she stammered in surprise, added that they were in want of a singer; that they gave their leading singer ten pounds a year, and that nothing was easier than to learn what it was requisite for her to know. That if she would come up to Mrs. Dodds' that lady would indoctrinate her in the requisite performances; that she would have several helps, and that if she was fond of music it would be a good opportunity for her to learn a good deal. In this assertion the man was wrong, because he knew nothing of Sarah's acquirements, or what music she was acquainted with. He had concluded all his life long that those Dissenters knew nothing, and had never given himself the chance to learn better.

Thus, in a moment, Sarah saw all her difficulties smoothed away before her.

The mere fact of earning money was promotion to her equal to that that made Sammy put on his hat "o' warter's," and the leaving the chapel was the first wish of her heart, so, with an excess of caution that only her careful education had taught her, she said—

"I'll ask my mother," and said it in such a tone that Mr. Dodds knew that his victory was gained.

"Very well," he said, "then if your mother gives you leave you will come up to Mrs. Dodds' and she will show you what you require."

"Yes, sir."

"Very well. Good morning, Miss Miles."

Sarah had to go through the usual storm of exclamations and remonstrance that welcomed every spontaneous action of hers. She did not seem to have the gift of coinciding with the general opinion, or the usual mode of action of her little world.

"Ye're going to leave t' chapel! Why, it would never have been built but for ye!"

This was not true, but things looked so.

"What, have ye taken up agin t' chapel? What's t' matter wi' Sammy?"

Sarah did not give the grand reason that there was money at the bottom of it. It might have resulted in an offer from her former associates; and it might have made Sam think that she was dissatisfied because of his not having offered her any. Though, according to the usual phrase, "he was nothing to her," she could not bear that he should think that money had made her leave, or would bring her back again. Besides, she rather liked being unintelligible to her associates, for she had something to conceal. Her real state of feeling she would not have touched upon by anyone. Let them think what they liked, she would give no clue to her quarrel with Sammy. Her mother knew this well enough, and said never a word, but—

"Well, Sarah, ye're old enough to take your own way; mind ye walk straight."

She saw no danger to her girl from the companionship of Mrs. Dodds. The lady was a fellow Christian from whom she differed, and Mrs. Miles knew nothing else against her. The worshipping in church was not to her mind, but if it was to her daughter's, she was welcome to go there.

Sarah struck up an acquaintance with Mrs. Dodds. The lady was informed that she was an intimate of the family of Mr. Turner's new partner; she asked about young Mr. Sykes, and was amused by the answer.

"Oh, Sammy!" Sarah said; "why, he's reight enough."

"Does he sing with you sometimes?"

"Aye, oft enough."

"And what do you sing?"

There came a list of musical compositions out of Sarah's mouth that bewildered Mrs. Dodds. She asked no more, but applied herself to instructing the girl in church anthems and hymns. Sarah led the singing with a vengeance. The half-incapable, half-timid young ladies that Mrs. Dodds got together to help, were roused to singing up to pitch, and with a will. The singing meetings became interesting, but they only half supplied to Sarah the want of those that she was beginning to lose. For Sammy, dispirited and unwilling, seldom arranged for a singing evening. He was deep in anxiety and almost remorse for other reasons than those that concerned Sarah. She felt she was a stranger to the greater part of his thoughts and cares; she attributed this to a wrong cause. "I am nought to him," she thought, "and he tells me nought;" while Sam concluded, "I am nought to her, and she never so much as asks ought about what comes o' me and my affairs."

Sarah wondered most at her mother. How had she let her come into this strait? She must have known that Sammy was not true; that he was playing with her, partly for his own ends and partly for the pleasure of doing so; for playing with lasses she had learnt was a favourite amusement of young men. To be sure Sammy, like her brother John, had not played to any such extent as the rest of them, but that was because they suited their blandishments to the nature of the victim they wished to deceive. All men were alike, and there was no good in any of them. (Most men and women go through this experience once in their lives, when some man or woman, not having pleased them, they revenge themselves by passing a sweeping condemnation on the whole sex.) Their habits of falsehood were repugnant to her. Their amazing faculty of being interested in a pretty woman, however false, mean, designing, or unprincipled, their demand for virtues and services which they did not return in kind, and, above all, their deliberate habit of living outside the circle to which they confined her, all raised a sort of disgust in her mind.

"Men's nought!" she exclaimed, while quivering under the wrench that had separated her from one of them. There was nothing left now that he was gone, and whether she suffered because he was gone, or because he was not worth keeping, she could not decide.

She was the more provoked that Sammy stood up stoutly in her defence whenever the desertion from the chapel was in question.

"She has a right to go where she likes," he would maintain, whenever she was blamed. "What must she stick to t' chapel for? She's going to be a singer, an' she's none bound to stick here."

"Why, for sure! it's reight for ye it seems! I reckon ye knew all about it!"

"Sammy had not known all about it, but he did not say so," she thought; "yes, as much as I knew about the partnership with Turner!" She did not say this either. They said little to each other now. There had sprung up a custom of meeting on Saturday night to practise the music that was to be sung on Sunday, but when Sarah forsook the chapel there was no more motive for meeting at all. Even before this interruption to their intercourse it had been formal to the last degree. A smile would have been a concession, so neither of them smiled. They talked over their business, and then ceased to talk at all. Sam's spirits sank. He began to believe that it was well that things had happened so, for how could a man in his position talk of courting? He accepted his fate, and said nothing. She would sometimes refer to his altered position as if he were out of her sphere; he never set her right, but drudged on with his burden and let her leave him.

Sarah saw that she was the only one who was not on the same friendly terms with the Sykes's that they had been all their lives. John was with Sammy very often, when his mother asked of his whereabouts. Old Sykes came in, as he had always done, not for long, but for confidential talk. Sammy came himself, and was as friendly as he dare be, yet they grew strange. Soon she had nothing to say to them, and wondered what, in former days, she had found to talk about. A little restraint stops the flow of conversation as effectually as a gag, and she knew nothing of what Sammy Sykes did or cared for.

Meantime she was getting promoted in the eyes of the community. The Miss Dunns came to sing with her in church, and then would ask her home with them to try other music; sometimes she went by formal invitation to a musical evening, and then Mrs. Dunn would talk to her, when she was for the moment left alone. There was a certain kindred between Sarah and the conscientious girls, but besides their conscience, they had fenced themselves round with such a tangle of proprieties that she could not endure the restraint, and fell off from them entirely, except in the matter of church singing. Even in this they were apart. Sarah sang for her wages, as she broadly said. They would have thought the wages a mark of degradation. Not that they thought Sarah degraded, but if our principles were to be all of a piece, most of them would want a deal of arranging. They did hold these two inconsistent principles, and plenty more; and then as she got more familiar, they let her know what politeness prevented them from telling her. They mentioned one of Sarah's acquaintances as being a very respectable man, observing—

"It is as much as you can expect from him; more, indeed, you know; he is but a Dissenter."

There was hardly room for a protest, but Sarah thrust one in, head and shoulders.

"So am I," she said.

"Oh, but, Sarah, you go to church!"

"But I belong to the old chapel."

"You do not see any objection to the church services, my dear?" Mrs. Dodds asked her.

"No, I've nought against the Church."

"No, of course not. Then we will say you belong to it, may we not?"

"How can ye say so when it is not so?"

The girls took an air of offence. Then, considering that they had not much ground for it, they relaxed, and wanted to be as kind as ever. The attempt was not successful. Sarah thought herself slighted, and the more so for the attempted equivocation about the Church she belonged to. Mrs. Dodds reproved the girls afterwards for their unlucky attempt at conversion. "The girl knows nothing about it," she said. "She would have come gradually to think herself belonging to us, and it would have been all right, but now you have set her on to stand up for the chapel!"

But then arose the question, How could they have a Dissenter singing in their church? They were more zealous than their teachers found it convenient for them to be. They would not let the matter alone, and were at last only persuaded to leave it for a while, for Sarah's sake, in order that she might have an opportunity of seeing the beauty of Churchism, and perhaps of joining herself to the Church. But the kindly feeling was gone, and she was held at arm's length, lest she should soil the purity of their garments. The difference between association with some and exclusion of others is so trifling and indistinct, that the attempt to try the one is very apt to end in the practice of the other.

CHAPTER XXII.

DEATH COMES TO ALL.

SAMMY was in the valley of the shadow, and how to save himself he knew not. He had entered into his new position full of hearty hope and good resolves. He knew that there was much that could be improved in the management of Turner's mill, and that the work entrusted to the sons had been neglected, or ill done, and the overburdened father could not always supply their place. He trusted to Turner's word that he would soon indoctrinate him with the book-keeping, &c., in which he was inexperienced; but this had not happened. At first the young man was respectful, and almost reverent to his unfortunate elder. As time wore on, and his patience got exhausted, his suspicions were roused, and he began to see that there was an attempt to keep him in ignorance. At this he at once rebelled, and began to maintain his own opinion. Then came disputes. Sam insisted that he could buy wool cheaper than they got it from Thelwal. Turner called him "a young man," and said he knew no better. However, Sam insisted, and brought proofs.

He was here on his own ground, and made it impossible for Mr. Turner not to see that he was right. The man, however, only yielded so far as to show that he was found out. He was very angry, and insisted that he had a right to decide for himself. This Sammy denied, but there could be no decision come to on the point, the thing needful being that they should be agreed.

As Sam with difficulty made himself acquainted with the accounts, he found full proofs that their business had not been profitable. He knew how little money he took out, and even had pretty good proof that Turner himself was as sparing as possible. With his very different habits Sam wondered how the family managed to do with so little. He therefore stuck to his point, and insisted on buying wool at Baumforth. Soon after this was done there came an unexpected visit from Thelwal, and a hot meeting of the partners with him. Sam did not know anything was due to him.

"We bought at three months," he said, "and I know you have discounted our bill. What more do you want? Are we to pay you before it's due?"

Mr. Turner interfered, trembling and excited.

"But, Mr. Samuel, Mr. Samuel! do not be so hasty! Mr. Thelwal, I can assure you, you will be paid! The bill will be taken up."

"An' if it is not," said Sam, "you're none the worse!"

"Mr. Thelwal," said Turner, in a begging voice, "I can assure you we will keep to the terms of the agreement; we will indeed."

Thelwal stepped back, put his hands in his pockets, and looked through his half-shut eyes from one to the other.

"You will, will you? Well, we'll see."

Then he took his hat, and walked out. Turner breathed more freely when he was gone, and turning to Sam, said with trembling, whining voice—

"You will ruin us if you are so impatient, you will indeed."

The old man looked so impressive and withal so broken down—so near to tears—that Sammy merely answered—

"We shall be ruined going on the way we do. Why cannot we stop it?"

Turner turned away and shook his head, and Sam turned towards his home.

When his father heard the history, he merely said, "There's summat behind, Sammy, an' ye mun find out what it is; there's more than we know.

Sammy hung his head as he walked about the village, and looked at Sarah, when he saw her, as from a distance that perhaps would never be passed over; while she mocked him, when she had the chance, about his "hat o' warters," as if it made him so far above her, that she could only speak to him with distant respect.

"What should you want with us nowadays?" she would ask, "we're none of us good enough for ye;" and Sam let the sneer go by, not thinking it needful to undeceive her, as the truth would come out sooner or later, "And then she'll laugh at me for having been so soon set up with being partner with Turner!" thought he.

Father and son did not know how much it added to their sadness when Harriet left them. Slow, honest James Hill, without any "gift o' the gab," had found out how to wile the heart out of her, and had taken her away, not without their consent, but yet without their rejoicing. It must be—like everything else. Why should she be made sad by their sorrow? Latterly they had in some degree kept it from her, and so James, having profited by the good times, had a home for her; it was all right, and they turned their faces toward the gloom without her.

Perhaps the most cheery person in the general depression was Maria Bell; she had in truth the most to sustain her, as being the best off of the sufferers. It is true she yielded at first to despair. She had begun to hope and to accumulate money, when the shadow came again, as if to teach her that her striving was hopeless. She stinted herself almost of necessaries, and felt the consequences in increased depression. She would sit by the fire at nights when the girls had left her, guessing how long it would last before she needed to put coals on. She thought she might as well sit without candle, as she had nothing particular to do. There was cold tea in the pot that would do if it were warmed. She would go to bed early to avoid putting coals on, and having to leave the fire to be wasted. Then she crept upstairs in the dark, and lay waiting for warmth, until the idea would occur to her that perhaps a little drop of spirits was the cheapest remedy for her misery; it would bring the sweet restorer, and she would forget awhile.

One morning after such a night she found the ground white with snow. Winter was come. She started back, at first, in affright. How was she to go on all through it? But sometimes a blow awakens the power of resistance. She looked up, as it were, and saw that she had dwelt on the dark side too long. What! with means in the house to live comfortably for twelve or eighteen months, and then a store laid by for necessities, was she to despair? She began to laugh at her own folly, to despise the distant danger, and take courage.

Having settled it that she had no need to think of herself for the next year or two, she began to think of her friend Dora. The only one who did not suffer from either want or the prospect of it was Dora. Her misery was not from poverty, Maria knew; yet she owned that she herself was not so ill off as Dora. She could not have borne the destiny that seemed to be preparing for her. For, looking back, Maria viewed the life history of the girl, and knew how much the past added bitterness to the present. How the teaching of her childhood, the hopes of her youth, would return to her mind and sting her with the contrast. The sorrow's crown of sorrow was hers to bear; and, think as she would, Maria saw no hope for her. She began to be afraid that she herself had raised hopes that must now be disappointed; had she not said, "Perhaps I can discover a way for you?" and now she must tell her that there was none. She asked Miss Everard what dependence was to be placed on her own mamma's words, "The chance will come some time; then take it." Miss Everard did not think the words gave much hope.

"Of course,' she said, "we live in a changeable world; but I don't see—things don't change for the better so often as for the worse, but I fear that Dora makes half her own miseries. She began wrong. I am afraid she will be headlong and passionate, and do herself as much harm as she can."

"What will she do when the old man dies? She says he is poorly. Will they turn her out without a penny?"

And then, half laughing, she continued—

"I wish they would! I hope they will! It might be the best thing that could happen to her!"

"I don't think she will be so very ill off, if she does not make herself so by her own temper; they want her services."

"But is it not a very wretched position to have to please unreasonable people—to fawn and flatter in order to get something given—especially if you think you have a right to it all the time, and owe no obligation at all?"

"I think it the worst curse we women have to bear," the old lady said, and Maria looked up surprised. "We go to the borders of falsehood, we keep our opinion secret, when we should speak out; and all to keep friends with the wrong-doer, because he is the bread-giver. We get a great deal of praise for doing so, but the world would be better if we had not to do it."

"I don't see how she could ever speak in friendship to them without belying her own feelings," Maria said. "She said that once she had announced her intention of seeking a place as a servant, but that Mrs. Greaves had persuaded her to wait; she did not know what for."

"A servant cannot live by service," Miss Everard said, sadly. "A month's illness would bring her to the work-house."

"Then what is there for her to do?"

"Nothing."

After a pause the old lady went on—

"Poor women spend their lives over an open grave, and by quick starvation, or lingering illness, they drop into it before they have lived out half their years. She may hold back and strive, but it matters not."

Maria looked again at the old woman with astonishment. Never before had such blasphemous words been uttered in the little lodge, and the girl saw that nothing less than despair had called them forth. The patient resignation, the quiet courage were gone, and a new side of Miss Everard's character was revealed.

"But you are not in danger, are you?" she said, suddenly. "You will get your rent."

"Have you seen Mr. Turner lately?" Miss Everard asked.

"No, I have not seen him; you know I only go out after school. Why do you ask?"

"He looks so old."

"He is old."

"And so worn and thin. His failure broke him down."

"Well, it is a pity for him; but why do you mention it? You have not lent him money, have you?"

"No, that is—you know I had forty pounds, and I did not like to ask him for money, and I waited. At last I asked him, and he said he was hard pushed, and I waited again, and now all my forty pounds is gone, and I asked when I saw him going by just lately, and wanted to stop him, and he got angry, and said he had no time to talk, that if we began on that subject there were two sides to it. He himself had spent a deal of money on the house. If an account were made out, perhaps it might bring me in a debtor instead of a creditor; that he had let me have this house for nothing, because he knew I could not pay any rent, but if he were not met in the same spirit, he did not know what he might be forced to do."

The two women looked at each other in blank dismay. Then Maria set to work to persuade Miss Everard to get some effective help to clear the matter up. Then came back the old frightened look to Miss Everard's face; she was almost in hysterics at the idea of such an offence.

"Oh, pray don't mention it to anyone! Pray don't! not a word. There is no one but himself knows my affairs, and if he got angry I should be ruined; he might charge me—Besides, I know nothing against him really—nothing."

Then Maria saw the impossibility of rousing this poor creature into an attitude of resistance against her foe. That at least must be left alone. She would lament—they both lamented—that they were so utterly ignorant of business matters. That business was so unwomanly.

"Then," said Maria, "I should like to get unwomanly as soon as possible!"

They both laughed, but they never told anyone of their

wicked wishes. The indefinite punishment of being unwomanly was too severe; what little unwomanliness they could get hold of, they grasped at eagerly, and kept it secret. Maria laboured to find the way to transplant Miss Everard to her fireside, but felt fettered by her friend's terrors of the unknown. Would a way open for her? It seemed absurd that she was not free; but there she was, bound hands and feet all the same.

On opening the door on her return home, Maria found a letter thrust under it by the postman. It was from Branksome, and it occupied the rest of her waking hours.

"My darling," it began, and every term of affection was still so new that she started back at the sound, and perhaps would have protested if she had heard a living voice. But the opportunity was lost, she carefully "disremembered" to correct it when she wrote, and Branksome was not the man to lose an advantage he had once gained.

"My Darling,

"I am depressed beyond common, and as usual I turn to you for comfort. You, yourself, are the subject of my present anger and despair; I know you are suffering, and I cannot help you. You stint, and work, and bend your head, and bear it in silence. You talk of the pleasure of being hand-in-hand, but we are at arm's length nevertheless. My arm aches, but I cannot help you; my own affairs are not going on badly. Indeed, considering how much worse off some people are, I have reason to be satisfied. But then this only leads to the conclusion that I cannot reasonably hope for anything better. Does not everything prove that such happiness as we hope for does not come in this world? Are we not bound to be separated, or to change? How long is this aching arm stretched out to be the alternative to absolute solitude? Yet would not people laugh at me if I proposed to take a wife to share my poverty?

"I am ashamed of myself for laying on your shoulders the burden I ought to bear. I know I ought to be cheering you, not complaining to you; but I am moved beyond my strength when I think of you labouring and suffering, while I look on helpless. I saw you the other day, and thought you looked paler than usual, and somewhat sad. Do you know, when you are unnoticed you always look rather sad, and now I think you begin to look wearied, not tired, but *ennuyée,* with sheer monotony. Is there no help for it? Work is hard enough, but monotony is worst of all. I remember what you say, you see. I almost wish I could do something outrageous to save you from it! What if I began to call on you every morning just when the children were taking their departure? It would be at least a new form of botheration, and then we could talk it over so pleasantly afterwards.

"I know your favourite recommendation, to look for someone whom we can help; but when I look I see *you.* There is none so near, none so interesting, and I cannot do it!

"Whatever may come of it, whether we shall die apart, or live in vain; whether I shall hold my outstretched hand to yours until my palsied arm can hold no longer, or I shall come nearer, and find you vanished in some mysterious way—betide us weal, betide us woe, still I thank God for you as my greatest blessing. You have been, and I trust you will be, for long, long years.

"Everard Branksome."

It appeared to Maria that it would be the height of cruelty and discourtesy not to answer it at once.

She began without preface—

"Rise up, sad heart! Why are you despairing? Are you any worse off than you were when you went to tea to Mrs. Dodds', some long time ago, and seemed merry and mischievous enough? Your despair hurts me, nevertheless. It is true that one's arm aches with being always on the stretch, but still, why despair? And I am conscious of a feeling which I am not content with. It seems to me we differ; if not, why do you only half enter into my position? You pity me outrageously for my poverty, but never enter into the circumstances that cause it.

"Now not to complicate the matter, let me tell you something. I am not worth pitying compared with two friends of

mine, that are now face to face with starvation. They are as
ignorant as cats of the how or why they came into such a position, and know no remedy. It is true they are guilty of the
wickedness of not having fallen in love with a man who could
provide for them, but as I am in the same predicament, I do
not pity them the less. I think their destiny is the most miserable that could have been invented for them, if, instead of
wishing them well, men had intentionally ordained them to
be miserable. Their education is the cause of it, and their
misery is made hopeless by the teaching that forbids to learn
anything about business or money. Tell me what you think
of this. Would you approve of the education that has brought
about this state of things? Or would you alter it? Answer.

"As for my opinion, I think of the words in the Jewish
liturgy, 'God I thank Thee that Thou hast not made me a
woman,' and I think too that if the present dispensation is
to last, I am of the opinion of King Alphonso concerning it.

"I do not fail to thank you in my heart for your pity. It
rejoices me and helps me to be patient. You bring tears to my
eyes with your aching arm, I understand it so well! It comforts me that you turn to me; may you always do it! This at
least no one can take from us so long as we both shall live.
There is light in our heaven yet, and perhaps sunshine will
come. At the worst there shall always be warmth between us.

"MARIA."

It sometimes happens that a number of small events, separated, perhaps, in time and space, give us such warning of
coming catastrophe that we forefeel it without knowing why.
The gloom gathers slowly, and at no instant can we say, "Now
it gets darker," until we raise our heads and look round and
find, all at once, that night is come. So for years Maria had
seen the clouds thickening, not round herself, but round Dora,
until she had learnt to be in wait for the storm that must
burst before long. She looked back on the whole of their united
lives, from the time when Dora had come in breathless to say
that the nasty man was come again, and that she suspected

more than occasional visits from him in future. How bright things had looked then! how easily she had talked Dora over to patience, and persuaded her that nothing more was needed. Dora had courage enough, and rose to the occasion when she found that that was the thing needed.

"Of course, if mamma likes him, it will be right," she said, though with a stifled sigh. "If he is nice, perhaps I shall get to like him! I would learn lessons to please him, just as I do to please mamma. I read all Rollin's History to please mamma, you know, and 'The Life of Columbus.' What would he like me to do or to read, do you think? And I would tell the sons that, though they were not my brothers, and never could be, yet, still, I would do them no harm, and, perhaps, we might get to be friends in time—not real friends, you know, like you and me, because I did not choose them." And she looked up in Maria's face as if to ask pardon for having used the word "friend." Then in unconscious forlornness and pride she asked, "Will you be my friend always, Maria?" and then, with sudden tears, the girls had kissed each other, and Maria told her that they were real friends, and whatever opposed, they could never cease to be so.

Then came the slow revelation of the actual fact—how the man was not "nice," how her mother's life had faded, and the girl was left in still deeper shadow; and now she saw that this was not the worst that was possible. The old man might die, and then Maria trembled for what would happen afterwards. It was pitiable; through all her life—almost, at least, before her childhood was gone—the girl had hoped against hope, looking forward to an unknown future. She had decked it out with pretty things, and used it to console herself for the darkened present. What if the future never came?

Maria thought of the Indian women who, when their nursling dies, dress up for themselves what they call a doll of sorrow, and dress it and fondle it in place of the reality. So we all of us do. Some coming time, or, at least, some possible time, we set before us, when we shall have pleasure, or affection, or beauty in our lives, and we enjoy it in part beforehand, or try to do so. Would it be wise to be sure that it could never come?

Maria and Dora had dressed their dolls, and talked of them together. First, when Mr. Woodman was to turn out nice, and then when Maria was to turn out prosperous, but all this had faded away. What was there now? Even hope was gone.

Here follows the last letter she had received from Dora:—

"I have nothing new to communicate, yet I must write to you. You are the only thing that keeps up in my mind a shadow of hope. You know a man will not give up hope till the rope is round his neck—and not then either.

"As to reasons for hoping, I have really but one. Do you remember your mamma's last words? 'Get away from there as soon as you can, Dora! You will think you cannot, but the chance will come if you look for it, and are ready to take it. Now, mind and be ready.' Now, the first half of her prophecy has come true, it is very sure. May not the second come true in time? And surely it cannot be long before—not when I am old and grown incapable by sheer inactivity—not when my life is nearly over, just to mock me! and it is very sure I shall be ready to take it!

"But I have walked all round my prison walls, and see no chink by which escape may be possible. Yet your mamma thought there was or would be one some day, else why did she say anything?

"True, I can go out of the house and not come back; but it would be to die of starvation, or to be brought back by the poor-law officers to Mr. Woodman as my nearest connection, and unless he positively denied all responsibility I should be left with him. If I got a place of any kind, it could not be one that would provide me with more than the meanest clothing, and the workhouse would rise up before me when illness or anything else threw me out of work.

"At times I think that we live here in a very narrow circle, and that you have somehow got out of it, and that possibly you may see more than I do. Yet nothing comes from you! Do not think I complain—at least not of you. I know you will help me whenever it is possible, but yet I grieve. Suppose I were to make the plunge, and inquire for a place as nurse or maid-of-all-work, and then trust to the chance of getting another place in time, and after a few such chances know more of the world than I do now? Would my knowledge be of any use to me? I should many times have to face the prospect of starvation, and would it benefit me?

"For the rest we change little here. We get more mean in our way of living, if not more economical. We live in the little room always. There is only one servant, and I do the rest of the work. As there are four men to 'do' for, I am well employed. I believe this is the reason I am let alone. They would get no other servant so cheap. I know what I can get, and ask for nothing else. Mr. Woodman once bought some diaper for a tablecloth, and saw that it was wrong somehow, but did not remedy the fault, and we dine without, as the diaper will not reach across the table, and is too short to join.

"If your mamma made me believe in the possibility of rescue—my own made me doubt it—why did she take the frightful step of marrying Mr. Woodman?

" 'For me,' she said. And the longer I think of this revelation, the more frightful it grows. I used to 'think scorn' of my mother every time I looked at the man, or witnessed his manners and his ideas. But now!—oh, I cannot get over it! She did it for me! and if this was needed, what must she have thought of my prospects when she was gone! Surely if there had been any chance at all she would not have done this! There was no glamour over her, she did it with her eyes open! From what terrible destiny did she try to rescue me when this was the price! Is it possible she could have believed, like your mother, that a time would come when I might rise out of helpless poverty? No, she did not believe it. She never in her life pointed out to me my future destiny, or the means of fighting against it. Once a beggar, always a beggar, she seems to have thought, and then accepted her position, and took the means that are supposed to make all things right for womankind.

"I wish you would write to me. If I could talk to you, would you tell me anything? Try, at least. What keeps up your spirits? Find out, if you can, and tell me."

Maria sat with the tears running down her face as she read this letter all alone at night. Then she took up a pen at once to answer it when the fit was on her.

"I have no answer to give you," she said, "that is worth the writing. I know no means, I see no opening; though I have made the experiment, and got out of the shelter, I have acquired no knowledge thereby. True, I have not yet come to the workhouse, but it is in sight. I got some work in teaching, but there is none now, for me or anyone else. I am not worse off than others. We all see starvation near at hand, and none know a remedy. For the moment you are better off than I. All that I can advise is for us to bend our heads to the weather in silence and, if possible, in patience, keeping ourselves meanwhile unspotted from the world. Let neither mean discontent, nor paltry dishonesty, nor anything of evil feeling stain our minds. Perhaps better times will come—perhaps not. In either case our course is clear. Let us hold fast to our faith and follow it.

"I wish I could talk to you. I would sell my shoes to pay for a letter from you. So much for the food and raiment wherewith St. Paul was content! Am I unreasonable? And yet I own I am better off than you, for I have a friend to whom I can talk. We do not say much, however. We find it best to keep silence, for we cannot help looking forward, and we will not talk of what we see before us.

"Yet remember, we two are hand in hand, and I do not forget my mamma's last words, '*The time will come!*' Let us rest on this and look forward. We may live to laugh at our present fears."

So Maria and Dora went on dressing their doll. The amusement has a little insanity in it, but which of us could do without it now and then?

She ended with the opinion that, "Perhaps it would not be right to throw away the bread you have until you see a chance of getting it elsewhere. We are both in deep waters, but we have helm and compass, and are still afloat, and if we should go down, why, many better than we have failed before us. We need not rouse the world with our exclamations. There is peace when the struggle is over, if we only act our part here."

Maria used to find a sort of pleasure through her tears in writing such letters as this. She spread all her own surroundings out before her friend, and got a clearer view of her own position thereby. She got used to the bracing air of poverty, and was strengthened by it. Nothing seemed to her so absurd, after writing such a letter, as to spend any time in keeping up appearances. She brought in her own coals, and carried her own groceries, without even thinking of the matter. She went to church in the old bonnet, and knew not that other people pitied her for being obliged to do so. We get rid of fancied burdens when we have real ones to carry.

And now Dora had been eight years in the house with her step relations. The time when she had received her notions of what was right, and true, and lovely, and of good report, was far distant and imperfectly remembered. Except her rigid honesty, and perhaps her shame of vulgarity, she had nothing left of her mother's teaching. Christian charity, Christian kindness, were hers in name only. The reserve of the savage that scorns to show pain, and the desire of the weaker to make herself feared, had taken the place of more cultivated feelings. All her minor morals and manners were imitated from those around her. For dress and appearances she cared as much—no, not so much—as a servant girl. It was really true what one of them had said, that she had forgotten to put on her better dress to go to church, and then had asked—

"Well, what does it matter?" amazing as the fact appeared to those who heard it.

Her clothes were seldom without a tear or two, her hair seldom straight, her shoes never whole, her voice and look seldom amiable, her help, even her civility, never ready. No wonder that if circumstances had not sent her to Coventry her own conduct would have done so. Only Mrs. Greaves laughed instead of taking offence, and said she did not know her own mind.

As a consequence of solitary confinement, it has been mentioned incidentally that it takes about five years to make a man insane. How long a time of confinement not quite solitary it would take to bring anyone half way to this conclusion we do not know, but uncongenial company, and very little of that, will bring one a good way towards it; and Dora's mind retained till death the warp given it in her youth. One circumstance only happened to her that gave her an insight as to the difference between herself and other girls. As Mr. Woodman failed more and more, when he found that the mild spring weather did not enable him to resume his outdoor habits, when at last he could not even go about the house, nor always help himself into his clothes, he yielded to Mrs. Greaves' advice, and she got him a nurse, and with this woman Dora had perforce to make acquaintance. She "wondered at her" when Dora did anything queer, stared when she was not dressed as well as her means allowed, and suggested the use of a comb and brush, until Dora used to call her to her face, "Brush it a bit." The woman wondered, too, at other things besides Dora, and finding out for herself the true state of the case, pitied the girl, and made her life more pleasant to her in various ways. And Dora became more humanized under the new *régime*.

But even with this wider horizon she often ran her head against the walls of her prison, as when she began to ask what women could do to make their own living.

"Oh, Miss Dora, my dear, what does that matter? You will not have to think of such things. You must stay at home and keep the house, and work, and—" She stammered while seeking another employment.

"But I can make no money by that," Dora said.

"It's not for ladies to make money like common folk," the woman said, just in the tone that she would have used if the girl had been guilty of impropriety. "It's only servant girls that think of such things."

"Then can one earn no more than a servant?"

"Well, there's governesses."

"I don't know enough to be a governess."

"Well, but you know, dear, a woman's place is in the home."

"I have no home to get into," Dora said, with a sneer. "When women have no home, what do they do?"

"Why, they wait. You may get one some time."

The nurse would not be more definite, and it was not necessary. Dora turned away with a gesture of scorn. The more she was driven towards the only remedy for her troubles, the more fiercely she fought against accepting it even as possible. She thought the world was indeed out of joint when her only fate must be to stand begging for chance alms, that perhaps would be repulsive when they came, or starve because they did not come. This puzzle the old woman could not explain to her.

"Nay, Miss Dora," she would say, "ye are like a bairn that they say can ask more questions than a wise man can answer."

Answer, indeed, there was none, and Dora sought round and round her prison walls in vain.

Still, the presence of the nurse was a benefit to the girl. It brought her into contact with the outward world. She began to ask how much a single person could live on, and to find an interest in the lives of those to whom "living" was the first thought in the morning and the last at night. The necessity of pleasing other people became more apparent to her. She spent more time over her clothes; she got clearer ideas as to what she could do when opportunity offered, and even began to ask why she should not make an opportunity for herself. She once asked the nurse why she should not go and offer herself as nursery governess, or at least, as nurse to a person who she had heard was making inquiry for one. The nurse was startled, and even frightened.

"Oh, dear, Miss Wells," she exclaimed, "whatever will you do next? You must not, indeed you must not! Mr. Woodman would be so angry! And they would say I had put you up to it, and I should never dream of such a thing."

"Why should he be angry? And what does it matter if he does?"

"Indeed, Miss Wells, you must not! You—you—"

Between the real difficulty of the subject and the woman's limited power of explanation, she gave no enlightenment to Dora as to why she should not put on her bonnet and go forth at once, and then, if such good luck befell her, come back and say "she was come for her clothes, as she was going to be servant at—" Then it would be done! She would be free! Why, how commonplace it was! How stupid she had been not to see it before!

"You always stop me, whatever I want to do," she said, and privately thought the woman had joined her enemies.

She talked to her no more. Yet she felt too ignorant and frightened to take the path that had seemed so straight and easy when she first saw it. Yet she could not drop the idea until she had had a visit from Mrs. Greaves. The nurse, in a fright, had told this lady of Dora's lunatic intentions in order to clear herself of all complicity with them; and the energetic lady undertook to set Dora right again.

"You must not think of such a thing," she said, holding up her hands. "You will ruin yourself and lose your position entirely."

Dora was dignified.

"Why should not I think of such a thing?" she asked. "I have no position to lose."

"You will ruin your prospects if you do. Don't think you will get anything out of Mr. Woodman by doing so. Don't think he will ask you back again, or promise you better dresses, or anything else. He is too ill—and too poor," she added, in a half-whisper. "If you would only be reasonable and be of use to him, he might be induced to put you down for your mother's fortune at least. He has quarrelled with his sons enough to do so. But there you go, wanting to force something out of him by going on in that way. You will never get a penny, I tell you!"

"I am not trying to get a penny!" Dora said, in a rage.

The old gulf was revealed between them. There was no understanding each other. Dora felt herself accused of design-

ing perversity, and did not see that Mrs. Greaves, in proposing another sort of trickery, could not be intending to insult
her when accusing her of such wonderfully far-fetched motives.

By accident, as it were, the angry lady hit upon an effective
argument.

"The man's going to die," she said; "can't you let him die
in peace, without disgracing him!"

Dora opened her eyes. She had known that Mr. Woodman
would never get better, but death seemed to her, as it always
does to the young, an indefinitely long way off. It was a thing
that could not be taken into calculation. Seeing her advantage,
Mrs. Greaves followed it up by adding boldly—

"People will say you have no heart at all!"

Then she saw she had conquered. She thought, "Oh, she is
content now to wait. I wonder if she thinks it is near? She must
have a bad time of it, to be thinking so. Well, she will not
be so much better off when he's gone. There's nothing for her
that I can see but another like him."

"You know nothing of the world," she said, aloud, "or you
would not be so impatient!"

"Sure enough I know nothing of the world," Dora said, and
the sudden agreement almost threw Mrs. Greaves on her face,
for she thought it followed that the girl should be docile to
those who did.

So the girl was wiled and frightened from her object.

"I see no way," she said to herself, sadly, when Mrs. Greaves
was gone. "I thought there was, and that I had found it; but
now it is closed. Am I a fool for listening to them all, or for
not thinking like them? What everyone says must be true,"
she thought, "and everyone takes me for a fool. Is it because
I don't want that I cannot believe? Can it be that there is
actually nothing to be done—that there never will be?—that all
my life?—"

She started back, literally refusing to accept the destiny before her. Then came a time of utter depression, which she
herself attributed to Mrs. Greaves' conversation. "The worst
of it is," she thought, "when friends come to help me. If I were

not roused by talking I should not feel pain. I will sink into
idiocy without thinking of it, since there is no help or rescue
for me."

Through all this time Maria's letters were all that held her
mind fast to the actual world, and soothed her feelings so as
to enable her to bear her lot. True, the closely-written sheets
could only pass between them at intervals of a month at least;
and soon Maria began to prepay her own letters, for she had
heard of some angry remarks made by Mr. Woodman, which
made her fear that he would some day angrily send back her
letter rather than pay for it. They told each other everything
they could think of to tell, much which they regretted afterwards when the necessity came of disguising misfortune or
misery. Yet it was best. They continued to know each other
thoroughly, and each to have a friend.

Maria was by much the better off of the two. The old timid,
hesitating woman to whom she had paid a visit of charity for
the sake of a change, proved a clear-headed, sensible, Christian
woman, with a great liking for her visitor; only when the Turners were spoken of she became humble, nervous, and sometimes actually frightened. She was dependent on them, she
explained. He—Mr. Turner—managed her business matters,
and she did not know how she could get on without him.
There was some suspicion mingled with her fear of him, but
whatever it was she could not shake it off. But with this subject out of sight she was always kind, helpful, and sometimes
entertaining. She listened as we listen to those who interest
us, and Maria saw that every deed and thought of hers interested Miss Everard.

CHAPTER XXIII.

ANARCH CUSTOM.

"WE have to go on living whether we like it or not," Maria said to herself, as she waited impatiently for the two little Miss Dodds to put on their bonnets after their music lesson. They were her only pupils. Mrs. Dodds had found out the necessity of their learning music when she lost all the others. Maria suspected that there was another cause, besides necessity, that brought them just at that time, and took the help gratefully, and did her best.

As she watched them dressing, she noticed one of them signal to the other, and they both moved towards the window, and, looking out herself, Maria saw a woman leaning her elbows on the little green gate.

"She has been before," said one of the girls, "and now she's come again; she waited ever so long."

Maria turned to open the door, and saw coming feebly towards it the most forlorn and desolate creature that ever met her eyes. Her torn frock was draggled to the knees, and the shoes soaked in mud. The bonnet was of shape and colour unrecognizable, and as she lifted a white face to Maria's, she said almost inaudibly—

"I had nowhere else to go."

"Of course not! Where else would you go but to me?" Maria exclaimed, as she put her arms round her, and helped her to the sofa, for it was Dora herself that had come begging to her door. The children hurried out full of news and curiosity, and at last the doors were shut, and Maria went back to her friend. She found her on her feet again, wandering about the room with bent head, as if looking at the pattern of the carpet. She brought her back to the sofa and made her lie down again; and bringing in a chair sat down beside her.

"Now tell me all about it," she said, caressingly, as she bent over the half-fainting figure. And Dora, looking up like the beggar she was, repeated pleadingly—

"I had nowhere else to go to."

"No, no! why would you seek elsewhere? Now tell me where you have been. Where have you come from?"

"From Long Norton."

"What! all the ten miles? This morning!"

"Yes."

Maria put her face to the white cheeks and said—

"You are here at last all right, so now tell me all about it."

And Dora took breath and began, after collecting her wandering thoughts for a minute—

"When old Woodman died—"

"Is Mr. Woodman dead?"

"Yes, he died some weeks ago."

"You never told me!"

"No, I thought—I don't know what I thought."

The fact was, she had thought she would not demand an asylum so long as she could live without one.

"After he died," she went on, "things went on worse than ever. I thought I would do my best, for I knew they might turn me out and let me starve. But the men would have more service and better dinners, and took more waiting on. They would bring in one, or two, or three people, and sit smoking in the little back room till midnight. Then they ordered me about with more authority and bad language; and at last Matthew—that's the eldest—swore so at the servant that she gave him notice and went off, or rather he turned her out. After a few days I told them I must have another servant. They took no notice, but at last, when things were not always right, and the dinner not always ready, they grumbled and scolded, and I said I could not help it, and then at last Matthew said there was one coming next day. The others looked surprised, but he did not explain. Next morning she came and took possession without saying anything to me, except to ask when the master was coming in. I said 'Not till evening,' and then she looked discontented, and walked about spying into everything. Then she went into the pantry and cut herself some cold meat. As soon as Matthew came in she asked him where her room was to be, and then went into it, unpacked her clothes and went to bed.

"Next morning after breakfast I asked where I could get some help, for I could not do without. They said I had got help; I insisted I had none. Matthew called the woman down, and told her she had promised to keep the house. She said she was ready, but she could not do all the work herself, and she looked at me as if to say I should help.

" 'Come, come,' he answered; 'you must do the work between you.'

"I was at a loss, and at last the men went away, and we were left to ourselves. I went mechanically about the most important work—the dinner; and after sauntering about a while, she began asking me questions as to our daily life. I gave short answers, and said she might do the rooms. She walked upstairs, but soon came down again and commenced sauntering about, and asking questions. At last she said, 'Now you need not be so cross, I don't see what harm I do you! Why can't you be friendly?' I said that if she would do her work I should prefer it. 'My work!' she screamed; 'who told you I had any work? Do you think I am going to be ordered by you?'

"I cannot tell you all; we quarrelled and shouted, and then I burst into tears, thoroughly ashamed of myself. Why is it, 'Ria that I always do so? and I cannot help it. I am getting like them, and"—here came another burst of tears—"I cannot help it!"

Maria comforted her, and heard the rest of her tale.

When the men came in to dinner, and found it was not ready, the quarrelling began again. Dora said sulkily that she could not do everything. The younger brothers, finding their comforts not provided, would have the woman in and make her promise to do better, or to go. She came in insolent and loud; she would do as she liked, and if she was scolded in that way she would go there and then. Matthew took her part, and at last, putting his arm round her waist, he said they should all turn out first. Then one of the brothers began to shout and laugh, and said, "Oh, oh! if that was to be the way—" and he came and tried to put his arm round Dora, who flew out of the room, and upstairs. After a time she came down with shawl and bonnet on, and ran to Mrs. Greaves. She was kindly received, and soothed into patience once more. "I will go and speak to them," the lady said; but Mr. Greaves, for once, over-ruled her, and went himself. He went, and returned scolding furiously. Those Woodmans were the most shameful people he had ever seen! They were a disgrace to the parish! He never knew such talk, nor such ways of going on! They deserved to be hunted out of all decent company!

"He went on a long time, and I waited to here if perhaps they had promised to do something. Now, to tell the truth, 'Ria, I was afraid most of all that they would make some ar-rangement for me to go back again; but I don't think he could. I stayed there till next morning, and then set off. She did not turn me out," said Dora; "but she won't help me."

"Did she say so, Dora?"

"No, but I know she won't."

"Yes, Dora; she is not ill-disposed."

"She won't, I tell you. I came to see if you would."

"Of course I will; but what can I do?"

"There is something—if you will."

"Is it a right thing, Dora?"

"Certainly it is."

"Then I will do it with all my heart."

"I'm come a-begging, 'Ria. If you don't like to help me, you must tell me so; but if you refuse me you take away my last hope of getting bread." She still hesitated and seemed to shrink from further explanation. At last, " 'Ria," she said, "did you ever hear the phrase 'as dark as the pit of hell?' "

Maria stood dumbfounded, and Dora, after waiting for an answer, began—

"I'll tell you what it means," she said; "the crown of misery is the helplessness that comes of being in the dark. And darkness means ignorance. Imagine anyone in the dark! A blow comes from one side, and he puts up his hand in self-defence, and finds he has cut himself against an unseen sword. He shrinks back, and another blow meets him from behind. He crouches down in terror, and is trodden on by some enemy in whose way he stands. All he can do is to lie still and suffer."

"Well, but, Dora—"

"Darkness is ignorance, I tell you. It is what is recommended to us women."

"But, Dora—"

"Maria," said the girl, "if people knew that the women in the churchyards were alive—those in the coffins, I mean—and were waiting for us to dig them up, do you think anyone would do it?"

"Dora, do be quiet!"

"Answer!"

"Well, of course they would."

"No, they would not! They would say ladies did not want to get up—that they had all they wanted, and that men did not like them to get out of their graves."

"Never mind what men say! You are not in a grave, and you can go where you like."

"Never mind! never mind! Men, and women too, have shut me up and left me in darkness."

She shook her fist and clenched her teeth.

"Do not hate people so, Dora!"

"Why not? They leave me to die by slow atrophy. They keep me in darkness, they shut me up! Look at me! I cannot live so! I am losing my faculties and my health, and have no prospect but to die by inches. Of course I ought to fade into an angel without complaint; and people will thank God and be glad when I am out of the way. The world is not my friend! And shall I not hate the world?"

"No, Dora, you shall not! You a lady! you a Christian! how come you to soil your lips with words only fit for a hired soldier, or a savage?"

Dora burst into tears.

"It is too hard, Maria! I cannot bear it!"

"Dora, listen! The time will come when you will care nothing for those who have opposed you. You will wonder how you could think so much about them. Once get a little success and they will all turn round."

"But how? how? how?" she cried. And then, bursting into laughter, said very quietly, "I won't hate my enemies, if you will show me how to get the better of them."

"First of all don't get it into your head that everyone is your enemy. You have no enemies."

"Well, then, take it as granted that I have no enemies. What next? What is the second step to be to get this little success?"

Maria was obliged to confess that she did not know.

"Now, Maria, there is just one plan. It may be a bad one, but except this there is nothing."

Maria felt relieved; she was ready to jump at anything.

"I want your help," said the girl; "your help for my one plan. Will you help me? I want to try and give a lecture here in Repton."

"A lecture!"

"Yes, a lecture."

"Here in Repton?"

"Yes, here in Repton."

"I don't know—"

Dora got up and seized her hand as if to prevent the coming refusal.

" 'Ria, you are my friend, I call upon you as my friend. I am not insane, I know very well that I go a long way to ruin you if I fall, but, Maria, help me. 'Ria! I am sinking under water, and I want a hand."

"Dora, is it right? Are you sure?"

"I am sure."

"Then I will help you with my whole heart! Never mind what comes of it, tell me what to do."

Dora sat up, and began in a slow, rational tone—

"One time when I was at tea at Mrs. Greaves', there was a man—Mr. Greaves brought him in for some tea just in a business way, and they began talking, and talked all tea-time, about ladies giving lectures. He said it was a good thing, and Mrs. Greaves said it was a thing she never could tolerate. Now, he was come to see if he could find hope for a lady lecturing there. He was a man that engaged them and looked after things; and she said she would never go, and began to say the lady must be a queer one, and she was sure—and then he interrupted her, and said she was a real lady, and was so stern, that Mr. Greaves said that there was nothing against the lady at all, and she tossed her head. It seemed to me that they made it just as they liked. The lady was to be a good-for-nothing, or a lady, just as they voted her, and both gentlemen voted her all right, and Mrs. Greaves was so angry that she talked all the evening after they were gone. And I believe she did her best to prevent the woman succeeding, but she did not succeed for all that. I never spoke, but I kept the programme and the man's address, and I have got them now. If I succeed once he will help me to another, perhaps, or show me what to do, or somehow I shall find out how to go farther. Now you know the people here, you will know half-a-dozen leaders whom all the rest will follow like sheep. Get me my chance, 'Ria, move heaven and earth to get it! It is all I have."

"I'll try," Maria said; "what is the lecture to be about?"

"About a play of Shakespeare's, *Measure for Measure.*"

"But, Dora, how can you? Why, you could not even read it aloud!"

"I don't intend."

"Shall you speak about yourself?"

"Yes, but they won't know, you'll see. If I get an audience, I'll interest them, and not shock them either."

"Tell me what you will say?"

"Get me the chance, 'Ria."

Maria looked into the fire, and was lost in the prospect before her. People would simply think they had both gone mad together. Dora felt that she must stop or change the current of her thoughts, or Maria would not keep up to the mark.

"Get me the chance," she repeated; "it has been done, and why may it not be done again? The man got the chance for the lady, and she was successful, and Mrs. Greaves says she will go if she comes again."

Dora burst into laughter—rather scornful to be sure—as she uttered the last sentence.

"Very well, we will go and do likewise," Maria said, and got up and walked about the room.

Then she bethought herself that they were both sadly in want of some dinner, and when this was despatched, Maria made Dora lie down, and cleared the dinner table. Before she had done Dora was sleeping peacefully, as if all her troubles were over.

"And perhaps they are only beginning," Maria thought, as she looked at the worn face and wet eyelids. A strong pity for the lorn girl swelled her heart. "I will fight for her till death," she exclaimed; "it is well to have the chance of fighting!"

We each think of our little private struggle as the thing of the most importance, but it is only when it is ennobled by fellow-feeling that it kindles into enthusiasm. And enthusiasm, in spite of the cynics, is the only thing that brings forth our best strength and noblest nature.

The thing she feared most was that Dora would take the opportunity to storm and scold; for of all means of getting help or kindness, the worst is to complain; loudly or lowly, but above all loudly. The reality of the grievance makes no difference, nor the extent of it; complaint is imbecile.

"You won't talk about yourself, Dora?" she asked again.

"Yes I shall, but no one will know."

Maria laughed.

"Well, then it does not matter."

Never, not even at the time of her removal to Repton, had Maria's mind grown so much older in a day or two, as it did during this Saturday and the Sunday after it. By the time the day was over she had become quite accustomed to the strange idea—and how strange it was no one of the present generation can imagine. It was new, and that was sin enough in the eyes of the majority. It clashed with the customary conventions, and that was wicked. There was in its favour only the curiosity that people will be guilty of, for things on the borders of impropriety.

"Let them come," Dora said; "I will show them whether it is improper or not. I'll throw the lie in their teeth."

It was such speeches as this that made Maria tremble. If this was the style of language she was going to use on the platform, both she and Maria would be ruined. She attempted to remonstrate, but Dora only answered—

"Let me alone; I know I have myself to take care of. I am talking so only to you, Maria."

On Monday evening Maria went to Miss Everard, with the whole tale. To her surprise she found her much more amenable to reason than she expected. The thing was against all the conventions, she acknowledged, but this was not with her a ground for objection. "When people's conventions are all wrong," she said, "they want someone to teach them new ones. But, Maria, I am very much afraid that Miss Wells is not the one to do it."

"We can only try," Maria said, despondingly.

"Well, my dear, try. I would not have brought this risk upon you, but—as it is—you must go on; you have promised. Perhaps the knowledge that you are concerned will make her careful of speech. Shall I come and see her, and encourage her?"

"Oh no! Oh no!" said Maria, in haste; "she is energetic enough now. If she found anyone of her mind, she would be overpowering."

Miss Everard laughed.

"You are quite mistaken," she said. "The knowledge that she is sailing with the stream would make it smooth water to her; she would cease to struggle. I think I will come."

And Miss Everard came and discussed the matter. She carefully looked shocked at every extravagant word, which at first brought out another delinquency of the same kind. But in a while the girl became aware of the enormity of extreme language; she moderated her tone, and talked well and quietly. Miss Everard told Maria that her opinion of her was much improved by the visit, and ended with prophesying at least escape from disastrous consequences, "and, perhaps, my dear, a certain triumph."

Maria's spirits rose, necessity drove her forward, and the terrible ordeal, sitting motionless in presence of danger, was over.

The three women got on well together. They discussed the subject from all points of view, and accustomed themselves to it. There was at least this one advantage in doing so: that they were ready with an answer to every argument against it. Then they abused their enemies to their hearts' content, an amusement which seems to be invariably popular in such cases, and which, therefore, must be at least pleasant and encouraging.

On Tuesday morning Maria came down in bonnet and shawl, and announced, "I am going," with a mock tragic air, that was not wholly without reality.

"Where are you going first? Tell me—tell me."

"To the Vicar's wife, of course."

"Oh, is she—has she got sense?"

"I don't know. I doubt it, but all the same, we must begin with her."

There had been nothing but kindness between Mrs. Dodds and Maria since she came to Repton. Miss Bell was taken as a sister in heart and belief, and a person to be helped and defended on all occasions. Maria loved the lady, and felt a safety in her friendship. She knew that now it was about to be tried, and perhaps broken, and steadied herself under the coming trial. Without the three days' cogitation, and the certainty she felt in her new position, she might have been moved out of her present belief by the efforts of her friend, but now she even had begun to hope to move Mrs. Dodds!

The lady received her eagerly; she had a reason more than usual for being friendly just now, for she wanted to know all about the visitor that Maria had got.

"You had no sisters, I think you told me?" she said; "have you any other relations?"

Then she heard the history, and was very sympathetic, and wrathful against the Woodmans, and then asked discreetly what was to come next.

"She must try some way of earning something," Maria said.

"Yes, indeed, my dear! I think you have been very kind already to her; she must, indeed, try something."

She thought a moment, and not finding anything, she asked—

"Have you thought of anything, my dear?"

"Yes, we have a scheme in hand."

Mrs. Dodds was evidently relieved, and even curious. A scheme by which a woman could earn her living was a greater rarity than it is now.

"Dora—Miss Wells—heard before she left, of a young lady who gave lectures to Mechanics' Institutes and such places. She thought she—"

"Lectures! Mechanics' Institutes!" Mrs. Dodds looked as if something improper were being enacted under her very eyes.

"Yes, a gentleman was saying—was wishing—Mrs. Greaves—that is an acquaintance of Dora's—"

"She seems to have some queer acquaintances! Is it not wonderful, however? But you did not encourage her in such an idea, I hope?"

"Yes, I did," Maria said.

"But, my dear!"

"What else can she do, Mrs. Dodds? She seems to think she can make a lecture interesting, and—"

"But, my dear!"

The repeated exclamation was as impressive as a whole vol-

ume of argument, and had this advantage—that it was quite
unanswerable.

There was a silence. At last Maria began—

"Perhaps I ought to have asked advice earlier; I could
recommend nothing better, in fact there seemed to me nothing at all. You know as a servant she cannot make a living. A
month's illness would land her in the work-house, let her be
as careful as she would. I thought she might as well try, at least,
to find something better. She can always fall back in service
if this should fail her. Will you advise me? we do indeed want
help."

"You do indeed, my dear," the lady said, severely. "You have
gone too far already."

"What, then, do you recommend?"

"Give up the idea at once, I should say."

"But what then?"

"What then, I am not prepared with a plan all at once, but
this you *must not* do!"

Maria began patiently—

"I know little of the world, I did what I thought best. Will
you advise us?"

"My dear, I can only recommend patience; something may
turn up."

"You see—"

"Yes, yes; I know you must not be burdened with her for
long. Is it not possible that the Woodmans may yield at last?
She has vexed them, no doubt, but they must see the girl belongs to them."

"No, Mrs. Dodds, she does not belong to them—there is no
relationship—she only asked for her mother's money, but they
do not choose to give it."

Mrs. Dodds had an uneasy idea that Miss Bell was getting
into a state of rebellion with things as they were, which was
much the same as insurrection against the powers that be. This
was altogether unorthodox, especially for women.

"Well, if it is not hers, you know?"

"Do you think it is not hers?"

The tone and look were still more rebellious. Mrs. Dodds returned the look with great severity.

"My dear, if she does not behave properly she will get no help at all."

"But she is not intending to behave improperly."

"I doubt it, my dear; I doubt it very much," and she added in her own thoughts, "She is teaching you to do so too."

"I hope not," Maria said. "But in any case, what can we do? Work she must, and what to work at—"

"My dear, you are on a wrong track altogether. A woman never gains anything by going out of the beaten road. She must get rid of such ideas."

"She did not seek them; she was driven to it."

"She thinks so, my dear; she is too impatient."

"How long must she wait? She is homeless and penniless." The tears rose in Maria's eyes.

"I know, my dear, it is very hard. But when the Woodmans hear the truth—suppose Mr. Dodds were to write?"

"Mr. Greaves has done what he could."

Mrs. Dodds recollected, too, that there were people in the world who were not impressed even by a letter from the Vicar.

"I cannot tell, my dear, but I will ask Mr. Dodds about it. You must not do anything hasty."

With this answer Maria had to leave. She saw clearly she could not come again, or expect any help in her present plan. She had chosen the dinner hour on Tuesday morning to make her first attempt at finding friends, and Mrs. Dodds was the nearest likeness to a friend she had. As she came in disconsolate, Dora met her and heard the words—

"She will do nothing. She thinks you ought to be quiet."

"Not even to try to jump out of the frying-pan into the fire! I wish she were in it herself!"

Dora's bitterness always acted as a calmant over Maria's perturbations. She said simply—

"Well, we must try elsewhere."

"Are not you going to get your dinner?" Dora asked.

"No, I think I don't want any."

"Then you are downhearted! You have been beaten. 'Ria! 'Ria! is there no hope?" and she sat down with her head on the table to cry.

Then Maria took up her old office, and in endeavouring to console her friend consoled herself.

"There are more people in the world than Mrs. Dodds! I will go somewhere else to-morrow!" and Dora's hopes were bolstered up again. When passion did not move her she was far more despondent than Maria. Maria had once made a plunge and had come to land safely, but Dora had always been beaten. The day got finished somehow, and the one after it. Then Maria put on the old black bonnet and mantle that had been new three years ago, and set off to see the grocer. "He's the next man of influence here," she said, "except the Turners, and I think he is a very intelligent man."

The curtains were already closed when Maria knocked at the door. It was opened by John, for Sarah was not at home, and she received a respectful welcome; the old people rose when they saw who it was, and she got a seat by the fire.

"I have come—I want help, Mr. Miles, and I think you can help me, if you will."

"I should be right glad to do anything I can for you, Miss Bell," said the grave old man. He spoke in the measured tone that belonged to his old-fashioned sect, and Maria felt disposed to lean on him at once. But what would he say when he knew what she wanted? His condemnation would be much worse than that of Mrs. Dodds, as he was evidently more friendly.

"I want to know—you may have heard, perhaps, that I have a visitor—a friend staying with me; she has come to me because she has no other home, and she is seeking some means of living."

There was an expression of pity, and Maria went on.

"She has heard of ladies giving lectures," this phrase she had repeated to herself so often that she thought her hearers must be as tired of it as she was. "There was a lady came to Norton, where she comes from, and gave lectures, and she made a living of it. She could live quite respectably out of it;

and Miss Wells thought she could. She could find something to say—she might try, you know, there is nothing else!"

Maria saw old Miles' face darken as she spoke. She saw him look at his wife, and his wife look at him. Partly from discouragement, and partly because she did not know how to go on, she stopped, but there was no answer forthcoming. She waited a moment, and then seeing very well that the pair were agreed on the subject, she asked Mrs. Miles—

"Is there anything else, do you think?"

"I cannot tell," said the woman, not without pity. "Of course, she could not do as we do. She could not go to t' mill, nor go to place."

Maria had dreaded, when she applied to the working class, being told that Dora was no worse off than other folk, but here she found the belief in class distinctions was even stronger than among those that were better off. She and Dora, in their discussions on the subject, had acknowledged that they were no worse off than multitudes of their sex, and Dora had declared her willingness to go either to place or to the mill, if nothing could be found. "But I have a right to try for something better," she had said with clenched fist.

So now Maria was quite ready with her answer.

"If she can do nothing better she must try that, of course. But can a woman live by that, Mrs. Miles?"

No; they must confess she could not. She must have a home to go to when work was slack.

"And she has no home."

Maria waited here, because her voice was becoming unsteady. She was not aware of the impression the short sentence produced. Mrs. Miles confessed it was very hard for a lass.

"It's hard for all poor folk," Maria said. "I think if they have a chance they ought to take it."

"Why, for sure," said old Miles, and Maria took heart and began again.

"Mr. Miles," she said, "I believe many people would be guided by you. If you would speak for Miss Wells, they would believe she was in the right to try to help herself."

"If I am to speak for anyone it must be because it's right," he said, not dogmatically, but pleadingly.

"Is it wrong?" Maria said, fiercely.

"I cannot say. I cannot make it up wi' mysen, seeing women coming out i' that fashion."

"It is not right," said the old woman. "Did ye ever hear o' women doing the like?"

Maria reminded them that she had told them of a woman who made money by similar work.

"Why, for sure," she said.

This phrase was in fact a large-minded yielding to the force of argument that Maria might have gone through the village without finding again. She tried once more. She knew her own character would have its weight with them, and she ventured to give her own opinion.

"I hold custom is not a law, and ought not to be a law, for women, any more than for men. If they find they can do better in a new way—"

She had not got half way before she saw that she had hit on a wrong line altogether.

"Nay, nay," said Mrs. Miles; "ye're wrong there altogether. Women sudn't be coming out into the world. They mun be stayers at home, you know."

Her husband agreed.

Maria sat for a moment in despair; then she rose, for anger came to her aid. As she walked towards the door she suddenly turned round, with tears in her eyes.

"You have spoken of right, Mr. Miles. When you refuse a helping hand to a friendless woman fighting for an honest living, does the action approve itself to your conscience?"

He stood up. Maria had thought that as the case was hopeless she might as well give vent to her feeling, but he took it as an honest argument. In a case of conscience he was accustomed to be thought in the wrong, and to have to maintain his point.

"I cannot say it does," he said deliberately, to Maria's astonishment. "If the lass has no notion but of gaining summat to live on," he added slowly, "I think she has a right to try."

"What sort of a lass is she?" Mrs. Miles said abruptly.

"She's a dark, pale, down-looking girl, not so tall as I am, but stouter built."

There was, as usual when women talk, a long ellipsis between these two sentences. They both understood that the question was as to Dora's personal appearance. Was she a girl who thought herself good-looking, and who wished to make the most of it in some irregular way? And the answer was direct to the purpose.

Mrs. Miles looked at her husband. For the first time he had not followed her, the pace being somewhat quick.

"If t' lass is in danger of wanting bread," she said, "happen she might be helped to an honest living."

"Ye know her?" he said, turning to Maria.

Maria stood with her hands on the back of the chair she had risen from, and told the history of her long acquaintance with Dora Wells. It was pathetic enough. The old pair hummed, and listened with pity in their faces, wary and excited, both. Maria did not repeat her mistake by mentioning any more opinions as to the rights of women. She gave a clear history of the part the Woodmans had played towards the mother and daughter, and when she saw scorn and condemnation in their faces she asked—

"Is the girl to ask charity from them?"

"No, no, no," said both man and wife at once.

Then, without sitting down, Maria detailed their plans. She would leave nothing wanting. She showed them what they had to do. If Mr. Miles would speak to his friends and neighbours, and say there was no harm in it, she was sure that they would be able to hire a room, and make it known that a lecture would be given.

"Aye, aye, we can get a room for you," he said. "We'll see about it. I'll call an' tell ye if there's any likelihood for her."

Maria hurried away, for had she stayed she would have burst into tears. In a minute after her departure John left the house, and ran straight down to the Sykes's. He burst in so suddenly that old Sykes took the pipe out of his mouth to ask if the house was on fire.

"Nay," said John, "but there's been Miss Bell in it, an' she's been a talking."

"Aye!" said the old man.

"Aye, an' her een shone like—like—like ought!"

"Now, come," said Sam, "tell us right off."

"There's a lass comed through Norton—"

"Aye," they both answered, "she's been wi' her sin Saturday."

"She's comed to give a lecture."

"A lecture?"

"Aye. It seems there's some women started o' lecturing. An' she wants to do t' same. An' father wouldn't have nought to do wi' it at first, but at last she talked an' talked!"

They both laughed.

"You dunnot mean to say that she talked your father over?"

"She did," he exclaimed, swinging his clenched fist.

There were roars of laugher.

"I mun go an' keep him straight," said old Sykes. "John, your father wants looking after."

"Nought o' t' kind," he said, still vehement. "T' lass is i' t' reight on 't. Women has as mich right to addle their living as men."

For John had swallowed the doctrine whole, only shaping it to the size of his mouth, and in this shape they both agreed to it. He told them the whole history of the evening's visit, and the young men resolved to do their share in arousing an interest in the new thing.

Their zeal was much stimulated by the fact becoming known that Mrs. Dodds had discouraged the attempt. Without knowing how, they got up a warm dislike of Mrs. Dodds, and stigmatized her as cruel and unjust. Very soon the general belief was that the question concerned Dissenters as against Churchmen. Now, the Dissenters made up three-quarters or more of the population, and though the Church people were the wealthiest portion of the community, yet their approving or disapproving of the experiment made not much difference.

John and Sammy promised to bring a whole regiment from Baumforth of young men who would pay their shilling willingly. The only place that the town afforded for such an assemblage as they wanted was the old chapel.

This building was the one known to all Repton by the title of the new chapel. The real old chapel was the small building, now pulled down, whose windows were broken by the Church people soon after its erection forty years ago. Things had improved since then, and the new chapel was the largest place in the village, and had frequently been used for assemblages of various kinds. Yet to lend it on this occasion would be to stamp the doubtful novelty with the approbation of the sect. Maria's supporters set to work with zeal, not to persuade Mr. Somers, their minister, still less to ask his advice, but to get the goodwill of the real leaders of the community. When Sykes and Miles and Saunders were persuaded, the only thing was to make their opinion known. When it was known that Mrs. Dodds had given her verdict against the lecture, all these members of the church militant rose against her. Many of the young men of the patrician order basely deserted their colours in search of amusement, though they did not speak of it at home. The isolation of the orthodox women became more complete, and they lost altogether the educating influence of the new movement.

Maria came home in rather better spirits, and ate her supper without pressing. Then they discussed the question how far this could be called good news. Dora thought it another mode of putting off the question; but Maria had got, she knew not how, an impression of the sterling character of the shopkeeper, and she looked for more from him.

"He did not say much," she observed, "but it was more to the purpose. He promised to come and tell us what success he had. She could not help confessing that both had begun by decided opposition. But then they pitied you so."

"Oh, they'll all pity you as much as you want!" Dora said, with a bitter sneer. "But they'll take care not to help you, not to let you help yourself."

"Dora, don't be so bitter!"

"That's another remedy! Be patient! Be patient!"

"Dora, be quiet! I have something else to tell you. There was a right side in their objections. They, like everybody else, could not get over the idea that you wanted to display your personal graces and accomplishments. Well, Dora, I have made you as ugly as I could," and they both burst into laughter.

Soon Maria took a letter out of her pocket which was on the table when she came in. She opened it and spread it on the table, put her elbows on each side of it, and her head on her hands. Dora took the hint, and went to bed.

"I have hurried home to write to you on account of some news I have just been having from Mr. Dodds. He says you have got a visitor of whom he and his wife strenuously disapprove. They are afraid your kindness is leading you astray, and Mrs. Dodds seemed to think even that this new-comer had infected you with some outrageous ideas. They spoke well of your kindly feeling, but were alarmed at the steps she was persuading you to take. So am I. Above all things, I fear to see you expose yourself to the careless mocking judgment of indifferent people. You little know the contempt and ridicule such attempts excite. You have hitherto been guarded by the respect of the community you live amongst. To them you are a living example of patient, quiet Christian womanhood. But once throw away the charm of seclusion, and you become a prey to all that slander can do to annoy and degrade you.

"My white flower in the shade!—till now untouched by stormy winds or too burning sunshine!—do you not know how sacred your solitude has been to those compelled to face the workaday world? With all my heart I beg of you not to soil your purity by mixing with those who misunderstand a woman's position and duties. Do not enter the arena where you are sure to be the weakest, and to earn nothing but contempt for your self-sacrifice. You do not know the people you must mix with, nor the faults you must condone in company with them. Oh, that I could see you and set before you the hopelessness of the course you are taking. My white dove! my helpless lady! wait! wait a little longer, and be sure that help will come! Do not laugh at me when I say that I am stronger than you, and to me belongs the right of helping you. I will move heaven and earth, but I will do it."

Maria threw down the letter, and with her face still streaming with tears she wrote the answer.

"I have undertaken to help a friend in extremity. Failing all other means, I shall try the only one we have. We knew we should meet with opposition and scorn, but we thought there was another public to turn to that would at least do us justice. Perhaps we were mistaken. I see with regard to you I have been completely so. I counted on you for encouragement and help, if help were possible, and I see you place yourself in the foremost rank against us. Perhaps you are in the majority. Perhaps we shall have no friends at all. Your white dove and white flower are merely decorations to hide fetters too heavy for me to bear. Offer me them no more, for I refuse to be helped on such terms."

She went to bed, and dwelt all night on the vanished vision that had been her companion and consolation for she knew not how long. She resolutely shut out all knowledge that it was gone, and dreamt of what might have been. In all her terror and anxiety she had looked with confidence to one supporting hand, and now her knight had started from her side, and would see her fall. How could it be? In the morning she was taken possession of by Dora's bitter spirit, and sent her letter. She had burnt her ships. If Mr. Miles could help her, how could she refuse his help? Nay, it was known that she was intending to do something, and according to Branksome her whiteness was soiled. In scorn and anger she promised herself to go on.

As one item of good news after another came to Miss Bell and her friend their spirits rose, and they made their preparations with zeal. Maria had none but black dresses, so one of them was fashioned for Dora. Black was at that time seldom worn by young people, which made the adoption of it more emphatic. It was a sign that good looks, if there were any, were to play no part in the evening's amusement. Mrs. Miles's question dwelt on Maria's mind. She could not explain why, but she let Dora know that black was the best colour. But Dora merely answered, "No, it's not; but it's all I can get." She kept Maria in hot water as to the sort of exhibition she would make of herself. Maria foresaw that Dora's failure would involve her own ruin. She would utterly lose her character if the evening's performance was such as the hearers would not tolerate. They were puritan in principle—not in conduct, certainly, but they kept their puritan principles to judge others by. To choose a play at all to talk about was a laxity that they scarcely forgave, and would not have tolerated had they known the play that was chosen. But they knew nothing about it, and looked to be informed by the lecturer, and for her Maria stood as sponsor. "She's a real lady, like Miss Bell herself. They were ladies long since." The thing that interested them was that their Vicar, worthy man, was against it, or at least disowned it, and they thought it their business to take it up, and to triumph, as their numbers always could, over the orthodox party.

Everard Branksome was as much astonished with his "setting down" as Sammy Sykes had been with his blow on the forehead. At first he was heart-sick with the dismissal so abruptly given, but soon, after reading the letter again, he began to find a pleasure in it that would have seemed to Maria the deadliest insult he could offer. He had never seen this side of her character before. He had thought her patient, conscientious, industrious, and half-a-dozen other things, but prompt, passionate, scornful! "I never dreamt it of her!" he said to himself, and added all this to the list of her good qualities. He was not a man to despair of winning the thing he had set his heart on. He would soon set that right. Had Maria walked into a river he would have just taken off his coat and plunged after her, so now he set himself to protect her from the danger into which she was running, and to save her name from the soil and mud that he thought would soon be gathering over it. He would have liked to knock every man down who did not speak of her with sufficient reverence. He explained, with very slight knowledge of the subject, her opinions, her principles, and her conduct. He soon brought his own belief into parallelism with her proceedings, and found them both perfectly just and noble. He half, or more than half converted a number of young men whose principles were in the same inchoate state as his own. Many of these resolved to attend the lecture, for the sake of maintaining order, which they would probably have done by the violent ejection of anyone whose conduct they did not approve. It was long since Branksome had such a pleasant hour as the one he promised himself in guarding and watching and listening to the lecture.

There was another cloud that Maria watched with ever increasing anxiety, and it seemed to darken as the time went on. One great danger to the leader of a party lies in the headlong enthusiasm of his followers. It is not easy to rouse people and put a new idea into their heads, but it is much easier than to put any sense into them besides. The new idea that John Miles carried into the Sykes's house was soon so enlarged, so distorted, that he himself did not know it. It involved not only a feud with the vicar of the parish, which, indeed, was there before, but also a quarrel with the decencies in general. There was no one who advocated the right to do what he liked, that was not a partisan of Miss Wells, and by implication Miss Wells was a partisan of theirs. In vain old Miles protested. All crude theories looked to him dangerous, and well he knew that whatever wrongs might exist, discontent was dangerous. He came at last to the conclusion that it might be his duty to rise in his place after the lecture, or even in the middle of it, and disclaim any participation in such doctrine. He would have done it with pain—no anger or self-seeking would have mingled with his condemnation—but he certainly would have followed his conscience, even if it had made him look like a fool.

With these anxious thoughts he took his seat on the end of the front bench, when the audience assembled—stringing himself up to the contemplation of a martyrdom he had faced more than once before, for he had not won his position without a struggle. No man does.

He had tried to elicit from Dora what her lecture was to be about. But, though she received him with great respect and gratitude, when he came to tell the news of the arrangements, and the prosperity that was coming upon her, he elicited no information, and went away still more anxious, and soon he found that in the rush of enthusiasm the management of affairs was taken out of his hands. The young men, without whom nothing gets done, and by whom it is always done headlong, would listen to nothing. He kept silence and kept to his resolve.

He seated himself patiently, as he was told, in the corner of the front bench, as became a supporter of the lecturer. He had refused to introduce her, pleading his ignorance of the custom in such cases; in fact, he had seldom attended a lecture in his life, and few people among the audience were more familiar than himself with the routine in such things. His wife sat beside him, and Sarah, with flashing eyes, came next. She was as much excited as her education allowed. She had never seen or heard of anything so likely to solve the questions that tormented her. Maria and Miss Everard took the two seats near the wall, in trembling silence. The strangers from neighbouring places sat in the middle of the chapel, and whispered to each other. The rest of the crowded audience were silent.

When Dora walked in from a door beside the pulpit, and took her place before a table in front of it, few knew she had come. A member of the old communion introduced her by name, and sat down. Then she stood up.

There was nothing to be seen but a white face and a black dress until she raised her eyes, and then there was a stifled hum.

"On the side of the oppressors is power, and there is none to help."

Then the audience settled themselves to a well-accustomed amusement. It was to be a sermon, since it began with a text, and they were well-used to listening, criticizing, and condemning a sermon. Maria and Miss Everard were in some degree comforted by the opening. They looked round on the crowd, from which they had before shrunk in terror, who might so soon become boisterous or mocking enemies. They had felt it was possible, as some people thought, that they were on the edge of a precipice, and that some unknown ruin lay before them? They had promised Dora to smile at every good sentence she spoke; they smiled not, but she saw them not. She dropped her eyes again and went on. Old Miles relaxed his attitude, well-pleased with the exordium. The foreign regiment exclaimed "She's reight faal!" and the same fact made Mrs. Miles content to be there.

It was a fact that Dora did not know when she said the first sentence what the next was to be. Her head, and heart and soul were full of matter, and she never dreamt that it could fail her. Without a thought of arrangement she went on at full pressure.

"Do you not know it, you who are come here to listen to me—do you none of you know of strong men who oppress the weak? Is there no injustice among you unredressed?"

Old Miles raised his frowning face.

She entered into details—of the prentice with a cruel master, of the servant with a harsh mistress, of the ill-paid labourer deprived of work for a fault perhaps not his own, etc. She went on at some length, warmly and clearly, and she spoke of everything but of a girl robbed by her step-father, and after every history she raised her eyes, and repeated wailingly—

"And there is none to help!"

It was fortunate that she had not prepared her words, for the momentary hesitation at times while she sought them prevented her from talking too fast. When she found an effective epithet, she flung it out, and her hand with it. Otherwise she used little gesticulation, until, after some signs of sympathy from her audience, she suddenly asked—

"Do not these call to you for justice, justice, justice?"

She raised her clasped hands high before her, and looked with flashing eyes at them all, as she dropped them again. A subdued roar ran round, for they knew not the custom of cheering. Old Miles saw clearly that the protest that was becoming necessary would have to be made in face of the whole assemblage, and if she had got so far when only half-way through, where would she get to before the evening was closed? She herself felt that to begin again in the same strain after such a burst would be in the nature of an anticlimax, and she had thought the subject so all-sufficing that she had not thought of anything farther. But on the spur of the moment it occurred to her that the object of her lecture was to point out a remedy. She found she had none except a reference to our common Christianity.

"There is none to help," she repeated, "and there will be none so long as each man thinks of himself only. If we wish for justice we must each one stretch forth his arms to help his neighbour. For so it is decreed, that no man can stand alone."

On this theme she dilated and was listened to. She soon fell into commonplace, and was approved by those who had doubted her before.

Her voice was many-toned and musical, as must be that of one who speaks from overflowing feeling. The very scarcity of her gestures made them impressive. They watched for, and remembered them, and well-pleased, Mr. Miles stood up at the end of the lecture, and proposed a vote of thanks for it. Amidst the tumult of applause, Dora was instructed that it would be necessary for her to return thanks, and she was utterly confounded. It was a detail she did not happen to have heard of, and was totally unprepared for. Two or three sentences rose to her mind as things she might say, but as they all wanted to come first, all she could do was to give a piece of each of them.

"I wish—I can only say—I do not see—I thank you all." The roar of fierce applause drowned her voice, and the close was well chosen enough.

They were all standing talking and endeavouring to get out. As Maria stood looking round at them, Dora put her arm into hers and pulled her away. Maria took the hand and pressed it hard. There was a momentary stop when they got to the vestry door, and raising her eyes full of water, Maria saw Mr. Branksome bowing to her with raised hat. It was but for a moment, and then she was past him, and the thought went through her mind—"I ought to have bowed," but it was gone in a moment. Beyond a sharp sensation of pain, arising from she knew not what, it made no impression. She was too deeply engaged with other things. There was a crowd in the vestry full of congratulations, and yet Dora did not seem satisfied.

"What on earth do you want more. Dora? Do let us get home."

"Did not you know," she whispered, "that that man said he would come and hear me?" and she looked into the chapel, over the people's heads. But it was useless waiting, and at last they got safely out, and hurried home.

They chattered wildly over their bread and milk by the fire, Miss Everard also being one of them. Nothing intelligible was to be thought or done for that night at least. But their talk was interrupted by a most unexpected knock at the door. With all their might they tried to put on grave faces, and Maria went to open it.

"Could I see Miss Wells, please?"

The speaker was a middle-aged man, with bald forehead, and excessively civil manners.

"Yes, she is here. Will you walk in?" Maria did not disguise her astonishment, and it was as good as a question.

"I promised to speak to her after the lecture," he said, bowing as he entered.

"Yes! yes!" Dora cried, and came to meet him full of sparkles and eager curiosity. "Shall I do, do you think?"

"Certainly you will do; I am ready to give you a trial."

"Where will it be?"

"At Baumforth; I think you have some admirers come from there."

Dora laughed.

"I will write to you very soon. Shall I address to you here?"

"Certainly," Maria said, and the man looked round at the keen excited attention which was being bestowed upon him.

"So I will wish you good evening, ladies," he went on, making play with his hat, and retreating to the door.

In two days Dora was a vanished form in Repton, though the talk about her did not stop so soon.

"I cannot tell what ye see in her," said those who had not heard her. "A throddy lass wi' her hair down to her een, and a face as pale as a corp!"

Dark hair and pale features were not in favour in that part of Yorkshire. Yet they came to hear her, and Maria was glad to find that she was here and there lecturing, and probably with success.

Dora did not remain constant to her resolution. Now she had "got her chance" she was surprised to find it was of little use. She had thought the subject of her wrongs inexhaustible, but now she found she had no more to say, she would not repeat herself, and knew nothing more. She saw that hers was the common lot. How could she dilate upon it? At this critical moment her guide and patron came in with good advice.

"You have a good voice and a good manner," he said; "but, of course, you have nothing to say." A week before Dora would have flung the assertion in his teeth. "You must take to declaiming, or to reading. I will show you what to read, and how to do," and now she was thankful to listen to him, and soon had a good repertoire of poetry and prose fit for declamation.

Everard Branksome followed the trio from the vestry door to the green gate. He saw them go in, utterly unconscious of his near neighbourhood. He waited till their visitor approached, and then, seeing him go in, he walked home and sat down to write.

"I have been leaning over the little green gate ever since you and your friends went into the house until now. What would I have given to be with you! If a stranger had not come I would have tried—I would have tried, all the customs of the country notwithstanding. I followed you from the vestry, and tried to join you. I even spoke, but you neither heard nor saw me. You were looking into the face of the friend you had helped, and you were all three talking at once. Why did not you own my existence when I faced you in the vestry passage?

"As I stood by the gate in the dark I heard your tones in mirth, or reasoning, or sudden humour, and the bursts of laughter that seemed to brighten the table and make the lights twinkle. Maria, why was I not there? Perhaps it could not be. But am I never to be welcome? Is it true what you wrote to me, that you wanted none of my help? I own I was utterly mistaken, and you have walked over the sharp sword-blade without swerving. Is there no kindness in your triumph? If I feared too much for you, is that an unpardonable offence? Never did you seem to me more worthy of worship than when you took the poor desolate girl by the arm and led her out with a look of triumph. Why might I not rejoice with you?

"I am writing in utter loneliness; I am not only shut out, but forgotten. I cannot share, even in thought, your triumphant feeling. You do not turn to me, as you have ever done till now, to hear my congratulations. Why, Maria? I will retract every word of advice I ever wrote to you. I never thought but you would do as you chose, but I never thought that it would end in casting me off! Come back, Maria! my life's hope, come back!

"There is but little in this world, and you are threatening to take the best of it away! And I dare to say it—to throw away your own happiness as well—aye, though it may make you blush with scorn and anger, I tell you you are throwing away the best thing that life has for you. At least, tell me how I shall reinstate myself in the place I have lost. Write to me, at least. Do not again pass me over with unseeing eyes. I will not give you up. I will not be shaken off. You have no right to turn away and ignore my existence. In grief and pain, such as nothing else could cause me, I wait your answer.

"E. BRANKSOME."

With abundant tears Maria penned her answer—

"Leave me alone. I have not made the gulf between us; you yourself have done it. Through all my troubles, almost in my despair, I was comforted by the thought of you. I believed that the time would come when you would hear my tale and be

thankful the dark time was over. Of your help and goodwill
I never doubted until you let me know I had not got it. I knew
before that I was the weakest, but did not think I lost any
good man's help for that. I knew, too, that there are some
who like to crush the weak from selfish motives, and who throw
their scorn at them afterwards. And you have joined yourself
to these. You threaten me with ridicule! I am lost in your
eyes if I mix with my kind without the assurance that I shall
triumph. Now that I have truimphed you come back to me.
Your language and your actions are alike offensive to me. For
God's sake let me alone! Leave me to my pain and solitude,
and do not remind me of what I have lost!

"MARIA."

CHAPTER XXIV.

EINE ANHANG VON SINNLICHKEIT DIE SICH NIEMALS CONCENTRIRT.

THE person that most puzzled Sarah among her new acquaintances was Mrs. Overton. Since the cook at the great house had pronounced her "a cut above Turners," Sarah had been desirous of her acquaintance, and had scrutinized her behaviour remorselessly. In the first place, Sarah saw no reason why she should come at all; she did not belong to the parish, nor, indeed, did she come to the Sunday performances, nor care to learn what was requisite to take part in them. She presented herself in a costly dress, with numerous accompaniments, and talked and smiled a good deal. She assured the girls that this was only an old thing, looking on the rich satin or velvet; that, in fact, she had given over wearing it, it was so shabby. But she thought it would do, "for, you know, I only just come to practice," so she hoped they would excuse it.

The truth was, she subscribed handsomely to the funds for the choir, and got leave to do what she liked. Her money was of more value than her melody, for she so seldom practised anything that Sarah wished for the power to put her out altogether. She tried to persuade Mrs. Dodds to do this, but that lady, without enlightening her, came to the conclusion that those Dissenters were incurably vulgar, and wanted much teaching before they could be admitted into the society of the Church. She herself was as much puzzled as anyone by the next move of the patronizing lady.

When Sarah talked over the singing-class with her mother she did not spare the will-o'-the-wisp beauty.

"But she's got no sense, mother; she does nought right!" Sarah thought.

"What does she do wrong?"

"Nay, I cannot say. When she wants ought they all say so it mun be, for all they had settled t'other way."

"Well, Sarah, ye have a conscience o' your own—at least, ye sud have. Keep yersen straight, an' never mind other folks."

This, however, was not enough for Sarah. She wanted a guide, and could not be satisfied with letting Mrs. Overton's character alone. She wanted to put her tendrils round the attractive lady, to be joined to her, and to stand by her means. Was she not a lady?—the best specimen in the universal opinion?

The carriage and pair that had at first roused such attention in Repton came in sight at the moment.

"There she goes," said the mother, "and I reckon ye'll ha' to go too."

It was Mrs. Overton coming for the Saturday's practising, and Sarah was going upstairs for her bonnet and shawl to follow the lady to Mrs. Dodds'.

"Why, Sarah," cried her mother again, "she's stopping here!"

Sarah went to the shop to verify the announcement, and saw Mrs. Overton descend from the carriage, with her stylish drapery, her waving ringlets, heavy eyelids, creamy white complexion, and the undulating gait that made her seem to be built without bones.

"Oh, how do you do, my dear?" and she kissed Sarah affectionately, while the mother looked on in rapt astonishment.

The lady's large bonnet, with her head in it, went about from side to side; her arms, with hanging ribbons and drooping shawl, waved to and fro.

"Now, my dear, I want you to come to Baumforth and pay me a visit. I never get a talk with you at Mrs. Dodds'."

"I was there last Saturday," Sarah said, bewildered.

Mrs. Overton laughed.

"Oh! but, my dear, as if one could say anything with all those people round you! The fact is, I want you to teach me to sing—to practise with me, that is. I am so fond of singing that I must have someone to sing with me. Mrs. Miles, do let her come! I should be so much obliged to you!—and my husband, too! We are such musical people!"

"She can please herself," the mother answered, with a scarcely veiled frown of repulsion.

"Now, Sarah, come away!"

Sarah stood stock still. Then she looked at her mother, but her mother had already given her decision, and nothing more was to be got out of her impenetrable face. Suddenly Sarah took the leap. She went upstairs for her shawl and bonnet, while the old woman asked her visitor to sit down, with icy coldness.

No, she would not sit down. She would wait in the carriage, and Mrs. Miles looked after her, wondering whether she were a veritable snake. Sarah came down and got in, saying, "Good-bye, mother," as she had seen the young ladies do at Mrs. Dodds'.

The mother left the shop and went in, and sat down by the house fire. She was stunned by the blow. It had always been her custom to make her daughter's path easy and clear before her, and then, if she wandered, to withdraw her countenance and protection. The means had always been successful, and the child had returned to her mother's skirts and held fast by them. But now she was gone!—gone with strange words on her lips, and with a strange woman! By-and-bye she told her husband the reason why her daughter was no longer there, and added, sadly, in the manner of a question—

"I could not do more, could I?"

He studied as he filled his pipe.

"I reckon she knows she can come back again."

"Aye, sure enough she does."

"Then never heed. T' lass, she'll come."

But the pair sighed, morning, noon, and night, for their lost daughter. They saw her far away, in mind as in reality, "with darkness and with danger compassed round," and moreover unconscious of the existence of any danger at all. Perhaps therein lay her safety! Perhaps to wake her too roughly would only bring about a fall! Her safety lay in her sure-footedness and in her upward look.

Meantime Sarah thought herself on the flowery road to Paradise. The comfortable vehicle, the pleasant motion, and the sense of future interesting novelties kept her spirits up in spite of her instinctive mistrust of her companion. Mrs. Overton hummed tunes, and Sarah went into a reverie.

At last the lady began suddenly—

"Do you know 'When we two parted?' "

"No, ma'am."

"It's a beautiful thing. I should like to sing it with you."

"Yes, ma'am."

"Don't say 'No, ma'am,' 'Yes, ma'am,' like a servant! Say 'Yes,' if you like."

"Yes, ma'am," Sarah said, and then they both laughed, and Sarah corrected herself.

"Do you know 'Lightly Beats?' "

"No, ma'am," and they laughed again.

"It's a beautiful thing—

> 'Lightly beats the heart that never
>   Felt the pangs that wait on love!
> Sadly sighs the breast that ever
>   Bartered peace its joys to prove.'

"Oh! it's a beautiful thing!"

"Is that a duet, too?"

"Yes, that's a duet, too. You must sing that with me, too. It's a beautiful thing!"

"All our pieces want bass voices," Sarah said. "There's always bass voices with us when we sing."

Mrs. Overton simpered—

"Well, we may possibly have bass voices at Baumforth."

"All right," said Sarah.

To which the lady answered—

"You funny girl, you!" a phrase the girl did not in the least understand, and put by in her memory for future examination.

Mrs. Overton showed her to her room, and watched her as she took off her bonnet, etc.

"What a nice, simple bonnet!" she exclaimed, taking it up. "I do so like a cottage bonnet. I must show you mine!"

The lady's own bonnet was the opposite of her liking. It was covered with ribbons and feathers, as, indeed, the fashion of the day required.

"Let me try it on you," she began. "Now look at yourself." And Sarah looked, and suddenly felt ashamed both of herself and her company. She hastily took it off again.

"It's too grand for me," she said, and laid it down.

Mrs. Overton put them together.

"Now, which is the prettiest?"

"Oh! yours is ten times grander than mine," Sarah cried.

"But do you know mine suits you very well?"

"Yours is best for you, and mine for me."

"But do you know I have heard people pronounce you very pretty?"

"Our folks say so," Sarah answered, turning the bonnet about on her hand.

"Ah! well, if they are judges! But do you know girls should not boast of their good looks?"

"Nay, I never heard so. All the same, it's a fond thing to do."

"Oh, you funny thing!"

Then the lady brought out a morocco leather case, which she opened, and took out a necklace of small pearls.

"Did you ever see anything like this?" she said, holding it to her neck. "I am so afraid; I always keep it locked up."

"Afraid for what?" Sarah asked.

"I am afraid of having it stolen! I should not like the servants to see it. It cost ten pounds—just think!—and I am always so frightened when I have it on!"

"If you are so frightened to wear it, couldn't you sell it?" Sarah asked.

"Sell it! Oh, I would not sell it for anything! Mr. Overton

gave it me when we were married. I *could* not sell it!" And she looked as if her feelings overcame her. "I *could* not sell it," she repeated, and put her head on one side.

"Well, but if it's such a plague to you—"

"Oh, of course you don't understand! Let me see how it looks on you," she said, suddenly, and fastened the thing round Sarah's neck. "Now, how would you like to be able to wear that?"

"It is not t' likes o' me," Sarah said, in her broadest accent, "and I shouldn't like."

Mrs. Overton twisted her shoulders.

"I see you have got to pretending that you don't care for dressing, nor for looking well. Now, you needn't do that! I can tell you the gentlemen don't like it! They like to see ladies well dressed. You should hear what they say of dowdy women!"

"Much matters!" said the girl (meaning, it does not matter), "but I mun wear what I've got."

Mrs. Overton went to another drawer and turned over the contents.

"I am seeking for something—a feather that I got the other day. I am going to put it into my bonnet. Oh, but look here! What do you think of this?"

She held up a small bag of white satin with a pair of crimson tassels.

"I think it is real bonny," said Sarah.

The lady put her arm through the strings and held it to her side, in the approved manner of carrying a reticule.

"And this, now. Which is prettiest?"

This was a black one with scarlet embroidery.

"It's well enough," Sarah opined.

"And I have another somewhere! I wonder where it is?" and she sought in several drawers, but at last gave it up and proposed to go downstairs, and there she began to discuss songs again, mentioning several, and saying they must practise together.

Some of them were for three voices, and Sarah pointed this out.

"Oh," said the lady, with a toss of her chin, "we shall find voices for them. You know one has visitors sometimes, and one must amuse them."

Sarah meditated on this piece of instruction, but found it indigestible. Mrs. Overton looked into the fire, as if absorbed in the contemplation of something a very long way off.

Suddenly she began—

"Oh! I must tell you what one of them said!—so impudent of him! We were talking about small waists, and Mr. Thelwal said—"

"Mr. Thelwal!" Sarah exclaimed.

"Yes, Mr. Thelwal. We were talking about small waists, and I said, I wondered if there every really was a waist one could clasp with their hands, because you know that people always talk of a waist that one could clasp with their hands, and Mr. Thelwal jumped up and said, 'Shall I try?' and wanted to try my waist. Was it not impudent of him?"

"Mr. Thelwal!" Sarah repeated, in utter bewilderment.

"Oh, he's a gentleman! you don't know him. He does not belong to this neighbourhood. But was it not impudent? and Mr. Overton was not in the room! What was I to do? Besides, I could clasp my waist for myself! See, now," and she stood up and did it.

"Well, then you knew that there was such a waist," Sarah said.

"Oh, yes, I knew it."

"Then why did you ask?"

"Oh, I just thought I would!" with another twist and toss of the chin.

Sarah sank more and more into silence, but this produced no effect on Mrs. Overton's reminiscences.

"Oh, he is such a man!" she went on. "I wonder if he's ever been in love? I should think he has; he's so nice with ladies. Oh, I'm sure he knows what love is, though he says he doesn't!" tossing her head. "I know!"

This was said as if someone had been contradicting her.

"And I know who it was with, too!" She waited for an inquiry, but, getting none, she went on. "It was myself! so he need not pretend to me!"

"Does he pretend?" Sarah asked.

"Oh, he always looks as if such a thing were quite beneath him! but I know! Of course it was all in fun, you know. There was nothing serious in it; but for all that I can tell when a man is in love. Can't you? Oh, I'm sure you can!"

"Can I?" Sarah said, thinking of the only case that had interested her, as to which she had not been able to come to a conclusion.

"Oh, I am sure I can! and then when they are jealous it is so amusing! Now, Mr. Thelwal is as jealous as jealous!"

Sarah felt as if she had plumped into a cold bath, and could not get her breath. She felt, too, as if indecent talk were going on, and she knew not how to stop it.

"What had he to do with you?" she asked, fiercely.

"Oh, it's all fun, you know. Just a joke!" and she got up and went to the piano.

"I want to look out some songs for us," she said, and took a heap on to her knee, sitting down again by the fire. "That used to be my favourite," she said, giving one to Sarah, "but I am tired of it now. I was told I sung that like an angel," she said, with a simper. "And this, oh, it makes me laugh to think where and when I sung this. Do you know there must be something strange about my singing! It seems to make some people go wild!—quite—quite silly, you know!"

To all this Sarah had not known what to say, and, as no answer seemed required, she made no farther attempt to say anything. This did not disturb the flow of Mrs. Overton's confidences.

"And this, too! Oh, how I do remember this—really! Do you know, this one, when I sung it, it made a man cry!"

"Is it so solid?" Sarah said (meaning sad).

"No, it's not particularly solid, as you call it, but"—here she became suddenly reticent—"it was the last time he ever was to hear it, and—oh, it was all so sad!"

She put her head a little on one side, and the curls drooped forward against the fair white cheek. Sarah began to see that the movement was habitual with her.

"There's Mr. Overton," she said, suddenly, and took up the music again, and when the room door opened she was giving Sarah one sheet after another with a word for each. The gentleman stood a moment at the door staring in surprise.

"This is Miss Miles, Ferdy," said his wife; "I have got her to help me to practise my singing."

The gentleman bowed and came in. He was young, slight, handsome, and looked rather wearied, and, though Sarah could not decide upon the point, rather in a bad temper. He sat down without a word, and his wife did not seem to think any words from him were necessary. She went on with her musical talk to Sarah, but without the recollections that had seemed before to hang to every separate sheet; and without this the work grew uninteresting, and was soon put aside.

The man sat leaning back in his chair, stretching his feet to the fire. His wife did the same, and Sarah began to wonder what would happen next. Quietude, however, did not suit Mrs. Overton. She jumped up and left the room.

"You live at Repton, don't you?" the man said, and Sarah looked up in surprise.

"Yes, sir."

"I—I don't remember the name. Whereabouts do you live?"

"At the grocer's at the corner. I'm John Miles's daughter.

"John Miles's daughter! I know John Miles. And where did you learn singing?"

"At Baumforth, sir. At Mr. Holroyd's; he taught me."

"So! You have had a good master; I like his way. I wish you would sing me something."

Sarah began "Comfort ye My People," to his great surprise. He had counted on some five minutes of hesitation before he should have to get up and open the piano. Mrs. Overton opened the door, and as Sarah did not see her she gave a stare of surprise. When it was finished she began—

"But, my child, you should not sing in that way, without accompaniment."

"I can't play," Sarah answered.

"Oh, dear! I shall have to play for you. But you must not sing such old-fashioned stuff as that. I will find you something better."

"That's a grand thing if it were right sung," Sarah said.

"Oh, I hate such humdrum stuff!"

Sarah laughed; so did Mr. Overton.

Then they dined. Then they spent a dull evening until Mr. Overton went out, and his wife proposed to try some of the duets. They did not practise. Sarah saw no object in turning over the music and beginning all sorts of things. There were two that she recurred to again and again, the two that she had mentioned on the way. Sarah should take the first part, then she should take the second; then that would not do, the reason for that, in Sarah's opinion, being that Mrs. Overton could not sing her part. Yet she did not try to learn it, nor go on as if she was satisfied with her performance. Her voice was good, and a small amount of labour would have produced an excellent effect. At length Sarah said—

"Your voice is high. You should sing soprano."

"Oh, I sing anything. I think sometimes I like the second part best."

However, she began on the first part, and blundered at the second bar. Sarah stopped.

"That is not it!" Then she sung the part.

The difficulty of confession once got over, the lady took her lesson, and could soon sing the piece. When Sarah put in the second it was charming, and when Mr. Overton came in he kept very quiet till it was done, and then applauded heartily. Mrs. Overton flushed with pleasure, but when he asked for another she said she had had enough for one night.

"Miss Miles will perhaps sing me something."

Sarah had no time to answer, for Mrs. Overton shut up the piano, exclaiming—

"I cannot play any more to-night, and I don't like to hear singing without accompaniment!"

Dulness reigned again, until Mrs. Overton said it was time

to go to bed. She took Sarah's arm and went upstairs with her, whispering as she went—

"I am so glad! I was rather afraid he would be angry!"

"Angry?" said Sarah, bewildered.

"Yes, I thought he might. You see I did not tell him. In fact, he said he would not—he would not have me fetch you. But I did it, and now you see it's all right."

"If Mr. Overton does not like me here I will not stay."

"Now, why? You'll see it will be all right! It is now!"

"But Mr. Overton said he would not have me here!"

"Well, but you see it's all right now. He is such a man! He is against everything that I want, but I am not going to be always put upon! Now you'll see I shall get my own way. I wish I had never told you!" she added, in a pet, as Sarah stood still, discontented.

So suddenly the bright prospect had clouded over, and Sarah's opinion began to resemble that of her father and mother, that she was in a dark and tangled path. Still she thought she would go right at it, and in the morning would ask Mr. Overton if he disliked her in the house, adding that if she had known of it she would never have come.

Mrs. Overton came into her room early next morning, and was very kind to her, wishing her to stay in bed for an hour longer, and then when Sarah found this impossible, telling her that Mr. Overton would breakfast alone. She heard the hall door close before Mrs. Overton sent for her; she was received with much friendliness again.

"Now he's gone at last," she said, "and we can breakfast together. I just thought you might not get on well together, and so you had better not see him."

She did not seem at all ashamed at this trickery, and when Sarah observed that she had wanted to see him, she grew angry, and exclaimed—

"What a girl you are! How can you be so perverse when I am doing the best I can to make you comfortable?"

From the time the breakfast table was cleared Mrs. Overton employed herself in getting up and sitting down again, and looking out of the window. She asked Sarah how her dress looked, and then, not trusting to her judgment, ran upstairs, and by-and-bye came down with another on. She carried also the three bags which she had shown to Sarah yesterday.

"Now which of these do you really think the prettiest? I must have you say one."

"I think this," Sarah said, taking hold of the thick chenille tassels that hung from the white satin.

"So do I!"

At length the door bell rang. Morning calls were then made in the morning. Mrs. Overton put herself in position in a low chair.

"Mr. Thelwal, ma'am," and Sarah looked up so much astonished that she almost echoed the words aloud.

Mrs. Overton was not at all surprised. She came forward with the undulating grace that suited her tall, slim figure, and held out her hand with her bend and smile.

"How do you do, Mr. Thelwal? Mr. Overton said you would call."

"I could not think of being in the neighbourhood without seeing you."

Mr. Overton had said no such thing, and Sarah and Mr. Thelwal agreed for once in their lives, for they both thought at the same moment—

"I doubt that is not true."

Whether the man were dull for want of amusement, or tired with the business already gone through, he seemed too sluggish to enter into a sprightly conversation. Mrs. Overton did her best; she took up the bag with the crimson tassels, and somewhat ostentatiously began to put the things out of her pocket into it.

"You see I cling to my old tastes," she said. "Do you remember this?"

"The thimble?—the pen-knife? Oh, the bag! Oh, yes, I remember."

"And I have found someone to admire it too," she said, "tassels and all."

She looked at Sarah, and Mr. Thelwal, who was puzzling his brain as to what sort of nonsense was connected with the bag, looked at her, too, with a languid curiosity.

"I am not the only one that is fond of tassels, you see."

Then he recollected having seen them before.

She threw the thing down, and set herself on a low chair, starting a new subject with all her usual want of continuity.

"So you are here again at last," she said. "I once thought I might never see you again."

"When I was in the neighbourhood, you see, I could not completely forget you."

"No, indeed! I should think not!" and the two sat down together; the lady joined her hands and laid them gracefully on her knee, bending forwards occasionally to look in the face of the gentleman, as if to better find the meaning of his words.

"And what are you doing with yourself here?" she said. "Have you many engagements? I make no doubt you are perfectly dissipated!"

"I am here on business; I don't know if you call that dissipation. If it is I wish I could lead a quieter life! I have not had a single evening's amusement since I came into Yorkshire!"

"Oh, dear me! and we have nothing to offer you! at least almost nothing. Will you come to dinner this evening? We will have some music. You know Mr. Overton's mania for music; and we have a young lady here who will sing to you; she sings beautifully! Miss Miles, Mr. Thelwal."

Mr. Thelwal bowed, and Sarah stared at him. She was in a fright at being called a beautiful singer to a Londoner who no doubt habitually heard the best singing in the world, and she bristled up at being promised as a performer without so much as the ceremony of asking her own consent. Mrs. Overton further explained that Mr. Overton had admired Sarah's singing—

"And that, you know, says a great deal!"

"Oh, I see, a *protégée* of the gentleman's?"

Mrs. Overton bent her head without speaking, and Sarah,

though she opened her mouth to give a flat contradiction, could not find words to explain. No further notice was taken of her, and the pair kept up a conversation about things and people that Sarah could not enter into. The gentleman was asked how long he should be in Yorkshire, and said at least a week. He could not get away sooner.

"I suppose it's that Turner business?" she asked.

He nodded.

"How is he getting on?"

"He is not getting on," he said, with a laugh; "he is getting down."

"Well, I suppose they never were much," she said, thoughtfully; "they never were real gentlefolks, you know. He had nothing, and she was a farmer's daughter. They will go back to their original position."

"Yes, they will go back to their original position," he repeated.

When he was gone, Mrs. Overton began to look busy, and grew communicative.

"We must have something," she began; "we must have a musical party and a dance, or both together. There won't be time for two in a week. He says he will only stay a week."

"Then you will not have time to sing with me," Sarah said. "I had better go home again."

Mrs. Overton's brow clouded.

"Now, Miss Miles, how tiresome you are! And you heard me say he should hear you sing!"

"You told him I was a grand singer, an' I'm nothing of the kind."

"I wish you would not be so stupid! I went for you on purpose because he was coming! And Mr. Overton said he should not ask him here, but I knew he would come here, and I resolved to have him, and got you to help to entertain him."

"You told him Mr. Overton got me here."

"No, I did not!"

"You nodded when he asked you."

Mrs. Overton had hoped Sarah had not seen or had not

understood the nod. She grew very angry. She would not have Sarah say such things! she could not understand conversation between ladies and gentlemen!

"No, I'm sure I cannot, if it's like that."

"Well, then, hold your tongue and make no mischief. It *is* mean of you! when I have done everything I can to make you comfortable!"

After sulking for a minute, suddenly she got up with her sweetest smile—

"Now, Miss Miles, do be good! We are to be friends, you know! close friends! and I will give you something to wear for the night of the party, only be amiable, and don't make mischief."

"I don't want to interfere in your affairs at all. I thought you brought me here to sing with you, but we don't seem to have time to sing, and I have nothing else to do. I don't know how to do when there's company. I want to be away."

"Well, you strange girl! you have to dress yourself and look nice! I dare say you know you are pretty, and would it not be far nicer to know some gentlemen than to have nobody but mill people, and such like? But perhaps you have already made up your mind?" she added, insinuatingly, with the coarseness of the one-idea female.

Sarah gave no answer.

"Ah, I see how it is! You won't confide in me."

As this was half a question, Sarah answered—

"Why should I?"

Mrs. Overton drew herself up, reddened, and sat down, and then got up again in a minute.

"Now, come, Sarah, I don't think you mean to be perverse and ill-mannered."

"No."

"Well, but you are! You don't know how you hurt my feelings!"

"No, I'm sure I don't. I've done nought to hurt 'em."

"Don't say 'nought'; you must talk better here; we don't like vulgar language."

"Well, I have learnt better, but I just forgot."

Again Mrs. Overton smiled and looked insinuating.

"You should remember, Sarah, you don't know much about the manners of respectable people. You should be willing to learn, and not be obstinate in your own way."

Sarah could not disentangle this confusion of ideas, and said nothing. Then they sang, and Sarah found she had to perform the same part to Mrs. Overton as she had done to Miss Raines. But as the lady was even idler than the mill-girl, it was much more difficult. However, they were both pleased with the effect produced, and as soon as the difficulty was overcome Mrs. Overton was very willing to sing the piece again and again.

"We'll learn these two for to-morrow, or to-night," Mrs. Overton exclaimed, jumping up in enthusiasm. "He is sure to come either to-night or to-morrow."

"Who is?" Sarah asked.

"Who is! Why, you child! Mr. Thelwal, to be sure!"

Sarah stared.

"Now, don't be off again on your tantrums! Don't you know that it is but civil for a gentleman to call on a lady? Especially when he is only here for a short time! Besides, you are going to be with me all the time he stays, so what more would you have? How can there be any harm?"

"I don't see how, whether I'm here or not. But what's he coming for?"

"Haven't I told you you don't understand the ways of respectable people? So now let it alone!"

She spoke with a sudden air of offence that made Sarah say—

"I never meddled with it."

"Oh, you are a funny child!" said the lady, twisting her shoulders as if the trouble caused by her funniness was almost unbearable. "Go on with the song, will you; and don't be tiresome."

The singing was the only point of agreement between them, and with that help they got the day over.

As soon as Mr. Overton appeared his wife told him that Mr. Thelwal had called, and added, "And I asked him to come again some evening, and said I would send him word. Now, what night shall it be? Of course we must do something to amuse him."

This was spoken without a pause to give time for a word. Sarah looked round, for she knew Mr. Thelwal had not been asked. Mr. Overton tossed his head as he answered—

"There was no necessity to ask him whatever. Why should you take trouble to amuse Mr. Thelwal?"

Suddenly there came a great disturbance. Mrs. Overton took out her pocket-handkerchief and sobbed, and, in a high-treble voice, declared she never knew what to do to please him.

"I just took all the pains I could to please your friend, and— 'I don't see why you should take trouble to amuse Mr. Thelwall' That is all the thanks I get!"

The tone in which she repeated the words was so insolent and provoking that they seemed to supply quite sufficient provocation for the tears and the flushing face—which had, indeed, seemed to be wanting before she began.

Sarah looked in alarm from one to the other, but was soon relieved by the expression of Mr. Overton's face. He scarcely turned to look at his wife, but, glancing idly at her from under the corner of his eyes, he remarked—

"Well, you've only had a little useless trouble, and you need not take any more, you know. Let the matter alone, I'll make it right with Mr. Thelwal."

Then she stood up in high excitement.

"Indeed, I shall do no such thing! I'm not going to be made a nobody of to please you, Mr. Overton! I have asked him, and he shall come! Do you think I am to be treated in that way? It is insulting!"

Mr. Overton gave a little laugh, and turned away his head to look into the fire.

"Well, if you will, you will," and he apparently dropped the subject out of his mind.

Mrs. Overton sobbed a little, and said a few half sentences.

Since the days when he had looked forward to the delightful prospect of being for ever united to his beautiful Lucy, Mr. Overton had found that what she called loving him meant looking to him unceasingly for stimulus and amusement. She exclaimed if he ceased for an hour to occupy himself with her or about her; she was cruelly used when he at last gave up the endeavour to supply her empty mind with ideas, and fill it with mental results that she spent no labour in acquiring. In a week he discovered that she used falsehood as an habitual weapon, and after that confined his intercourse with her to short commands, or acquiescence equally short. She spent infinite trouble in getting small advantages, and infinite cunning in going round the commands that she did not wish to obey. To Sarah she posed as a patient sufferer, but never forgot to look well.

The next morning Sarah woke with a feeling that she never had had in her life before. She did not know what to do. With an oppressive sense of something to be accomplished that would be very difficult, she sought in vain to discover what it was. Every item of her late experiences was repulsive to her, and she turned her mind away from it in disgust; she could not dwell on them sufficiently to see all sides of them, or come to a conclusion concerning them. She came down to breakfast silent and absorbed, and had not Mrs. Overton been just the contrary her silence would have been noticed. As it was the lady was talking herself without ceasing.

"Gone!—all at once like that! Whatever made him go so suddenly?"

"His work was done," the master answered; "why should he stay longer?"

"Now, I'm sure you have done something or said something—"

She stopped, for Mr. Overton raised his head with a warning glance, and interrupted her.

There was a silence, and Sarah was glad when the servant came in saying there was a man wanted to speak to Miss Miles. She rose in a moment.

There was a carter at the kitchen door, whom she knew well, and she walked up to him quickly, asking—

"What is it, Bob?"

"T' missus telled our Sally 'at I were to tell ye ye mud come home; she wants ye."

"What's t' matter, Bob?"

"Nay, I know not. She wants ye."

"Why, what can it be?"

"Nay, I know n't. There mun be summat up."

"Very well, I'll start directly."

She went back to the breakfast-table and announced her departure. Very little was said, and it was evident the pair were otherwise absorbed.

Like a dream when one awaketh, the world in which she had lived for the last few days dropped out of sight, and the world in which she had grown up reappeared. She walked into the house with her bundle just as she might have done coming home on the Saturday from Mrs. Gracehurst's.

She entered by the shop door, as she saw her mother there. The old woman looked up well pleased.

"Eh, lass, I'm fain to see ye," she said. "We've trouble afoot."

"What is it, mother?"

"It's old Sykes. He's going, I'm feard. The doctor says there's little chance for him. He went to Baumforth and got wet through, and then they were very throng, an' he never changed his clothes till midnight, when he went to bed, an' when he wanted to get up t' next morning he fan out he could not move for rheumatism, an' there he's laid ever since. I go down a good deal, an' I wanted ye home."

The tears were running down Sarah's face.

"Mother, let me just run down to 'em, an' then I'll just start an' do t' work."

"Run off, then, lass, an' dunnot stay so long. Ye willn't see him, for he can see no folk. But it's just gone twelve, an' Sammy will be there for his dinner."

Sarah opened the door quietly by which she had so often entered into the once happy home. Sammy had done his dinner, and was sitting blinking into the fire. He stood up, embarrassed, and the unusual welcome pressed Sarah's heart together with a sense of guilt. She had not seen him for long—it seemed to her—so long! and it was she that had cast him off! Yet now she knew there was none like him. She had left Repton four days ago in hope to find something better than what she had been used to all her life. She came back with the feeling that here, and here alone, was what made her life worth living. The atmosphere of truth that had always pervaded the old place came round her again, and she felt that nothing else was possible for her to say or do.

As she looked at the empty chair her tears flowed again, and she sat down on the fender facing Sammy, and asked him how it came about. He repeated her mother's story, and she listened, watching him.

"He's gone on ever since he began from bad to worse, and now he thinks there's nought for it but to die, an' he wishes it were over. He was well five days since."

"He knows, then, that he must go?"

"For sure he does!"

"What does he say about us—about us 'at's left?"

Sammy meditated a little, Sarah still watching him.

"He cannot say so much. He's in a deal of pain. It's noan t' first time he's talked of leaving us. We all know what he had to say."

She continued looking at him with her wet eyes, waiting for more, but she saw there was nothing more for her to hear, and owned to herself that she had no right to expect a place in such communications. Had she not herself moved away from contact with the family? And how could she now intrude?

She rose to go, taking a look round at the furniture and the fire; so desolate it seemed, though everything was just in its old place. "We return no more," said the ghosts of the departed!

"I'm going now, Sammy," she said, and he stood up.

Such a ceremony until to-day had never been gone through to Sarah Miles; she hurried out with a nod, and he saw her wiping away her tears as she passed the window.

Soon the mother came in, and they nodded to each other. She passed gently through the house, and ascended the stairs, saying as she went—

"Sammy, ye sud mense up a bit! Throw t' cinders up and sweep t' floor!"

He laughed a little, as if that would be a rather strange thing to think of doing, but when she was gone he brought a sweeping brush and began, but the chairs were in the way, and he gave it up, wondering why people ever cared for such things. He had never noticed the cinders up to the grate, nor the dusty furniture. The discomfort had mingled with the general stream of anxiety and misery with which he was surrounded.

It was true that Thelwal had been beaten off, and there was a prospect that work and patience might bring them through. But when his one friend became incapable, Sammy found that he was tired.

But the old man's life was not to end there. In a few days' time there were signs of improvement, and soon it was acknowledged that he might come round.

CHAPTER XXV

EVERY HEART KNOWETH ITS OWN BITTERNESS.

Poor old Mrs. Turner sat by the breakfast-room fire and meditated sorrowfully over her fallen fortunes. She was reduced to
the one small room, in order to save fire and labour to the
one servant, and the one daughter, who willingly put her
hand to the work. She thought of the time when it had been
her hand that had aided in the struggle to rise, of the slow
but hopeful course of the fight, of the almost success that she
had attained to, of her noble boys and beautiful daughters,
of the last and best of them all, and of her failure. And then,
as most people do who suffer, she asked why should she suffer
so? What had she done that she should suffer so? She saw not
the connection between her actions and their consequences,
when she looked back over her life. Had she not vigorously
held her head up, and struggled against her lowly position?
She was a farmer's daughter, and a beauty, and did not this
last quality make her worthy to rise in the world?

And the pair had succeeded, they had risen, at what cost
of anxiety and falsehood. How often she had stinted herself
to save appearances! How often insinuated falsehood to hide
the truth, or add to it! How often scraped with difficulty odd
shillings to give to her darling boys, that they might appear
to be spending more than they really did! Their lives were
made up of avarice and prodigality; as they were taught to
claim a position higher than really belonged to them, they

were at secret or open enmity with all their neighbours, and they were gone! Even she could not regret their absence; the tax on her now empty purse, the constant quarrelling with their father, were more than her nerves could bear. Even the diminution in the household expenses was welcome to the harassed mother.

Matilda's failure, too, was a misfortune, though one long since past. According to her teaching and belief, a woman's worth was nothing after five-and-twenty at latest; and Mrs. Turner's eldest girl was nearly thirty. Eliza, too, might as well be classed with the failures, her case having been hopeless from the first. But her last treasure, if ever one deserved success, surely she did! On all hands her superiority was acknowledged; her beauty, her goodness, and her wit had made her the pride of the house, and had nearly won her a position better than her mother's. Ah, how nearly, and now she saw this poor cast-away fading slowly before her eyes. What could she do? What was there she had neglected? Her mental eye wandered over all these ideas in a tumult of emotion as first one and then another rose to prominence before her. And then suddenly—at last—there came to her an idea! As to her husband, two years before her misfortunes, and mingling with her ignorance and her prejudices, suddenly solidified into a guide, and determined her mode of action.

Was it not the woman's place to use her peculiar weapons for the benefit of those dear to her? Woman's weapons" was a phrase very much in fashion at the time. They were given to understand that they would get very much more by the use of them than by any other means, and Mrs. Turner armed herself with them, having no other.

One day at breakfast, she began asking why her husband had not told her that Thelwal was in the neighbourhood.

"For I know he is, though you never mentioned it to me."

"Mention it! Why should I? Thelwal came purely on matters of business."

"But why could not you ask him to dinner as you used to do? Why should you keep up a quarrel so long?"

"Ask Thelwal to dinner!" her husband exclaimed, in bewilderment; had his wife forgotten all the events of the last two years, he thought.

"Well, why not?"

And as the girls all began to wonder, she ran on into a perfectly unintelligible maundering about the advantages of being kindly, and the duty of forgiveness, that brought out continual exclamations of, "But, mamma! but, mamma!" Even Amelia was roused, and flushed up, and stammered. Mr. Turner left the table as soon as possible, and then the girls began openly to express their astonishment.

"We all know what Thelwal has done, and now we are to be friendly, and ask him to dinner. Oh, mamma! how could you?"

Neither mother nor daughters knew anything about what Thelwal had done; but their course had been decided for them long ago, and now they were to love their enemy! No wonder they turned restive! They had duly hated him as ordered by the higher powers; and now Mrs. Turner left the table hastily and went after her husband. She caught his arm as he was taking down his hat.

"Do stop, George," she said, in tears. "Do stop! Do you not see how Amelia is pining away? There is nothing else for it, we must try what we can. Is she to die because you cannot give up your revenge? Why not forget and forgive? I am sure he liked her, and if he could see her he might—I am sure he ought to return to his former state of feeling. But he has had no chance; we do not even know. Perhaps he has been longing to come, but how could he? Now do, do listen, we must try! Let me do it, you need not do anything."

Between anger and despair Turner stood speechless under this new blow. He wondered at his own misery. He had wished for a wife to crown his house, for a daughter like Amelia to brighten his old age; but now! Oh, that he had never seen them! Oh, that he were alone and knew them not!

She had to let him go without an answer, but she saw that she might go on, and she went back to her daughters standing by the breakfast-room fire. Here again she had to fight. They met her with anger as well as astonishment, her teaching could not be accepted. For two years not only had Thelwal been made responsible for the wrong he had done (in being Turner's creditor), but for all the insult and suffering that the worn and desperate father had endured, while fighting for his life. With little exactness, and speaking to his family, who knew nothing of the matter, he had often accused his grasping creditor of wrongs that did not fall to his charge, and the household held Thelwal responsible for most of their sufferings.

Amelia went upstairs. Whenever their misfortunes were discussed she went away to cry in peace. Then the mother went on more freely—

"You see we must do something! And how do you know but what Thelwal is just as sorry as Amelia, that they parted?"

"Why, mamma, sorry? Amelia hates him."

"Yes, yes! But if you knew, don't you see how she is pining? Of course she won't say more, poor girl!" and Mrs. Turner took out her pocket-handkerchief. "Of course, how do you know they are not both pining because your father still keeps up his anger?"

In vain the girls called out, "Thelwal pining!" with scornful laughs.

"And you too, I wonder you don't know your duty better. It is your place to soften anger, not to stir up hatred. If only Thelwal could see Amelia, I feel convinced that he would take the opportunity to—to—oh, you are cruel, all of you!" and again came the handkerchief into play.

There was not the slightest hypocrisy in it; the mother persuaded herself as she went on that she was the good angel, and the household was to be brought out of darkness under her leading.

Finally the girls could not but admit that such a consummation was devoutly to be wished. They even acknowledged that, should the chance occur, they must not lose it.

With Amelia, the task was more difficult; but at last she was brought to see that, if Thelwal had only been an enemy through a misunderstanding, "if your father is so soon angry, my dear, if he had offended Mr. Thelwal so that he could not possibly come here again—men are so, my dear, but it is the woman's place to persuade, not to strive and fight; if the opportunity offered, you ought to explain and be kindly towards him."

Amelia suddenly left the room again, and the mother waited hopefully. She had never felt deeply in her life, and knew nothing of the whirlwind she had raised in her daughter's brain; and Amelia lay on her bed feeling, nothing but feeling.

Was it possible that the door of Paradise was opened again? Was there no inhuman monster in the way, who had ruined her father, and insulted them all? Could a few kind words bring him back again in human form? Oh, how she would pray for forgiveness, not only for her father, but for herself. For she had often, in imagination, poured out her torrents of indignation on the absent man, and now she thought, "I have been perhaps unjust."

But then the darkness came again. "Who am I," she thought, "to guide a man?" She looked back at her former self and knew herself different; she was then a child, it is true, but full of noble aspirations, and good practices. She was educating herself, and was resolved to rise in character as she rose in position. She would learn, and practise, all that was lovely and true, and of good report, and now she saw herself as she was, idle and self-indulgent, for she did not own to her own ill-health. Constantly quarrelling, of no use, selfishly wrapped up in her own troubles, what would he think of her? and her tears flowed in quiet despair. No! she had lost him and there was no help for it. She had rather never see him again.

But here the mother came to the rescue. She pointed out how it was possible that Thelwal, too, was suffering. Would she leave him to suffer? It made slight impression at first, but it is said that repeated taps at regular intervals would set Menai Bridge in motion, so that it would swing itself asunder;

and so it was that by slight half-sentences the mother kept Thelwal's possible suffering before her daughter's eyes until her intellect and sense veered round, and she began to long for the chance of owning all her mistakes, and asking his forgiveness—not to return to her, she would carefully avoid doing that! She would hold out her hand and say, "I wish to say farewell to you in peace. I shall always think of you in kindness;" the farewell would get rather long, and she would have to pull herself up.

The girl's mind was in one sore that nothing could heal. No wonder if she moved convulsively.

Then came an unexpected blow, as severe to them as it was to Mrs. Overton. Thelwal was gone! Then only they knew how much they had hoped from their wild experiment, for the smallest spark of hope is infinitely better than utter darkness. The mother only looked forward as became her age and experience, and after a few weeks she informed them that Mr. Turner had said that Thelwal was in the neighbourhood again. Soon she learnt that the scheme for an entertainment to Thelwal was afoot again, for the fact was that the world, that we never think of, that observes us all the more because we take no notice, had found out that there was always a scheme of the kind when Thelwal came.

"She's sure to have him," was repeated from mouth to mouth; "he may say what he likes," *he* in this case, as in many cases, meaning the husband.

After a time, a harassing time full of alternate hope and despair, the Turners learnt that the day was fixed; and it was a long notice, which implied something extraordinary. But now a new difficulty came in sight. The mother had professed to hope that invitations would be sent to them; but when none came she had recourse to another plan.

"I don't see why we should not be there!" cried Mrs. Turner. "We are as good as Mrs. Overton, any day."

This was a phrase she had used all her life, when there seemed any doubt as to their pretensions being acknowledged.

"Why, you were at school with Lucy Overton, and have been friends with her ever since! I don't see why she should not ask you to her dance; she was asked to ours two years ago."

"Yes, but you'll see she won't," Eliza muttered. She could never go on with the efforts of her relations to build up a false position, and then to believe in it.

Her mother thought a little, and then began quietly—

"Well, but I don't see at least why one of you should not go. Of course," with a little laugh, "if all three of you were to go it would be too much."

Eliza repeated her objection. The mother would not be beaten.

"Well, but I dare say it is all forgetfulness. Lucy was always the most selfish creature you ever saw. But still"—she staggered over the next bouncing tarradiddle—"but still, she would do anyone a kindness when it was brought to her mind."

No more was said just then, but the leaven fermented in the feminine mind, and next day a note was written, not by Mrs. Turner, but by her daughter Matilda. It contained many expressions of love, and many recollections of school days when they had been such friends. Then it lamented over their present estrangement, and explained how the Turners had suffered, and how impossible it was for them to keep up the friendship now. "But still Matilda was sure that Mrs. Overton would do them a kindness if it lay in her power; and now it was in her power. She was going to tell her a secret! It had never become known, but the fact was that Mr. Thelwal was, before their misfortunes, almost engaged to our Amelia. You remember Amelia? Such a pretty child she was a while ago; and now to see her! And all because papa had quarrelled so with Mr. Thelwal that we never see him now. I am sure you would pity her if you saw her, so patient and resigned, and would help her if you could. Now we have heard that Mr. Thelwal will be at a small party of yours that is to come off soon, and I feel sure that if you asked Amelia, and they could talk to each other, things might come round. She would have no escort, for we should not think of coming ourselves, but she would be under your protection, and would not that be enough? People might think she was living in your house, and there would be no difficulty. Pray, pray let her have that pleasure, and we shall always remember how you helped us."

Then came some more recollections of old friendships, some endearments, and some flattery. The missive was sent, and the four women suffered from hope deferred for the next two days. Amelia's face got at times a weird, flushing beauty, that made her mother say in whispers—

"Yes, why should it not do?"

Yet when a formal note came in the third person they were as much astonished as if they had never expected it. They read it again, and remarked that the writer might have said something more, and then began some more building up of their artificial world.

"Oh, she was too busy. No doubt she would have too many to write. Perhaps she got someone to write her notes for her."

"No, it's her own hand-writing," Eliza said, perverse as usual.

"Well, what does it matter?" asked Matilda. "Amelia, mind you be more civil. Say we all sent our love to her, and wished we could see her again."

Then the dress was brought out and examined. It was a world too wide. The puff on the sleeve was upon the shoulder, instead of being fastened half-way down to the elbow. There was not material for alterations, and the whole sisterhood had seen nothing of the present fashions for two years. Under these disadvantages they did their best, and were not aware of their utter failure. They saw, indeed, how thin and woebegone she looked, and kept telling her to hold herself straighter. She faithfully did it for a minute or two, and mamma looked to the excitement to do the rest.

The father was casually informed that Mrs. Overton had remembered to ask Amelia to their dance.

"And I am sure I don't see why she should not go!" she added. "We can send her without its costing much, and I am sure she wants a little pleasure, poor girl!"

She went on in rambling talk, until the strangeness of the invitation was quite out of sight.

The poor man wondered what women were made of to wish to dance at such a time. However, he said nothing in opposition, and the better half of the household went on with their preparations.

He was himself living in terror of his creditor, to understand which a little explanation is necessary.

When Thelwal had stood with his hands in his pockets looking alternately at his two debtors, the old man had more meaning in his eager assertions than Sammy understood.

"Mr. Thelwal," he kept repeating, "we will keep to the agreement, we will indeed," while Sammy looked at him puzzled and silent.

What agreement was there, except the usual one to pay what they owed? But Turner alluded to something different. The fact was that when he got possession of Sammy's thousand pounds Mr. Turner was in a much worse position than he let his partner know. In order to stay Thelwal's hand, he had been obliged to promise him to buy his wool only from his creditor, of course with many promises on the other side that he should lose nothing by being so bound. This reckless engagement, entered into in sheer despair, he succeeded in keeping from Sammy until the latter broke it in spite of him. Then occurred the visit from his creditor, in wrath and suspicion. By a flash of intuition the man saw the true state of affairs, and left the two partners to fight it out, thinking there would be time enough to come down upon them when he thought proper. Turner soon found it was useless to try to persuade Sammy to abide by the unknown agreement, and they went on working as hard as possible, and seeing at last that there was some sign of profit at the end of it. Only Turner knew of the drawn sword that hung over them, and he wondered why it had not fallen before now.

Sammy thought the position desperate enough. He laboured on, but was not cheerful. True, there came to him the comfort that his father would be spared, and that was of more use to him than he thought. He went also while Sarah was away a good deal to the Miles's house, where he was kindly received and listened to. He ceased when Sarah returned home. Since her association with the young ladies of the church choir she had taken up the habit of speaking good English, and she gave Sam the benefit of it. She implied that that was the most suitable for him in his present exalted condition as partner with Turner. He knew that Thelwal had been to Mrs. Overton's while she was there, and he believed that she was fully acquainted with his position. Well, he must let her go! He could do no other!

CHAPTER XXVI.

"Now the serpent was more subtle than any beast of the field."

WHEN Sarah left the banker's house at Baumforth she certainly thought she should not enter it again. She had never made out with certainty the reason why Mrs. Overton had invited her there, and she made no doubt that that lady had seen so much difference between her visitor and herself that she would never want her again. She was, therefore, proportionately surprised when the smiling lady entered the shop, and began without preface—

"Now, I really must have you for a day or two, if no longer! You surely are not so busy, Mrs. Miles, that you cannot spare your daughter for a few days at least? You took her away so suddenly!"

Sarah was angered at the selfish indifference of the lady to all concerns but her own. But the melancholy illness of the old friend, the sorrow that his danger gave to his neighbours, the solemn gloom in which the two families had lived, all this was not fit for Mrs. Overton's ears. Sarah rather gruffly answered—

"Aye, we mostly have our work to do."

"Oh! but my dear girl! for three days only."

"We have never one day without its work."

Mrs. Overton looked proud, angry, cunning, and suave, all in the course of one instant.

"But surely you could. Mrs. Miles, I am sure you would oblige me?"

For she had detected some astonishment and disapprobation in Mrs. Miles's face.

"If it's only for two days, Sarah?"

Sarah remembered that her mother was but imperfectly informed of the reasons for her dislike to Mrs. Overton, and would probably think that her daughter should not be disobliging.

"If my mother says so."

"Yes, she says so. Don't you, Mrs. Miles? So come now, get your things ready, and what you have not got I can supply you with, you know."

So, still in the dark as to why she was wanted, Sarah was whisked off to Baumforth. Mrs. Overton chattered disconnectedly all the way there, but gave Sarah no information. But as soon as they went upstairs she began pulling out of drawers and cupboards all manner of dresses.

"This one will do for you, I think," holding up a large flowered muslin.

"Oh, I shall do very well with this," Sarah said, without even looking at the flaring thing.

"Impossible! It's for the dance, I mean!"

"Dance!"

"Yes, for a dance," said the lady, cross and determined. "I would not tell you till I had got you here, for fear your mother should object. But I wanted to give you a pleasure. So now try this on."

"I can't dance," Sarah said, without moving.

"Well, but you will want a dress all the same."

Sarah thought manners were the most troublesome fetters that the human race had ever forged for itself. She was on the point of throwing the thing down, and declaring she would wear nothing but the dress she had on. But Mrs. Overton took her by surprise by exclaiming—

"Oh! oh! I see how it is, you don't like this one! Well, choose for yourself! There's this silk; it will do, though it has long sleeves. It will make you look older, but you pretend not to care how you look!"

There was temper in the remark, and the accusation of falsehood in it put Sarah in a passion, but the whole matter seemed to her so ridiculous to quarrel about that she yielded, and accepted the silk. The dress was tried on, and a brooch added, "to make you a little bit smart," and the rest of the litter left on the bed.

Downstairs came on the vacancy that seemed to dwell there as soon as Mrs. Overton's freaks were in abeyance. She yawned and turned over the music, and proposed to try some of it. But she had already studied two or three things, as she thought, sufficiently, and could not be brought to give attention to them any more.

After dinner she got more energetic, and ordered the carriage, and asked Sarah to get ready for a drive into the town. There was no end to the things she must have; but though they went to many shops Sarah did not find out what they were. Some streets she would pass through twice or thrice, but without buying anything.

"Now I wonder if I can get what I want here?" she said, as she passed into a street without any shops at all.

"But these are all warehouses," Sarah remarked.

"No, not all," Mrs. Overton insisted. "At least, I think not, and I am going to see."

She kept a sharp look-out, and sometimes leaned her head out of the carriage, looking up and down the street.

"There's Mr. Thelwal!" she suddenly exclaimed, and straightened herself into order. The hanging bracelet, the drooping curls, the heavy eyelids, were all correct. But the carriage was passing, and Mr. Thelwal had not given a glance that way. He was talking to a businesslike man at the door of one of the warehouses, and looked anything but amiable. Mrs. Overton put her three fingers on to the carriage window, and leaning so as to bring the curls forward, she exclaimed—

"Why, Mr. Thelwal!"

He woke up, looked up, and came perforce to the door of the carriage.

"Well, really I do believe you were going to let the carriage pass without speaking. Really you don't deserve that I should speak to you."

Thelwal had been, in fact, somewhat deeply absorbed in his own concerns, but gathering himself together he declared that he was—"that is, I should have been—in despair if I had missed you."

"You don't deserve that I should. No, you really don't. Will you forget that you have to come to my dance on Friday?"

"Oh! dear, no, I could not possibly—"

He was at a loss how to finish the sentence. Suddenly he bowed to someone in the street, and then turning to Mrs. Overton—

"I really must leave you, but I will not forget the dance," and he walked after the man.

Mrs. Overton was forced to give directions to the coachman to drive home, and remained for over a minute silent.

"How dull he was!" she exclaimed at last. "I think he was out of temper. I shall tell him so to-morrow night. He had not a word to say."

Sarah was tired of the woman and the subject, and leaned back in the carriage, wishing she was at home. She disliked Thelwal more than ever, without being able to give a reason for it. Mrs. Overton opened her parcels, and took out the bits of finery in turn.

"Are not these pretty?" she asked, holding up a pair of white gloves with pink tassels.

"Why, they're just gloves," Sarah answered.

"But look at these!"

"Well, you can cut them off if you do not like them."

"Cut them off, indeed; They are just the thing I was seeking."

"This can't be a real lady," said Sarah to herself. "These cannot be the real employments of ladies—to spend so much time over the details of living!"

There could be nothing learnt from such a person as Mrs. Overton of the duties and employments of ladies, and she wished again she had never come, and that she was going away.

"I shan't be here at your dance if it's to be on Friday," she said, suddenly. "I was only to stay two days."

"Oh, but you must stay. I find I cannot possibly have it before Friday."

"You did not tell mother so."

"Well, because I did not know. But you will have to stay till Saturday morning at least."

As she said this, Mrs. Overton thought, "And then I shall be glad to be rid of you."

Sarah was silent. The dilemma was beyond her. She knew her mother would have helped her out of it without a foolish quarrel, or even without offending Mrs. Overton at all. But she could not do it. She was in a tangle of falsehood, which she wished to tear through all at once, yet she knew this mode of proceeding would not do.

Next morning she changed her mind about going entirely. And this was how it came about. As Mrs. Overton sat at breakfast she suddenly gave that unmistakable twist of her shoulder that showed she was not well pleased.

"How tiresome! Here's those Turners again. I wish they would forget all about me."

Her husband looked sharply at her.

"What about the Turners?" he asked.

"Here's that tiresome Matilda writing to tell me all about how—what friends we were at school together. Why does she always bring that up? She knows very well that I was ever so much younger than she was—such a little thing I was when I first went to that school—and she was one of the old ones."

"Has she written to you to remind you you were at school with her?"

"No, but she must always be mentioning it."

"Then what has she written about?"

"She has heard that I am about to give a party, and that Mr. Thelwal is to be there, and wanting an invitation for her sister Amelia—the young one that left school just before they failed. She is sure there is something between Mr. Thelwal and Amelia, and it would be such a good thing to bring them together, and so forth. I don't believe a word of it. Thelwal admiring Amelia Turner!" This came with an accent of scorn. "I don't believe a word of it. She's just wanting to get him to do it—that's what it is."

"Who's written the letter?"

"Matilda."

"Oh!"

"Well, what does it matter who wrote it?"

"Only I thought the old folks had something else to think of."

"She says her mamma begs me to ask her."

Mr. Overton grunted at the unaccountable idiocy of women. "Why, ask her, then."

"I'm not going to ask her. They would never be away from here if I did."

"Send her a note of invitation," Overton answered. "Write it at once."

When he left the house he took the note with him, remarking that the Turners were ill enough off without anyone refusing them a small service if they could do it.

His wife shook herself once more as he left the room, saying she wondered why she was to help them. Mr. Turner had failed once, and she really believed he was going to fail again. And what business had they to be going to balls? She was a nasty thing, was Amelia, and when she came she would let her know it. What business had she with Mr. Thelwal? But she did not believe a word of it. She would ask him if there was any truth in it. Whereupon Sarah exclaimed—

"You surely would not do such a thing?"

"Well, I should like to. But it's not true. What business has she to come here after him?"

"She likely does not know anything about it."

"Oh! don't she? However, I shall put him on his guard."

"But if he cares nothing about her, as you seem to think, it won't be needful to put him on his guard."

"No, I'm sure he does not. But I shall warn him against her all the same. Nasty mean thing!"

When the important business of dressing was finished on the Friday evening, Mrs. Overton came into Sarah's room to inspect her, and receive her commendations. She brought with her a handsome brooch, and insisted on Sarah's putting it on. Sarah made no objections, but suddenly Mrs. Overton exclaimed—

"Ah! there's the bell. There's somebody," and ran downstairs in full excitement.

Then Sarah quietly took the brooch off again, and left it on the table. Then she slowly went down and entered the room.

Mrs. Overton was seated on a low chair, with her lap full of music, which she was giving to the gentleman, with a remark on each piece. Thelwal, for he it was, made an attempt to rise, which her action prevented, so he merely bowed. Mrs. Overton was annoyed that he should do even this.

"It's Miss Miles," she said; "you've seen her before. Mr. Overton is so music mad that I asked her to come and give us some to-night."

Sarah sat quietly down. She cared not a whit for the lady's lie. There was the slightest wrinkle between her eyebrows and a purpose in her face that made Thelwal look twice at her, and then not make her out. In spite of Mrs. Overton's intentions, he would begin a conversation with her.

"I am very glad to hear it, Miss Miles," he said. "I think I have heard you, have I not?" turning to Mrs. Overton.

"No—yes—what does it matter? She is not going to sing yet. Oh! by the way, I have to warn you. You are in danger."

"In danger?"

"Yes, indeed! I warn you! The lady is coming to-night."

"In danger! And a lady in the case? Oh, where shall I hide?"

"Oh, you false man! But you know I don't believe it all."

"But how am I a false man?"

She tossed her head.

"I shan't tell you. You will see when she comes."

Thelwal saw she only wanted pressing, but he was too little interested to press her. Sarah Miles attracted him more than the stale flirt. He turned to her and asked her if she did not sing.

"Well, she sings with me sometimes," Mrs. Overton interrupted.

"Oh! you have been practising, then?"

"Oh! you horrid man! How do you know what I have been doing? I shan't sing a line unless you sing with me."

They got up and went to the piano. Before they had sung a line he had no doubt about the practising. When the duet was finished, he turned to Sarah Miles and asked if she knew "Lightly Beats."

"No, she does not!" Mrs. Overton exclaimed, in a loud, angry voice. "She never saw it before she came here."

"And has not tried it since, perhaps?" he said, in his softest, most insinuating voice.

"How should I know?" the lady asked, with a twist.

"We sang it last night, you know," Sarah said, quietly, from her seat.

She knew this would enrage Mrs. Overton, but she did not say it for the purpose of enraging her, but only to break the web of falsehood that she felt tangling round her.

Mrs. Overton cast a lurid glance at her, and then said with her sweetest smile—

"Oh! yes, so we did. I had forgotten. Shall we try it again? But perhaps you don't care about it?"

"Not care! It is one of my greatest favourites. I am so glad you have practised it."

"You horrid man! How do you know what I have done?"

They sang the duet. Mrs. Overton was at ease in it, and sang it well. Then Mr. Thelwal asked Sarah to favour them. She did not know what he meant, and Mrs. Overton, suddenly standing up, closed the piano, saying she was tired, and would play no more. She sat down in the sulks, and the company began to arrive. She was again all smiles and undulations. As she passed him once, she took the opportunity to shake her finger with a threatening gesture, whispering—

"Your lady is late in coming."

"Pray protect me," he said, with begging voice.

She shook her head once more, and passed on. It was a little mystery, and with a mystery she was always delighted.

Mrs. Turner would have liked to hold her poor daughter's hand in her own when she entered the large room full of people, and bespeak a little kindness to her. As it was she stood at the door alone, with forward stooping head, blinking in the unaccustomed light. The Turners had forgotten, or had never known, that ladies' dresses had been lengthened. Instead of ending at the top of the boots, they came down quite to the floor, and only a small portion of the toe was allowed to peep out occasionally. She was eyed from head to foot as she advanced, and people made way for her. Her old-fashioned sandals, her scanty muslin, her bony neck, her sunk and earthy face, with wild eyes, roused a look of astonishment as she passed along the lane made for her with a convulsive smile, holding out her hand to Mrs. Overton.

The lady stepped back a pace or two and made a tremendous obeisance, and the hand fell down.

"How do you do, Miss Turner?" she said, and Amelia looked round for a way of escape. She could not see the way before her nor the people round her, but she felt her hand seized and Sarah Miles's voice saying—

"How do you do, Miss Amelia? Shall I find you a seat?" and with a firm grasp Sarah led her away.

Mrs. Overton suddenly seized the other hand. She had seen Thelwal's cynical eyes following her every movement.

"Allow me to introduce you to Mr. Thelwal, though I suspect you know him already." She looked in the girl's face maliciously as she spoke, dragging Amelia forwards. "Mr. Thelwal, here is an old acquaintance wishes to renew her friendship with you."

There was an accent on the word "friendship" that brought a scarlet flush to Amelia's face. She looked at the man with wild imploring eyes as he made a most formal bow.

"I hope I see you well," he said at last, and Sarah, holding her arm fast, led her away.

Amidst the whirl in her brain, her over-strained senses heard the comments round her—

"It's one of Mr. Turner's daughters."

"They have no business to come to balls."

"Why, they don't go out often."

"What a fright she is!"

"How could she afford any better?"

"Let's go and talk to her, poor thing!"

Sarah, finding that Amelia was scarcely able to stand, whispered to her to come upstairs, and led her to the door.

Mrs. Overton watched them with angry eyes.

"Miss Miles, you are wanted here," she cried after her.

"I'll come by-and-bye," Sarah answered, not in the most courteous of tones.

"Where are they gone?" the people asked.

"Gone?—into hysterics, to be sure!" said some joker, and the incident passed over; but there was much whispering, and some confusion.

"Never mind, Miss Amelia," Sarah said, upstairs. "It is nothing. You have only to leave the house. You did not come to be insulted. Where is your cab? I will send for it. Where is your shawl?"

Amelia could neither speak nor cry. She only gave assent by a gesture. There was a taste of defiance in the plan of leaving the house that gave her a momentary strength.

It took half-an-hour to get the cab to the door, the man not understanding that he would be wanted so soon. The rooms were full as they came down, and a number of gentlemen were on the watch. They pressed up to her, looking into her flushed face and flashing eyes, and veiling their curiosity by eager offers of assistance. When the cab rolled off they re-entered the drawing-room, and announced, "Miss Turner is gone away," not caring much whether Mrs. Overton heard them or not. As Sarah slowly followed them in, she noticed the dead silence, and in the midst of it, Mrs. Overton standing, with a sheet of music in her hand and a deep flush on her face.

"Gone! Why?" and then seeing Sarah, "Miss Miles, why do you go away when you are wanted?"

As they met the two women stood with fierce eyes facing each other.

"I have been with Miss Amelia Turner. She is gone away."

Then Sarah turned her shoulder very decidedly to her hostess, and walked towards a seat.

Thelwal came up, impertinent and obsequious.

"Miss Miles, we were waiting for you to try some singing. Will you allow me to lead you?" and he offered his arm.

She turned her back upon him, and went in another direction. Several people rose and offered her a seat.

The affair had been an amusement to Thelwal, but now he was roused and angry. A scowl came over his eyes, which he could not quite efface as he went, smiling like Satan, to another group of men who had been watching, like everyone else, in silence.

"We are on the high horse," he said, to no one in particular.

"You know the girl?" some asked him.

"A singing girl of some kind," he said, jerking his elbow contemptuously.

"But the other one?"

"Oh! she's one of Turner's daughters."

"I thought Turner's girls used to be pretty."

"I think nothing of a girl that does not know how to dress herself. This was a perfect fright."

"Was she better when you knew her before?"

"Well," with a shrug, "I think nothing of girls that thrust themselves upon one."

"Was she of that kind?"

There had been a sneer in the questions all through, and now it became so undisguised that Thelwal walked away without answering.

Mr. Turner's name was known in the neighbourhood, and his insecure position was not quite a secret. The people spent their time in quietly discussing it and them. When at last the gentlemen were told to find partners and lead them into the other room they seemed to forget what they were about, and talked to the ladies instead of leading them away. In the dance they each and all kept forgetting their part in the figures, and came to an end all lost as to their places. There was a whisper that someone was going away. Mr. Overton was seen with a cigar in his mouth and a bewildered air, coming out of the smoking room, with a few old cronies behind him.

"What—what—what's this?" You cannot be going now?"

"Yes, Mr. Overton. Good-night."

"And we, too, must say good-night, Mr. Overton."

He gave his hand with stately silence. By degrees the principal people dropped off, and the rest sat or stood about, idly whispering.

The ball was a failure. Thelwal had slipped away without the ceremony of leave-taking. Sarah went to her own room, away from the angry recriminations of the husband and wife. She was disgusted and bitter, yet triumphant.

The weary mother sat with her two girls, waiting for the home-coming. They had persuaded the father to go to bed, and found it easier for them to be without him. They could better discuss the overpowering subject that filled their minds. They had a kind of hope floating in their heads, but it would have brought out its absurdity too much to speak of it.

"She was to come home at twelve," said the mother. "I hope she won't be much later."

"Why, what's that? There's a carriage coming! It can't be her! It's only ten or half-past, at most."

They all stood at the door and helped Amelia out. Help was needed. She staggered into the room, and rested her hands on the table to steady herself.

"Well, Milly, have you enjoyed yourself?"

"You are back early!"

And the mother put her arm round her, asking, quietly—

"How was it, Milly?"

Amelia looked from one to the other—white, open-eyed, and wild.

"I will never again do what you tell me, or believe a word you say."

She took up a candle and staggered out. They heard her stumble on the stairs, but they only looked with dismay in each other's faces, and did not go to help her.

"Well, I never!" Matilda exclaimed. "After all the trouble we have had!"

The mamma sat down and sobbed.

"She's ill! she's ill!" she said. "Don't scold her!"

"What can it be?" Eliza asked, and no one spoke.

Then a fear, more than they could account for, fell upon them. After a while they took the light and went upstairs. Mamma listened at Amelia's door, and heard the girl moan. She was deep in the sleep of exhaustion, but not at rest. She was dreaming she was on a wide moor, without a sign of life about her or knowledge where warmth and shelter lay. There was a light that she must follow, and she laboured after it in pain and fear. It was so far off! And now she sank in swamp, and now fell in a hollow, and now climbed in desperation up a craggy hill. Still the light came no nearer. She struck her foot against a stone and fell. As she rose the light stood on the top of a steep scaur. Breathless and moaning, she began to mount the steep crag-side. She caught at the bushes, and climbed on her hands and knees. It seemed as if her chest must burst with straining. She looked up once again, and the light was gone. With a stifled cry she threw her arms above her head, and lay groaning through her clenched teeth.

"Amelia! Amelia! what is it?" her mother cried, in a passion of fear. "Look up, my child! See, we are all here. What were you dreaming about?"

The girl looked round with wild eyes and blackened lips.

"I don't know," she said. "Let me alone."

She sank down, and in a minute she was again on the rocky soil and without the light. They tried to raise her up, and dispel the terror. At last she grew aware of what was going on. She listened to the inquiries and offers of help.

"What can we do, dear?" the mother asked, caressing her.

"Oh! mamma, let me go to Aunt Bankes!"

"To Aunt Bankes, child! Why, it is in the middle of the night!"

"Let me go! let me go to Aunt Bankes!"

"Well, well, dear, we'll see about it when you are better. Lie down now, there's a good girl. You must get a little stronger, you know, before you can go to Aunt Bankes."

Amelia sank down, and spoke no more.

"She'll sleep now," the mother whispered. "Go to bed, and don't wake her."

Amelia did not sleep. She recognized the tone and manner of her mother's answer. It was not satisfactory. The girl unwittingly carried out her promise. She never again believed a word they said. She moaned and cried, and now and then sank into unconsciousness, awaking with a start as she saw the light disappear, and found no consolation in waking. In the morning there could be no question that she must stay in bed. Her illness was discussed at breakfast, and the question mooted whether it would be better to write to Aunt Bankes and say that they would like to send her there. Her mother would have postponed the discussion till her husband was gone out, but Matilda, faithful to her stiff gentility, began, in spite of warning—

"What folly of her talking always about Aunt Bankes! I wish to goodness she would leave it alone!"

"What is that about Aunt Bankes?" Mr. Turner asked, and the wish was explained to him.

"What in the world can she do there?" Matilda asked again. "Does she want to weed turnips?"

"She is very poorly! She's very poorly, Matilda!"

"What could Aunt Bankes do for her?" Mr. Turner repeated, impatiently.

"Well, papa, she always wanted to go there. Why should not she go? It is one of her queer schemes. You know it is all nothing."

"It is not all nothing," said Matilda, "for her to disgrace us with her nasty low ways—talking about earning, and work, and sending home some money!"

"Why, Matilda—why can't you let her have her way?" Eliza broke in. "I'm sure there's nothing so pleasant here that she should not be allowed to get out of it!"

"Be quiet!—be quiet!" cried the harassed mother, and the discussion ceased.

Mrs. Turner thought much of management. If she did not succeed in getting her way it was always for want of dexterous management. If Matilda would only not object and Eliza would not speak out so plainly, she felt sure that Mr. Turner might have been "talked to." But now he rose angrily, and said—

"The girl must stay at home, whether pleasant or not. I do my best," said the hunted man, "and you will have to be content."

"There's no need to talk about it now," the mother said. "She can't get up yet."

"Not get up!" cried Matilda. "I don't see why she could not come down to dinner. She was not so very late last night."

But Amelia never came down again till she was carried out feet foremost. At first she only wanted leaving alone. When at last this was refused, she said nothing, and never expressed a wish. The doctor thought her very weak, "dreadfully weak," he kept repeating, wondering how, because she had been "a little ailing lately," there should be no spring at all in her young life. The girl quietly accepted her destiny. She knew that she must end here; that for her there was no more life on earth. She would never more share with her kind the hope due to endeavour, or the pleasures of success. Only in imagination could she know the varied emotions of active life—"the shout of them that triumph, the song of them that feast." She would be sitting apart, and slowly dying! Not growing first fair and gentle, and then ethereal, and sinking quietly to rest, amid the help and admiration and sympathy of all the world. She was to drag on till she dropped, always a burden, always blamed, till she fell down at last and could be carried out of the way. She almost heard the judgment pronounced on herself, "A happy release, I am sure, poor thing!" and could imagine the relief her absence would be to those to whom she was nothing but a burden. They appealed to religion for her, as people do when they have lost all other hope, and misunderstood her bitter confession—"I have never done my duty." They helped her to the shore of the dark river, and pointed out the lovely land of Beulah, and were forced at last to leave her in the deep waters. She died suddenly, they said, as people do who have got used to watching; while everyone else knows well enough, so dies "a wave along the shore." "What shall we do for her?" had been the question every morning, and now there was nothing more to be done. But the question recurred again and again, for long after the fiat was gone forth. When they drew round the fire at dusk they discussed the necessity of informing the relations of the death. They must write to Aunt Bankes. Eliza whispered to her mother—

"I wish she had gone there!"

"I wish she had," her mother answered, with tremulous emphasis.

"Should we write to Miss Forbes?"

This was said with some dim idea that Amelia would have liked it, and Maria would have liked her to have had her last wish.

"Miss Forbes! Why Miss Forbes?" Mr. Turner exclaimed, and passing over in his mind all his daughter's acquaintances, he recollected all her enthusiasm for her teacher when she came from school. He was rather approved of it at the time, thinking that it was quite right for his daughter to patronize Miss Forbes.

"Yes, write and tell her," he said, rather to their surprise. They thought he was rather repenting of his decisions as to Amelia's wishes. He was simply ignorant of them, as an outsider might have been—as ignorant as a master always must be, and as little conscious of it.

He went out, as his custom was, to break the terrible monotony of the evening, by a walk in the dark. He too was lonely, and his life was nearly done. For years he had climbed, only to be struck down again infirm and helpless. Surely, he thought, he had been hardly used! The curious logic by which debtors always come to this conclusion, is not to be explained. But they had made it impossible for him to provide for his family? Had they not hunted him till they had done to death his youngest girl?—his pretty child! Revenge would be far more fitting for his ruthless creditor than patient begging, yet beg he must! He had indeed beaten him off, as he had expressed it to his wife, but the man would come again. There was to be another assault, and neither fight nor flight could avail him now. He almost laid hold of the decision that any means were good against such a foe.

CHAPTER XXVII.

"Tearlessly, fearlessly,
    The day of trial bear,
For gloriously, victoriously,
    Can courage quell despair."

Worn and broken with misery, Mr. Turner, dragged himself about the house and the mill. He spent much time sitting by the counting-house fire, and watching Sammy, active and vigorous, pushing the work and seldom coming to him for help and advice, and Sammy, conscious that he was not trusted, let him alone. They both wondered why Thelwal did not come and make an end. Sam thought they were, at least, making something, and ought to take the opportunity as long as it lasted. Perhaps they might be able to make terms when the man came.

"Never! never!" said the old man suddenly. "I may as well tell you he never will!" He then explained how he had made a promise—that they were breaking every purchase they made.

After getting over his astonishment, Sam told him that perhaps the offer to pay off the debt by slow instalments might content him.

Turner was too hopeless, and would neither speak nor act in any way, and Sam went home for the moment utterly discouraged.

"What's gone is gone," he said, as he walked home with bent head. "I've been two years at work, and I've lost a thousand pounds! This is the simple truth. This is how it looks to all my friends." He thought of Sarah, whom he associated in all his fortunes.

"This is what ye can do when ye set up for yersen," he almost heard her say. "Ye start o' wearing yer hat o' warters as if it wor all done, an' ye ha' not begun on it yet!"

And she was staying at the house where Thelwal was a visitor! Gossip had not failed to inform him of the fact that there had been a dance, and Thelwal there. In those rooms where he never entered, she was given over to all manner of influences against him. No doubt they might discuss the affairs of Turner and Co., and Thelwal would stand before her as the magnanimous creditor, who had once graciously forgiven a breach of agreement on the part of the crumbling firm, and was willing to promise to try them again, if only they would understand that "a promise was a promise." He would say it contemptuously, and Sarah would understand that they were at the mercy of their indulgent creditor.

And he saw himself helpless, floating out on the ebb tide, while she stood on the shore, momently receding from him. He would never have the chance of setting himself right with her, for their lives would drift apart. Perhaps she watched him even now, and thought his ruin was only what was rightly due to his incapacity and self-conceit.

"If I could only keep it from *him*," he thought, as he turned into his father's house. "If he's to go too"—thinking of Amelia's death—"why should he be grieved? I'll tell him he shall know all about it later on, when he's a bit better. Why should he be troubled?"

His father met him with a smile as he came to the bedside.

"Well, lad, ye're down enough, I know! I know more than ye think on! but ye'll get over it yet. First of all, I'm going to get over it mysen. I am going to get better, I tell ye."

"Why then never heed," cried Sam; "never heed all else! We'll talk o' t'other stuff later on."

"Nay," said the old man, holding his son's arm; "we'll talk on 't just now! Bless you, lad, I know all about it; but never heed. Ye're young yet; it's none so bad for ye as for him. He's an old man!"

At once Sam rose to the new point of view, and began to think himself well off. There was some miserable work before him, he knew. But the day would wear through, and the time come when he would be free of the anxiety and tension of mind under which he was suffering, and every step after that would be upward.

"I were flayed to tell ye," he said, with a smile; "we are noan getting on, it seems to me we had best stop altogether."

"I heard 'at Thelwal had said there mun be an end on't."

"An' *he* always threeped me down 'at we could never buy wool cheaper than there! We've done it, however, an' now he's been a' done nought, an' we know nought about it how soon he'll come again."

"Go ye on wi' yer work an' say nought," said the father. "an' take care an' make it no worse for t' old man."

And Sam went on his way wonderfully comforted, brave, and quiet, if perhaps somewhat stern and silent, and still the partners wondered why they were suffered to go on unmolested. It might be the death in the family, it might be other business of his own that made Thelwal let them alone, but after a few weeks of respite a letter came from him.

Turner had laid it on the desk, and pointed to it when Sam came in, as he sat by the fire.

It said that Thelwal had found a new plan by which he hoped to set them afloat again, without proceeding to extremities. He would be with them that morning, and he hoped he would be able to come to terms.

Sam asked what it could possibly be. Turner knew nothing.

"We'll make no more promises," Sam said, sturdily.

"But you don't know yet," the old man replied, and Sam let him talk without contradiction. He would not grieve him, reserving all his strength for the coming assault. "Dunnot be hard wi' t' old man," his father had said, and he felt almost as if the father had begged for himself.

It was the unconscious habit of his mind, the effect of his

religious life, that enabled the old man to speak so cheerily. All his life he had striven to be just—to see the other side—to help and pity the fallen. Instead of loud lament and angry execration of the man who had ruined his son, he took the misfortune patiently, and taught his son to follow his example.

"It will soon be over now," Sam said, laying his hand on the old man's shoulder; "and then we can start free."

Turner sat blinking at the fire and gave no signs of hearing. He had his elbows on his knees, his fingers in his hair, and his head in his hand, which did not improve his appearance, when at last he raised his head.

"Aye, it will soon be over now! ye've ruined me!" he said. "Mr. Samuel, do—do promise to keep the agreement, it is our only chance! Perhaps we might, we ought to get the wool on better terms. Perhaps he would promise."

"He promise! I would not take his word for a doit! (a coin). Did not he promise our wool as cheap as anybody else would?"

"It is our only chance! Think, Mr. Samuel, do not be so hasty. We can but try!"

Sam knew not how to answer him. The old man's face as he looked up at him was too despairing, but the door opened and the "faal beggar" preserved himself jauntily and smiling before his debtors.

At once Turner drew himself erect and smilingly gave him his gracious bow, invited him to be seated, and asked after his welfare.

"I hope you have enjoyed your visit to Yorkshire this time," he said; "you have been here some weeks, I think."

"Yes, I have been here longer this time than usual," said the man, settling himself at ease in the chair offered him, and looking alternately at the partners. Turner sat down almost from necessity. After a moment spent in collecting himself he tried again—

"Did you try Mrs. Overton's again? It used to be a pleasant house."

"Ah, yes, but I was not there. One gets tired of always the same thing."

"Well, yes, one does," said Turner, with a fatuous smile. "Ten years ago, perhaps—"

"Ah, yes, ten years ago, but people should know when to leave off! By the way," said Thelwal, suddenly, "who is that young lady—governess or something—that was staying with them at the dance a while ago?"

"Governess! There are no children."

"There was a young lady, anyhow. She called her Miss Miles."

"I don't know, I'm sure. There's a Miles here, but he's a grocer; it would not be his—"

"I don't know, I'm sure, but she's worth ten of Mrs. O."

"Indeed! so you were struck!"

With a fatuous imitation of interest, Thelwal laughed, folded his arms, and looked at his boots.

"Well, she really was the best there—much the best! She carried herself like a queen—cares for nobody! gives you a word when she can't help it." Then, viciously, "I should just like to bring that girl down from her high horse—I should just! If I had time to follow it, I would just make that girl glad to be spoken to."

"You would soon do that, no doubt."

Another laugh.

"Well, I think I could. And those quiet ones! I know them; if once they listen they stick to it!"

For once the thought of the two men fell on to the same subject—the dead girl, Amelia. The father started up, and catching his breath, began—

"Well, we have business before us, you said, Mr. Thelwal."

"Yes; I said I had a proposal to make."

Sam turned round, still leaning against the desk, and both men looked for the proposal.

When it came it was simply this: that they should give him a mortgage on the mill, and *afterwards* declare themselves bankrupt; after which they might begin again clear, and go on as before.

"Then," he added, "you will be free again."

A look of terror passed over Mr. Turner's face when he understood the matter. He began a stammering objection, but Sam interrupted him.

"The mill belongs to the creditors," he said, and not a word more.

Thelwal looked at him for the first time.

"But, Mr. Samuel—Samuel," as if he did not quite recollect the name of such an unimportant personage.

"The money must be divided among all the creditors alike," said Sam, putting his hands in his pockets and returning Thelwal's stare.

"But, Mr. Thelwal, we cannot do that!" the old man began. "But listen to me, Mr. Samuel; let me make a proposal. I think we might—Mr. Thelwal has always been so considerate—you know we may have better times in future—if you would only try again—and if" (with bated breath) "we could only have the wool a little cheaper," and as he saw Thelwal's face darken he put up his hand to deprecate interruption. "We do not want to have it cheaper than other people, Mr. Thelwal—no, no!"

Thelwal shook his head.

"I must have some security," he said.

"But, Mr. Thelwal—" said the debtor, despairingly.

"We have none to give," said Mr. Samuel.

Thelwal went up to him coaxingly and laid his hand on his arm.

"Just listen to me," he said. "You might—"

Sam looked down at the white hand on his sleeve.

"Take your dirty hand off my arm," he said, showing all his snarling muscles.

Thelwal turned round and sat down. It was a new face looked at them now. Mr. Turner started and came between them, and laid his hand on Sam's arm.

"Pray—pray, Mr. Samuel, do not be so hasty! Mr. Thelwal 'll give us time!"

Sam looked at the wild eyes and trembling lips, and could not shake off the suppliant. He knew not what to do.

But Thelwal decided for him.

"Then you decline my proposal?"

"We can't accept it, being honest men."

"Mr. Samuel! Mr. Samuel!" said the wailing voice before him.

"Then will you pay me my debt?"

"We will do our best, Mr. Thelwal! We will, indeed! We might be able with a little time, but just now we cannot, really!—but soon!"

"Then I need not stay. There can be no more time given."

The man put on his hat, and gave a fierce growl to "Mr. Samuel," and then walked towards the door. Mr. Turner dropped into the seat and put his fingers through his hair.

"I'm ruined—I am ruined!" he wailed, as he sank together.

"We're noan so much ruined as we were afore," Sam said. "We are free now."

Mr. Turner rose in haste.

"Get out o' t' gate," he said, as he tottered to the door, using the broad Yorkshire dialect, that was as familiar to the masters as to the men. Sam watched him for a moment, and saw him enter his own house. Then he, too, left the place.

"Ye've done it?" said his father, as he sat down in silence.

"Aye, we've done it," Sam said, and looked up with sorrowful face.

"Why—why, lad!" said his father, in the tone and for the purpose that he would have used when he patted the little boy's head long ago to encourage him, "now you can begin clear."

Sam looked up and met the smile.

"Aye, for sure I can; but what can *he* do?" he asked, suddenly.

Turner entered his house without seeking to hide his disturbance.

"Where's your mother?" he asked Eliza—the first one he saw.

Eliza took him into the drawing-room, and followed him in. She shut the door quietly, partly that no one should hear his voice, and partly that he might not notice that she had followed him.

"Get ready, all of you. You must be off directly. You must go to Aunt Bankes and say that I begged for a shelter for you until I could look round."

"Off!—Aunt Bankes!" said the bewildered mother when she came. "How can I?"

The thing was slowly made clear to her with Eliza's help. She wanted to know why they must go just then?

"How can we—all at once?" she asked; but when he persisted she said, in a low, awe-stricken voice—

"Are you in danger of arrest?"

His gestures grew angry at the question, but he did not answer her. His silence frightened her.

"Let the girls go," she begged; "I will stay with you."

"You must go!—you must go!" he shouted. "I am going to get a carriage for you. Eliza, pack up what you want."

He was off, leaving them to solve the question what they should want.

Soon he helped them into the taxed cart that was the only conveyance for hire in Repton. They were all in tears, and with tears he saw them drive away. Then he turned into the house again, but soon came out without sitting down.

Talk of railways and telegraphs! For speed and suddenness the world ought to go to inquire the means by which news is communicated in a small village community—news that concerns them. By "drinking" time all Repton knew that Turners had stopped again, and Harriet walked into her father's house with her baby on her arm.

We have rather neglected Harriet lately, but she would not have minded it, if she had looked round to consider. She was quite content with her own employments and position. She lived halfway to Baumforth, and came over on Sundays and discussed with her father and brother all the heap of news that had accumulated during the week. As soon as she had laid the baby down she proceeded to set the house to rights and prepare the tea. She said James would come as soon as ever he could get away, and she was sure he would find something or other to help them.

Tea was scarcely over when Zachariah Flocks came in, and said that Nancy and his brother were coming in a bit. One by one half-a-dozen people opened the door quietly, including Sydney Wynde and his fiddle, and then the blind being drawn, and the fire stirred up to save burning a candle, Sam gave an account of the matter.

"There was nought else for it," he ended; "I were like to do it. If it had not been for t' oud man I'd ha' gi'en him a good deal more than I did. I just said, being honest men we could not do that way. T' beggar wanted to take what there was, an' leave nought for anybody else!"

There was great laughter and applause. The slap in the face given to Thelwal gave personal satisfaction to most of them.

Then they began to talk of the Turners. There was nothing but pity for them. Their utter helplessness was acknowledged, yet it might be seen through it all that their wretched fate was in some way the "teind to hell" that they had to pay for their superior position. It came seldom, but it had come, and they must acquiesce in the inevitable.

In the midst of this Sarah Miles walked quietly in and up to old Sykes.

"Please, father says ye mun keep up your spirits, an he's coming i' t' morn!"

"Thank ye kindly," the old man said, and there was a stir to find a seat for Sarah.

Sam left his own, and took his place half sitting on the table, with his hat on and his pipe in his mouth, but not smoking it. Sarah took her old place on the fender, and leaned back against the chimney post. She was thus in face of the whole assemblage, whom she liked to look at when she was talking, and was herself in the shadow. The friendly civility, the old cosiness, the well-known sincerity of them all opened her heart and made her at home. She had nearly begun with, "Now, Sammy, tell us all about it!" when she suddenly recollected that she was not on speaking terms with him.

After a little hesitation one and another began to congratulate her on having come back to them.

"We thought happen ye were going to set up for a reight lady an' never own us any more."

As she did not answer, Harriet began again—

"Tell us summat about fine folk, Sarah, lass."

"Why, I think nought so much about 'em."

"Why, what hev ye again 'em?"

"Nay, I've nought again 'em."

"What do they do wi' theirsens all t' day?—t' wimmen, I mean?"

"They lake" (play).

"Folk cannot lake all t' day."

"Aye, but they can. I never seed ought like 'em. When they reckon to be working right hard, they get agate playing music or making pictures; an' then by t' day together they'll be laking wi' their clothes."

"They're like to make their clothes."

"They never do nought o' t' kind. As soon as ever there's ought to be done—ought to speak on, I mean—they go to t' dressmaker, an' they fair deave her wi' talk."

"What's Mrs. Overton like?" Harriet asked. "Is she no better than t' rest?"

"No; she's waur."

Sarah and Harriet had unconsciously taken up the opinion that if there was anything in ladyhood, Mrs. Overton would be a good specimen thereof. She was unknown to them from her living at some distance, and her style of dress and surroundings showed her far removed in wealth from any other who might claim to be ladies. Sarah's opinion brought forth several inarticulate sounds from the women when the question was asked, and an assenting grunt from the men that said—as well as a long speech could say it—that they thought lightly of Mrs. Overton. When Sarah's answer came the whole party burst into laughter.

"Ye're reight," they said, and she knew that they admired her penetration.

"What do ye know about Mrs. Overton?" she asked.

They laughed and said, How should they know ought o' such fine folk?

"An' what's Mrs. Dunn like?"

"Why—weel enough."

The tone was even more hesitating than the words. In fact, Sarah had yet her own opinion to form before she could communicate it to others.

"They're allus agate o' summat 'at's nought," she said. "They'll talk by t' day together about pictures or ought o' that—what they call art—'at thcy reckon folk sud know. Ye'd a'most think they were to get to heaven by art."

Sarah made a mouthful of this last word.

"Art means pictures," said somebody, doubtfully.

"It means ought 'at they lake wi'—music, an' stories, an' verses, an'—ought 'at's nought."

"An' do they keep agate o' that all t' day?"

"Aye, that an' such like. They reckon that's what makes 'em better than other folk 'cause they've gotten a taste."

This too was a mouthful.

"That's what makes 'em ladies?"

"Aye, an' that they had ancestors."

"What's ancestors?"

"Their fathers afore 'em."

"Why is there folk 'at comes into t' world any other way but by having fathers afore 'em?"

"Nay, ask 'em."

"But what's taste, Sarah?"

"Why, it's just to teach 'em to lake wi' their pictures, an' music, an' such. They cannot do it right without *taste*."

"Then I reckon ye cannot sing, nor nought! Have ye gotten a taste, Sarah?"

"I reckon if it does not come of itsen it never comes?"

"Taste! Ye mun have a taste! That's like grace! Ye mun get grace, but it mun come—"

Old Sykes had taken his pipe out of his mouth to look at the speaker, and the sentence was never finished.

"Why," said Sarah, "they think more of taste than of the grace of God. They would rather teach it to a bairn than teach him the ten commandments."

"For sure they would. They know nought about right and wrong. There's nought right but what pleases them, an' nought wrong if they happen to like it." This from Sammy.

"Ye see they have nought else to do but to please theirsens," said Sarah, pleadingly. "Why shouldn't they praise up what they like best?"

"Aye, let 'em," said Sam, with emphatic scorn.

Sarah had some notion that in condemning her new associates Sam was intending to condemn her. She began to defend their pursuits with great warmth.

"Well, I like their ways o' laking," she said. "If I had plenty o' brass I'd be like 'em."

"Aye, I daresay ye would!" he retorted, without changing his contemptuous intonation.

"I'd have plenty o' pictures an' plenty o' music," she went on, defiantly; "they are grand things."

"What is there so grand about picturs?" they asked.

"Why, if it worn't that they are allus agate wi' women they would be grand! They'll talk for ever about just a lass wi' a bairn, an' say it stands for the Virgin Mary. Why, it's just like another lass, nobbud a bonny 'un, ye know. An' sometimes they get together three Marys at once. Where do they find 'em? Why, there were t' Virgin Mary, ye know, an' Mary Magdalene—"

"What do they want wi' her?"

"Nay, I know nought about it, nobbud she wor there."

"An' they mak' pictures on her?"

"Aye."

" 'Cause she wor a nought," said Sam, from the table.

"Where does it say so?" asked several voices at once, meaning in the Bible.

"Nay, I never seed it mysen, but they fun it out somehow. That's t' reason they talk tull her."

"It says she wor a sinner; why, so are we all."

"Well, they've fun it out somehow. An' there's nought them folks like so weel as a nought."

" 'Tworn't for that," said Sarah. " 'Twor for—she goes wi' t' other Marys."

" 'Twor for that an' nought else. There's nought they like so weel as a nought, I tell ye. Find a lot o' folks 'at taks up wi' art, an' ye'll ha' fun a lot 'at's given up to wickedness. There never were a nation given over to art 'at worn't rotten."

"It's grand, for all that," said Sarah, stoutly; "and if I had lots o' brass I'd have lots o' pictures."

"Aye, ye tak' tull 'em."

There was a dead silence. Sam's eyebrows covered his eyes as he scowled at the circle. Harriet was almost in tears. Sarah blushed, a thing she was not given to.

All the brains in the room were working to find something commonplace to say which should bring the conversation down to the common level. In a somewhat milder tone Sam went on—

"If 'tworn't that she wor a sinner they'd think nought on her. They fill rooms an' rooms wi' 'em. More art they have an' more noughts they have allus about 'em. Show me a nation 'at's given over to art, an' I'll show you one 'at's rotten."

But the silence came again.

"What's Thelwal like?" said Harriet, suddenly, in a cut-and-dried fashion.

She had held the sentence ready for the first pause, but could not command the intonation.

"Him!" said Sarah, her face darkening with scorn, "there is not an inch on him nowheres but what wants kicking out o' t' door."

A general shout relieved the suppressed excitement. Sam left the table, and took his old seat in the circle. Sydney's fiddle set up a fearful dancing tune.

"Now, then, we'd better start," he said; "we've talked enough."

"Nay, it's time to be off home," some of them thought, and Sarah set the example by giving them all a quiet good-night.

In half a minute Sam put on his cap and went quietly after her. Sarah dried her tears of rage and sorrow when she heard his footsteps. She did not turn or speak when he came alongside of her, but kept on her way.

"Sarah," he said, "I never telled ye what father said about ye when he were ill, an' we thought he wor going."

"I knew that well enough, Sammy. Ye would not tell me. What did he say?"

"He said, 'Stick tull her, lad; she's worth having.'"

She had stopped full of eagerness to hear the father's words, and now got them full in the face.

"But ye did not think so, Sammy. Ye lightlied me afore them all."

"I never did, Sarah. Ye nobbud thought so. There shall nobody lightly ye when I'm there. Ye're aboon all others for me, Sarah, an' whatever ye say or do, I'll go on thinking so, an' trust to your thinking better o' me, an' I'll wait till ye do."

She laid hold of both sides of his coat collar, and looked up in his face.

"Sammy, I believe ye're an honest man and a good one, and I should like to help you."

"Then you're mine," he said, clasping her round, "ye're mine! An' you've been mine all along, an' I thought ye had left me. So now, for all I am a bankrupt and a beggar, I'll ask ye to take me for better or worse."

"Never mind being a bankrupt, Sammy. I can add ten shillings i' t' week mysen," at which Sammy nearly fell on the floor with laughing.

"Ye'll addle! Ye'll start o' keeping me! How much lounce am I to have i' t' week, Sarah?" he asked, with his face close to hers.

"Ye'st ha' nought if ye do not behave yersen," she said, and they walked on.

It was late when she got home, and when Sam quietly opened the house door and found the room empty, he walked upstairs to his father's bedside, and finding him wide awake he called out—

"I have her, father; I've got her!"

"All right, lad; ye've done it in a queer fashion!"

Sam laughed as he looked back on his long misery, and his bankruptcy at the end of it, all wiped out by the words—

"I should like to help you, Sammy!"

CHAPTER XXVIII.

IF WE CAN'T HELP OURSELVES WE CAN HELP ONE ANOTHER!

SOMETHING like this motto came into Maria's mind when she was left to herself after Dora's departure, though she knew nothing of its reckless composer. She was not happy. She did not like thinking, for the smiling future that used to occupy her forward-looking eyes was vanished out of sight. She was almost guilty of the fatuity of wishing something to happen, and soon her wish was gratified, though, as usual when we get our wishes, not after the manner she would have liked.

The little Miss Dodds came in one morning all excitement and wonder.

"Oh, Miss Bell, do you know Mr. Turner is gone away?"

"How, my dear? He often goes away—"

"But he's gone quite away! He sent Mrs. Turner and the Miss Turners off yesterday, and now he's sent the servant away and locked up the house and gone."

Maria went through the music lessons in thoughtful silence, and when the little ones were dismissed she set about putting the house in order. She lighted a fire in Rik's room, as it was called, and put the bed before it. Then she filled the grate downstairs with coal, a thing she had not done since Dora went. She put all in trim order, and as twilight came on put two candles ready for lighting, and set the two arm-chairs near the fender, put the kettle on the hob, and set the tea-tray on the table. When all was ready she drew the curtain, put on her shawl and bonnet, and locking the front door, took her way to Miss Everard's. Flakes of snow were falling; the earth was lighter than the sky, for dark, heavy clouds seemed nearly to touch the earth.

There was no light in Miss Everard's window, though the shutter was not closed. Maria knocked, at first gently, and then louder, but heard no sound. Then she gently opened the door, and saw the little old lady sitting in her accustomed place on one side of the fireplace. She was looking into it, though the fire was dead out. When the door opened she turned feebly round.

"Good evening. How do you do?" she said, shuffling feebly across the floor.

Maria took her icy hand, and after a wandering look in her face she exclaimed—

"Oh, it's you, Evelyn," and drew her in and found her a seat. "I am sorry the fire is out," she went on, as she fumbled about for the tinder box, and tried to light a candle. "If I had known you were coming I would have lighted a fire," she said, and looked towards Maria with a piteous appeal, as if lost.

Maria looked at her, almost dumb with sorrow.

"I see," she said, "you have heard of Mr. Turner's failure, and you are overwhelmed."

"Yes, he is gone, and I cannot help it, you know!"

Maria went and clasped her round.

"Now you know, Miss Everard, you can come to me. Get your bonnet and a warm shawl, and let us go."

"No, no, Evelyn! I have thought it over, and I always resolved that whatever my fate would be I would burden nobody, least of all you. Do you know I have not a pound in the world? How can I come to you?"

Maria laid her cheek to the white, shrunk face.

"Miss Everard, won't you come to me? You don't know how I want you! Mamma said you would befriend me, and I have no one—no one. If you won't come I shall have no one!"

She burst into tears, and laid her face against the old woman's shoulder.

"My dear, my dear! I will come to you! I will do what you want!" and she wiped Maria's eyes and kissed her.

Maria fetched a shawl and bonnet. When they were ready Miss Everard took the girl's face in her chill hands, and whispered—

"You know I have always dreaded this—that I should come to charity at last, but I never thought it would be so pleasant when it came!"

She was soon muffled up, and the pair slowly went their way. The snow already whitened the ground, and it took a painful time to get Miss Everard to the school. They went through the little gate, and unlocked the door.

"Now we are at home at last," Maria exclaimed, and threw open the door, showing the fire, the table and tea-tray, and the two arm-chairs. Miss Everard made a sound almost like a laugh when she saw them. Soon she was seated with her feet on the fender and looking round. Maria put the kettle on, lighted the candles, and arranged the tea-tray. There were two salt herrings for tea, as it was a special entertainment. There were no such things in those days as the abundance of fresh fish and fruit that the valley now enjoys.

They talked disconnectedly during the meal. The unwonted pleasure of warmth and food and company, all at once, made them excited. When the meal was over they both turned round and put their feet on the fender again. Miss Everard had a little colour in her cheeks and brightness in her eyes. She looked at Maria and began to call her Evelyn, for the girl's reference to her mamma had brought back her old train of thought. She had not mentioned it much to Maria before, as she saw her friend did not like it.

"Evelyn," she said, "you see! Do you still think your mamma had no influence in bringing us together?"

"I cannot tell."

"She was wiser when alive than most of us. And she foresaw the fate of the Turners. I always dreaded this failure because of her prophecies."

"But what had she against him?"

"He was somehow not true. He made people wonder. They thought he went on too fast. He was nobody. People understood that he came to help Bentley with his accounts, when his affairs went wrong. He lived in lodgings down the lane then. All at once we heard he had taken the mill. And to mend it he took a wife, and the great house soon after. Of course he got it cheap. Still, people said he went too fast."

Miss Everard had a confused way of telling a story. Some years elapsed between Turner's taking the mill and his taking the great house. But it looked short as she reviewed the past.

"We were all young then—your mamma, and Eliza, and all of us. And now, how strange it seems!"

She leaned back in the easy chair holding her hand up to shade off the blaze.

"Evelyn," she began again, after a pause, "do you believe in presentiments?"

Maria looked up a little anxiously.

"I don't know," she said.

"Your mamma always said Mr. Turner would never stand straight through fair and foul. Was that a presentiment? He always said that the old-fashioned notions of caution and economy were unsuited to these modern times."

"Was that all mamma had against him?"

"No, there was something else. But I don't know now what it was."

She spoke in all seriousness, and Maria began to wonder if she was still conversing with the dead.

"When did he come to Repton?"

"He came just when I left the house. I could not keep up the house when Charlie married and Eliza died."

"But how are you poor if the house is yours and the ground rent for the mill besides?"

"Well, you see, I could never do any repairs. And he told me at last—he paid rent for ever so long—and then he told me the house wanted a great deal for repairs and alterations, and he said it would be better for me in the end. And as I could not do them he did them, and was to take them out of the rent. And I came here. I don't know what they all cost, but I have never got any rent for the house latterly. When I asked about it he got angry, and said he might bring me in a long bill if we began on that subject; but where would be the use?" She looked reflectively into the fire and then began again. "But the fact was I knew it all along—though I dare not say it even to myself. He was not to be trusted. And your mamma put it into my head. Maria, there are such things as presentiments. You know some people have a consciousness of things to come, or perhaps now here, of which no intimation has been given. You know it is said that a sleeping person will wake if you look at them awhile, and if the sleeper does not like you, he will be uneasy in his sleep."

"Yes, I have heard that. And one may sometimes know other people's thoughts without being told them."

"What makes the thought of a person at a distance come into your head quite suddenly when there was nothing to call him to mind? Or perhaps a sudden dread of misfortune comes over you when you cannot see from whence it should come."

Maria began to be uncomfortable. She reasoned thus: "There are signs of the future that show plainly enough what it must be. And we forget the signs and remember the thing itself. Now there are plenty of signs of future misery for me. And she knows them well enough, though she does not connect them with me. And she thinks the future that she sees coming is revealed to her by occult agencies."

"What kind of misfortune do you apprehend?" she asked.

"Nothing to either you or me. It is not exactly misfortune, it is death; but it comes to neither of us."

Maria laughed rather hysterically.

"Then since there is no one else here it can't be coming."

"I don't know how that is. But it is coming. I don't know how it will come, but the feeling is not brought on by our surroundings. Here I am quite comfortable, with a bright fire, and a good friend by my side, and candles burning. Maria, what extravagance, two candles! But there is a dark cloud. There is death coming, though it is neither for you nor me."

"We are getting crazy," Maria said as she rose to shake off the eerie feeling. She snuffed the two candles and went across the room to look out into the night. "How it snows!" she said. "Everything is white, there is a white cap on the gate-posts. Oh! and there is a man coming down the road. How he stoops! and his shoulders are white, and the back of his hat. Oh! I hope he will soon be at home, poor thing. I am sure he is old."

She dropped the curtain and came back to the hearth, but did not sit down. She stood looking into the glow, and trying to regain a composed frame of mind.

"The presentiment concerns me," she thought; "my friend knows all the facts of my life, and she knows the conclusion that must come! But she will not look at the facts, so she confuses herself with thinking it must be some thing unknown that will come. A death! Yes! that may be too. She says 'Not to you nor me.' But may it not be to me, after the misfortune? And it would not be much of a misfortune, either. There is nothing much left for me on this earth, so I will go cheerfully on, and then drop into my grave without tears over my departure.

"We will not turn cowards for shadows only," she said.

"Maria, there is someone coming," Miss Everard said, not in the least responding to the spirit of Maria's remark. The girl listened, and heard the dull, heavy footfall of a man treading on the soft snow, and started at the sound of a knock at the door. With white features and set teeth she went to answer. The front door and the parlour door were very near together, and Maria threw the latter wide open in order to have some light. Then in desperation she opened the door, and the whitened, stooping figure stood before her.

"What is it? Who are you? What do you want?"

"I want to get warm," it said, and the deadly white face was raised towards her, while the foot was already within the door, endeavouring to enter.

"Mr. Turner!" Maria said, and flung the door wide open.

There was the well-known gracious bend, as the staggering man came in. Miss Everard came hurrying out from the room. Between them they lifted his cloak and snowy hat off, and helped him to a chair before the fire. He murmured as he tottered on, "I only want to get warm, it is so cold!" He stooped over the fire, stretching his hands out.

"I have been to Manchester to find my sons, I thought they might have helped me; but I could not find them. I will get a little warm and not trouble you any longer."

Maria put a glass of wine to his quivering lips, or rather to his chattering teeth. He swallowed it greedily and went murmuring on.

"My son was not at the address he had left. I sought about a long time, and at last I was tired, and I went into a small eating-house, but there was a man there whom I knew and I went out again, else I would have got some dinner. And I saw I was near the inn where the coaches start for Yorkshire, so I resolved to come home. We were four hours in coming, and it was so cold, and I saw your light when you drew back the curtain, and I thought there would be no fire in my house, and I came in. I will go soon, I only want to get warm."

Maria sought for food; there was not much choice, but she soon came back with a basin of hot bread and milk. He took it eagerly, but after a few mouthfuls he gave it back, saying it made him sick.

They quickly arranged Miss Everard's room, piled the coals on the fire and blankets on the bed. Then they gave him more wine and helped him upstairs. He made some feeble protest, but he was too far gone not to be under command. They told him they would come again shortly and went down. In silent wonder they sat by the fire till midnight, speaking seldom, and then went upstairs again. His broken sleep was very like rambling, though when roused he was clear-headed enough. They offered him milk again, but he turned from it; then they gave him wine.

"We will send for a doctor to-morrow, or had we better send to-night?"

At once he started up in alarm.

"No, no! no doctor, by no means. I will go home, I will go home!"

They soothed him with the promise that they would not send, and putting wine by his bedside they left him again. They came downstairs baffled and rueful; tears were in their eyes as they thought of his piteous begging.

"Just this one night, I will go in the morning."

In vain they told him that the doctor would tell no one. He did not always answer connectedly, and always reverted to his son and not being able to find him, and "Oh, it was so cold."

As they stood by the fire Maria spoke out—

"I think we ought to send for a doctor directly," she said; "you see he cannot eat, and, did you see it, he was picking the bedclothes."

Miss Everard nodded, without speaking.

A doctor was brought before it was quite light. The half-dozing man made no remonstrance. The Vicar's wife came shortly after, for the doctor found the case too serious to listen to the patient's wishes, and soon from other neighbours came wine, jelly, and what not, but it was too late. His coffin was carried out in two days' time, followed by the doctor as chief mourner. There was some difficulty in finding the address of Mrs. Bankes, and the distance was too great for the invalid women to come over. They came no more to Repton, and their name was soon forgotten in that small community.

After this the two ladies soon fell into a regular way of living. It was a new surprise every day to Maria to find the room tidy and warm when she came in from the schoolroom, and a cosy tea provided, and the whole house in trim order.

"We ha' been provided for an' sae will we yet!" the old lady used to exclaim, as she shut the door at evening. She brought her furniture into the new home, and they were merry over its arrangement. In a week or two after the failure, Miss Everard was astonished to receive a business visit from an assignee of the Turner estate, as he described himself.

"Surely I have nothing to do with that?" she said, in terror; "I did not owe Mr. Turner anything."

"No, but you are a creditor, I believe," and as she did not appear to understand, he asked, "Did you not own the house where Mr. Turner lived? and also the ground rent of the mill?"

Yes, she knew that she had the ground rent; but the other, he had not paid any for a very long time.

"Then you have many years' rent owing?"

"No, no! I have the ground rent, but I never asked for the other—not for a very long time."

"The house rent was a hundred a year, I think?"

"Yes, it used to be; I had the ground rent. I have never asked for the other for this long time."

"How much was the ground rent?" he asked.

"It was thirty pounds a year."

"And you got that?"

"Yes, I got that until lately."

"How much of that is owing to you?"

"Oh, I don't know; I have had to spend my savings. I got ten pounds a good while ago, and then five, and then seven, and I think some more, but I am not sure. Mr. Turner kept all my accounts."

"And you don't know what is owing for the house rent?"

"No, I don't; I never did anything about the house rent, I had the ground rent, at least until lately."

"I do believe she thinks thirty pounds is more than a hundred," the man thought to himself. The fact was that Miss Everard was in mortal terror of a tremendous bill coming to her for repairs and improvements to the old house, and she had a confused notion that by never mentioning the subject she might somehow escape her liability.

"Well," said the man at last, "we shall perhaps find out from the books; you appear to be a creditor for a good round sum, but I cannot say that you will get much of it, unfortunately. Excuse my troubling you; good-morning."

For some time after Miss Everard remained subject to the spectre of a long bill for repairs to the house. Who would present it, and how she should pay it, were equally mysteries to her.

With all her troubles and fears, Miss Everard was happier

than she had ever been before, since she lost the shelter of her father's home. There was the daily employment, one which she dearly loved, and then there was the evening's pleasure of relating it in detail. She enjoyed exceedingly the pleasure of closing the schoolroom door, and entering the warm, bright Paradise, and hearing the quiet, affectionate murmur of the presiding genuis thereof. Maria had her skeleton, it is true, and she firmly believed that she would never lose it. Yet the bright picture of the golden age to come, that she had once had, grew every day dimmer and more distant, and the world she lived in was after all getting to be a very pleasant world.

It was brightened by a small, but laughable, event that came about one day. Miss Everard was more occupied, and more energetic than usual, for the next day was Sunday; there were more preparations to be made. In the midst of her labours there was a knock at the front door, and when she opened it there stood, to her astonishment, a lady dressed in black silk and dignified bonnet, who seized her hands, exclaiming—

" 'Ria! 'Ria! 'Ria!" and then suddenly dropped them again, and begged pardon. "Oh, I beg pardon, I meant Miss Bell, and it's you," she added, looking at Miss Everard.

"And you are Dora," Miss Everard said, laughing; and brought her in. "I did not know you, you are so much changed, you are so—" respectable, she would have said, but she stopped in time.

"Yes, am I not?" the girl said, and she stood before Miss Everard and turned round to be admired.

She smiled comically on the old woman, and nowhere was a smile of so much effect as on Dora's face.

"I knew it was Saturday, so I came to talk to Maria all Sunday long. I was at Baumforth, so I came."

"Was it to show your new dress?" Miss Everard asked, archly.

"Yes, partly; it is my lecturing dress."

"Then it is all the decent dress you have?"

"No, it is not; I found two others that would mend up. They do very well; I don't wear this every day."

"Then you should not put it on to travel in."

"Oh, but—!"

"Oh, but, how can you help with the dinner in that dress? for I must go and cook the dinner."

"I can go and lay the cloth," and she flitted about, and exchanged a word when the two came in contact.

It was a merry time, and the cloth lay on the table all the afternoon, because they could not interrupt the talking to take it away. At last Miss Everard got up and put things in order, and Dora standing up said gravely—

"Now, Maria, I have something for you," and unfolding a five-pound note, laid it on the table. "I know you have lost nearly all your pupils, and are having bad times, so I brought this. See, is it not pretty? It is the first I have saved, so I thought it should be for you. You are not so ill-off as I was when I sought your help, but you *are* ill-off," and she stroked Maria's cheek, and kissed her.

"Put it by, Dora," said 'Ria, "put it by, I may come to want it, but I do not want it now, so take care of it. I promise to turn to you for help when I need it; you are my friend, you know."

And Dora took it up again, and contented herself for the present without giving it away.

Then they sat down, and Dora explained what had enabled her to come into possession of such a sum. She had left them in the trembling hope that her second lecture would prove as successful as the first, but it did not. It was not a failure, but it was evident the subject was exhausted, to Dora's utter bewilderment, for she had thought she could speak for ever on it; but the truth was, that her bitterness had melted away in the sunshine, and her half-suppressed passion was her main attraction. In this predicament the man who had undertaken to exploit her (begging pardon for the bad English), came to her help; he advised her to try reciting or reading, and to take lessons in elocution, and she succeeded. She had naturally a musical voice and a lively action, and she carefully suppressed her exuberant vitality. With this outfit she was ready to face the world, and had already done so with a certain success. It was a miserably poor one as things go on in these days, but to her it was heaven. Stepping out of the seclusion that was, according to public opinion, her proper position, was Paradise. In vain Maria insisted it was a piece of luck, and luck was not to be rejoiced over, because one could never hope it would be permanent.

"I care for nothing now," Dora said. "Do you remember, 'Ria, telling me that I should forgive my enemies when I had conquered?"

"I remember how you looked; you made a private vow you never would."

"No, but I thought I never could, it was not possible."

There was a pause full of remembrance, as all three brought back the heat and struggle of the fight. Then Dora half yawned and asked suddenly—

"Why do you keep looking at me so, Miss Everard? Do you think I am somebody else?"

"There is more changes in you than your dress," she answered; "you are different; you are—I don't know how."

"Pray find out; do, please!"

"Well, you are grown more; you are like a man."

"How? In what way?"

"Well, as if you had something to do—business-like; and then as if you could do it—confident."

"Well, I suppose I am getting improper, is that it?"

"Well, yes."

"And I am determined, as most sinners, to go on in my own way. I think I will come here to Repton and lecture furiously on the rights of women."

Had they known, the impropriety was marked on them all three, though owing to their greater age, which had marked the character of the face already, it was not near so prominent as on Dora's. A victory won increases the strength, as, indeed, we go on in any way we have begun, be it for good or evil. The three women were bound by a tie that included no one else, or at least not to their knowledge. For though England held many thousands of women suffering from the same misery, they bore it in solitude and without hope. Had they all met together to make their wants known, and asked for help, no advice could have been given them, except to win a living for themselves, and not beg for it.

CHAPTER XXIX.

AS THE MORNING SPREAD UPON THE MOUNTAINS.

DAYLIGHT was visible to Sammy Sykes, though he still walked in the darkness of the valley below. But he looked round and saw no opening for his willing labour. "Who would take me for an overlooker?" he asked, "after such a failure? I must just take to wool sorting, and stick to work. There is nothing else for it." His father hoped for better things with time, but Sammy saw that better men than he were seeking work and finding none. Those were not times in which men could hope. Men were thankful if they could get a living from the surrounding poverty, and he had a load of debt to bear besides!

As he stood by the fire with his hands in his pockets he became aware of a gentleman standing at the house door, and went towards him.

"You are Mr. Samuel Sykes?"

"Yes."

"I wish to speak with you about this bankruptcy."

"Are you a creditor?"

The man smiled.

"I am a banker. Overton is my name."

"Will you walk in?"

"It seems you were a partner with Mr. Turner in this—"

"Yes, I was a partner."

"Well, you have made a nice mess of it, or at least the old man has. Perhaps you did not interfere with it much?"

"No, I did not. I understood little about it. I think now I ought to have interfered. But I did not even know how it was."

"Well, now, Mr. Samuel, what do you think of doing?"

"When I have given up all I had? I suppose you have nothing to do with that?"

"What had you? There is almost nothing for the creditors."

"Nay, nay, not so bad as that! There's the mill, and there's some good machinery in it."

"Don't you know we have a lien on the mill? The title-deeds are in our office."

"I never knew," said Sam, hanging his head to hide his trouble. This was a great deal added to the burden of debt for which he considered himself responsible.

"So it is," the banker said, gently. "You seem to have been taken in."

There was a silence, for at the moment Sam could not speak.

"And now, Mr. Samuel," began Mr. Overton again, "allow me to ask you what you mean to do in the future?"

Sam had acquired a perfectly irrational hatred of the words "Mr. Samuel."

"That's my concern," he said, sullenly.

"It may be ours, too," the banker returned, patiently. "What if you were to take the mill from us? I am told you understand the business."

"How can I begin such a concern as that when I am just cleaned out?"

"We might help you."

Sam's brain could not make so complete a revolution in a moment. The first thing that made itself clear to him was that he was not ill thought of by everyone. Mr. Overton was the last man in the world from whom he should have hoped for help, or even trust. He was relieved when that gentleman rose and said—

"Well, now think it over. You see, we want someone to run the mill, and we think you seem to us to be the one best suited to do it. We have known your father many years," he added, "though he does not do so much business with us as we should like." He turned to the old man, who had listened silently, as if not concerned, "and we hope to have as long a connection with the son. Good-morning, just now. We hope to see you again soon."

Sam sat down and covered his face.

After a while his father spoke.

"Could ye do it, Sammy?"

"I am sure I can!" he said, with a sobbing voice. "We could ha' done it before if we had not had so much to pay to that London chap."

"There was fraud in it all t' way afore. Now, thank God, we're rid o' that. Ye mun think on it, Sammy."

"Aye," said his son, and walked out of the house.

"He's gone to tell the lass," old Sykes thought. "Well, it's nought but reight."

As daylight comes to the silent wood and the still fields, so the sound of gladness woke over Repton as the news flew that the mill would soon be working again. First a twitter here, then another twitter there, and soon a full clamour of noise and activity. The boys shouted, the women sung over their work, the men walked with emphasis about their accustomed business. One could almost feel it in the air that there was good news afloat, and it became a pleasant thing to behold the sun.

Maria soon felt the warmth of the new day. She got three or four pupils, with the promise of more, and moved about with energy as heretofore. But now, one day, all at once, as she sat teaching, came a sudden stab of pain—pain almost physical, from she knew not where. When she collected herself, she knew how it was. She had seen Branksome coming through the little green gate up to the house door.

"I must not have that!" she thought, as she cringed with closed hands. "He must keep away." Somehow it must be done, for this she could not bear.

She finished her work; the children ran off. She set the room to rights, and closed the door. Then she entered the parlour, and saw two people sitting cosily by the fire, and evidently enjoying their conversation. The man rose and shook hands, and then rather suddenly sat down again. Miss Everard went on—

"Yes, the house is empty. I passed it yesterday. It did look desolate."

"It does!" said Branksome. "Do you know, I climbed over the wall yesterday, and got down by the pear tree, and walked round the garden. The poor man did not spend much on it lately. There was a year or two's growth of weeds."

"Poor man!" Miss Everard said, and began, according to her old habit, looking over the melancholy past.

"I suppose you will be going there now?" Mr. Branksome asked, quite as if it were a matter of course.

"Going there! Going there! I never thought of such a thing!"

"Well, but is it not the best thing you can do?"

"Why?"

"You will pay no rent there, and the house is always the better for being lived in."

"We! Well, Maria, do you hear? Are we to go and live in the great house?"

"How should we furnish it? You know that was Mr. Turner's idea to get a great house."

"But when you get it for nothing?" he suddenly asked.

"But we do not get the means of furnishing and living in it."

"But, Maria, we don't need to furnish. We can get our goods over there for very little, and not have to pay rent, and the fruit out of the garden will pay for keeping it in some sort of order."

"I could help you with that!" the man said, eagerly. "Do you know, Miss Bell, I used to have a little garden of my own there when I was a lad."

"Yes," said Miss Everard, laughing; "and used to get over the wall by the pear tree to come and look after it."

"You knew Branksome so long ago?" Maria asked, opening her eyes.

"Miss Everard's father was my best friend. It was he gave the advice to my father and to me to get myself apprenticed,

and learn a trade, instead of loitering about without means
and without work."

"Then you are fiftieth cousins, or something of that sort?"

"Well, we are Scotch."

Miss Everard asked if his proceeding had come to any good.

He said it had, that since he was out of his apprenticeship
he had had plenty of work, and he was prospering fairly. And
then he suddenly rose.

"Well," he said, "I have intruded long enough. I am glad
to find you so comfortable and happy," and he held out his
hand to Miss Everard, going across the hearth rug to do so.
She stood up and took it warmly.

"Thank you," she said, "I am glad to see you. You must not
forget us now, but come again."

"Well, I always liked Everard Branksome!" said the old lady,
walking about and rubbing her hands, "and I like him yet.
I am pleased to see him again. I hope he will come often! He
was always a nice boy!"

"I never knew before—" Maria said.

"Don't you know his name is Everard? And we are more
than fiftieth cousins, though my grandfather left Scotland before the Branksomes did. Old Branksome came here because my
grandfather was here, and they both seemed to get entangled
in the same old-fashioned ways! They must spend more than
their income! Aye! aye! they've taught their children something in that respect! But, Maria, I want to talk to you about
moving into the great house. Why should we not?"

"Miss Everard, do you know" (with intense gravity), "you
are getting like a man!"

"I'm feeling so," said the old lady, striding about the room
and laughing. "I have found something to do, and I am doing it."

And the feeling seemed not to go off next day, nor the day
after. She seemed nowadays always to be energetic and busy.
She would dress herself in all her war-paint, to wit in the wonderful bonnet and satin gown, and sally forth, and never say
where she had been, and write letters, though Maria had never

known her to have a correspondent till now, until at last Maria declared she must have an explanation.

"Well, I had begun to think I could not get on any longer without telling you, so I may as well do it. Now look here, Maria, we must try and get up a boarding-school in the great house, and we must do it directly!—this coming summer."

"A boarding-school! And I am all in disgrace for favouring the impropriety of a girl lecturing!"

"You are all out of it! Mrs. Dodds thinks there was, perhaps, no harm in giving a lecture, but it ought not to have been in a chapel, and it ought to have been under clerical patronage. She was glad to hear that at Baumforth it was under the auspices of the Vicar that she appeared."

Maria laughed as she thought of the visit, when she had asked for help and encouragement at the Vicarage.

"And don't you see, we are paying rent here! and we might as well save the money. And Mrs. Forbes is giving up her school, and will recommend you as her successor, and that you are a clergyman's daughter, and that I am going back to the home of my ancestors."

"What is all that for? We may be a couple of fools for all that."

"Well, I don't see the use of it myself, but some people do, so make up your mind to accept your position, and assume a dignity, if you have it not. Now write to Mrs. Greaves and ask her to send you her two girls for the finishing quarter that she used to talk about, and then persuade her to make it half a year."

"You propose one thing more impudent than another! Don't you know that Turner's opinion was that I should lose caste for ever if I took day scholars?"

"Well, I know how much you value Mr. Turner's opinions, so you need not quote him to me."

Maria found her head in utter confusion. She could not get it all into order, and applied continually to Miss Everard for explanations. How could they fill the great rooms with furniture? and where were the books to go? and, oh, where were they to find beds for the boarders? By slow degrees the confusion settled down, and only the real difficulties became apparent. And about this time came an unexpected help; the same gentleman who had already frightened Miss Everard once appeared at the door again.

"I know what it is," she thought, "I am to pay for the improvements."

She led him in, and asked him to sit down, and then strung herself up to wait for the announcement.

"I thought I had done with it all," she said. "What can there be now?"

"First of all, I have to inform you that the mill having been taken and in work, you will get the ground rent, and then that there will be a small dividend on the sum owing to you for the rent of the house. It is over five-and-twenty pounds, and I have brought it to you. Will you please give me a receipt for it?"

Miss Everard caught her breath, and said at last, holding the receipt at arm's length—

"To what does this make me liable if I sign it?"

It was a very suspicious document, being already written out, and a part of it in print.

"The woman's maddling," thought the man.

"For nothing," he said. "It is merely to show that you have received this," and he began to count out the money on the table.

She thought herself in the toils, but, helpless as ever, she could not see how she was to refuse to sign the paper. Then she wished the man good-morning, and stood trembling before the heap of gold that would not disappear, as she looked and half-expected it to do.

At last she went in haste to the schoolroom door, and called—

"Maria, I want to speak to you!"

Maria hastened to the parlour, where Miss Everard stood, still contemplating the money.

"Maria, that man has just brought me this!"

"Oh! very well; it's the dividend, I suppose."

"But shall I have nothing to pay?"

"Nothing at all."

"But Mr. Turner said—"

"He wanted to make you liable for improvements. That was nonsense. Take your money and be thankful."

"Then you take it up, Maria, and put it away before I spend it right off. It's too much for anyone to have in their hands at once."

Maria took it, and put it in the drawer where the money was deposited for housekeeping purposes, and it lasted till it was done. It relieved them of all anxiety about the absolute necessary expenditure for moving when the time came.

"Listen here," Miss Everard called out one night, as Maria came in after the day's work—

" 'Miss Forbes begs to announce to her kind friends and patrons that she intends giving up her school at the end of the present half-year, and she begs to recommend to them her successors, Miss Everard and Miss Bell, as being well qualified to instruct and train their pupils in all the accomplishments and duties of their sex and station.

" 'Miss Everard is the daughter of the late Charles Everard, Esq., of the Great House, Repton. Miss Bell is well known as having being already for some years engaged in tuition. She is the daughter of the Rev. Mr. Bell, late Vicar of Long Norton, and was mainly instrumental in bringing into notice the talent of our popular lecturer, Miss Wells.'

"You see, I come first," Miss Everard explained, "because I belong to a family that was once rich, and am supposed, therefore, to know by nature how to teach girls to behave themselves."

"Give me that to send to Dora," Maria exclaimed, "and I will make her pay the postage!"

> "And hope again elastic springs,
> Unconquered though she fell,
> Still buoyant are her golden wings,
> Still strong to bear us well!"

There were the blessings of change and activity, though her own castle that she had been building for her own delectation had been swept away by a tornado, and she had resolved in vain to turn her eyes another way, and not to look upon the wreck. Now it was growing over, but she felt she should always know what was there concealed.

> "For as long as the heart has passions,
> As long as life has woes."

"I shall turn to the picture that I have painted for myself, and that I knew could never take shape in this actual world."

She shed a few tears over the vanished paradise, and went sadly about her work.

In early summer Maria walked over to the great house with her old friend, for the sitting-room was dismantled when she came out of the schoolroom, and Miss Everard told her that the upstairs furniture was gone. She remembered the time when, with anxious, desolate heart, she had entered the house before. And now!

Miss Everard unlocked the door, and opened it to her, exclaiming—

"Now we are at home," and showed her into the breakfast room, where the tea tray was set, and a fire burning, and the two old arm-chairs on each side. Maria took possession, and smiled and cried.

"Miss Everard, whose cart was that, that was loading with furniture when we left?"

"It was—I don't know what they call them, where Mr. Branksome is; he offered it. He said it had nothing to do for the time, and he might as well bring it."

"Then has it brought all the furniture?"

"Yes, every bit of it."

"We should not accept—"

Miss Everard laughed.

"Yes we should; Mr. Branksome is an old friend, and I am thankful to receive help and kindness from him."

"I never heard of this old friendship until lately," Maria

said, discontentedly. "You scarcely ever mentioned him to me."

"No, we did not talk of him much, but I told you all you asked me; and, Evelyn, I like the man, and I want him to come here and be friends with us. Don't be so stiff with him if you can help it!"

"Do you think you will agree?"

"Well, perhaps not. But what then?"

"Well, nothing."

"But there is something."

Maria laughed, while her lip curled bitterly.

"There is not likely to be anything more," she said.

"It is a pity," the old lady said, after considering awhile. "There is not such another man in Repton."

"I am glad to hear it."

"What is it all about?" said Miss Everard, crossly. "What is the matter with the man?"

"When I was fighting for Dora's life, and was wanting help, he wrote me a letter to explain that he did not like to see me doing it, and that he hoped that, for this excellent reason, I should give over; that he liked to see me keep quiet and not struggle. Moreover, he informed me that most other men thought with him, and that in consequence of this I might lose my position and be disgraced by my efforts, and lose the small means I had—as if I did not know that! And then he owned that he did not know what I could do better, only I was to do that—and all the stuff you know about! We had plenty of it at that time."

"Oh, but, Evelyn, that's all past!"

"The cruelty of it remains."

"Fiddle about cruelty."

"Was it not cruelty to point always to the precipice where I might fall, and assure me that he thought women who did as I did generally fell; and then wound up with an acknowledgment, that he knew no other road to take? I looked so for one helping hand! Just one word of encouragement."

She stopped for fear of tears.

"Fiddle about cruelty," said Miss Everard again. "He knew nothing about your affair. He would have helped you had he known how; the mistake was in your wanting guidance, and being willing to take his, until you found you could not possibly go on with it."

"That is true. It is a mistake I don't intend to repeat."

"Evelyn, you seem to think that men are a bundle of principles that you can understand and count upon. They are no such thing. Every day spreads over their mind a deposit of its own colour, and they think that is their opinion. Comes another day, and they change again. You have changed Branksome. He has lived another day, such as he had not experienced before. If you take men's advice and are ruined by it how can you blame them? It serves you right."

"So it does," she said.

"Come into the garden, 'Ria."

Maria awoke to a consciousness of the bitter feeling that had overwhelmed her, and, shaking it off, she followed Miss Everard through a little side door that she had never noticed before into the large overgrown garden.

"I shall need some time to get acquainted with the place," she said, as she turned round to look at the struggling, overgrown fruit trees and the moss-grown walls.

The evening sun was still warm, and they sauntered slowly along the grass-grown walks.

"Now, look here, 'Ria. We shall have ever so much fruit from these trees, and we will sell what we don't want. Look at these strawberries! They want planting out afresh. And then we can make preserves! This is the pear tree where Everard used to climb over. You see it slants, so you can run down the trunk once you get on to it. I used to do so when I was young. Look! Who's coming?"

Branksome entered the garden from the kitchen door.

"You knew he was there!" Maria said, reproachfully.

"No, I did not," she answered. "Now we must thank him for his help with the furniture."

"I have just been placing your furniture in the kitchen," he said, gaily. "I suppose you will find it all wrong to-morrow morning."

"Thank you all the same," Miss Everard said. "Now come and look at the old pear tree. It leans ever so much more than it used to do."

"So it does," he said. "You will have to cut it down."

"Cut it down! Don't talk sacrilege!"

He looked round sadly at the departed past.

"I left all this long ago," he said. "Shall I ever see my fortunes united with it again?"

"It has happened to me," Miss Everard said. "Why not to you? We made our plunge, and are come to the surface again!"

"No one could tell you beforehand," Branksome broke in.

"No; there was the difficulty! We thought we might be ruined by the deed, but the case was too sad! It was Dora's last hope! If her effort failed she had nowhere to turn to, and no bread to eat, and we had not much to give her," she added, in a lower voice. "Were we not bound to try?"

"Surely you were," said the Scotchman. "You may well be proud of the help you gave! I congratulate you both," he added, hastily, offering his hand, "and I am glad the good times we are getting are coming to you too!"

"Are they coming to you?"

"They are," he said, emphatically. "I am making money!—not before I wanted it! I wanted it badly!" he added, mournfully, turning to Maria, and looking into her eyes as he offered his hand.

His change of tone brought her to tears. She took his hand like a schoolmistress—the incarnation of wooden propriety.

"Look, Maria; these are jargonelles," Miss Everard said, when the man was gone. But Maria forgot to answer.

The sun was gone, and they went in, to avoid the chill air of evening.

"Now, is it not nice by the fire?" said the old lady. "I wish Branksome had come in with us."

Maria wished so too, but she said nothing. She was looking

at the overgrown ruin, and thinking of what lay beneath it. When would she forget to grieve?

The man continued to come. During the long evenings he found time for a short visit, and a sentence or two addressed especially to Maria. When he had received the chilling answer he would go, either as if he could not bear it or because he took offence, and would not need two hints that he was not welcome. He showed wonderful invention in finding errands to Miss Everard, but no invitation could persuade him to stay beyond ten minutes after Maria had entered the room. She knew he could sit comfortably when she was away. He took care that she understood his reason for cutting the visit short, but she gave no sign that he would have been welcome had he stayed longer.

"I wish he would not come," she said to herself, when he was gone. "It would be less pain if he stayed away."

And after a month in their new home Maria began the half-year with five little girls. There were no more quiet evenings, for the girls sat with them until they went to bed, and Branksome gave over coming. But he did not wait a week before he resumed his old plan, and Maria could not but read his letter.

"Once more I ask you! Is it unmanly in me to persecute you? I do it because I cannot believe I have your final decision. Am I become all at once worse than a stranger to you? Am I not worthy of a chance to justify and defend myself? If once I thought this of you I would never see you more. But how can this be? I will not believe it! Maria, give me the opportunity to explain and justify myself! I have a right to ask it!"

Maria carried the letter in her pocket, and hoped somehow to escape the pain of answering it. But not a day had passed when she saw him before her on the road, as she walked with her five little pupils. He was on the opposite side, and he walked on until they were nearly past. Then he looked, raised his hat ceremoniously, and crossed the road to her, holding out his hand.

"Will you name a time when you will see me again? You dare not refuse me that! Give me a hearing!"

"I do not want to discuss anything with you. I wish—"

"I will not take that for an answer! You cannot be so unjust and cruel! You shall hear, at least, that you may know in future on what small grounds you have rejected me. I have no longer free access to you. Are you going to let the customs of the country" (with infinite scorn) "stand in your way?"

"Those are for women only, it appears, for you to quote when they do something you don't approve of."

She spoke in scorn, and then, suddenly aware of the little troop gathering round her, "I will see you to-morrow evening," she added.

There was another ceremonious flourish of the hat, and the man was gone.

Maria told Miss Everard that Branksome had asked to see her. "He says he has a right," she added, in explanation.

"*He* says," Miss Everard thought, but she answered not a word.

Branksome was shown into the drawing-room. As soon as she entered he came to her and took her hand.

"Now, tell me," he said, "why you wish to cast me off? What have I done?"

Maria was angry. A culprit so unconscious of crime she had never imagined.

"I wonder you care to know," she said. "You cast me off in my extremity. You told me to expect the contempt and ridicule of the world unless I followed your advice. You were clearly of the opinion of my enemies, and did your best to prevent my going on. You did it when I was at the last gasp and had no friends. Do not talk of my casting you off."

"You wanted me," he said, "and I failed you! My poor girl! you did not know how ready I was to help you!"

"That is past," she said. "What do you want now with a woman who has made herself ridiculous and contemptible?"

"Good God, Maria! Do you suspect me of despising you? I was wrong in my advice, and you were wiser than I! Yet I could not see you in danger without speaking! How was it possible? But you have won, Maria!"

"The opinion you threatened me with has changed, and you too, of course."

"I never wavered! I never for a moment thought you less than perfect. I come here now not to lose my treasure. I cannot give you up, Maria! Take time to think! I will bear your scorn, your contemptuous looks, your mistaken insinuations. Take time to think!" He had come closer to her, and spoke in the beautiful tones of pleading love. "If you throw me off you will repent, for I am true to you. All my life long I shall dream of you, if you cast me off, and all your life long you will repent having done so!"

As Maria listened she covered her eyes, and let the tears fall down. Her paradise was in sight, and she could not turn away.

"Do not ruin us, Maria. We love each other!"

He laid his arm on her shoulder.

"Do not ruin us, Maria. We love each other!"

Then she raised her eyes to his face with a wandering gaze, as if seeking something there.

"I cannot tell," she said. "I thought I could have gone on my way and passed you by. But I have no hope, no prospect, no heaven without you!"

Then she kissed him, and was folded to his heart.

They said little more, but promised soon to meet again. When she had let him out she went to Miss Everard in the breakfast room, and told her she had fallen in love with Mr. Branksome.

"You have done quite right, my dear. He is the frankest, most truthful, most fearless man I know. Why have you been so long about it?"

"If you were not a Scotchie I should say you knew nothing about it, that I had been long."

"You were quite right to be cautious."

"Have you done it all from beginning to end?" Maria asked, turning suddenly round.

"I begin to perceive that you are of a suspicious temperament, Miss Maria!"

Maria seemed to have acquired something of Scotch caution, for she asked no more.

There was pleasant sunshine over Repton valley in those days. Sarah Miles would not give up her teacher, even in the great house, and Maria somehow heard that she was engaged to the new mill-owner, and had a fellow-feeling for her. She introduced her to Miss Everard, and the three spent some cosy evenings together, at least until Branksome came and Sammy would come and fetch Sarah away. Then the pair would go indifferently to either the Miles's or the Sykes's house. Sometimes a neighbour would come in seeking one of them, and ask with humorous gravity—

"Which house do you live in now? A body never knows where to find you."

And this had to last for some time, for the two young men were mere penniless beginners.

"Who is that old man?" Branksome asked one day, as Maria took leave of him at the gate.

"Mr. Miles."

"Who?"

"Sarah Miles's father."

"And who is she?"

"She is engaged to marry Mr. Samuel Sykes. Her father helped me better than you did," she went on. "I was not a white lily to him, but a suffering fellow creature in want of help."

"I forbid you to mention that again," he said. "Don't you know it hurts me?"

"Then I never will," and only under necessity did she ever mention that time again.

One evening Sam came into his father's house to find Sarah there, as had been agreed upon beforehand. He began—

"Now, father, I have something to say. I've been talking to Branksome, and he's put something into my head. He thinks it won't be long before he will be getting married; and it would be a right good thing if he could settle down in the half of the great house, and Sarah and me take the other half. It is big enough for both of us, and ye see, father, we are going to be pinched for room. We want a bigger warehouse.

He had stopped several times for a word of approval, but he got none from either of them, so he went on without—

"If we pulled this house down—"

"The house has done well enough so far," old Sykes said, not approvingly.

"But are we never to do more than we have done?"

"What do you want to do now?"

"I'd like to pull this house down, and add it to the old warehouse."

Sarah said—

"Eh, Sammy?"

The father said nothing. Sam went on—

"Now, you see he just gave me a hint that Miss Everard has none so much to live on, an' it would just set her up if we could take t' half o' t' house; an' t' wimmen folk would be right glad besides."

He waited now for a response of some kind, and the father spoke at last, without answering his son's appeal.

"My lot has fallen to me in pleasant places. I shall be content to die in the place where I have lived."

There was a silence, and both Sam and Sarah knew that the old man was grieved. Why should the "sturm and drang" of youthful energy press him out of the way? He had thought to rest in his old age in peace. Must it be that life's turmoil was not yet over?

"It munnot be, Sam," Sarah exclaimed, suddenly. "We're noan going to leave t' oud spot."

"Come here and give us a kiss, lass! Thou'rt t' best o' t' pair."

"Dunnot ye set her up so mich," said Sam; "she'll get too good a conceit of hersen."

"He allus thought better o' me than ye did," she said, saucily.

"Nay, 'twere nobbud ye that thought so."

The old man died in the house where he had lived. He and old Miles spent their time indifferently in each other's houses, and lived surrounded by their children's love and care. Sam pressed forward to independence, and Branksome fell into the rush of prosperity that followed the introduction of railways. He took the great house, and left Miss Everard room in it, which, with a hundred a year which he paid her for rent, made the old lady happy. Then came a little Sarah into the Sykes's house to toddle about the floor and amuse the old men, sitting on the fender and asking her questions with wide-open eyes, and confident fluency, as her mother had done before her. The two couples had many changes and many sorrows, so we had better leave them in sight of that paradise which never comes but at the end of a novel.

THE END.